# Recollections and Reflections of an Unknown Cyprus Turk

# Recollections and Reflections of an Unknown Cyprus Turk

## By

## Süha Faiz

**AVON BOOKS**
1 DOVEDALE STUDIOS
465 BATTERSEA PARK ROAD
LONDON SW11 4LR

Printed and bound in the U.K.

## Avon Books

London
First Published 1998
© Süha Faiz , 1998
ISBN  1 86033 227 7

*To my Family -*

*Past, Present and Future*

. . . . . .

*For All whose Task is Building Bridges*

*To every thing there is a season
and a time for every purpose under the heaven*

Book of Ecclesiastes

*So much depends on when*

Anon

*When your task is complete
toil again and turn fervently to your Lord*

The Qur'an

# Acknowledgements

p23 quoted from p.46 of E.M Forster's *Abinger Harvest*, Penguin 1976 [© Estate of E. M. Forster, 1936].

p200 and 201 quoted from pp63 & 67 of Harry Williams's *The True Wilderness*, Constable, 1965 [© H.A Williams, 1965].

p225 quoted from p.71 of Constance Padwick's *Muslim Devotions*, SPCK, 1969 [© Constance E. Padwick, 1961].

p271-272 quoted from the Introduction in *Discovering Turkey*, Batsford, 1971 [© Andrew Mango].

p274-275 quoted from pp335-6 of Carl Sagan's *Cosmos*, Macdonald Futura, 1981 [© Carl Sagan Productions, 1980].

p285-286 quoted from p.178 of Colin Thubron's *Journey into Cyprus*, Penguin, 1986 [© Colin Thubron].

p308 quoted from p.88 of Godfrey Goodwin's *A History of Ottoman Architecture*, Thames & Hudson [© 1978 Thames & Hudson Ltd].

# Contents

# POINT OF DEPARTURE

"Well actually, I could never live in the Close," I said. Just why I spoke so categorically I don't now remember. Nor indeed how the subject of the Cathedral Close had come up. Possibly someone had mentioned Edward Heath and his mansion there. We had no personal connection with the place; and no particular interest, though we shared the general wonder - almost awe - at the Cathedral itself as a supreme example of England's magnificent mediaeval architecture. As for the city, it was a useful place for occasional shopping beyond our usual weekly visits to Warminster.

For ten years or so we had been living in about as remote a Wiltshire village as you could hope to find. Right in the middle of Salisbury Plain, Chitterne was in a hollow almost completely surrounded by downs, though with plenty of handsome sheltering trees. Our house was virtually in the centre of the hollow - a suntrap in the summer and a frost-pocket in the winter.

We were sitting outside the drawing-room French windows. The lawn stretched down to the wooded area beyond the drive which separated the garden from the orchard. Beyond the orchard's boundary wall the church, of Wiltshire flint, made a scene almost ridiculously picturesque.

"Oh, and why could you never live in the Close?" asked my wife's sister. And since I had spoken unthinkingly, on impulse, I had to find some reason in justification. Of course reasons of sorts then flowed into my conscious mind. It is, I suppose, arguable whether any words or behaviour can be really impulsive in the sense of being entirely born of the moment. Without having tried seriously and systematically to review my own such words and actions over nearly seventy years, I do have a sense that when I have been impulsive I have been driven

1

not so much by the moment as by some great accumulation from my past. The reasons which now presented themselves to my mind, to justify dismissing so peremptorily the Close as somewhere I could ever possibly choose to live, were perhaps predictable. I rationalised. Life in such a place would probably be rather "precious" and somehow inward looking. The kind of community within a community I should expect there, would very likely be full of the hot-house emotions which that sort of environment could so easily breed and spread. One could suppose it to be the stamping ground not only of an established hierarchy of Dean and Chapter, headed - and yet not headed - by the Bishop, but also, in some measure at least, the haunt of other nabobs such as former prime ministers, literary notabilities, historian didacts, and the like. (At that stage Sir Arthur Bryant might recently have died; and neither Susan Howatch was, I believe, in residence, nor, I think, had Leslie Thomas yet moved into his imposing house.) To all such marshalled debating points against living in the Close I added, for good measure, that being in such a place would seem to me to involve a kind of retrogression to undergraduate existence, more especially in the considerable inconvenience of being locked in after hours. I had heard that all three gates of the Close were shut and barred after a certain hour at night and, though hardly a night bird, I thought I shouldn't like the sensation of being imprisoned or excluded without there being, so far as I knew, a surreptitious way of escape and entry which had at least given a certain spice to the closure of the college gates at Oxford. Whether I carried a case against living under the shadow of that tallest of all the spires in England I doubt; but memory doesn't tell me that anyone actually said I was talking fairly ripe rubbish. More to the point my recollection is unclear whether my *ex post* reasoning had carried much weight even with myself.

Had any of us wanted to argue the matter, it would have been just as valid to use much of what I had said about the Close also to denigrate living even in our very secluded village on the plain. My picture of a Cathedral Close as a place which could generate antagonisms, bred of conflict of personality or ambition in a relatively sequestered environment, might possibly have had some merit; but if so, that prospect was not necessarily absent in a small rural community which included its share of retired service officers. Indeed that aspect of village living may well be in the minds of those who look with disfavour

2

on bucolic existence, but are too polite to say openly that they consider those who choose it to be a bit off their heads.

As it happened, Chitterne was almost entirely free of that phenomenon which my wife and I once heard described to us by a local artist, while we were spending an Easter break away from London in Dorset, as "the amusing competition between the retired Air Commodore and the retired Brigadier to be the village squire". Quite the contrary. When we first arrived in Chitterne a retired Colonel had said he was glad to see in me a possible new member of the "four C's" - an entirely mythical "Chitterne Clapped-out Colonels Club". When I pointed to my ineligibility, as an ex-member of the Colonial Service and now retired from the Foreign and Commonwealth Office, he conceded that the club had better be redesignated the *"five* C's" to include clapped-out civil servants.

However, in dredging up a response to my sister-in-law a thought *had* crossed my mind - but which I hadn't voiced, as being almost certainly irrelevant in the 1980's, by which time Anglicanism was very much infused by the spirit of ecumenism. (It was at least a decade later that I was to hear - how well may be warrantably questioned - that even at the turn of the century only Anglicans had been allowed to live in the Close.) What had occurred to me was the pleasing paradox - even irony - were I to be breathing daily the quintessentially Anglican atmosphere of the Salisbury Close as a grandson of a Mufti - the religious leader of the Turkish Moslem people of Cyprus. For that was what my father's father had been at the time I was born in Cyprus in 1926.

# PART I : THE NEST

## (1878-1926)

# ~1~
# Nicosia - Egypt and France

*The island of Cyprus was in the year of my birth an utterly different place from that which is now visited by tourists in their thousands each year. Somnolent, much more nearly Near-Eastern than Mediterranean, Cyprus had only become a British Colony a year earlier. The British had arrived in 1878 under a treaty signed that year with the Ottoman Sultan, by which Britain undertook to safeguard the Ottoman Empire's borders against Czarist Russia in the wake of the Russo-Turkish War of 1877-78. By reason of that British guarantee, and to provide her with a base from which to honour and fulfil her promise, the Turkish Sultan in effect leased what was then an Ottoman island to Britain. In return for Turkey's continuing to receive a yearly payment, equivalent to the annual revenues previously derived from Cyprus, Britain was to be allowed to administer the island as Ottoman territory, the inhabitants remaining Ottoman citizens.*

**********

*(Following the Congress of Berlin in 1878 the Ottoman Empire had, separately, also been forced to cede the administration - but again not the sovereignty - of the province of Bosnia-Herzogovina to the Austro-Hungarian Empire. In this latter case however, and even without the excuse of war, Austro-Hungary had, quite illegally, annexed that province in 1908. Six years later a Bosnian Serb, Gavrilo Princip, assassinated the Austrian heir Archduke Franz Ferdinand in the provincial capital - Sarajevo. This murder of the heir- apparent to the throne of Austro-Hungary sparked the explosion of the First World War in 1914.)*

\*\*\*\*\*\*\*\*\*\*

*When, in July 1878, Sir Garnet Wolseley's redcoats entered the Cyprus capital, Nicosia, through the Famagusta Gate (one of the three gates in the town walls locked up each night), they had marched, in the terrible heat of a Cyprus summer, twenty five miles and more across the plain from the coast at Larnaca where they had landed. Just how hot it must have been, and how unacclimatised the troops, can be understood from a pathetic inscription on a tombstone in the English cemetery at Kyrenia, on the coast sixteen miles to the north of Nicosia: "Number 141 Sergeant Samuel McGaw, V.C., 42nd Royal Highlanders (Black Watch) died on the line of march to Camp Chiftlik Pasha of heat apoplexy, 22 July 1878. Aged 40 years".*

\*\*\*\*\*\*\*\*\*\*

The walls of Nicosia in 1878 (and even in my childhood) were still the boundaries of the town. Something over two miles in circumference in a perfect circle, with eleven equidistant and identical great heart-shaped bastions, they were a fine example of a post-mediaeval military circumvallation. In a panoramic photograph I still possess, probably taken in the 1870's, the photographer is viewing the town from the south-east, with the range of the Kyrenia hills as a backdrop. The fading sepia shows not a single building outside the ramparts. Above them, within the walls, appear the roofs and upper walls of houses and other buildings, overtopped by many mosque minarets. Just out of the picture to the west is the mosque of *Bayraktar*, the "Standard Bearer", erected on the southernmost bastion on the spot where, in 1570, the Turkish Standard was first planted - and where its bearer was cut down - when the Ottoman Turks captured the island from the Venetians. The town had been taken by assault, despite the formidable new fortifications which the Venetians had built during their rule of eighty years or so. These new defences (those in my photograph) had been constructed by the Venetians, after they had destroyed the old mediaeval, crusader walls so as to reduce the circumference of the defence line by more than a half. Rupert Gunnis, who was the ADC to

7

the island's Governor at the beginning of the 1930's, wrote in his *Historic Cyprus* that, under the Venetians, "everything outside the new walls was destroyed or blown up so that a field of fire would be left for the artillery mounted on the walls. In the general destruction nothing was spared; churches and palaces alike perished in the general demolition irrespective of their interest or beauty".

North of the walled town was a broken plain stretching some seven or eight miles to the foothills of the two thousand foot high Kyrenia range. The colours of that line of mountains I can see now through childhood's eyes, as they slowly change between dawn and dusk from shades of palest mauve, through blue-green, to dark purple, before the sun sinks behind the peaks over to the left.

Outside the walls to the north and west was the area known as *Köşklü Çiftlik* ("the farm with a pavilion"). In the flat, unbuilt fields and gardens, with trees separately and in stands (of which date palms, cypresses and eucalyptus remain most sharply in my memory) were no more than a few scattered and isolated houses. One of these was the *köşk* in question, which had been enlarged into an unpretentious but beautiful house in the old Turkish style. A couple of hundred yards to the south and west stood another house in the more modern version of that style, but constructed of local, golden, cut sandstone, rather than the old traditional mud-brick of the *köşk* and other similar houses inside the walled town.

The word "mud-brick" conjures up a very misleading impression nowadays. It produces a picture of some kind of primitive building, even a hovel. The "bricks" so-called were in fact something like eighteen inches or so square and three to four inches thick. Made of local clayey earth mixed with straw, fed into wooden moulds and dried in the sun, these slabs were the age-old traditional building material of the Near and Middle East. Seeing these being made gave sharp visual point to the biblical admonition not to attempt the futile task of trying to make bricks without straw. Walls of these building blocks were strongly plastered inside and out; and, either with or without cut stone door and window surrounds, the result produced was that harmony which comes of combining simplicity with natural materials, the whole blending perfectly with the surroundings. Buildings made in this way were also wonderfully suited to the climate: the warmth of fires, stoves and braziers was retained inside to a remarkable degree in winter, just as the oppressive heat of summer was kept out.

It was in houses of this kind, in the "Arab Ahmet" *mahalle* (quarter) within the walls of Nicosia, that my maternal and paternal grandparents lived. No-one's memory I suppose, can, before the age of about three, carry any but rare and fleeting images, if it carries any at all. My own during those early years brings me nothing of my mother's and father's parents. And this for the very good reason that from the age of about eighteen months I never saw any of my grandparents for some three years - or indeed the land of my birth.

\*\*\*\*\*\*\*\*\*\*\*

In 1927 my father went to England to read for the Bar at Gray's Inn. Accompanying him were my mother, my brother (senior to me by eighteen months) and me. The importance of that decision by my father in the shaping of my life can, perhaps, be imagined - at least in part. But egregious (very much out of the ordinary - in the strict sense of the word), and indeed bold, as it was for a Turkish father, still more for a mother, to go to England *en famille* in this way, and in those days, the decision has also to be viewed and understood against the general background of Cyprus's position after the First World War, and judged in the particular context of the situation of the island's Turks at that time; and not least having regard to the individual circumstances of my father, my mother, and their parents.

\*\*\*\*\*\*\*\*\*\*

*1927 was a bare five years into that totally new and wholly strange era which had opened in Turkey. A revolutionary, a volcanic, change had taken place. The Ottoman Empire had been defeated in the World War of 1914-18. That defeat had itself followed on the two calamitous Balkan wars of 1912 and 1913; and those had been preceded by the Italian attack on, and seizure of, Tripolitania (Libya) and the Dodecanese islands, including Rhodes, from the empire, in 1911. Twelve subsequent years of continuous war had prevented anything*

9

*approaching adjustment to the dislocations and upheavals which had themselves been produced by the disastrous loss of territories in the Balkans fifty years earlier as the result of the Russian war of 1877-78. A third of the populations of those territories had been Turkish, families who had lived there up to five hundred years. In their tens of thousands, men, women and children, had poured as refugees into Istanbul, the Ottoman capital, in wretchedness and penury. From there they had been dispersed throughout the Anatolian provinces. By 1918 nothing remained of the Empire save Anatolia. And that too had been carved up on the map: the south-west allotted to the Italians; the south to the French; and the south-east to Britain. (Palestine was to be separately disposed of.) In 1915, in order to rally the Czarist empire, Britain and France had offered the Russians what for centuries the Czars had coveted - the city of Istanbul (Constantinople). But the collapse of Russia in 1917 had aborted that part of the plan to share out the expected post-war spoils. In 1919 Istanbul was occupied by British and French forces. The government of the Sultan was absolutely under their control. The Ottoman state was at the Allies' mercy.*

*It was at this moment that the Greek state, which had stood aside militarily from the battles of the First World War, was urged on by Lloyd George to embark on the adventure of seizing the Aegean hinterland of Turkey so implementing its megalomaniacally ambitious* Megali Idea (Great Concept) *of a new Byzantium, or Greater Greece. In 1915 Greece, as well as Russia, had been lured by bait intended to induce her to come into the war on the Allied side. The aim was to rally the Greeks to the support of the British and ANZAC troops who were hemmed in by the Turks on the Gallipoli peninsula. Churchill, the architect and fierce exponent of the "Dardanelles strategy", in the face of equally ardent "Western Front" strategists, fought for his Eastern strategy with every weapon he could deploy. He offered Cyprus to the Greeks as their prize. In 1915 they failed to take the bait. Now, four years later, in 1919, with the Ottoman state defeated and exhausted, Greek armies were landed at Izmir (Smyrna) and, spreading outwards, advanced into Anatolia. What to the Turks is their War of Salvation ended, after another three years of battles and hardship, in the rout of the Greek armies.*

*The achievement was that of the patriotic, popular (and populist) forces motivated largely by Mustafa Kemal Pasha - later surnamed Ataturk - who had been the Turkish commander at Gallipoli. There followed the abdication of the Sultan, the declaration of a new republican state, the abolition of the Caliphate (the Headship of the* Sunni *Moslems of the world, which the Ottoman Sultans had held since 1517), and a deluge of social, economic and cultural changes - each one of which, even singly, was a cataclysmic "culture shock". The changes included the abolition of the Moslem Religious Foundations (the Evcaf) - to a great extent comparable with the 16th century English Dissolution of the Monasteries; prohibition of women's veils, and of the fez, which had been the headgear of Turkish men for virtually a century; the abolition of the Arabic script (which was quite unsuited to the vowel-harmonic Turkish language) with the substitution of a new Latin script which everyone had to learn from scratch; and the establishment of entirely new and wholly strange State Economic Enterprises at all levels of commercial and industrial activity. The Republic's parliament, the Grand National Assembly, formulated and proclaimed the National Compact. This declared the boundaries of the new state and renounced all other territories previously part of the old Empire. The Allied Powers, and Greece, recognised all this (so far as it concerned them) in the Treaty of Lausanne in 1923. Turkey's sovereignty in Cyprus ended with that treaty; and Britain's legal sovereignty began, enshrined in the Cyprus Orders in Council of 1925.*

**\*\*\*\*\*\*\*\*\*\***

Born in the middle of the 19th century, my father's father might well have been among those who had seen the British troops march into Nicosia, and had witnessed the raising of the Union Jack at the start of the British administration in 1878. But I cannot know this. Such great matters would hardly have been discussed by a Turkish patriarch with his grandchildren; nor did the subject ever come up with my father. What I do know is that grandfather, after finishing his education in Cyprus, had gone to Istanbul, and from there to Cairo to the great Islamic university, *medrese*, of Al Azhar (whose foundation predates those of all the Oxford colleges). He emerged after the usual long

11

years of study as a rounded Islamic scholar with, naturally, a complete command of Koranic and classical Arabic. In due course he was appointed to be the Mufti of Cyprus. And he was also elected by the Turks of the island as one of their representatives on the Legislative Council presided over by the Governor. *Haji* (one who has made the Pilgrimage to Mecca) *Hafiz* (one who has "preserved" the Koran, by committing it to memory) Mehmet Ziya ed-Din Efendi was now both the supreme Moslem religious dignitary in Cyprus and the leading Turkish political figure in the island. In this latter capacity he would have seen, frequently and at close quarters, the *ex officio* members of the Council, who were the leading representatives of Britain, the country which would now determine the future of the place. He would, too, have similarly observed the elected members of the Greek Cypriot community, numbered among whom was their Archbishop.

At the time we sailed from Cyprus for England the riots of 1931 were still four years in the future. But the embryo of the Caliban yet to be born had already been conceived in the womb of the innocent island; the seed impregnated by a rampant political ambition, wildly incited and excitedly urged on by men supposedly pursuing religious - even holy - ends. As in Bosnia seventy years later. The early evidences of the pregnancy would have been visible to my family. They would, too, hardly have been unaware that they were now members of one of the many Turkish communities which, with the Turkish Republic's National Compact, could not look to Turkey for support in trying to hold their own in lands outside the new Republic - though those lands in which they lived had been their homelands for centuries.

We can today see fairly clearly how the British Empire had, after the First World War, already passed its high point in history. That clarity of vision was not possible at the time; and certainly not to the peoples of Cyprus. Many of the island's Turks had indeed been so despondent about their future that they had emigrated to Turkey a mere forty miles across the sea. (It is sometimes forgotten, even by those few Turks today who knew it, that under the arrangements by which Cyprus was ceded to Britain, all Ottoman citizens in the island - who of course included Greek as well as Turkish Cypriots - were given two options: either to remain in Cyprus, though as British subjects; or to retain their Turkish citizenship, but at the price of leaving the island. It is even less in the consciousness of very many Cyprus Turks nowadays that, in the mid-twenties and early thirties, the government of the new Turkish Republic, very understandably, actively encouraged inward immigration from Cyprus to help in rebuilding the shattered and debilitated country that was the new Turkey.)

\*\*\*\*\*\*\*\*\*\*\*

Something also needs to be sketched in of my mother's family. She was the daughter of one of two sisters. They were the only surviving children of Ahmet Beligh Pasha. His native village was Kilani in the Limassol District of Cyprus, where his grandfather was the Hoja. The word had in those days two separate connotations. In the first place it meant "teacher"; but it also designated one who officiates at religious services, though not in a priestly capacity - there being no priesthood in Islam (sacerdotally understood). The Hoja is more nearly akin to the Rabbi in Judaism. Perhaps "Minister" would best describe him in English in respect of his religious functions: instructing children (and adults) in religious practice; leading the prayers, and preaching, in the village mosque; and officiating at weddings and burials.

Born in 1851, my mother's grandfather Ahmet was exceptionally bright. His family was respected, but poor. His father died when the boy was still a child; and his father's paternal uncle married the young widow - this being a meritorious act, though not a duty. In fact Ahmet was not happy with his stepfather. The family went to live in Egypt, then an Ottoman province, governed under a *Khedive* (Viceroy), a rank unique in the Ottoman Empire (as it was to be, virtually, in the British - in India and in Ireland). In the Turkish case, however, it was hereditary to the family of the founder of the dynasty, Mehmet Ali. His family came originally from Konya in south-central Turkey; from there his forebears had moved to Edirne (on the present borders of Greece and Turkey), and eventually settled at Kavalla near Salonica. Ahmet's stepfather went to Egypt as an officer in the army, and the boy was placed in a school funded from the Khedive's revenues. There he did extremely well. It was at this school that he was given by his teacher, as was the custom, a name additional to his personal name. He now became Ahmet Beligh (meaning in Arabic "Eloquent").

13

## The Nest

In 1869 Napoleon III's Consort, the spectacularly beautiful Empress Eugenie, came to Egypt for the opening of the Suez Canal, which had been planned and constructed by the French engineer Ferdinand de Lesseps. The Empress's programme included a visit to Beligh's school. The headmaster had set the boys to compose an address of welcome, and had chosen Beligh's. The Empress was much struck by the speech, delivered by Beligh himself, which had to do with the exceptionally high level of the annual Nile flood that year - on which the country's agriculture depended. (Beligh talked of the Nile's having broken its bounds in wishing also to lay itself at the Empress's feet. This ability with diplomatic floweriness has not descended to his great grandson.) Eugenie's gratification led to Beligh's being included among a small contingent of youths to be sent at the Khedive's expense for education in France. There was at this time huge competition between Britain and France for paramount influence in Egypt. France's political influence began, relatively, to wane after the British naval bombardment of Alexandria in 1882. This led to the effective control of the country by Britain which lasted, in various forms, until 1936. In matters cultural, to use that word fairly widely and loosely, France's influence continued strong. At Court, as also among the ranks of the landowning and commercial plutocracy - which included an ever-growing European and foreign carpet-bagging element in the main cities and towns, especially Alexandria - French developed as the preferred first European foreign language of those whose mother tongue was Arabic or Turkish. Beligh was to the end of his life a warm admirer of France. His career culminated with his appointment as President of the Supreme Appellate Court of Egypt, with the honour and rank of Pasha, a sort of non-hereditary peer. He returned in retirement to the island of his birth before the First World War.

Just as on my father's side of the family it would have been the Mufti, his father, whose word would carry the most weight, so in the case of my mother's family it would have been her maternal grandfather, the Pasha, who would have the decisive say when matters of consequence needed to be resolved. The evidence, or rather the lack of it, suggests that the Mufti did nothing to discourage his son's wish to go to England, and indeed that he materially enabled him to do so. The Pasha had died in 1925, the year before I was born and two years before we left the island. But I think there can be little doubt that he

14

too would have looked favourably on his grandson-in-law's keenness to improve his chances by qualifying as an English barrister; and that he would have approved of his granddaughter, my mother, accompanying her husband during the three years of life in Britain which would be involved. With his world view, even wider than that of the Mufti, his near neighbour in Nicosia, the Pasha could, in the mid-twenties, only have concluded, like the Mufti, that the future security of the Turkish population of Cyprus lay in reliance on Britain as the sovereign Power able justly to hold the scales in this island colony containing two peoples of different languages and religions. Both men, it seems to me, would also be likely to have shared the conviction, from their own personal experience, that for an able man living in a small, restricted environment the only hope of fulfilment (in the mundane, career sense of the word - which is not to be belittled) was to expand one's horizons by going abroad for higher education. There was no education in Cyprus beyond the secondary level in those days.

But my father had, I believe, a rather more specific reason for wanting to go to Britain and to become a barrister. After he had finished his Turkish secondary education he had spent some time at a newly founded "English School" in Nicosia. This took boys of what might be called "fifth and sixth form" age, Greek as well as Turkish - and Armenian and others too. Apart from the benefits of the academic education which they received, under the headship of an Anglican clergyman, Canon Newham, the products of the place usually became very proficient in English, spoken as well as written. Father's ability in both was notable. At whatever age I was first aware of such a thing as accent, I was conscious that when he spoke English he sounded in no way different from an Englishman. From the English School he was accepted into the police. That body's official name was the Cyprus Military Police - the C.M.P. There were about half a dozen British officers, equivalent in rank to Majors or senior Captains, and about the same number of Inspectors or Sub-Inspectors recruited locally. At the time my father joined all members of the force wore the Turkish *fez*, as photographs I still have show. From the earliest days of the British administration many of the posts in the civil side of the government had also been filled by officers from the British army. Indeed the list of the first High Commissioners reads like a military roll-call. Even

15

with the change in designation to Governor, after Cyprus had become a Crown Colony, there were to be such ex-military men holding that most senior of British appointments in the island. The British officers of the C.M.P. would, apart from Canon Newham and a couple of masters at the English School, have been the first, perhaps the only, British men with whom my father would by that date have had close acquaintance. One at least (whom I know he regarded highly) was Scottish.

My father must have been fortunate in these people who were to form his first impressions of the country they represented. That such impressions are powerful in shaping future attitudes would seem to have been borne out in my father's case, as was to be clearly seen in the view he took of Britain generally at this important stage in his life. The thought of improving his career prospects was naturally the direct impetus to his going to England and the Inns of Court. As a barrister he might reasonably look to advancement in the government by transfer to the Legal Department as Crown Counsel; and from there he could hope to rise to becoming Solicitor General (at that time the highest legal appointment open to a Cypriot, the Attorney General being British). But, as I now judge in retrospect, he would also have set out for England not just in the expectation that he was taking an adventurous step towards furthering his career but also to grasp an opportunity to see the country whose few representatives he had so far met. He would, I think, have been more than merely mildly interested to see for himself the British on their own ground. I believe he was not disappointed.

# PART II : NESTLING

(1927-1934)

# ~2~
# London

I find it extremely difficult to try to recapture in truth for the written page the few visual memories which I think I can faintly discern from the three years that I spent in England while my father was studying for his Bar exams, and while he and my mother were seeing the British at close quarters, "in their native habit as they lived" as it were, and learning by direct experience of living amongst them the ways of the ordinary people. By "ordinary" I mean to differentiate them from the British in Cyprus, who almost all occupied official positions, and those ones of authority.

**********

*I sit down now having just come back from my daily constitutional, advised as the best prophylactic against recurrence of heart attack. My walk took me along the Salisbury Avon just outside the Close through the Harnham Gate in the south-east angle of the walls. The day is crisply clear, the air fresh, cold and still, with an unusually bright sun low in an unclouded blackbird egg-blue sky, a couple of days before the December equinox. The scene was almost unnaturally like the picture in plain and nearly primary colours that small children paint when they succeed in capturing what is so real to their as yet undeformed innocence. Perhaps for that reason what I was seeing on my walk powerfully conjured up what I had once seen in infant vision as my conscious self now strained to remember what has in reality probably passed beyond memory. Yet what I saw, or seemed to see, was Hyde Park and Kensington Gardens in the England of 1930. The similarity of Salisbury today and London sixty-five years ago is not quite as incongruous as might appear. Physically the two scenes had*

18

*much in common.  The level green expanse of grass, the trees singly
and in clumps, the hint of buildings on a near horizon, the water of the
Avon so smooth and slow as to be as still as the surface of the Serpentine
or Round Pond.  Even, however odd the comparison may seem, the
unique spire of the cathedral, almost bisecting the sky, recalled to me
a church spire somewhere in Bayswater which to my mind's eye had
also somehow linked green grass to blue sky so many years ago.  More
than that, the two scenes, visions almost, were to me then and now
something beyond mere "Englishness"; rather it was a sense of
"being" in some way to be universally apprehended.  I suppose this is
the vision of the artist, the poet, perhaps even of the mystic.  I have not
seldom wondered if those of us who are none of these may sometimes
be able to capture, or be given, some share in that deeper vision by
seeing a place through the eye of the foreigner.  The mystics seem to
be telling us that in seeing, or feeling, themselves as partaking of the
sights, the sounds, the sensations of the world in which they live they
do so, at the same time, in a real sense, as strangers to the place - as
those whose true nature and being is elsewhere.  In this the mystic and
the child (at any rate the infant) seem to me to be sharing a state of
existence in which they sense the eternal.  In any event what I was
seeing, as I approached sixty-nine, had that of it to stir in me intimations
of what had been part of my infancy.*

**************

I think I can only be sure I am not running the risk of deceiving myself
if I say that the single direct memory I have of Kensington Gardens is
of what must have been the large stump of a once very big tree.  Out of
the solid wood, as the buildings are hewn out of the rock-face at Petra,
were carved life-sized birds and creatures which I was to learn were
images taken from Peter Pan.  Even that is an imperfect vision.  I *think*
I saw rabbits and owls and squirrels; but were these remembered
squirrels in reality perhaps the live ones I could well have seen
scampering about on the grass or in the Hyde Park trees?  And the
rabbits and owls fashioned out of a tree-stump could possibly have
merged in my mind with the illustrations in A. A. Milne's *Winnie the
Pooh* books, then only recently written and which I know were read to
us during those three years in London.  Read to us either by my mother

19

when her English had reached the stage when she could do this, or by the young nanny who looked after my brother and me for a good deal of the time.

There were then, north of the park, in the area between Shepherd's Bush and Bayswater, lots of large houses which were run as residential hotels. The costs of maintaining and running what had until fairly recently been substantial family homes were becoming beyond the means of the owners; and that slide was beginning into what was to produce "bed and breakfast lodgings" for such as medical students, among whom were to be numbered my mother's younger brothers in due course. However, when we arrived in London only the early steps in this descent had been taken through the conversion of the houses, probably by their new owners, into places where those whose fortunes were also declining could find virtually permanent accommodation in an agreeable neighbourhood (albeit " unfashionable", as I would later learn, by comparison with that other Kensington which lay "south of the Park") and in buildings of generous and fine proportions, of the sort to which they or their immediate forbears would have been accustomed. With their commodious and comfortable bedrooms the guests, decayed and decaying gentility, shared one or more drawing rooms and a spotless dining room where they were served, by aproned maids, their thrice-daily fare of wholesome English cooking. Homes for the genteelly impecunious, and all for a modest sum. But "modest" is a relative measurement. It is for me a matter of conjecture how my parents managed financially. Certainly my father's salary would have been nowhere, even remotely, adequate for more than a proportion of our expenses - even without the part-time nanny. Clearly my grandparents must have subsidised their children.

Although both pairs of grandparents owned land in Cyprus, this yielded little in the way of cash income. For example, the Mufti had bought olive groves in a village a mile or so out of Kyrenia from which the extended family got all their olive oil, used for all cooking, but it was quite beyond the villagers' means to pay rent. It was only a couple of years ago that I learned, from a local villager, that my grandfather had arranged for the purchase of properties in this Turkish village to forestall foreclosure of mortgages at hugely exorbitant rates of interest by a particularly notorious Greek money-lender. And yet, in the years following the coming of British rule, a sense of stability, even of permanence, was in the air. Beligh Pasha, with a pension from the Egyptian government, was at this time to be counted a wealthy man by Cyprus standards. He had been engaged in improving the Arab Ahmet *mahalle* of Nicosia. The British community asked him for help in providing a suitable building for use as an English Club. The Pasha was no doubt happy to combine personal with public interest by obliging the small but important British community. He did this by building, and renting to the club, premises inside their own walled grounds in the heart of this Turkish quarter of the old town of Nicosia. (The place, no longer such a club, still stands.) From this rent, and those from other modest houses and shops, I surmise that he would have been well able to help with the expenses of my parents in London. I can only assume that this happened. But I feel more sure that I would also be right in thinking that - with what hindsight now tells us was even then the twilight, if it was not the gathering dusk, of the British Empire - my father would have been looking to a future which appeared increasingly bright when he should return to Cyprus.

As for my brother and myself, I can really only recall those days with the help of the camera's lens. Photographs show us variously accoutred, and often very like the child who features in Shepherd's illustrations to the Christopher Robin books: the same shirts and velvet-looking shorts; the same style of hat varying with the season; the same gaiters or leggings in winter. Two small boys outwardly no different from their British counterparts also being taken on walks by their nannies in London's parkland. Some photographs show us on a beach, which I have learned was at Broadstairs in Kent, then a favoured and genteel resort - so, again, I have been told. (The thought amuses me now, as I glimpse the roof of Edward Heath's residence from my small flat window, that we might just possibly have shared that beach - and even the beach photographer's services - so long ago.)

I think we must have had a series of nannies then (the only time we were in the charge of such a being) rather than a regular one; I like to think I would have had some sort of a memory of the girl, had she been the only one - but I have no such memory. And I also have in any case the impression that my mother perhaps managed to get the services of the more junior of the girls in training on an *ad hoc* basis. The

Norland Institution was close by in Holland Park and our nannies (if indeed they were in the plural) were certainly from Norlands. How my parents were introduced to this essentially English institution I think I can correctly speculate.

There was at Gray's Inn a young man from Devon, Edward Duke. His father, Lord Merrivale, was President of the Probate, Divorce and Admiralty Division of the High Court - and it is for me a nice idiosyncratic British touch to lump together in one of the many "mansions" of the legal "house" these three disparate and unrelated aspects of human existence. But be that as it may (as the lawyers not infrequently say), Edward Duke and my father took to each other and became friendly. The Duke London house was in Holland Park, close to the Norlands headquarters; and I think it not unlikely that it was on Edward Duke's advice, and very likely through his introduction, that my mother applied to Norlands for help in coping with two small children in a strange London.

Whether it was through acquaintance with my parents that their English friend became sympathetic towards the Turks, or whether he was already among the many British people who had come to admire Turkish courage and steadfastness both at Gallipoli and afterwards during their War of Salvation, I cannot know. The old Gladstonian hostility to all things Turkish still lingered on - though Lloyd George himself was no longer in office or power - even if such hostility was mainly subconscious. (My father long afterwards told me, with amusement, how as a three-year-old I had been behaving obstreperously in a barber's chair. The barber admonished me with, "Don't be a little Turk!" - to be told by my father, to the man's discomfiture, "Well, actually he is".) But there was also much sympathy for a people who had come to be seen as the underdog in the calamitous wars in the Near East over the past half century; and Edward Duke may already have shared that sympathy before he became the friend of an individual Turk. Who can know?

There is a telling, and moving, vignette from those days: "Our Graves in Gallipoli" in E.M.Forster's *Abinger Harvest.* It is dated 1922, the year Lloyd George's ambitions sought to involve Britain in yet more war against Turkey, after the Greek defeat in Anatolia. (The direct result was his loss of office, never to be regained, and the annihilation of the Liberal Party.) Forster's short piece is a conversation between two dead soldiers in a Gallipoli cemetery. They are musing on a *Punch* cartoon in which "Lloyd George, fertile in counsels, is urged to go to war 'to protect the sanctity of our graves in Gallipoli'". The First Grave ironically advises that "it is well for a nation that would be great to scatter its graves all over the world ... each with its inscription from the Bible or Rupert Brooke". The Second Grave from time to time asks questions and ponders on the motives of the rich and the powerful. After the First Grave has explained how Lloyd George has unsuccessfully "tried to enter Asia by means of the Greeks", he adds that "they have mostly been killed there, so English young men must be persuaded instead". The colloquy ends after the First Grave bitterly parodies the politician's desire, with further fighting, "to sanctify Gallipoli" by making "our heap of stones forever England, apparently".

'Second Grave: "It can scarcely do that to my portion of it, I was a Turk."

First Grave: "What! a Turk! You a Turk? And I have lain beside you for seven years and never known!"

Second Grave: "How should you have known? What is there to know except that I am your brother?"

First Grave: "I am yours."'

That my parents were able to meet and know and make friends in the England of those years with people in Britain for whom such sentiments rang true is one of the gifts with which providence blessed their lives - and, through them, their children's.

# ~3~
# Nicosia; Kyrenia; Nicosia; Amiandos

*As I now begin to try to summon up my memories of the time after our return to Cyprus, when the direction and course of life was to be significantly set, I first record what happened half an hour ago. One of those things, small in themselves, which serve to remind how providence, at least as much as we ourselves, determines the outcome of our lives - how, if you will, "there is a Divinity which shapes our ends". (How far it may be the case that fate is influenced by others, and how far it flows quite independently of other humans, is something I have to leave to Ibn Ghazzali or Augustine or Aquinas.) I had stepped out this morning to buy bread. In the bakery I had dithered between two different kinds of loaf. The assistant, a kindly woman, was prepared to spend time to help over such a momentous decision, instead of just being irritated by my inability to make up my mind. The precise moment, therefore, that I passed through the gate of the Close on my return was at least affected by our discussion at the counter. About twenty paces after passing under the arch there was a sharp crack behind me. I turned and saw on the pavement a broken tile, dislodged no doubt by the recent high winds. It must have missed me by a fraction of a second. A variation of pace, too, would have ended these recollections at the previous paragraph.*

**\*\*\*\*\*\*\*\*\*\***

By the end of 1930 we were back in Nicosia. We lived in one of the houses built by Beligh Pasha outside the walled town, the one I have mentioned, of cut sandstone not very far, to the south and west, from the *Köşk* of the old *Köşklü Çiftlik*. Though only about thirty years old, the house was laid out in the old style. On each of the two floors there was a large central hall with rooms opening off it on three sides. The house stood about a quarter of a mile to the west of the town ramparts, virtually in open country. To the north the well remembered line of the Kyrenia range, violet, purple and even azure. All around us tall cypresses and shady eucalyptus. The faintly oily scent of the latter and the sharply dry smell of the former need no effort to recall. To the south, on the road that led past the Armenian cemetery to the Paphos Gate, there were one or two smaller houses. In reality these were at most only a couple of hundred yards or so from us, but they seemed to me at that time very distant. Our house had a walled courtyard, at the end of which, I remember father's horse was stabled. The warm smell of animal and of manure mixed with straw is, even now, vividly strong with me. Father was still in the police and had a policeman orderly. I have memories of two at different times; one, a Greek, Karpi; the other, a Turk, Mehmet. One, or both, would make us a shepherd's pipe out of bamboo with finger-holes for playing. Mehmet also used bamboo, together with paper and string, to make kites with long tails.

In one of the houses to the south lived the Stone family - father, mother, and son Michael (the same age as my brother). Mr Stone was the Director of Public Works; I don't have any memory of him at that time. The fact of his being in the Public Works Department (PWD), really only impinged on my mind many years later when I heard the anecdote - quite untrue - about the two young men on the P and O steamer. (It is revealing of the social *mores* of the time and of the "imperial hierarchy".) The young men were travelling out to take up posts in an Egypt which was still effectively under British control - even if not, strictly speaking, under British rule - exercised through a Consul-General, later a High Commissioner: a personage somewhat in the nature of a Roman Proconsul. The two newly appointed youths enquire of each other which government departments they are destined for. The one says, with becoming modesty yet pride, that he is taking up a post in the Treasury. The other, glancing around furtively, whispers, "I'm going to the PWD. But for God's sake don't ever let on to my parents - they think I'm going out to play the piano in a brothel." I was, over the years, to be educated in the particular niceties and distinctions, official and social, as they once existed. No longer, thank Heaven. Yet I was, too, very often conscious of the British capacity for gentle self mocking, a characteristic finely balancing a tendency to be somewhat acutely alive to the existence of class

25

distinctions. The latter is very much on the wane; the former seems to me to show signs of moving in the direction of a corrosive captiousness.

It was no doubt with a view to companionship for her young son that Mrs Stone organised and ran a kind of small nursery school in her house. To this my brother used to go; and I have a vague remembrance of feeling a bit excluded.

**********

*Ramazan Bayram* is the Turkish for the Arabic *Id ul Fitr*, the three day holiday which comes at the end of the fast lasting from daybreak to dark each day of the Moslem month of Ramazan. This was the only knowledge I had of anything Moslem during my childhood; indeed of anything that could be called formal religion, as distinct from moral upbringing. Children do not, of course, fast during Ramazan; but I knew that my father did, if only because the fast ends early enough in the winter (the lunar calendar comes forward eleven days each year) for us to join in the eating of the *iftar* - the meal with which the fast is broken. In Cyprus darkness comes swiftly; it almost literally falls, with no dusk. Sometimes the *iftar* was a larger family affair in the Mufti's house, opposite the lovely small Arab Ahmet mosque, which gave the *mahalle* its name, close by the English Club.

A block to the north was the main government administrative building. It stood at the edge of the central square, known then as "Konak Square" in English and *Saray önü* in Turkish: "Konak" being the Turkish word meaning "government building" or "residence"; and *Saray önü* meaning literally "the front of the Saray". Strictly speaking this latter word signifies a palace or any imposing official building. (It is the first part of the word we have latterly become all too familiar with in the name "Sarajevo"; and which we know in its italianised form from Mozart's *Abduction from the Seraglio*.

When the British arrived in Cyprus in 1878 the Turkish Governors occupied a building on the site and this still included a portion of a Gothic structure dating from the Lusignan crusader dynasty, which had ruled the island from the 12th to the 15th centuries, and from whom the Venetians acquired Cyprus by means of a crafty dynastic marriage. The Victorians of the second half of the 19th century, full of energy and self-confidence, were not so dedicated to the preservation of ancient buildings and monuments as we are now - in fact nothing like so dedicated. At a time when early mediaeval Balliol was razed and the ghastly buildings which still exist were put up in its place (almost as hideous as the contemporary Randolph Hotel facing it across from the Martyrs' Memorial), it was perhaps not to be expected that the exiguous revenues of the newly acquired island of Cyprus would be used to restore the old Lusignan building in Konak Square. In fact it was levelled; and in its place was built the dim but utilitarian standard "British Colonial" structure (to be seen in variously modified guises from the old Gold Coast to Ceylon: double storied, plain, rectangular, with a wooden balcony or verandah running all the way round, supported by wooden or stone pillars at ground-floor level.) The Nicosia building still stands today.

It was in the square beside the Konak that the *Bayram* fair was held. Roundabouts, swings, balloon-sellers, sweet stalls, cake - and pastry-sellers. Into this crowd my brother and I would be taken by Mehmet the orderly. Early in the day we would first have gone with our parents dutifully to kiss the hands of our grandparents - and to receive our *Bayram* presents. Out of these coins we were allowed to spend at the fair.

***********

Just about the time of our return from England two English girls - they couldn't have been more than in their mid-twenties at most - opened a small school in Kyrenia run on Froebel lines. (I have never known in what exactly this method consisted.) They may indeed have started the school while we were still in London and my parents may have heard of this before we left, or had news of the proposed project. Whatever the case, within a year of our arriving back in Cyprus, when I was on the verge of my fifth birthday or had just passed it, we two brothers became boarders at this school on the coast sixteen miles to the north. Neither this distance nor the journey time, of about an hour by car, conveyed anything to me and I did not suffer any feelings of separation or homesickness. In retrospect I wonder why.

***********

**Nestling**

The school was in a building which had once been a private house, almost fronting on to the main road into Kyrenia, with a large garden at the back. In those days Kyrenia was a very small and compact town, not much more than a large village. The school was in easy walking distance of the sea, around and on the far side of an immense crusader and Venetian castle. There were only around a dozen of us at the school, and apart from one or two who were English, we were all Turkish. For the next three years my life alternated from the "Froebel School" to home in the holidays in Nicosia, and back. I suppose I might conceivably have begun as the youngest boarder in the lands then coloured red on all those lands' school atlases. My time at that school and the intervening holidays bring to me my first distinct personal memories of the island of my birth. (As an incidental detail, I was the only member of our widely extended family who was not born in Nicosia. In 1926 my father had been serving in Famagusta, on the coast some thirty five miles to the east, since his marriage three years earlier. A silver salver inscribed "To Inspector Faiz Bey, from the Famagusta Division of the C.M.P. on his Marriage, 5th April 1923" is still with me - having survived three burglaries in England. It was in Famagusta that I was born.)

**\*\*\*\*\*\*\*\*\*\***

A "crocodile" of small girls and boys - there were actually only two or three girls - is being taken by Miss Millen and Miss Chatterton for a bathe off the "slab" below the eastern curtain-wall of the castle. We walk along a winding incline down a drowsy path fringed with asphodels and saturated by a smell of dustiness. A passer-by seeing us in our brown sandals, grey shorts or skirts, and floppy felt hats, could well have thought us English as we burble away to our teachers. (It was only the other day that I discovered the Editorial Note at the beginning of Joyce Cary's last, unfinished, novel *The Captive and the Free*, in which the editor acknowledges the encouragement she received in her difficult work from "the invaluable help of his secretary, Miss Edith Millen". Our Miss Millen's first name was Edith. Would that I had known earlier of this connection with a writer whom my wife and I so much admire.)

28

**********

Round the walls of the room are white cardboards with black lettering and pictures in colours. Was there ever a time when these were not words but simply shapes and patterns? Whether this is a commentary on my inability to achieve total recall, or a tribute to the Froebel "method", I do not know - but I have no memory of actually being taught, or learning , to read. What I do recall is a sense of "belonging" in that bright room, with the wooden verandah outside the green shuttered windows.

**********

School and toys I do not associate. (At home one of the few toys I remember was a Noah's Ark and animals which one made of cardboard cut-outs.) Our amusements at school were primitive by today's standards. We would make pipes, to smoke in pretence: the small, as yet ungrown, fruit of a pomegranate tree is shaped sufficiently like the bowl of a pipe, and into one of these we would stick a straight twig, and with this between our teeth imagine ourselves grown-ups. The odd thing is that I don't actually remember ever having seen anyone in Cyprus smoke anything but cigarettes or, in a coffee-shop, a *nargileh* (once known as a "hubble-bubble"): a device in which the smoke is drawn through a bowl of water, making a bubbling sound, before being inhaled - nicotine-free, judging from the colour of the water. We would also wait for black hornets (perhaps bees, too, but it's the black hornets I remember) to get right inside a hollyhock flower and then seize the petals, imprisoning it - as a test of courage, I suppose - before releasing it by hurling away flower and hornet together.

**********

Once, refusing to eat something I didn't like (what, I don't remember - fatty meat most likely), I was told I would have nothing else until I had finished the rejected food. The test of wills continued till the next meal-time - and possibly to the next. The outcome was that I fainted.

**Nestling**

So I made, and I assume gained, my point; whatever it was. Others at the time remember this better than do I. It was in the company of another of these, a cousin, that after a production of Goldilocks and the Three Bears, the two of us found the unfinished "prop", or inducement to get us to perform, and finished these off - bowls of real cold porridge.

**\*\*\*\*\*\*\*\*\*\***

In an upstairs bedroom with three iron bedsteads we are lying in the dark after our baths. My cousin Necati, a year and a half older than me, asks me if I say my prayers. I do not know what he means. His mother, my paternal aunt Vesime, has taught my cousin a prayer to say by heart. I have a very retentive memory and am soon repeating with him: *Bismillahi errahmani errahim, elhamdulillahi rabulalemin, errahmani errahim, maliki yevmeddin...* I do not know what this means, and neither does my cousin. It is nearly fifteen years later at Oxford, when I begin to take an interest (extracurricular and personal) in Islam, that I discover that, aged five or six, I had learned by rote what could, very loosely, be termed the Moslem "Lord's Prayer", *El Fatiha* (the opening chapter of the Koran): "In the name of God, the Merciful, the Compassionate; praise be to God, the Lord of the Worlds, the Merciful, the Compassionate, King of the Day of Judgment ..."

Like many of the women of Cyprus, Turkish and Greek, my aunt also pays regard to what we would consider superstitious observances. It is she who has also passed on to me, through her son, what has no root in Islam. If you get a severe momentary shock - say, by hearing a very sudden loud noise - you lightly tap in turn your right and left cheeks, then press the end of your thumb hard up against the palate inside your two middle upper teeth, and finally pull with the same hand at the lobes of your right and then left ears. I never heard any explanation of what this achieved; but for quite a long time it became a conditioned response in me to any shock of the sort which makes one's heart jump in fear or apprehension.

**\*\*\*\*\*\*\*\*\*\***

30

After our swim, as we are coming up the road on the last stretch back
to the school, a group of boys and girls at the roadside, not much older
than ourselves, hold out something in their hands and call out to us in
a jeering sort of way. I do not know what they are saying but can see
that what they are holding out are two pieces of what seem to be thin
wood, fashioned cross-wise. And I can sense their unfriendliness. I
ask my cousin, who seems to understand what is going on. He tells
me that they are Greeks, who speak a different language from us, and
are "Christian". He doesn't explain what this means; but there is no
doubt as to their antagonism.

**\*\*\*\*\*\*\*\*\*\***

We have had our swim in the clear, glassy, turquoise sea behind the
massive castle and are coming back by the small harbour on the farther
side of the fortress. The rich, succulently sweet scent of carobs in the
stores on the quay mingles with the damp, decaying smell from the
rusting metalwork in the harbour. And above the harbour buildings
the single, sharpened pencil of the mosque minaret and the white bell-
tower of the church are outlined against the sky to the right of the great
curtain-wall of the keep. Beyond rises the purple of the Kyrenia range,
so much closer than in Nicosia.

**\*\*\*\*\*\*\*\*\*\***

We have been told that we are not to go out into the school garden, so
we are scuffling about on the verandah. Suddenly two very curious
looking machines can be seen on the other side of the low garden wall,
passing down the road leading into the town. These have wheels like
an ordinary motor car, but are completely covered - like a tin box on
wheels. Our teachers tell us that these are "armoured cars" with soldiers
inside. The Greeks have been rioting, and last night burned down the
Governor's house in Nicosia; however, he is safe, and now that the
soldiers are here we are alright. It was not until I was a schoolboy in
England that I was to read that same Governor's autobiography, Sir
Ronald Storrs's *Orientations*, and understand what the riots of October
1931 were all about. Demonstrations had been organised by the

31

Orthodox Church in the main towns; violence had erupted under inflammatory prelatical urging; in the capital the mob had surged on to Government House, and burned the place to the ground. The object of all this was the pursuit of *enosis* (meaning "union"): that is, to bring the island within the boundaries of Greece - a never-ending campaign, as part of the *Megali Idea*. (It was also to be many years later that I learned that father had been in charge of the police sent to Government House when the mob were marching on it and that he got the Governor away in safety across the dry river-bed at the back. I suppose it was for this that he got the King's Police Medal for gallantry. He never told me why he had it and I never asked.)

\*\*\*\*\*\*\*\*\*\*

Once, in Nicosia - I imagine we had again been taken by father's orderly - I was among the spectators of some sporting occasion in the moat across the road from and below my maternal grandmother Hidayet Hanım' s house on the ramparts; perhaps it was the police sports. One of the events was "tent-pegging". Wooden pegs are driven into the ground (presumably not so deeply as an ordinary tent peg) and then, in turn, horsemen gallop down from about fifty yards away and try to hit the peg and carry it off on the point of a lance. In father's case the manoeuvre is carried out with a sword. Did he succeed? I don't carry a vision of him triumphantly bearing away the peg on the tip of his sword - but I do faintly see him hitting it. Wishful thinking? (It had been in this same moat that, up to 1878, equestrian events like this, *jirit*, had provided a popular spectacle.)

\*\*\*\*\*\*\*\*\*\*

There is a huge hall-like room on the first floor of Hidayet Hanım's house. (I don't know why, but I never thought of the place as my grandfather's, always as hers - as in fact it actually was, having been given to her by her father the Pasha when she married.) Down one side of this hall is a line of green shuttered windows looking out on to an enclosed garden, at the far end of which a single very tall date palm rises up against the sky. But in summer the only view of the garden is to be had by squinting through the chinks between the louvres of the shutters closed against the great heat outside. Along the whole length of this wall, under the window-sills, runs a continuous box-like seat covered with flat white cushions, a *minder*. Though it wasn't used by the family as a room but merely treated as a hall through which were reached the rooms opening off it, to me it felt like the heart of the place. These spaces, leading into other rooms, were in old Turkish houses the *sofa*, a word which has passed into English, but with the changed meaning of a couch-like piece of furniture, possibly because a *sofa* nearly always had a surrounding *minder*. In Victorian and Edwardian England that article of furniture was also known as an "ottoman", or "box-ottoman", since it was in fact a lidded wooden chest on top of which the quilted cushions were placed.

In Hidayet Hanım's house there was a room off the *sofa*, on the left at the far end, opposite the entrance door, which had an ornate, carved wooden ceiling. It was in this room that father and mother had sat at their wedding celebration, or *düğün* - when the bride and groom are, as it were, on show to the guests who on this occasion, included many British officials bidden to the wedding of the Mufti's son to the Pasha's granddaughter. (By which hangs a tale - as I shall tell.)

**********

On visits to my grandmother's house with my mother I used to wish I could be allowed upstairs to sit on the window seats in the big room above and leave the grown-ups talking among themselves. Sometimes I think I had reading books with me. These would have been in English - I don't have any memory of reading in Turkish. One such book I remember - what must have been a children's version of *Uncle Tom's Cabin*. I also recall reading this when Sedat and I, then aged eight, were on the ship going to boarding school in England with mother and father in 1934; but the two memories are not necessarily contradictory. On one occasion my grandfather Rasim Bey was present. He sat me next to him on the settee-like seat (which is today in the same place in the arched and stone-flagged open area of the old house where my mother's brother Fikret now lives) and gave me Turkish coffee to drink. This he pours, glistening black, out of the small cup so like my egg-cup at home, but with a handle, into the saucer to cool it for me. Years later I was to learn that English politesse frowned heavily on this mode of cooling one's drink. I didn't therefore relish the full flavour of the schoolboy joke of the two tramps when I first heard it as a schoolboy. The one tramp, with an insufferably superior air, rebukes his companion and friend for ill-manneredly pouring his tea into the saucer. Although I laughed heartily (because of its grotesquerie) at the genteelly acceptable method advised - "You should fan it with yer 'at" - I didn't quite cotton on to why drinking from the saucer should have been frowned upon.

Because of his kindly disposition it was, I think, Rasim Bey whom I asked about a picture in vivid, even lurid, colours which hung on the the upstairs landing outside the *sofa*. The picture was striking because I had seen no other picture of any kind in the house, or in any other house that I can remember, except for photographs. There were in this picture about a dozen fierce looking men in the foreground, and a great many more in the receding distance, clubbing and hacking at each other with what looked like knives on the end of their guns. The men were clearly in two distinct groups, some in greeny-brown clothes and the others in a bewildering costume - white (including close-fitting stockings and short frilly skirt) except for a black tasselled red skull-cap and pom-poms on the ends of their shoes. It was this second group who were getting much the worst of it: many were stretched out on the ground dead or dying, and of those still fighting several were being bloodily stabbed. This, I learned was a picture of a battle in the Great War in which the Turkish people had just defeated the armies of Greece who had come to take their country away from them. But the Turks had driven off the invaders and were now safe. Was it indeed Rasim Bey himself who had explained about this picture, or might it have been his son Fikret?

\*\*\*\*\*\*\*\*\*\*

At this time my uncle Fikret must have been about seventeen or eighteen years old. He went around on a motorbike, which seemed to me very dashing. (I had a different view of motorbikes when my son was to take to them at about the same age in London some thirty-five years later). Fikret had been, and perhaps still was, at a school called the American Academy in Larnaca, about twenty-five miles distant from Nicosia, and the American high school culture, as I was subsequently to identify it, was outwardly evident in the coloured pennants which were draped on the walls of his bedroom. A memory I have of him at that time is of seeing and smelling eggs being fried by him on the covered upper-floor balcony which looked out west over the moat towards Shakespeare Street, where our house was. (Since then the Ledra Palace hotel, built just after the last war, the haunt of newspapermen during the time of EOKA terrorism in the 1950's - of which more later - and from which in 1963 my mother's house, with her in it, was to receive its portion of Greek strafing, has blocked out that childhood view. Indeed the vista from that balcony is nowadays dominated by this large building, currently being used as the United Nations headquarters, standing in the otherwise uninhabited no-man's land of the so-called "Green Line".)

For some reason which I can't put my finger on, I always felt a bit intimidated by Fikret in those days. But he was to make amends later, during the war, when I was at Oxford and he at Saint Bartholomew's hospital. He was then rather in the position of the perpetual medical student in the *Doctor in the House* series, taking about a dozen years to qualify. I occasionally visited him in London and he would stand me a meal in the Istanbul Restaurant in Frith Street (I believe the only Turkish restaurant in London - perhaps in England - at that time), which was owned by a Turkish Cypriot. It was possible, if you had the money -which I didn't - to eat at restaurants throughout the war without using the food coupons which otherwise regulated the limited consumption of food rations. Though I couldn't afford this Fikret could, having got himself a job with the B.B.C. Overseas Service, broadcasting to Cyprus.

**********

Instead of walking inside the old town Rasim Bey sometimes used to use one of the "gharries", known in Turkish and Greek as *karotza*, presumably from the Italian. This was an open carriage drawn by a single horse. It usually had the hood up, more from protection against the heat than to keep off rain. I myself only very rarely had a ride in one of these; but the "ping-ping" of the bell is very much a sound of my childhood. This bell, operated by the driver with his foot, was to warn pedestrians but the "clip-clop" of the hooves would have been enough for that purpose. I imagine the driver probably took pride and pleasure in announcing his presence to everyone in this way. I admired the confident figure on his perch with his stiff silvery moustache and *fez* on top of his head.

The *fez* was still to be seen in the Turkish quarters of Nicosia, and elsewhere, at that time. It had originally been brought in by the modernising Sultan Mahmut II in the early part of the 19th century as a head covering for Turkish and other Moslem men in the Ottoman Empire, by way of a Europeanising influence, in place of the turban, something like a *fez* being frequently worn by the non-Moslem males of the empire's European provinces in the Balkans. After having become the hall-mark of the Turkish male for nearly all the preceding hundred years, it had, in the middle of the 1920's, been peremptorily banned by law in the new Turkish Republic, where men were required instead to put on the *şapka* - hat or cloth cap. However, in Cyprus, with no legal sanction against it, the *fez* continued to be seen into the mid-thirties. And until then it had in fact remained the headgear of the police, apart from a very brief trial period with the Australian-style slouch hat (a curiously insensitive move for Turks who still remembered Gallipoli - and not in the healing spirit of E.M.Forster). This was at once followed by the standard colonial police cap which we still occasionally see in news reels of events in, for example, ex-British territories, including Israel.

In the 1930's nearly everyone to be seen in Konak Square was a man. Such few women as might be there, and elsewhere in the Turkish quarters and in the villages, would nearly all be wearing the *çarşaf*, a headcovering which came down to the waist. Nearly always black, this could occasionally be brown and, extremely rarely, white. The face was not covered but the costume included a transparent veil which was thrown back over the top of the head and could be let down to hide the face if desired. The *çarşaf* too had been abolished in Turkey by the republican government but it was only slowly that the Turkish women of Cyprus, without the authority of the law to compel them (or to support them - according to the individual viewpoint) began to discard the customary habit. Mother's passport photograph when she went to England for the first time shows her in her *çarşaf*. She abandoned this in England - and must have been among the first Cyprus Turkish women to do this - never to wear it again.

\*\*\*\*\*\*\*\*\*\*\*

On a little rocky promontory on the northern coast there is a plain white-washed building with a flat roof. It has a covered, arched extension. Silhouetted against the glowing sea in the seaward arch sits an old man, bearded, wearing a black robe and a *fez*, around which is wrapped a thin white cloth. He is the *imam* of the place. The word means, essentially, "prayer leader" in congregational prayer, but in the present context "guardian" would be a suitable rendering. The place is the unpretentious shrine of *Hazret-i Ömer*. To outward appearance the man looks not unlike my grandfather the Mufti. But my father's father is someone I know as a person and there is no mystery about him, indeed he is human in his bodily infirmity - he is now frail and needs help to rise from couch or chair. The man at the edge of the sea seems, in my memory, to have about him something more permanent. Is this clear visual memory one of a real scene, or perhaps only a photograph I might have seen?

\*\*\*\*\*\*\*\*\*\*\*

The Froebel School leaves the sticky coastal heat of Kyrenia in mid-summer to spend that term up on the Troodos mountains. The place is Amiandos, where asbestos is mined a little way down the mountain from the houses where the foreign staff of the mining company live. The school building is one of the company's houses, a second house being used as a dormitory. Under a hot sky the air is yet cool; and the scent of pine is all about us, with occasional wafts of the smell of hill-scrub. Sometimes - or was it only once? - we are taken down to see the mines. Hideous overhead funiculars, white-smoking tall chimneys, wagons clanking in and out of great sheds. The seeds being sown, perhaps, of dislike of the noises and dirt of mechanical and industrial processes.

**\*\*\*\*\*\*\*\*\*\***

One or two children from the mining company families come to the school. Walking along a mountain path on our daily crocodile I am hand in hand with a Dutch girl - or is it that I wish I was? I cannot remember her name. But I can identify her from a group photograph in my album.

**\*\*\*\*\*\*\*\*\*\***

Whenever we go up to Amiandos for the summer term, or return to Nicosia, the part of the journey along the hair-pin bends on the mountain roads, so different from the level central Messaoria plain, has to be broken for me to be car-sick.

**\*\*\*\*\*\*\*\*\*\***

These were the years when my parents must have been full of anxiety for the future of their children and especially concerned over the pressing question of where we were to go after the Froebel School. When I am with my grandchildren - and the two older ones are now at just the ages which spanned my brother's and mine at that time - I can in some measure share my parents' feelings when they must have come to the decisive point at which they concluded that our education ought to continue in England. All the clichés about being "cruel only to be kind", that "this hurts me more than it hurts you", that "love brings pain and hurt", rise up in my mind, ready to be given the standard derisory dismissals as clap-trap and hypocrisy, though never once did my parents in fact use such formulas with us - I doubt very much whether they even knew these expressions. In retrospect I can in all truth say (especially after having just shared the joy of taking all our grandchildren to a family pantomime) that my response to my parents' decision is simply admiration for their fortitude, and intense feelings of sympathy for them at that difficult time and the years which followed. All considerations of financial sacrifice and strain apart, I call to mind that in those days, before general passenger air transport, Cyprus was at least a ten days' voyage distant from Britain by ship through the Straits of Gibraltar and the turbulent Bay of Biscay, with a day or two saved if one disembarked at Marseilles and arrived in England *via* Paris and the Channel crossing. To be in Cyprus with your small children in England was then real separation. And yet, God knows how, we seemed to take it all in our stride.

You may of course, particularly if you are one of my generation, react by wondering what all this fuss and drama is about. Was it not after all merely common form for parents so to distance themselves, physically and emotionally, from their young children? Wasn't it the lot of all children whose fathers served in the outposts of empire to be despatched "home" to Britain? "Look at Kipling! Look at Saki!" you might say. "Indeed," I would reply, "Indeed. Look at them!" And remember too that we were not being despatched home; nor were our parents inured by the knowledge that *they* were simply acting as their own custom and tradition dictated.

**\*\*\*\*\*\*\*\*\*\***

To turn from my studied reaction more than sixty years after the event to what I recall of my sensations at the time. I am astounded that there was seemingly no trace of any anger or resentment in me. Am I therefore unconsciously determined not to remember any such feelings of hostility, or was I truly at that time so insensitive? Either way I am grateful that I was not turned against my parents. The only recollection - and that but faint - which remains to me from the time I learned we were to go from a school in Cyprus to one in England is being told by the sister of Miss Millen that we were going to be taught by men not women. This gave me a sense of foreboding.

# PART III : FLEDGLING

(1934-1950)

# ~4~

# Ashburton; East Allington; Ellesmere; Cyprus; Ellesmere

The voyage to England was a happy one. Whether or not our parents were deliberately steeling themselves to an appearance of stoical fortitude they did not convey to us that this was how we, eight and nine year olds, should conduct ourselves. I think children are very sensitive to a contrived attitude, and I was not at all conscious that my mother or father were acting a part. We might just have been going on an adventurous sea voyage, remarkable in nothing but its novelty. There were ship's games, of which I remember obstacle races for the children; and, for the adults, horse races using wooden model horses (from which, and from guessing the ship's daily "log", I first learned what a bet was). Curiously, being no great sailor since then, and considering my propensity to car-sickness, I wasn't seasick; and I did a fair amount of reading (and I have an impression that my parents derived some pleasure from this fact being noticed by fellow passengers).

**********

We are being introduced to Mr Evans Prosser at Ashburton Grammar School. Again I wonder how it was that this should have been the place, in a then remote Devonshire, chosen by our parents from all the various possibilities; though of course finance would very largely have reduced the field. I suspect now, from Ashburton's being a Devon country town, and not very far from the smaller place Merrivale (from which Edward Duke hailed, and from which his father took the title of his barony), that Edward Duke played some part in the selection of this school for us. The headmaster was, so far as I know, not strictly speaking to be a guardian to us in England but he did stand, at least unofficially, *in loco parentis*. That being so, it seems to me now, much more than "forty years on", passing strange that after no more than one term at Ashburton we were to find ourselves a hundred and fifty miles or so to the north, in Shropshire. While I don't think it at all likely that my parents would have known of this imminent change at the time they left us with Evans Prosser it is, I suppose, just possible. I have always thought that among the considerations which could have weighed quite heavily with them in their choice of Devon was the reputation which that county had, especially its southern half, as the "English Riviera". We were after all going to spend not only the seven months or so of the three school terms a year in Devon but also the rest of the year during our holidays; so somewhere in this bleak England which enjoyed a climate somewhat tempered to their shorn lambs might well have had a strong appeal.

**********

My first impression, and one of the most lasting, of Ashburton is of Evans Prosser introducing us to Mrs Lucas (henceforward aunt Dorothy), the wife of the Rector of East Allington a few miles away. It is to be at the Rectory that I and my brother are to spend our holidays - and, as it turned out, for the next five years, even after we had left Ashburton to go to Ellesmere College. Aunt Dorothy, I remember, asked me about Father Christmas. She was in no way disconcerted, but on the contrary rather amused, by my stout denial of belief in his existence.

I write this having just heard on the news that the Japanese are to develop an electronic model of the human brain which they hope to have completed by 2005. From this they are said to believe they will understand the processes by which the (I think) five thousand million separate nerve endings of our brains, linked in an inconceivably intricate network with each other, enable us to retain information and retrieve it. By which process I should, supposedly, be able to discover how - but even then not why - among all the things that happened on the day my parents took their leave of us, two things only are called up now by my brain. First, that I was taken by my father alone to another school, just across the way from the grammar school, called "The Wilderness".

43

**Fledgling**

(That is how I saw the name at the time; but I now recall that when Bertie Wooster discovered that, in the face of his express instructions, Jeeves had inveigled him into taking a cottage - from which Jeeves would be able to engage in some fishing - the following dialogue had taken place:

"I should find a little fishing most enjoyable ... while we are at Wee Nooke."

"Did you say "Wee Nooke?"

"Yes, sir."

"Spelled, I'll warrant, with an 'e'?"

"Yes, sir."

I suspect the same applied to the place of which I recall the headmaster saying to my father, to his evident gratification, that I was "as sharp as a razor". I can see now that the expression is, and quite possibly was then, capable of more than one interpretation.) My other memory of that last day is of our parents giving us each a toy like a wooden pistol with a cardboard or celluloid cup on top, out of which, when you pressed the trigger, a ping-pong ball shot up for you to catch it in as the ball descended. It is a grievous disappointment for me that I shall not be around when the Japanese electronic brain reveals the secret of the process by which this significant event is still retained in my brain while memory of others at that time is fled.

Except for one other, which now comes back to me. Psychologists, or psycho-analysts, might I suppose be able to theorise why this latter episode has been retained since my eighth year. It must have been some sort of singing class we presumably shared with some girls at The Wildernesse. A choir of girls rather older than me are singing: "Early one mo-o-rning, just as the sun was ri-i-sing, I heard a maiden singing in the va-a-lley below: O don't decei-eive me; O never lea-eave me..." That song still has power to draw tears from me.

\*\*\*\*\*\*\*\*\*\*\*

Ellesmere is the most northern of the Woodard schools. Of that Foundation, Lancing is the senior, a school nonetheless which Evelyn Waugh was seemingly ashamed to have been to. (Though he would probably have been unashamed only of Eton - or, in his subsequent days as a Catholic, of Downside.) Ellesmere was in those days in that category of public school which was the subject of the waggish comment: "The sort of school which when asked which school you had been to, you begin: 'Well, actually....'" The way this reflects a then typical, and specifically English, attitude and nuance is evident in the fact that the witticism is incapable of being rendered into Turkish, and probably other languages. Evans Prosser had been appointed to the headship of Ellesmere; so with him to Ellesmere we went. Now ordained and become "the Rev." - as I believe the heads of all the Woodard Schools were then required to be - his ordination must have happened in pretty rapid order.

Before taking the reader up to Shropshire it is to the rectory at East Allington that I now turn, that being the place where, more than at school, the self I once was, and to a fair extent am still, was first "rough hewn" - though more gently than roughly.

\*\*\*\*\*\*\*\*\*\*

The nominal head of the Lucas family was the Rector, John Lucas (to become to us "Uncle Jack"). A tallish, craggy, and ascetic-looking cleric, from him we felt remote. The only times we met were at family meals. Met, that is to say, to speak with. He was, I believe, a conscientious visitor to his parishioners; and respected by them, so far as impressions go - which derive mainly from such functions as the village *fêtes*. From overtones of conversations across the dining-room table between Uncle Jack and Aunt Dorothy (or, more familiarly "Aunt D") I caught some hint that the village did not consist entirely of parishioners of their church; but I have only a vague recollection of a plainish building which was "the Chapel". In those days the gulf between the Church of England and "Dissent" or "Non-conformity", still existed to a degree now inconceivable.

Of the three Lucas children, Bridget (in her very early twenties) had already left home and either then or very soon afterwards was a nanny with a family in London. (I later learned that the father was a barrister and M.P., Henry Willink, who was, very briefly, to be Minister of Health in the short-lived Conservative government of 1945 when, immediately after the end of the European War - Japan was still some months away from experiencing the first atom bombs on Hiroshima and Nagasaki - Labour left the wartime coalition to win by a landslide the general election of that year.) Pam, the next eldest Lucas, left to take up a secretarial job in the Scilly Isles after our first holiday at the rectory. She had been at Cheltenham Ladies' College (I believe with a scholarship - she was much the cleverest of the three Lucas children). Michael, known as Mick, was about a year and a half older than my brother.

The village of East Allington was deep in the Devonshire countryside. Kingsbridge was six miles away, Totnes nine, Paignton five miles beyond Totnes, and Thurlestone (with the beach at Bantham) some miles on the other side of Kingsbridge. Dartmouth was about ten miles away in the opposite direction and not a place we went to - except once to see the Naval College. Only occasionally did we go into the village, either to Mrs Penny's tiny shop for sweets, or to the small post office where Cyril , a red-headed postmaster (a sort of Postman Pat before his time), sold Cidrax and other teeth-rotting fizzy drinks.

The rectory itself was completely isolated. About a quarter of a mile from the village, it was approached off the tarmac main road down a long track through a large field, after which a drive continued to curve down a slope, at the bottom of which stood the house. Mid- to late-Victorian, the grey building was not aesthetically particularly attractive, even rather forbidding at first sight. But it grew on one. Built in typical Devon granite and slate, it was the kind of house a country professional of the time would have lived in. There was no electricity - lighting was by Aladdin oil lamps, and we used candles going to bed. Looming shadows as we climbed up the dark stairs. In the 1930s the finances of a remote Anglican living were no longer what they had once been fifty and more years before. Uncle Jack and Aunt Dorothy must have fairly recently decided to augment his stipend by taking in children as "paying guests" for the holidays. A PG was by no means a rarity in the hard economic times of the 1930s slump.

When we two boys turned up there were already two other PG children, Peggy and John Taylor; Peggy I think was about fourteen or fifteen years old, and John was around my age or a very little older. They turned out to be related to Aunt Dorothy; their parents were in India, he being in the Indian Police. Before the 1939 war there were very many British families living abroad - in India, Burma, the Sudan, and the colonies - whose children were at boarding schools in the UK; and for those who couldn't be taken by relatives, holiday homes had to be found. Where and how father found the Lucases I can only surmise. Most likely it was Evans Prosser who had arranged for us to go to them as soon as he had accepted us for Ashburton.

Thinking - and feeling myself - back to those mid-thirties, I have a curious sensation that we were somehow caught up in an era which was not quite of its time. The thirties had just about managed to seep into this remote place through a few gramophone records which had been left behind by the lively, smart (in today's term "with it") Bridget when she had gone off to London with the Willinks. From such numbers as "Red sails in the sunset" and various Jack Hulbert and Cicely Courtneidge songs, I became aware of a different, metropolitan, world of theatres, musical comedy and "romance". "Smoke gets in your eyes" is a song which still vividly evokes that period for me and plays on my emotions - though when I first listened to it I had no idea of the pathos of the words in its title! These records also introduced me to such gems as "Where do the flies go in the winter time?", which I also confuse with "The flies crawl up the window". But on the whole the general atmosphere of the place was that of an epoch scarcely emerged from pre-1914 Edwardian England. This impression can, naturally, only be retrospective. I couldn't at the age of nine or ten have had any idea of what the country had really been like a generation earlier; and in any case isolated villages like East Allington, and indeed small rural parsonages, may all have somehow been capsules of an England as yet not too deeply affected by the coming of the motor car, wireless, ribbon-development, and all those other changes so wonderfully evoked by George Orwell in his relatively unregarded novels like *A Clergyman's Daughter* and *Coming up for Air*.

Socially the Lucases would have been what I was later to know as impoverished gentry, but without being in the least resentful or negative about it. It was, I imagine, very largely for the purposes of seeing Mick through his public school that we PGs had been taken on. It must have been a heavy responsibility for Aunt D to have us, but she was all that my parents might be thought to have looked for. Never once did any of us, as far as I know, feel anything but entirely part of the family. Certainly I think of my time there with warmth and affection.

It would only have been a year or so after the rectory had become our holiday home that Michael Stone arrived from Cyprus. This had come about as a result of our parents' recommendation to the Stones, who were now living, as tenants of my grandmother, in the house in Nicosia in which we ourselves had lived while going to the Froebel School. Immediately opposite it there was now a small modern thirties-style house my father had built and in which my parents had their home. (This house has its own place in my story thirty years, and more, later.) From the rectory we must, directly or indirectly, have conveyed very good reports of the place in our regular weekly letters home - which, curiously, I have no memories of writing - and these would certainly have been retailed to the Stone parents. Michael was now to go to Blundell's, the minor public school at Tiverton about twenty miles away from East Allington. Mick on the other hand had just started at the like school, Kelly College, no further distant. *Apropos* which, the peculiar role which the public schools then played in the social scheme of things was again nicely demonstrated with the appearance on the scene of the Milner-White family.

Rudolph Milner-White had just retired from the Indian Civil Service. He and his wife had bought a very large house, Sheplegh, in the neighbouring parish of Blackawton. There, with their three daughters, they came to live - in about a third of the house, the rest remaining empty. Such large houses were then, during the depression, virtual white elephants and could be acquired very cheaply. Whether on doctrinal grounds or not I do not know, nor have I been interested enough to find out, the Milner-Whites found the church services at East Allington more to their taste than those in their own parish; and it was outside Uncle Jack's church that I first met the family. One day Rudolph Milner-White, as unpompous a man as could be imagined, and with not a shred of snobbery in him, was told by Mick that he was at Kelly. "And when," enquired Milner-White politely, "will you be going on to your public school?" - wholly unaware that Kelly was in fact one and, of the minor kind, well-regarded. Yet totally unknown to the Old Harrovian ex-ICS man - to his own intense embarrassment and discomfiture.

**\*\*\*\*\*\*\*\*\*\*\***

The only communal place inside the rectory was the dining-room, which had a big open fireplace. In the winter I spent a great deal of my time in a wicker-work chair reading books from a bookcase by the side of the fire-place. Among these books were bound volumes of *Punch* going back very many years. I feel sure, looking back, that these added to the sense that we were living in a kind of time-warp. As I have said, there was an almost pre-First World War atmosphere about that remote house. (Aunt D's clothes, as I see them through memory's eye, were surely Edwardian. From reading, and looking at the pictures in those old *Punch*es, my eye became, and remains, attuned to recognising periods in history from the clothes of the time.) Other books I remember are Edith Nesbit's stories of the Bastable family. I only came upon the same author's other books, like *Five Children and It*, when my daughter was moving from infancy to childhood. There were also the P.G.Wodehouse school stories, in bound volumes of the magazine *The Captain*. In these I was introduced to the character Psmith, in whom one may discern the chrysalis which was to develop into those later butterfly figures exemplified in the likes of the Hon. Galahad Threepwood, the Earl of Ickenham, and those others whose persiflage is that of the Fourth Form schoolboy carried into adulthood - and none the worse for that, in its place. The first time I made my acquaintance with this mode was, I suppose, when Psmith is asked at school why his name is so spelled. His response is that "Smith" is much too ordinary; that he despised the device of hyphenating it - and as for "Smythe", he regarded that as "a cowardly evasion". (The 1890s being more decorous times than the 1930s, he only pointed out that "the 'p' is silent - as in 'pshrimp' ", rather than, as the comparable wag of my own middle school days had done, "... as in swimming".)

## Fledgling

I suppose that I was at that time something of what was known as a "book-worm". But no-one at the rectory reproached me for this, though Aunt D did sometimes try to encourage me to get out a bit more often. I was not then at all interested in the two horses in the stable at the top of the drive (or rather in the pony-like stocky 'Penny' and the old retired polo pony 'Swift'), on the smaller of which my brother certainly used to ride. I found more companionable the two dogs - who often lay by the dining-room fire, rather niffily, as I recall, but not offensively so: 'Bobbie', a kind of *mélange* of sheepdog and conceivably, given his rather short legs, bassett hound; and a terrier, very far from short-haired, called 'Scrap'.

Outdoor activities included bicycle-polo on the lawn; and tennis of a kind, very rarely, with a very superannuated net and rudimentary court markings. And in the early days there was a good deal of tree climbing, especially of the conifers whose regular and straight branches enabled us to shin up very high and quickly. The art was to tread at the point where the branch emerged from the trunk, so leaving a wedge-like foothold if ever a branch were to give way. (I try now, but am unable, to recapture the glorious sensation, something I imagine of what a bird must feel, as we looked far out over the fields and the house from our perches at the top of those trees - high and free.)

But my favourite activity was juvenile woodwork. I used to envy Mick Lucas, who 'did' carpentry at school and had a real set of tools in a tool-chest. I started with a hand fretsaw with which one could do 'fretwork', producing things like pipe-racks, corner wall-brackets and objects of that sort. From this I progressed, *via* kits at a shilling or two, (obtained by post from 'Hobbies Ltd, Dereham, Norfolk' - odd that I have remembered that) to making models. I believe my first was one of Sydney Harbour Bridge, which I think had just been built in Australia, and a fair amount of fretwork was involved. I coveted a treadle fretsaw which I saw in the Hobbies leaflets, but could never afford one. I then moved to ship models - the *Golden Hind*, the *Hispaniola* (the schooner in Stevenson's Treasure Island), and Columbus's flagship the *Santa Maria*. I pursued this hobby in a little room at the end of the upstairs passage opposite the bedroom my brother and I shared. I realise now that these rooms which the PGs occupied were what would have been the maids' bedrooms when Victorians and Edwardians could afford domestic servants; they were on the north of the house with no sun and with direct access from the backstairs which led down to the kitchen passage below.

When we first knew the Lucases they had no motor car. On our second or third holiday a small 'baby Austin' made its appearance. Its number is still in my memory - OD 7886. What the number is of our car now standing outside our flat I am not absolutely sure. The Austin was no bigger than a five-seater at most, but into it we crammed on the infrequent occasions, a couple of times a year or so, when Aunt D took us to the cinema. This was always in Paignton and sometimes preceded by a tea, with eclairs, at Dellers tea-shop. The films were obviously chosen carefully as being educational and 'improving' - however bland they might appear today: *Fire over England* (Flora Robson as Elizabeth I), *The Thirty-nine Steps*, *The Lives of a Bengal Lancer* - particularly enjoyed by John Taylor, *Captains Courageous* (Freddie Bartholomew as the spoilt millionaire brat to be toughened on the fishing boat into upstanding boy), with the occasional touch of comedy and even of satire in *The Ghost Goes West*.

I recall two occasions when I was in disgrace at the Rectory. Once my brother and I had a flaming row - I have completely forgotten what it was all about. I flung at him one of my 'house shoes', as they were called. I was on the top landing and he was running down the main stairs. I missed him and the shoe went through, or anyway broke, the landing window. I don't remember being punished - no doubt the cost of repair was added to father's bill - but I sense again in recollection an overhanging air of dire disapproval - very different from the usual benign sunniness of Aunt D. The other time I got into trouble was when some grown-up relative of the Lucases had come for a meal from some way away - it could have been from Norfolk which was the part of the world that Mrs Lucas's family, the Armstrongs, came from. Uncle Jack was teasing me, in some fairly innocuous way I imagine. I don't remember any one particular thing getting my goat; but a furious feeling of "this is too much" swept over me and I flared at him. I have a distinct memory of flinging gravel at him - perhaps at him and the guest - not at the moment I must have snapped, which I think was at the meal, but presumably as the guest was leaving. I was ticked off by Uncle Jack - in terms which have not remained with me; but the heavy

51

atmosphere of disgrace has. It is curious how no punishment seems to have attended on either of these incidents. In fact I don't recall anyone being punished in that household. Were we really such a lot of near prigs? Or was the whole place wonderfully well conducted, without it seeming to be? This seems to me now to be a pretty fair definition of how things ought ideally to be. To the extent that one has to resort to punitive sanctions, that is itself a measure of failure in the system; though an unfailing system would seem to be a human impossibility. However, as it happens, I don't actually remember punishment from our parents either - perhaps a psycho-analysis would reveal something? We must have had prohibitions, but again these are not in my conscious memory. I think we may have been fortunate in somehow imbibing a sense of what was acceptable and what was not, largely unconsciously, through the example of our parents and the Lucases - the very opposite of the "Do as I say, not as I do" philosophy which seems to me to be even more destructive than the "Do as you will" variety. If indeed it were the case that we passed our formative years in surroundings where, without it being preached, we were learning consideration for others, then (to misquote St. Paul) we were indeed of all men the most fortunate.

Every Sunday at the rectory we trooped off mid-morning to church. We walked across three fields. The route seems in memory to have been quite a long hike, although it was pretty much in a direct line; but this was preferred to what would have been three sides of a rectangle: going right up the drive, left along the main road and on through the village. Although I am sure Mr Lucas was a good country parson, I remember very little of substance in the services - while much of the liturgical language has nevertheless been retained in my memory. I think I do have a recollection of feeling that the music was, compared with Ellesmere's High Anglican services, pretty awful; but how could a village 'choir' compete with a very drilled and trained one? A powerful female voice from the congregation comes to me as I think myself back to that Devon village church. It seems to me now that at the time I had no sense of anything specifically 'religious' about going to church. Any more I suppose than the memorising in Arabic of the opening *Sura* of the Koran had, at the age of about six or seven at Kyrenia, given me a sense of another and deeper dimension of life. But then, indeed, why should any child develop in this way a spirituality apart from its growth in true, ordinary humanity?

**\*\*\*\*\*\*\*\*\*\***

It was at East Allington church that we rectory boys first became aware of the three Milner-White girls. The middle one was almost exactly my contemporary, the eldest almost my brother's, and the youngest was about five years old. It is of this youngest that I have the earliest anecdotal memory. She would have been with her parents and sisters talking with Aunt D after a service and observed, "I am the brains of this family." I cannot swear that I heard this myself, but if I didn't then I must have overheard Aunt D retailing the incident to Uncle Jack over the Sunday lunch. In the way of nine or ten year old boys - readers of Richmal Crompton's *William* books will recognise the situation of the Outlaws and Violet Elizabeth Bott - this insignificant child, and a girl at that, was regarded by John Taylor and me as beneath contempt, and to be avoided if observed to be coming, or known to be, for a visit. In such circumstances we took off and disappeared beyond the far end of the lawn to shin up trees. But this tree climbing also had an element of drawing attention to oneself - not so much from the five year old Rhodope, but from the elder sisters. My only quite sure impression from that time of these Milner-White girls is that the dark-haired pig-tailed eldest one was the 'beauty of the family'; and that my feelings were of being much attracted by her, while at the same time thinking that I owed it to myself to present a front of indifference. This sense of what was proper to a boy derived - and I feel my retrospective analysis is more than likely to be right - partly from John Taylor, and partly from the attitudes of the boys as depicted in the adventures of the fictional Bastables, especially the elder - and the narrator of the stories - Oswald.

**\*\*\*\*\*\*\*\*\*\***

On Boxing Day 1936 I woke up with pain under my ears. I told no-one, but went with the others, as foot followers, to the local hunt. Next day, however, the mumps were very obvious, and I was extremely unwell. I spent what seems a very long time in bed. It was then, and I remember it clearly, that I made the acquaintance of the world of English pantomime - with the classic "Why did the chicken cross the road?" joke in a book of stories. What Charles Lamb's *Tales from Shakespeare* is to the Bard this book was to the pantomime scene: narratives of the standard plots, with some dialogue and jokes, of the main pantomimes - *Jack and the Beanstalk, Aladdin, Cinderella* and the rest - none of which in fact I ever actually saw in my childhood or youth. I wasn't allowed back to school for a great part of the Easter term. In those days boarders had to take back at the beginning of every term a 'health certificate' in case they had come into even remote contact with infectious disease. When I did get back to the Junior School at Ellesmere, I had of course missed a large number of lessons and I still recall my sense of a break in the even flow of those lessons and my feeling that things, especially maths, were not now as smooth and easy as they had so far been, without knowing exactly how. Which doesn't say a great deal for my initiative I suppose - or, if it comes to that, for the school's direct concern with individual boys. Possibly Evans Prosser had been more concerned with his charge's physical health than with this academic hiccup. On which note I turn to my time at Ellesmere from 1935.

**********

Sitting on radiators trying to keep warm - and being told that this merely encourages chilblains. Perhaps it did too, because while I remember very precisely chilblains as something quite new in my experience, and itchily painful, they don't feature in my memory as a continuing torment.

There are more than enough works of literature - from mediocre to high art - which tell of life at a British public school. For me to attempt even a prosaic descriptive account would be otiose and, paradoxically, somehow irrelevant. The period is, I suppose, one of the great formative times of a person's life - those years between pre-puberty and about seventeen or eighteen. Yet I am conscious of only very few significant happenings; scarcely indeed of anything much more than the almost automatic passage of time through a procession of organised activity taking place in form rooms, rugger fields, cricket pitches, chapel, dining hall, and country lanes on school 'runs'. These latter, which I loathed, were known as the 'big grind' and the 'small grind' - about five miles and three miles respectively. A memory of these ghastly runs: an Indian (though he would, I think, now be a Pakistani) donning a pair of white gloves as a mark of distaste for the whole lamentable proceeding and coming in last, by a very long way, at a gentle, and gentlemanly, lope. It might even have been a stroll for the final short stretch. I seem to remember him getting a fair amount of amused approval, and even applause.

There were studies only for school prefects, of whom there were no more than around ten. The three senior prefects wore purple gowns: the Captain of School, the Prefect of Chapel and the Prefect of Hall. Looking back on it all we seemed to have practically no free time, and in any case there was nowhere to spend any such time in any kind of privacy. Each House had a 'House Room'. These common rooms were really no more than places to sit around in. At Meynells, my House, we did have a small billiards table. In these rooms we could read, and write letters - though I seem to recall there was nothing to stop you doing this in the various form rooms.

Ellesmere was a reasonably musical place, possibly not unconnected with the fact that we had a lot of Welsh boys. Those with the same surname were identified numerically, and at one time the Joneses went up to Jones IX. In a sort of crypt underneath 'Hall' (the dining hall, quite separate from the even larger 'Big School' off which opened many of the form rooms) there were quite a few music practice rooms. Here I practised the pieces set in my (voluntary, and 'extra') weekly piano lessons, reaching eventually the easier Beethoven sonatas or movements from them, and Chopin nocturnes, mazurkas, waltzes and preludes. My *pièce de résistance* (and not too difficult of resistance) was Chopin's E flat major nocturne.

The school buildings were even more isolated than the rectory. A single huge Victorian 1870s pile set in extensive grounds, it was about a couple of miles from the town of Ellesmere. School houses were not individual buildings but consisted of separate wings or blocks of the H-shaped school - two big open quadrangles. There was no contact between boys of different Houses; we mixed with those of other Houses only in the course of lessons, as players or spectators at matches, in the Officers' Training Corps (OTC), or in a few school societies or activities. For those who acted - I didn't - there was the annual Shakespeare play.

**Fledgling**

The OTC symbolised and embodied the class nature of public schools, and indeed of the armed services, in those days. It was, generally speaking, assumed that officers in the services were to be drawn from a particular social class and that members of that class would be educated at public schools. There seemed to be some blindness to the fact that the range of such classes represented in these very disparate schools, with Eton, Westminster, Winchester, Harrow and the like at one end and the 'minor' schools at the other, was so immense as to make this classification to a large extent meaningless. In retrospect I realise that at Ellesmere - and for all I know at other such places - we were living in an atmosphere several school generations behind the times. It is odd that this should have been so when, as I have already remarked, our holidays at East Allington, too, seem to have been passed in a mental climate that was a throwback, probably closer to the Edwardian era - at any rate pre-First World War - than the immediately post-1914-18 War of Ellesmere in the thirties. The outward evidence of this at school was that, right up to the Second World War, beginning in 1939, our OTC uniform was still the heavy serge high-collared tunic and 'plus fours' together with 'puttees' (khaki bandage-like material rolled round and round from tops of boots all around the calves up to just below the knee). We looked exactly like the troops in the trenches of the Western Front during those appalling four years in Flanders which I used to read about in the illustrated volumes of those ghastly campaigns to be found in the House 'library' - that is, on the shelves at one end of the House Room. These were no doubt intended as edifying reading matter in the spirit of the previous generation. The school motto - and this for an Anglican foundation - was *Pro Patria Dimicans*: Fighting for the Fatherland. I had been under the impression that this had been changed since my time; but I have recently been told that this is not so. A pity, if so - shades of the grim picture in grandmother's house of the battle in the Turkish War of Salvation in the very wake of those battles in Flanders.

\*\*\*\*\*\*\*\*\*\*\*

There was chapel every weekday morning between breakfast and first lesson; and twice on Sunday. It was always evensong on Sunday evening, and I think I am right in remembering that the Sunday morning

56

service was Sung Eucharist. It was only at East Allington that I heard Matins. While I believe I can say that I managed to compose myself to a reasonable sense of devotion in chapel, the extravagant ritualistic to-ing and fro-ing at the altar end conveyed to me a general air of fussiness and even of ostentation which made me uncomfortable. Nor did I warm to the chaplain, who struck me as someone anxious to ingratiate - though not with me particularly. I felt unsympathetic to the *coterie* from which were drawn the chapel 'servers', irritating in their surplices and general air of 'holiness'. If I have a tendency to 'puritanism', I suspect that, paradoxically, the 'High Anglican' Ellesmere chapel has played its part in forming, or at any rate in inducing, this. It was not in chapel, however, that I had any sense of being in any way 'different'. To the extent that I was to feel this it was to derive from more mundane matters.

***********

It was in chapel that one day prayers were said for my brother. There had been a measles epidemic. I had gone down with it, but had been passed fit again. My brother had in turn joined the dozen and more in the sanatorium I had left. (I believe that quite a lot of boys had been taken off home by their parents, as there were a large number of boarders who lived within twenty or thirty miles of the school.) Whether or not I had received any forewarning is not clear in my recollection, but in retrospect I can still feel the great shock of learning from an intercessory prayer in chapel that my brother was dangerously ill. In whatever terms the prayer was couched the very fact of God's being addressed on his behalf meant that divine intervention was being asked to enable him to live. The measles had developed into what was called 'double pneumonia' and, in those pre-antibiotic days, the chances of recovery were slim. In the event he pulled through. I remember as if it were yesterday being told by my Housemaster that the "crisis has passed" and that my brother was "out of danger"; but I have no memory of having previously been told that such a crisis, marking the danger point in the progress of the disease, was inevitably to be expected. (It is I suppose because of this experience, and the way I was later to hear of the unexpectedly early death of my father, that I have ever since recoiled from giving bad news to anyone and have avoided doing so if I possibly could.)  During my brother's immediate convalescence in England he was prescribed stout; and I can still see him drinking down the black stuff with no evident sign of enjoyment.  This was at the time the Guinness advertising  slogan was widely displayed on billboards : "Guinness is good for you" - a claim I suspect which would today run foul of the Trades Descriptions Act.  It was considered essential by the doctor that my brother should not spend the next winter in England. And so back to Cyprus he went, missing most of a school year.

**\*\*\*\*\*\*\*\*\*\***

At Ellesmere we slept in House dormitories of twenty or so iron beds, a Junior and a Senior dormitory for each House.  We cleaned our teeth and washed in cold water every morning, winter and summer, at a row of basins at one end of the dormitory. Baths, as I believe might have been the case generally at that time in England, were weekly affairs - though we had regular soaks in a steaming communal rectangular 'tub' in the changing room after rugger.  It was after all not very much more than some fifty or so  years earlier - about as far distant in the past then as those Ellesmere days are from today - that the head of an Oxford college had remonstrated against a proposal to install bathrooms: "Bathrooms! But the undergraduates only come up for eight weeks at a time!"

Our meals were all in Hall, which accommodated the whole school, but here again we sat grouped in our separate Houses.  It was in Hall that we were handed out any letters or other mail we had received.  A parcel I particularly remember contained a handsome iced birthday cake ordered by father for delivery on the day from the Army and Navy Stores.  Their thick bound red annual catalogue had its place in the lives of many 'overseas' families.  Short of the traditional, and mythological, "cleft stick for carrying messages", which features hilariously in Evelyn Waugh's *Black Mischief*, practically anything could be ordered from that volume. I only recall getting such a birthday cake once; perhaps it was while my brother was in Cyprus and it was some kind of consolation for my being on my own.  Another item I remember getting was *The Children's Newspaper* which arrived regularly, I think weekly.  This, in much the same format as an adult daily paper, was I think aimed at diverting me from that staple of many of my contemporaries - comics. Yet I also received what could have been regarded as a comic, a not unwholesome and innocuous magazine called *Film Fun*.

**\*\*\*\*\*\*\*\*\*\***

My recollection of first having a feeling of being in some way set apart relates to a memory in Hall. Breakfast consisted of such traditional fare as bacon, eggs, tomatoes and sausages - sometimes with fried bread - not all together but, as I recall, in combinations of any two of these. I believe it was during the war, when eggs in particular were rationed, that while the others were having bacon and tomato, I was given egg and tomato. I deduce this to have been on instructions from my father - bacon being of course impermissible for Moslems, as for Jews. But this could have happened *before* the war and following on my brother's arrival in Cyprus after he had been so ill. Anyway I was conscious of being differentiated from the others in a way I had not until then known.

**\*\*\*\*\*\*\*\*\*\***

It was in the summer of 1939, when I was thirteen and a half, that my brother and I came out to Cyprus for a holiday which was supposed to last about a month. This was the only time I had been there in the five years since I had gone to school in England. And the gap between one's eighth and thirteenth years is a huge one. The Polish crisis boiled over while we were out in Cyprus. On the 2nd of September, following Hitler's invasion of Poland, Britain gave Germany an ultimatum to withdraw within twenty four hours. The next day Chamberlain announced over the wireless that, as the withdrawal had not been made, Britain was at war with Germany. We were unable to return to England.

My immediate reaction was youthful excitement and pleasure that I was going to stay on indefinitely in Cyprus. I suppose, given my age, I might be forgiven for being so unimaginative. Father and mother must have been desperately worried and anxious - whether to accept that all their plans and expense so far on an English education for their children must be abandoned or whether, against the odds, they should try to get us back to England, with all the separation, and danger, that this would involve in conditions of world war. They must have agonised over this.

Father was then the Superintendent of Police in charge of Larnaca district and also, for a period, additionally responsible for the adjoining district of Famagusta while the English Superintendent was on leave. In Larnaca we lived in the official house allocated to the Superintendent, a typical PWD building, solid, roomy, with the usual verandah running all round; not unlike the old Froebel School house in Kyrenia. There was a small nine-hole golf course nearby, which father would very occasionally go round with my brother. This was quite near a little landing strip for light aircraft, which has now I believe become the site of the post-1974 main airport of Southern (Greek) Cyprus. A mile or so away is the *Tekke*, shrine, of Hala Sultan, a delightful small mosque by the edge of the salt lake, yet surrounded by greenery - cypresses and palms. It is the site of the tomb of the Prophet Mohammed's aunt and wet nurse Umm Haram: a place traditionally visited, and especially before setting out on a journey.

**\*\*\*\*\*\*\*\*\*\***

Of those months in Cyprus my recollections are very 'bitty'. In Larnaca we were cut off from the family in Nicosia, and we knew no one of our age nearby. I can see now how extremely busy and preoccupied father must have been during the weeks while war was looming and then when war was declared: administrative preparations for all the civil defence wartime controls must have filled his time and mind, quite apart from the normal running of district police work. When he went on inspections he sometimes took us with him. I remember a visit to Famagusta, where he had served during his early married life. We went to the beach there, which I well recall as miles of clean, bright, unspoiled sand. There was a single old-fashioned red-tiled building - the George Hotel where we had a meal. (Against the background of my subsequent political experience of the island I can now see that the name was a subtle way for the Greek owner to ride two horses at the same time: the name of the Kings of both England and of Greece was at that time George.)

60

Photographs of my brother and me enjoying ourselves on that beach and plying a rowing boat relive those days for me; as also does one of me reading a book just inside the verandah.  I must have spent a great deal of my time doing that and I feel pretty sure that it was then that I was first introduced to a P.G.Wodehouse book that wasn't one of the school stories I had read in the bound volumes of *The Captain* at the rectory.  My first 'real' Wodehouse book was one of the Mulliner volumes - and the first of those stories I read was, I think, about the stutterer who gets his girl nevertheless.  My abiding appreciation of the English language I owe in very large measure to that master stylist.  Good style I understand to be such writing as cannot be improved by adding, taking away, or changing even a single word.  By that stern and rigid test Wodehouse cannot be faulted.  I owe him a huge debt for the pure pleasure I have enjoyed reading his gloriously funny books over a lifetime.  I did not know then that what I was reading was beautiful, impeccable, English; merely that I was very happy doing so.  And when I was to learn much later that the University of Oxford had accorded him the honour of a D.Litt. my gratification would have been somewhat akin to that of the Wodehouse character who had "discovered that alcohol was a food well in advance of medical science".  Just as watching the stars at Wimbledon tempts one never again to touch a tennis racquet, so the thought of Wodehouse's prose urges me to stop trying to record my memories.  But I plough on.

Our being away from school was clearly worrying father - especially as my brother had already missed much of a year when he had been so ill.  He managed for a while to get hold of a young man, George Meikle, who was an assistant master at the English School in Nicosia, to come and tutor us once or twice a week - for maths and Latin, I seem to recall.  My very faint memories of these sessions are more of social occasions than of pedagogic instruction.

On one of father's tours of inspection he took us with him up the Karpass peninsula in the far north-east of the island.  This I recall as quite an expedition with some fairly hair-raising roads - though oddly enough my days of being car-sick seemed to have passed.  But I still gave myself nausea by trying to look through binoculars out of the car window.  I was struck, and I think impressed, that father seemed to know individually every policeman he came across even outside the police stations, especially as we were not in his own district but at the far end of Famagusta district.

**\*\*\*\*\*\*\*\*\*\***

A dim memory of helping my brother to rig up a small golf putting course in the garden by digging out little pits in the sun-baked solid earth. We had to soak the ground first and I remember using this clayey material to fashion heads - especially that of the Führer which was very easy to reproduce, with its square shaved moustache and 'lick' of hair across his forehead.

**\*\*\*\*\*\*\*\*\*\***

Very occasionally we went to Nicosia. Curiously enough I can't remember that we ever went to our parents' own house, built about three or four years earlier, and where my brother had lived during his recuperation a couple of years before. The house, my mother has told me, was simply shut up, awaiting a hoped-for return if and when father should be posted back to Nicosia. In the event this happened, and by the long-desired promotion to the Legal Department, to which he got his appointment as Crown Counsel - ten years after he had come back to Cyprus as a newly qualified barrister. He was in his very early forties (mother was thirty five) and he could very reasonably have expected to be appointed in the course of time to the next senior post of Solicitor General. But within the year he was dead. He died of cirrhosis of the liver, a disease normally brought on by alcoholism. Yet father was an observing Moslem, and therefore a teetotaller. In his case the disease was diagnosed as being the result of malaria in his youth, which had been somehow 'incubating' into his middle years. Since it is the liver which is affected, it occurs to me as a possibility that this could well have had something to do with the fact that he would occasionally show evidence of a strong, but never violent, temper.

His father, the Mufti, had been known to display irascibility. One such anecdote illustrates this aspect of the Mufti's character (or is it temperament?). His house was right opposite the Arab Ahmet mosque.

The signal for breaking the *Ramazan* fast each evening was the firing of a blank cannon shot from the ramparts by the Kyrenia gate about a quarter of a mile away to the north. The Mufti was said to have been seen once, around sunset, standing in his doorway calling out irately to the *muezzin* (who gave the call to prayer, the *ezan*, from the minaret) to get on with it - presumably because he, the Mufti, had judged, as he was entitled to do, that the time for the *iftar* had in fact arrived.

My grandfather also had a reputation for a certain tight-fistedness - or anyway a regard for the value of money (which I suppose doesn't necessarily equate with lack of generosity, but is rather a sort of 'look after the pence and the pounds will look after themselves', a 'waste not want not' attitude, which I think I have inherited from him - and which my impecunious years at Oxford did nothing to weaken). The Mufti was in his room with instructions that he was not to be disturbed. His wife, Hurmuz Hanım, tried to tell him that someone had called wanting to see him. "It's Hasan," she said. "Send him away," replied the Mufti, testily. "But he's come about the olive oil harvest." "Send him in," said the Mufti, equably.

The Mufti had died two years after we had gone off to England in 1934 (as also had my other grandfather Rasim Bey), and the Mufti's old house opposite the Arab Ahmet mosque no longer stands, having been demolished and replaced after the war by unattractive flats. In the autumn and winter of 1939-40 trips with father from Larnaca to Nicosia, when he had to go there on business, included large gatherings at family lunches given by the Mufti's widow in that old house. At these lunches I remember the meal not beginning until the entry of Munir Bey (my aunt Vesime's husband) who would walk in from his office just down the road. He was the Director of Evcaf, the institution responsible for the administration of Moslem ecclesiastical, charitable or trust properties. By virtue of this position he was an appointed member of the Governor's Executive Council in the capacity of the Turkish community's representative. With Munir Bey's arrival the small servant girl would bring the brass bowl and pitcher, *ibrik*, with soap and towel for him to wash his hands immediately before eating - a Moslem practice, indeed habit, which I do not always see being observed in Cyprus these days.

## Fledgling

It must have been either at Christmas 1939 or the New Year of 1940 that the Stones, still living in the 'old' house in Shakespeare Street - which had been our family home until 1934, and which Lalage and I with our two children were ourselves to occupy more than twenty years later - gave an evening party for about a dozen people. Father, mother and we two boys were also invited. (It now seems pretty clear to me that by this time final arrangements had been made for a return to England by my brother and me, father having managed to get us on a ship to Alexandria, transferring there to another going to Marseilles, from where we were to travel across France by train. That journey was also to be undertaken by Michael Stone; and his parents' party must have been in the nature of a farewell.) Perhaps we had used the opportunity of this evening invitation to spend the day in Nicosia taking in also the last of the family lunch gatherings. Anyway we had driven up from Larnaca earlier in the day. In the course of the morning father discovered that the Stone party was to be a black tie affair. And there followed an afternoon drive all the way back to Larnaca (normally a good hour's journey in those days on a far from well-aligned road) at what seemed to me - and as I recall to mother as well - an almost terrifying speed in order to change before returning for the party. It had been on this same road that, a few years before, as I later learned, father had nearly killed himself by falling asleep at the wheel on a tree-lined stretch, crashing into a tree. Many years afterwards I was to experience for myself how hypnotisingly soporific is the effect of driving along such a road with the rhythmical alternation of sunshine and shadow on the eyes and brain.

Whether on the night of the Stone party I can't be absolutely sure, but there was a night (the only one I remember) when we slept in Hidayet Hanım's house on the ramparts. The room we two brothers slept in was the same one which had been Fikret's (now a medical student in London) six or seven years before. A clear memory, early the next morning, of the itinerant *yoğurt* seller's cry of *"Yoğurtcu-u-u!"*. My last aural memory of Cyprus as a child.

\*\*\*\*\*\*\*\*\*\*\*

In early 1940 father, mother, my brother and I drive out to the Larnaca salt lake with its clouds of pink flamingos. (Possibly my memory is playing tricks and I am confusing these with the flamingos on the Limassol salt lake where Lalage and I used to ride in sight of that pink cloud there many years later: flamingos came to both places in their season). At the lakeside, down a shady tree-lined roadway, is the great iron gate set in the carved stone arched gateway opening on to the peaceful garden which surrounds the *Tekke* of Hala Sultan with its domed mosque and shrine, and cloister-like adjacent buildings. We come to this venerated place before we two boys leave Cyprus for the war-time voyage to England.

\*\*\*\*\*\*\*\*\*\*\*

Of the time between our visit to Hala Sultan and our actual embarkation no memory remains - nor of the departure itself. Probably the visit to the *Tekke* was followed by driving directly from the salt lake to Larnaca to board the mail packet the *Fouadieh*, which was to take us to Alexandria where we would join the Egyptian Khedieval Line steamer *Mohammed Ali el Kebir*, bound for Marseilles. The Mediterranean can be rough in winter - as St. Paul's shipwreck at Malta testifies. I lay on my bunk feeling ill. After partial recovery, but still supine, my spirits were lightened by reading one of the new Penguin books (just out at sixpence each - two and a half pence in today's money). It was *The Good Soldier Schweik*, a fictional and highly satirical account, by Jaroslav Hasek, of an unwilling Czech conscript's doings in the multi-ethnic army of the Austro-Hungarian Empire in the First World War. Representing, as in some kind my life did, a sort of transhipment from the beached wreck of one imperial hulk, to another similar - yet still sea-going - vessel (though far less fitted than was known at the time for the tempestuous waters that lay just below the horizon beyond), I was then quite unconscious of the symbolism of Hasek's book, so redolent of the last days of that other, leaking, Austro-Hungarian ship heading for the rocks.

\*\*\*\*\*\*\*\*\*\*

On arriving back in England we travelled straight back to Ellesmere. It was the Easter term of 1940, just before Hitler ordered the opening of the *Blitzkrieg* which, in a matter of weeks, gave him victory over the whole of north-western mainland Europe. (And I need to remind myself that although we have come to identify the word *Blitz* with the aerial bombardment of Britain which began in the autumn of 1940 it was actually the land offensive for which the German term 'lightning war' was first used, and seen in action - swift movement by armoured units, in combination with infantry, and supported by tactical dive-bombers.) We returned to Britain just about the time when the inactivity which was to be known as 'the phony war' ended and war in reality burst upon us. What my poor parents must have suffered, in full realisation of what they had sent us back to, I can now only faintly imagine. At the time, to my shame, and as far as I can remember, I did not even think of this.

I now note as a curious fact that in writing the earlier part of these recollections I found the episodes, and even the words to record them, came reasonably freely; but having now reached these later Ellesmere years, I find I have to strain - and even urge myself - to try to recapture that past. Those years seem to exist in a somehow strangely unreal dimension of being. This may of course be the consequence, more or less direct, of the fact that the arrival of puberty coincided with the onset of the first part of the real war so that the core years of my schooldays from 1940 to 1943 were the ones during which things were darkest on the war front. And from our return to Britain until I left school in the summer of 1943, we also no longer went down to Devon for our holidays, but used to go to different places nearer to the school. Only one of these places has left a mark on my memory. This was another rectory, at Erbistock on Deeside.

\*\*\*\*\*\*\*\*\*\*

It was while we were there that we learned of father's death the previous winter. As I think back to that moment when my brother told me the news - which had, unbelievably, reached him first by way of a letter of condolence from Miss Millen who was now in England and had just heard - I remember three things. First the absolute emotional numbness. I did not cry for a whole day - could not - and wondered why I wasn't crying and couldn't. Then, at breakfast the next day (over a boiled egg as it happens), the dam bursting, but soundlessly. And last, a quite new feeling of closeness to my brother.

**\*\*\*\*\*\*\*\*\*\***

The fall of Dunkirk; the blitz on London and other cities; the sinking of the *Hood*, and then of the *Repulse* off Malaya; the fall of the supposedly impregnable fortress of Singapore; the German advances in the Western Desert and the seemingly increasing likelihood that Cyprus would be in the front line - these were the background to our school years between 1940 and 1942. And yet, in retrospect, I seemed to be living detached from these epoch-making world events - only very infrequently aware of what was going on in the world outside - the 'real' world beyond Ellesmere. I imagine now that I was emotionally desensitised; but whether this was something which fitted me the better to cope with the 'unreality' of the position I was in, or was the dire consequence of it - who shall say?

**\*\*\*\*\*\*\*\*\*\***

It was also at Erbistock, as it now comes back to me, that I first felt the inner personal appeal of classical orchestral music. In the rectory there was a gramophone with a few records. Among these were Tchaikovsky's *Nutcracker Suite*, and Debussy's *La Cathédrale Engloutie*. But the record I played most was Haydn's 'Clock' Symphony. There is no accounting for why a particular piece of music should especially resonate with someone at the deepest emotional, even spiritual, level - or, if there is, I have never discovered the reason; but that Haydn piece became a part of me. And among the very first half dozen records I bought in the first year of married life was the 'Clock'. It was one of the first 'long players', which had just begun to replace the old 78 rpm's. Their reproductions were presumably relatively very expensive because my record, which I still have, has retained what sounds suspiciously like the clatter of one of the players dropping a violin bow (I have just interrupted this typing to confirm that this is indeed the case) - yet the recording was not scrapped.

***********

Two domestic breaks I recall from the continuous sights and sounds of school are of times I was invited to boys' homes. One was Stanley Roberts, who lived nearby on a small farm. His father would I think have been a tenant farmer. I don't recall whether or not he was away at the war, but it was Stanley's elder brother (who was not at school with us) who presided at the lunch. I well remember that very welcome change from school food - though that wasn't in truth at all bad. We ate the meal - roast beef, potatoes, Yorkshire pudding and vegetables, followed by apple pie - in a large kitchen, the elder brother sitting in his shirt-sleeves with detachable collar removed and front stud in place. A rather D. H. Lawrence scene - not that I knew anything of that at the time. Stanley and I went out shooting rabbits with a small 'four ten' single-barrelled shot gun. I don't recall whether either of us actually bagged anything. Stanley was the 'brains of the family' (even if on the analogy of the rather cruel but kindly intended Victorian adage: "Always remember, dear, that the least unattractive girl is the beauty of the family"); but the height of his ambition was to get his School Certificate and so get into a bank - a safe and reliable job in those days when agriculture was anything but a desirable occupation in the depression. The other time I visited a boy's home was when I was a House Prefect, the highest I ever reached, and my House Captain, Lambert, who was Prefect of Chapel, had me to stay during part of a holiday in, or near, Gloucester - where I have an idea his father was a Canon.

***********

Ellesmere was progressive, or modern, in that we did physics and chemistry up to Higher School Certificate (for those who wanted to). I acquitted myself up to School Cert. level. Demonstrations of the various experiments as a rule worked out as intended. But I was never to see successfully 'demonstrated' the 'electrolysis of water' - of which I remain ignorant to this day, as the experiment invariably failed. Two things I remember distinctly in 'science'. First that the text-book definition, in 1940-41, of an atom was: "the smallest indivisible particle of matter", although that had already been split quite a few years before. Second, the very striking effect of sprinkling iron filings into a bunsen burner so that, when lit by the unsuspecting master, a most satisfyingly picturesque, sparkling jet of fireworks is produced. Innocent merriment the intention, but not so regarded by the object of the jest.

I was only once beaten at school. In fairness it should be said that Ellesmere was not a place where beating was common, though it was generally taken as acceptable - or at any rate regarded as a normal punishment in its place (which I imagine begs a question or two). I was fifteen years old and in the Sixth Form, the youngest but one. Half a dozen of us were in the school Library during a free study period. Among us was a School Prefect - as I recall he was the Prefect of Hall, a Welshman and a great rugger player, as well as a fast bowler whose run and delivery were much guyed by the unregenerate. He had taken off his purple gown and left it draped over the back of his chair while he went out of the room, presumably to go to the lavatory. In his absence, for a joke, I put his gown on. I still had it on when he returned much sooner than I, at least, had expected. The beating was my punishment; but whether in retaliation for the affront to authority and dignity, or whether as retribution for supposed impertinence, was not made clear. Probably by now I was regarded by my elders as needing to be taken down a peg or three and this was an opportunity to make the required downward adjustment.

I was beginning to rise in some spheres. House colours and the School Cricket XI - though my place in the team was I suspect due at least as much to 'keenness' and 'pluck' - words much used in those days - as to any prowess. And I became a member of a slightly self-conscious group called the Seven Club, at which we read papers on a variety of subjects. I can't remember what I spoke on, but I do recall the title, if not much of the content, of a dissertation on 'Dialectical Materialism'. This was delivered by David Henderson. He and I were in different Houses and had scarcely any acquaintance with each other, other than in form - we had been in the same form for quite a long time.  I think I sensed that his arrival at Ellesmere, which happened quite a few terms after mine, was in some way significant for me, but without being able to put my finger on a specific reason.  He was younger than me by about a year and came to the school after I had moved up into the Senior School from the Junior, which was in effect the prep school for the Senior with, so far as I could judge, automatic progression from lower to upper school.  In which form it was that I stopped being top I don't remember, but certainly with Henderson's arrival I did - as well as, of course, no longer being the youngest in the form.  That I had lost this fortuitous distinction I am pretty sure I felt at the time.  What I only now suspect is that the school was then aware that it had a better bet (in Henderson's undoubtedly prodigious talent) for obtaining the very rare accolade of a Major Scholarship to an Oxford college.  This in fact Henderson achieved.  I myself was never put in to sit for any Oxford award. Having got my School Certificate with various 'distinctions' and about twice the five 'credits', which I think were then regarded as the equivalent of university matriculation at fourteen, I merely went on to take the Higher School Cert.  (I had failed to get the French 'credit' which was a *sine qua non* for an Oxford entry and took this again though only by way of a *viva voce*, and got through.)  With my Higher I had, at sixteen, another year still to go at school; and I simply took the exam again the following year - to what precise end, beyond marking time during my last year, was not explained to me.  The result was seemingly commendable enough to get me to Oxford, as a Commoner at Worcester College; and there I went at the beginning of the Michaelmas Term in October 1943.

# ~5~

# Oxford; Cyprus; London; Oxford; London

Late afternoon in October. The dank mist as I walked from the station didn't dampen my exhilaration. Nor do I recall that this was perceptibly diminished by the formidable, bulky, six-foot-four, bearded Head Porter, Bryant, in his Lodge at the college gate. This ex-Regimental Sergeant-Major Coldstream Guardsman, who dwarfed me, was distinctly intimidating to the view; but I was told early on that he was only to be feared if you let him overawe you. "Don't take any nonsense from him!" Sound advice. Luckily I never needed to take the measure of that other Coldstreamer, the redoubtable ex-Colonel, the Dean, Wilkinson - known as "Horse". I do not have any memory of his ever having spoken to me during the four years I was up - three as an undergraduate (when Worcester was my home in vacation as much as during term), and a further year when I was on a 'Devonshire' course under the aegis of the Colonial Office as a cadet member of the Colonial Administrative Service. Had I had to contend with both the Coldstream Colonel as Dean *and* his RSM as Head Porter, I would have found, as did Bertie Wooster when coping with various aunts, fellow Drones Club members, Sir Roderick Glossop, magistrates, *et al.*, that "the mixture was too rich".

The most striking change introduced by Oxford into the life I had so far known was the sense of being a free individual. This independence was symbolised, and conferred, by the fact of my having, for the first time ever, a place of my own: a sitting room or study, with a separate bedroom. That the sitting room was narrow and almost minute, and the bedroom only big enough to take the bed and an old-fashioned washstand, in no way detracted from the wonderful feeling of possessing my own space, to which I could retire, or retreat, whenever

71

I might wish. The sitting room had a tiny coal-burning iron fireplace. (Fires were then still laid by our 'scouts'. An age away.) The intense pleasure, even joy, of sitting in front of that fire, reading for work or recreation, is something I look back to with immense gratitude. My rooms were at the top of a college 'staircase' and had, theoretically, lovely views of the Worcester gardens, but in fact I would only have been able to enjoy the vista by pressing up against a narrow window. Beauty almost out of sight, though not out of reach.

One of the oldest of the Oxford college foundations, dating from 1283, Worcester College was originally Gloucester Hall, a hall of residence for Benedictine monks sent by their monasteries to study at Oxford. It fell on evil days after the Dissolution of the Monasteries and by the middle of the 16th century the buildings were in a parlous state; the chapel indeed had become a total ruin, as a Loggan print of 1560 shows clearly. The property became part of the wealthy St. John's College but was re-founded in 1714 by a Worcester baronet as the college it has since been. The founder had aimed to build a wholly new college in the magnificent new Palladian style, so excellently exemplified by The Queen's College. But the money for the Worcester rebuilding ran out after the new Chapel, Hall and Library to the east, and the new wing to the north, of the main quadrangle had gone up. And so future generations were bequeathed a college which combines the old mediaeval with the new eighteenth century architectures in unique but unintended harmony.

The Worcester buildings seem to me now, in retrospect, to provide some kind of object lesson which I have, in the course of my life, only sporadically, and then more often than not but semi-consciously, hoisted in. Making the best of a bad job, not letting the best become the enemy of the good; platitudes these may be - and even sententious. But for me the Worcester buildings are a lovely, visible example of a characteristic of this country and its people. It could even be counted as a virtue. The best of the British way of doing things lies, I believe, in the capacity to avoid pursuing an end at all hazards to its logical conclusion, rationally and coldly calculated in advance; in a readiness to see that one might be wrong so that instead of vainly, and possibly disastrously, pushing an original plan to the limit, choosing rather to adapt the plan to circumstances. In short to be pragmatic - dread, and despicable, though that word may be to the zealot and the fanatic. And, as I have after many, many years come to learn for myself, another aspect of this many-sided virtue (of finding, if you will, the truth of things) is in the Islamic quality of resigning one's self to providence - to God. Not in blind fatalism without prior personal effort, but after having first done to the utmost everything that one can do. This is after all no more, and no less, than what is contained in that saying, not infrequently heard in this country in my youth, "Man proposes, God disposes". For those for whom theistic language loses its meaning - if it does not actually offend - I can only say that, for myself at least, I have found that I am happier when I can accept my limitations. And even more when I am content with them.

\*\*\*\*\*\*\*\*\*\*\*

A year earlier than me my brother had decided that he would take up his acceptance by Worcester for one year, after which he would join the Navy, so that I could come up (if I were to be accepted) in his place and with a view to staying a full three years to take my degree. The point was that mother, widowed, could not possibly finance the two of us together even for a short period of overlap. There was then in existence a scheme providing 'cadetships' (though I'm not sure whether specifically so called) by which people liable to be 'called up' for military service could be selected, as possible potential officer material, to come up for six months to the university, at government expense, where they would in all other respects be regular members of the various colleges to which they were sent. My brother was not one of these 'cadets'; but on arrival at Worcester he joined the University Naval Division, nearly all the members of which were in fact such 'cadets' who were due for the navy. Each 'cadet' at the university knew at that stage for which of the services he was destined. By no means all of these successfully completed their training at university, or later, in a process which included the system of selection involving psychological testing of the kind which was then very strange (though it has since seemingly become almost universal in many walks of life). At that time it was sardonically put about that among the methods of seeing if you were the right kind was checking whether you ate your peas off your knife! But perhaps there *could* have been some element of sifting

73

out those who were not "one of us", to use the political jargon of a more recent generation. (It used also to be alleged that if two applicants for the old Sudan Service were otherwise neck and neck, the selection was determined by casually offering a cigarette from a silver case: "Turkish this side, Virginia that." If you took the Turkish you were in.) Always, and to a fault, modest, my brother alleges he got through his training and selection process - including his service on the lower deck - to emerge, some six months after leaving Worcester as a Sub-Lieutenant, Royal Naval Volunteer Reserve, because D-Day was imminent. The invasion of Europe by the Allies was generally expected from the winter of 1943; from this time the whole of southern Britain was full of American troops. According to my brother the first wave of assaults on the beaches was to involve a very large number of landing craft, and each of these would have on board a junior naval officer. High casualties were to be expected, and so the number of Sub-Lieutenants who passed out after training was disproportionately high. That at least is my brother's story - which I take with liberal spoonfuls of salt.

**********

When I arrived at Worcester there must have been few in the country who had any idea that we were already well past the chronological mid-point of the war. I could (when I thought about it) envisage my three years as an undergraduate lasting the full course of the war, for there was still the grim prospect of a long drawn out struggle against the Japanese, who occupied and controlled the whole of South East Asia and much of the Pacific, even if - though not long after D-Day we began to see the prospect as being "after" rather than "if" - victory in Europe were assured. As colonials neither my brother nor I were liable for 'call up'. The possibility that my brother might not survive I resolutely declined to contemplate. Had that happened I do not know whether I too would have joined up - or whether I would have felt I owed it to my mother to save her from losing her husband and, possibly, both her children. She was, in 1943, only thirty eight. As it was, the war in Europe ended towards the beginning of my second year at Worcester; and with the Doomsday-seeming bombs on Hiroshima and Nagasaki within a couple of days of each other, the Asian war too was over less than six months later.

The Worcester Law Tutor, Alan Brown, an Australian, had been away at the war, in the Scots Guards; so during my first four terms I had tutorials with dons at Balliol and Trinity. By that time I had taken my Law Mods and it was Alan Brown who saw me through the Final Honours School. I was a disappointment to him in declining to read for a BCL, though I don't remember informing him, in terms, of the fact that I couldn't have afforded further time up as a graduate anyway. In any case I wanted to go down as soon as I had taken my degree, with the intention of returning to Cyprus in the hope of an appointment there in the government service. Alan Brown's tutorial method, if such it could be called, must have consisted in what P.G.Wodehouse has called "encouraging with word and gesture". In a letter to an old school friend he (P.G.W.) tells of becoming president of the library in the German internment camp where he was held in the early part of the war. "The President of a camp must not be confused with the Librarian. The Librarian does the rough work like handing out books and entering them in a ledger. The President presides. He stimulates and encourages. I, for instance, used to look in once a day and say 'Everything okay?' and go away again. It was amazing how it helped. Giving the Wodehouse Touch I used to call it." *Mutatis mutandis* such also was the Alan Brown Touch, as recollected in tranquillity. Nothing whatever remains in my memory of what I suppose must have been an actual weekly essay session. No doubt Alan must have directed my reading to some degree, and I imagine we would have had discussions. My mind is, however, curiously bare of any pictorial image of such sessions, in contrast with those I retain of the ones during Mods in Balliol and Trinity. Lectures I went to in a very sporadic fashion: de Zulueta on Roman Law; Cheshire (the father of the V.C. founder of the Cheshire Homes) on Real Property; Fifoot on Tort; and others. But in general what one needed for the specifics was available in tomes on these same subjects - often the work of the dons lecturing. And, frankly, I found it easier, more comfortable, and quicker, to wade through these in my room in my own time.

For exercise I used to hire a 'skiff' from Salters at Folly Bridge and scull for half an hour or so. But mostly I played squash. Among those with whom I played was the Chaplain, Bobby Milburn, though I was no attender of Chapel. An incidental attraction of the squash courts, situated at the far end of the college gardens, was that they provided the favoured illicit entry into college after lock-up, so evading the mandatory fine. One of the other ways of getting in was through a particular ground-floor bedroom window; but that was very much a last resort as the successive occupants not unnaturally took a dim view of these trespasses.

Of outside college activities my memory is of political societies - including what now sounds the rather archaically named O.U. Conservative and Unionist Association where, with memory's eye, I see in a headscarf - a usual wartime woman's headcovering - a Somerville girl: a determined, yet demure (yes) Margaret Roberts. And the Union. I went regularly to the weekly debates on, I think, Thursday evenings. I recall speaking only once, at the invitation so far as I remember of the then President, Godfrey Lesquesne. The subject was United Europe: I wish I had any memory at all of what I said, or even the line I took. The Union was attractive to me for its atmosphere of that essentially British institution, the club, with its library, billiards room, and tea with toast as the light faded.

As I have indicated, my time at Worcester divides into two, overlapping, periods. The transition from the first to the second was to me almost imperceptible: the change from wartime to peacetime Oxford. Stark though the contrast must have been for those coming back from the services (some from actual combat), for those up in 1944 the difference in 1945 was rather less evident. The bigger change for me came in Michaelmas 1947 when, accepted for the Colonial Service, I came up again, this time in a Bachelor's gown, for a year's course of instruction intended to give us budding colonial administrators a general grounding in our coming responsibilities. The minute I had learned that I had been successful in the Schools I had managed to get a passage to Cyprus. How this was achieved in 1946 I have no recollection, but it was almost certainly through the Welfare Department of the Colonial Office, who then had a general sort of 'consular' responsibility for colonials in Britain. Anyway, there I was, in June 1946, on a ship returning Italian prisoners of war to their homeland - and me to mine.

The ship decanted me at Port Said, after off-loading the Italian POWs at Naples. From Port Said I managed to get a deck passage on a small schooner bound for Cyprus. We landed at Limassol, or rather disembarked by way of small boats since there was not then anything like a quayside there but only a jetty. By chance the Collector of Customs at the port was at the time yet another uncle! I didn't know him from Adam but, from my passport details, a policeman, having known my father, made the family connection and took me over to him. A taxi was summoned and I found myself travelling to Nicosia, accompanied by a Turk returning there from a business day-trip to Limassol. The two hour journey was broken at the half way stage of Skarinou where, in the village roadside coffee shop, my companion and guide sat down to a hearty lunch, at which he asked me to join him. I could only have dreamed of a meal like that in war-time and post-war Britain: delicious meat, rice, potatoes, vegetables, and fruit in abundance. Truly a new and different world of plenty, swimming in sunshine - blazing light and crisply sharp, defined shadows. A sense of paradise attained, if not regained, almost overwhelmed me.

But there was a serpent in that Eden. It was the horrible embarrassment, and even shame, which I felt in not being able to converse with my companion. His English was practically non-existent and to his determinedly inquisitive efforts to be friendly I was only able to try to respond with the odd half-remembered Turkish word or phrase. At the end of the journey he delivered me to my mother - and, with supreme natural good manners, immediately took his departure.

It is quite beyond me to describe my mother's controlled joy when she opened her front door to me in my twenty first year - to see me for the first time since I was thirteen, and after an intervening war. I had in fact asked the ship's wireless officer to telegraph her to give her news of my coming, but that message from mid-Mediterranean had presumably been misdirected to that other Nicosia in, I believe, Sicily or Sardinia. At all events my arrival on her doorstep was a total surprise to my mother, the shock of which is hard to imagine.

**********

I now lived with my mother in her single-storey house, immediately opposite the large one still tenanted by the Stone parents. (Michael was as yet in England, on the point of being demobbed as a corporal in the Signals.) That house of my mother's may have had only subjective aesthetic appeal - its style being what I tended to think of as 'Tel Aviv thirties', after the brand new town which had grown up in that decade on the Palestine shore alongside the old town of Jaffa. (I have recently seen a description of another house which might suitably be used of mother's: 'Bauhaus crossed with Deauville'.) It was however wonderfully well designed and not least in taking maximum advantage of the climate as, for example, in having the main bedroom facing west to catch the summer evening *meltem* breeze - a huge benefit in those days before air-conditioning. This was the first, and only, time my mother and I were to live in a house of her own; so that small unpretentious place has always meant a great deal to me even though - and possibly because - I never shared living in it with my father as well. Here I stayed during the six months or so which brought in the end of 1946.

**********

In the middle of my twenty first year I was a stranger in Cyprus. It was some little while before I could so much as produce a simple Turkish sentence; and I eagerly threw myself into becoming at least modestly fluent within the circle of my immediate family of uncles, aunts and cousins. This was of course the first time I had lived in Cyprus during my adult life. I revelled in it. I was enchanted by the place, spell-bound. From the flat roof of our house I had a clear view of the well-remembered Kyrenia hills. The sight stirred up deep feelings from my childhood recollection of those hills to which I now again "lifted up my eyes", their colours eternally transformed through each day as the sun moved from the direction of Famagusta away over on the right to Morphou Bay as far out of sight on the opposite horizon. Beligh Pasha had built a small retreat, for relief from the mid-summer heat of Nicosia, in the little village of Dhiorios some twenty miles to the west of the capital. It stood on a bluff facing the bay into which the sun set, producing an effect which, when I was to see it from that place, is among my treasured memories of that Cyprus of half a century ago.

At that age I didn't find the torrid daytime heat of mid-summer oppressive, but almost invigorating. Or, rather, I thought I did. I overdid things, riding the sixteen miles to Kyrenia, and back again, by bicycle. The ride out, in the early morning, was delightful. But after a day's bathing (again behind the great castle, as in the Froebel school days) the ride back finished me and I collapsed with heat exhaustion. I learned to treat the Cyprus sun with more respect and caution.

A cousin had an old motor car and we drove out together to Famagusta and Larnaca. I was able to visit again the *Tekke* at the salt lake where my brother and I had gone with our parents before returning to school a bare six and a half years ago - though it seemed like a lifetime. Constantly in my cousin's company, I made good progress with my Turkish. In Famagusta I saw again the house where I had been born. Of course I had no memories of the place at all, but that it was the place was not in question since I was shown it by my mother's second brother who was then the District Medical Officer for Famagusta district, having transferred back to Cyprus from his first posting, before the war, in British Honduras (now Belize). He was to retire thirty years later from his last post, in Hong Kong, and died a few years ago in Hove. A well-loved man by all who knew him. I wish I had met him more often and been able to know him better; but our lives only briefly intersected.

I also luxuriated (there is I think no better word for it) in the historical associations evoked by the uniquely varied cultures represented by the buildings still remaining from the times of the successive rulers of the island. I resist the temptation to be sidetracked into attempting a travelogue description of 'sites'. But as an account of my own experiences I have to mention the Roman ruins at Salamis on the east coast north of Famagusta, the mediaeval fortresses of Kantara and Hilarion on peaks of the Kyrenia range, as well as Kyrenia castle itself (of which I had never seen the interior before), the Venetian walls and ramparts of Famagusta and Nicosia, and the Latin abbey of Bellapais. In all these I breathed the very history of the place. So too in the Turkish buildings from the last three hundred years of Ottoman rule, such as the *Tekke* of the *Mevlevi* Order of Dervishes; the colonnaded and arched 16th century *Büyük* ('great') *Han* (merchant hostel or caravanserai) and the much smaller, almost domestic, Kumarcılar ('gamblers') *Han*; the *Bayraktar* ('Standard-bearer') mosque amongst others; the numerous water fountains with old Ottoman inscriptions;

and, not the least lovely, much of the domestic architecture of the towns - especially the houses within the walls of old Nicosia with their enclosed court-yards and overhanging first storeys making even narrower, but also giving shade to, the already narrow streets. (I had not then known Sidney Smith's *bon mot* when walking down an Edinburgh street and hearing two housewives arguing furiously overhead from the windows of just such upper storeys. When I did, I was to find it sadly apposite to the political surge of argument on the future of Cyprus: "They will never agree, for they are arguing from different premises".)

What was for me quite wonderful was how the various differences in building styles yet combined into a synthesis of new beauty, even in such minor points as the way (which my untutored eye couldn't then identify, nor now specify) the three gateways into the walled town of Nicosia merged the later Turkish into the original Venetian. The captious could make a distinction and regard the result as being incongruous - synthetic, rather than a synthesis. So be it. For me it is not so. It was in the two main mosques of the island, in Nicosia and Famagusta, that I found this blending of style, and indeed culture, most attractive and fascinating. Thirteenth century Lusignan gothic cathedrals over topped by minarets. To some this might, even in these more ecumenical times, come as out of place, or even shocking. For me it is deeply satisfying, as much aesthetically as it is symbolically - a house of prayer owing an outward form to humans who believing themselves separate from others of their kind have, despite themselves, produced a monument to their real community with each other. The whitewashed, columned interior of the Nicosia mosque especially produces very much the effect of paintings I have seen of sixteenth century Dutch church interiors.

\*\*\*\*\*\*\*\*\*\*

It was now that I began to go to mosque services for the first time in my life. The very first occasion was the early morning service on the first day of the Bayram holiday following *Ramazan*. I didn't have to know either the words or the sequence of prostrations for the liturgical prayers - the *namaz* - since at congregational services you need only follow the motions of the prayer leader, the *imam*. But I taught myself the minimum of these, and the meaning of the Arabic words, to pray the *namaz* privately.

**\*\*\*\*\*\*\*\*\*\*\***

Soon after my return to Cyprus I had consulted my uncle Munir Bey on how I should set about applying for a post in the Cyprus administration. (He was the husband of that sister of my father from whose son I had first learned to memorise the words of a Moslem prayer.) He advised most strongly against any such move. He himself had been, since the late 1920s, on the island's Legislative Council as an elected Turkish member (until that chamber was abolished following the Greek riots of 1931), and then an appointed member of the Governor's Executive Council, from which he was to retire in 1947. (It was in Council that, as I was later to be told, he had delivered himself of the unconsciously felicitous observation, combining two idioms in his otherwise faultless English: "But, Your Excellency, these people are hand in bosom with each other.") His advice was not to be lightly set aside. In his view I should put out of my mind any thought of obtaining a 'local appointment' in Cyprus. With the seeming likelihood, even probability, of post-war constitutional changes in the island, as in other colonies - though the possible time-scale was highly conjectural - the course of events in Cyprus would be problematical: the best thing to do would be to apply, from Britain, direct to the Secretary of State for the Colonies, for appointment to the Unified Colonial Service. The almost certain outcome, if successful, would be a posting outside Cyprus; but there would always be the possibility of a transfer, in which case I would then be in Cyprus on the same basis as an Englishman posted there. There was the implication, if it wasn't more specifically stated, that in such an event I should not be so much at risk as would be a local Turkish appointee, in an island which might well move to internal self-government. In that event the situation of a Turk would be that of a member of a vulnerable, powerless minority.

Whether there was a further implication, or even a more direct hint, that beyond the prospect of possible self-government lay a more ominous vista opening on to *enosis* I couldn't now say for sure; but the burden of the advice was more than clear: on no account become an official in Cyprus unless you can obtain a Secretary of State's appointment. This I determined to apply for.

**\*\*\*\*\*\*\*\*\*\***

The decision made, my mother and I went for a week's break from the mid-summer heat of the Nicosia plain to stay at a newly opened, tourist style, modest hotel up in the Troodos mountains, midway between the villages of Pedhoulas and Prodhromos. It seems in my memory to have been very quiet, very simple, catering largely if not wholly for Egyptians and others from the nearby Arab countries. Rich islanders, I learned later, used either to go abroad, or to patronise two hotels on the Limassol side of the Troodos summit, the Forest Park at Platres especially, and the Berengaria at Prodhromos itself.

In the Greek village of Pedhoulas my father's eldest brother had rented a village house for the summer. He had been a judge first in Cyprus and then, during the war years, in the Gold Coast (now Ghana). Just retired from there, he was now busy in Nicosia establishing himself as an advocate in private practice - a proceeding which presumably had the acquiescence of his Inn of Court or whatever the relevant barristers' ruling body would have been. My uncle was himself only occasionally up at Pedhoulas, during week-ends. While I and my mother were at the hotel I was invited by his wife to spend a day to provide company for her daughter, one of only two girls who leaven more than a dozen of the roster of my first cousins. There I found someone a couple of years older than myself, whom I hadn't seen for twelve years since the time she, too, with her elder sister and younger brother, had been at the Froebel School. Entirely naive as I was, I had not the faintest idea that this was a move by my aunt (and no doubt my uncle also) to bring us together with a view to a possible match. My mother, as I was to learn, was of course perfectly aware of what was afoot, but was not party to it. She was also much too wise to try to influence her son one way or the other. Had this been the usual *pourparler* towards setting in train the procedures for an arranged marriage, the parents of one of the intended parties would have made approaches through intermediaries to the other side. Though no intermediaries had been used in this case, the set-up was that which would have been the desired outcome of such an initial approach to which a favourable response had been given - to get the young couple to meet and discover their reactions to each other. For contrary to what seems to be the widespread idea that an 'arranged marriage' is an imposed marriage, in which the wishes of the possible spouses are not taken into account, this is not in fact the case. But what was for me simply a social call on my aunt, and an interlude in an otherwise unexciting stay at the hotel, was perfectly well understood by my cousin for what it was intended by her mother to be. She therefore, as soon as she decently could, told me that she had no thoughts of marriage. Whether the point was made in general terms only, or by specifically ruling me out as a prospective husband, hasn't registered on my memory. What that does recall to me now is that I was rather put out and disgruntled. Marriage was just as far from my thoughts too at the time, indeed the idea hadn't even approached them; nor was I in any way smitten by my cousin. Yet I was discomfited in being so summarily dismissed as a possible suitor. My mother, on the other hand, decidedly was not.

\*\*\*\*\*\*\*\*\*\*

When the time came to arrange a passage back to England, so as to put in hand my application to the Secretary of State, my mother decided she wanted to come too. She had endured the strain of having sent her children back to Britain in wartime; she had faced that separation from a great distance, in deeply anxious uncertainty, when the outcome of the war seemed to be in doubt and Britain was beleaguered and for one year totally alone against the Axis powers; she had coped with all that was involved in her husband's tragically untimely death and the financial insecurity of living with stringent economy, indeed austerity, so as not to erode her small and dwindling capital. She wanted, and richly deserved, a break. In England she would also again be close to her other son, whom she had been able to meet briefly during the last year of the war when he had been on mine-sweeping duties in the eastern Mediterranean and had managed to get to Cyprus on leave. He had by now been demobilised and got a place back at Worcester, this time with an ex-serviceman's grant, which relieved mother of any need to contribute financially. The decision to return to Britain together was rather a calculated gamble. If I were to be successful in my application for the Colonial Service, financially all would be well; but if not ... well, that would have to be considered if the case arose. The post-war world, even in the euphoria of a victorious Britain, was in any event one of uncertainties - though also one of hope.

In January 1947 we got passages on the *Ascania*. Barely a year had passed since the war had ended and shipping was still extremely limited. I think the *Ascania* was on demobilisation passages, taking troops home from various theatres of war but also carrying cargo and passengers. What I remember is that women and men were separately accommodated (though they could come together for meals) in cabins into which the maximum number of bunks were fitted, like small dormitories. There were six people in mine, all but me Greek Cypriots, and I knew virtually nothing of their language except for a minimal "courtesy of" Greek, to adopt a term used by Colin Thubron to describe such Turkish as he had when he was in Cyprus in 1972 a quarter of a century afterwards. (About which I suspect I shall have something to say later.) In the present instance one of my fellow passengers - and "fellow traveller", it appears, would have been as accurate, though an anachronistic, a description for him - had good enough English for us to be able to talk. Without in terms avowing membership of AKEL, the Cyprus Communist Party, he was extremely far to the left in his political views. This was, of course, still the time when the dreadful, vicious, civil war was raging in Greece between the communists and the (scarcely crypto-)fascist royalists, and my interlocutor wasn't formally identifying himself with one side in that bitter partisan struggle. But his ideological position was pretty patent. Nor did his general political and economic views prevent him from being an ardent and rigid proponent of *enosis* for Cyprus. Again, it was abundantly obvious that what he looked for was a new, communist, Greek state of which Cyprus would be a part. His general political stance seemed to me to sit oddly with the relish with which he told me of a very clever priest who had recently completed theological training in America (or was he then *going* to America for that purpose?) of whom much was to be expected in the cause of *enosis*. It seemed to me that this clerical involvement in the campaign would surely be difficult to square with the outcome he wished to see. But I kept this to myself. Wouldn't priest and church together get their come-uppance, I thought, if only by being simply suppressed, in the new Greece, just as in Russia? I really couldn't take all this seriously; it seemed to me to be almost vapouring. Events were to demonstrate just how wrong I was. The priest was a certain Mouskos. Within the year he was to become the Bishop of Kitium (Larnaca) and by 1950 Archbishop - that Archbishop Makarios, to whom the Greek, no less than the Turkish, people of Cyprus owe so much - of grief.

\*\*\*\*\*\*\*\*\*\*\*

And so we came to England. It was just before the fierce onset of what was to be that most horrendous winter of 1946-47. We stayed at a residential hotel in a square behind Notting Hill Gate. For my mother it was a return to the London of eighteen years earlier. The place was almost a replica of the one where she had lived *en famille* on that first visit to the capital of the Empire. For myself, with no memories of that previous hotel, the character of this one seemed to be epitomised in its dining-room. There the guests, for the most part permanent residents, came together regularly. They were all, in my recollection, elderly women. Compared to my mother, by then turned forty, they appeared in fact positively aged. And now, on the verge of seventy myself, I realise the falsity and unreality of age relativities, simply considered.

The scene in that dining-room, with each guest's private and personal jam and marmalade jars and sauce bottles stacked in front of them, was like a stage set for the play 'Separate Tables'. Looking back, there comes to me an impression of a place somehow bathed in an indefinable air of melancholy. It was, I suppose, a sort of silent epilogue to the era of empire. Yet I did not then consciously see things in that light. On the contrary, I was full of anticipation, in which, though mixed with a certain apprehension, optimistic hope predominated.

During the early months of our stay in London we were very much concerned with just trying to keep warm in what was probably the most bitterly cold winter the country and the capital had experienced for at least a couple of centuries - the papers were even harking back to the great freeze-up of 1666 when a fair had been held on the frozen

Thames. The freeze arrived just at the time the country's coal stocks fell dangerously low. Yet with that steadfast determination - and again that *démodé* word 'pluck' comes to mind - which had been shown by all during the war, everyone once more gritted their teeth and, though grousing, endured. In a way it needed even more resilience now, when the war had been won. Perhaps newsreels on cinema screens showing the devastation of German cities, and the awful conditions the people there were coping with as they scrabbled in the ruins, helped to stiffen resolve and strengthen patience. I do not ever remember, watching those news-reels, any sense of gloating in the audience, but rather sympathy. I think it is true that self-pity debilitates, just as sympathy and compassion strengthen.

I obtained the necessary papers - I think from the Oxford University Appointments Board, but possibly from the Colonial Office direct - and put in my application for the Colonial Service. Whatever machinery might have been turning behind the scenes in the way of sifting applicants and assessing their qualifications and merits, so far as the candidates themselves were aware - this one anyway - the actual process of selection was in the hands of a Board which interviewed the hopeful 'Sanders of the River' for about half an hour, as best I can remember. Of my interview I can recall only that at one point I was asked what I thought I would do in my spare time in a 'bush district'. The exact words of my reply I obviously can't now remember; but the general sense of it is certainly clearly with me - if only because I was acutely conscious of the complete bogosity which underlay it. I would venture out, I said, in the hope of a bit of shooting. It is true that in the OTC at school I had been pretty proficient on the range with the old Lee Enfield rifle, of 1914/18 vintage, but apart from the rabbit hunting expedition when Stanley Roberts had kindly had me over to his place from school, I had never used a shot-gun. I *do* remember at least having the *nous* to disclaim in my reply any wish to go in for big game. Not because any such inclination would be likely, as nowadays - and quite properly - to count against me on grounds of cruelty: that was far from the ethos of those days. I was simply aware that there was not the slightest possibility of my being able to carry off such a pretence with any hope of its sounding at all convincing. So, contrary to the injunction of the master-propagandist Goebbels - "when you tell a lie tell a very big one. It is more likely to be believed" - I produced my feeble little one:

by implication I would only be 'shooting for the pot'. I was not taken up on the point by the Selection Board. And I must otherwise have satisfied them - by a wide or small margin one was never to know - on whatever else they were looking for. The terrible winter passed. Some time afterwards, during a wonderful spring which renewed hope, I learned that my application had been successful and that the submission by the Board to the Secretary of State had been approved by him. I was accordingly offered the usual appointment as a Cadet Administrative Officer. My posting was to the Gold Coast (today's Ghana).

The news of my success was not the first time in the course of my life that I was to know that sense of all things being now "for the best in the best of all possible worlds" - if I have correctly quoted Voltaire's words poking fun at the foolishly false optimism of Doctor Pangloss: a feeling that a line had now been drawn separating the past from a future in which the old fears and uncertainties would be no more. An earlier premonition of just such a state of immature, if not positively childish, fantasy had come on me not so long before at the moment I had seen posted on the notice board in the Porter's Lodge at Worcester the list of successful candidates in the Honours School of Jurisprudence, which I think I headed - though not with a First.

But however ungrounded in reality was *my* sense of elation in knowing that I was to be a member of the Unified Colonial Administrative Service, my mother could truly breathe more easily in now being able to enjoy her release from the strain of our living in London on a diminishing capital hoarded against the need to secure the future careers of her sons. (We still used to think in terms of careers those days - or at least the staid and unadventurous of us did). The weight of responsibility my mother had so long carried, to provide for us, she could now lay aside and, in freedom of spirit, live her own life quietly back in her home in Nicosia. Or so we then thought. There she returned in the autumn of 1947.

\*\*\*\*\*\*\*\*\*\*

My brother was due to go back to Worcester in the coming Michaelmas term to resume life as an undergraduate in company with the great majority of his Oxford contemporaries who were also ex-servicemen with government grants. And there, too, I went the same term, on one of those 'Devonshire' courses, named after a Secretary of State for the Colonies, instituted to give training for cadets to the Colonial Service before they went out to their different territories. We received allowances, on which we lived very adequately and, in my case anyway, comfortably - compared with my undergraduate days, during which I had subsisted, in term and vacation, on the small amount with which my mother had been able to fund me.

These courses lasted a full academic year of three terms at Oxford (or Cambridge) followed by one term in London, where our time was divided between the London School of Economics and the School of Oriental and African Studies. Since such aspects of colonial administration as concerned economics, constitutional development, anthropology, and kindred matters had, naturally, to cover a very wide spectrum of dependent territories (colonies, protectorates, United Nations Trust Territories) as far apart as, for example, Africa, Malaysia, the Caribbean, and the Pacific, these topics had necessarily to be treated rather broadly so as to encompass the great divergences. To that extent, the ground mapped out by our lecturers (eminent authorities in their fields, like Margery Perham) could scarcely be traversed other than by way of an academic approach. Excellent though they were in content, within that limitation, it was questionable how directly relevant the lectures were to the actual work in which we were to be engaged. And even such monumental works as Lord Hailey's *An African Survey*, and discussions on the system of 'indirect rule' through local chiefs and 'Native Authorities', though useful enough, hardly warranted a year at Oxford at the taxpayers' expense.

Interestingly, I have found among such of my books as have survived the vicissitudes of my career moves - "careerings" might perhaps be a more accurate description - several which date from that Devonshire course. One in fact was published in the very year the course began. *The Colonial Office from Within* was among our recommended reading. It is a slim autobiographical memoir by Sir Cosmo Parkinson of his time in the Colonial Office, from which he had just retired as Permanent Secretary, after thirty six years service in that Department of State. The reader should perhaps be reminded that

Colonial Office staff were quite separate from members of the Colonial *Service*; the former, being home civil servants, did not normally serve abroad - save, very exceptionally, on occasional secondment. In his book Sir Cosmo writes: "There has been considerable difference of opinion as to the value of courses of instruction for administrative officers appointed to the Colonial Service. Some have queried the usefulness of a course of any kind before a cadet takes up his duties; others have held that the syllabus is overloaded - or deficient; some maintain that a course during leave is more valuable, and exactly the contrary opinions have been expressed by others. In the old days the newly appointed administrative officer went out to Africa or Malaya or Ceylon or the Pacific without any such preliminary training, and he learned his job by doing it." I myself could hardly have called the "syllabus ... overloaded"; nor, with hindsight, would I now consider it "deficient". But from a general standpoint I felt distinctly doubtful as to the need for these courses at all - without being in any kind of position to judge whether they might still have been an improvement on the previous arrangement under which the new officer "learned his job by doing it". In fact, as I was to find, learning on the job was what to a large extent still applied in practice. However, regarding the matter from a purely personal, and selfish, angle I couldn't at the time have found it in me to cavil. Not only was I enjoying a year back at Worcester with no money worries, I was also being allowed a period during which I could rub shoulders with men who, though only a few years older than me, had nevertheless had very much greater experience of life. By no means all had seen 'combat service' in the sense of being in the fighting; only a minority of those I knew had. (My brother had been on active service during which he had been engaged in mine-sweeping in the Mediterranean.) But all had seen a world beyond the school and university of my own cloistered youth.

**********

I was myself now an adult, in the technical, legal sense. But I was unquestionably dreadfully immature. Circumstances had brought me up to the university at seventeen and a half - by any reckoning much too young. And the Oxford of my first two years was a kind of limbo, an unreal place of transients, and transience. In the phrase of the time

I was in any case probably "young for my age". But there was, as I now think, rather more to it than that. How does one measure immaturity? How different is it from merely being callow? Are the two things indeed but the same thing? Or aspects of the one thing? I was certainly grievously lacking in experience. But that is primarily to be without *savoir faire*, which is easily, if not almost automatically, acquired in a place like Oxford, though less quickly in the conditions of wartime. Even during the war the correct way of doing things was still being upheld and imparted. During my first term I had received an invitation to tea from the Provost - "Jacky" Lys. (A dear old man of whom it was, as affectionately as it was inaccurately, said that, having been head of the college for so long, he was due for a second term as Vice-Chancellor of the University, that position going - so at least it was also incorrectly alleged - to the heads of colleges in rotation.) In my reply, correctly cast in the third person, I had written that I was "very pleased" to accept the Provost's invitation. During the tea, in the most fatherly and benevolent fashion, my host corrected this lapse, assuring me that the proper terms in which such an acceptance should be phrased was by writing that one was "*much* pleased"!

An instance of *savoir faire*, of knowing not so much the "manners and customs of good society" but the ways of the world, was brought home to me in reading a newspaper in the Junior Common Room in 1947 or 1948. I think it could only have been the *News of the World* of those days - the JCR Committee being nothing if not catholic in its selection of papers and periodicals. A steward of a Union Castle liner stood accused of murder. Under examination or cross-examination either the accused or a witness had described the victim as "sophisticated". Asked what was meant by this, the reply was that she always carried a french letter in her handbag. If indeed maturity equates with *savoir faire*, and immaturity with callowness, inexperience, and lack of sophistication, then I was at that time unquestionably in the latter category. (It was about this time that I first heard, and had to have explained, the hoary joke of the Englishman on holiday in Paris whose wife dies, and he goes into a shop to buy a black 'Anthony Eden' hat for the funeral, explaining what he wants by saying, *"Je voudrais acheter un chapeau anglais* (pronouncing 'chapeau' as though it was the French *capot). Noir, vous savez - parce que ma femme est morte."* At which the assistant, raising eyes and hands to heaven, comments in admiration, *"Ah, ces anglais; quelle delicatesse!"*)

But the thing went deeper than that. I heard on the radio today Ted Dexter, test cricketer and captain of England in the fifties, being interviewed in a series called *On the Ropes*, in which he referred to his experience in the army. The code of his regiment dictated that they should excel in carrying out their duties; but in such a manner as to convey no hint of exerting oneself. He used the vivid, if unoriginal, image of the swan sliding serenely along - but paddling furiously underneath the surface. The same idea of proper comportment was expressed in that supposed "effortless superiority" once claimed as the mark of the Balliol man. It seems to me that these are but particular instances of what was once considered a characteristically admirable trait of the English: presenting a calm, unruffled, and emotionless front to the world (without, as also with the "stiff upper lip", this necessarily calling for an assumption of Curzonian superiority or arrogance). In so far as concerns what I see as my immaturity half a century ago, I feel sure that to a great extent a big contributing factor was this kind of suppression of feelings, which results in retarding, and sometimes stultifying, the development of a person's true self. I do not think that in this regard I was all that different from other products of the class of school of which Ellesmere had been but a minor one. And if immaturity is indeed one consequence of what might be seen as unnaturally holding back the development of one's self, then I was probably in very good company - at any rate a very large company - of people similarly produced. Those who come out of that stable and can yet claim to have been truly mature and balanced individuals at that age are, I suspect, rare birds indeed.

Yet my immaturity at that time, my undeveloped state, by seeming comparison with my contemporaries, comes to me now as something different. Possibly it was not just that the others were merely more accomplished in presenting their outer *persona*, but that they were in reality more advanced down the road of integrating their real selves. For myself, though I certainly couldn't have analysed the case in such terms then, I think that there was a very deep and unresolved inner divide between the satisfactions of the outwardly completely British Oxford graduate and the frustrated longings of a person wanting unconsciously to be somewhere else, even someone else. My pretending to be the sort of person which my mind told me the Colonial Service Selection Board would find acceptable is revealing. This had not just been a slick bit of interview technique (which could well have backfired - and had deserved to); what I had been doing - and knew it at the time - was playing a part. In that case it had been for a specific purpose; but there seems to have been a more general, deep-rooted, semi-conscious kind of role playing which might possibly have been deleterious.

How far what was happening in the way of an inner irresolution, a failure to determine what, or who, I really was, did not I think arise from any sort of clash or dissonance between 'Turkishness' and 'Britishness' as such (whatever those two conditions might imply); rather it was, I believe, a kind of inner instability having its birth in a degree of emotional deprivation inevitably caused by being separated so young from my parents. It was in no sense tragic or dramatic; nothing so horrific as what we now vicariously experience when recoiling from the by no means uncommon lot of children who had once been sent back to Britain to languish among unkindly aunts while their parents did their duty to Empire in insalubrious lands under the Union Jack. My childhood in England was certainly not consciously unhappy, yet I suppose my real self was slowly being stifled or stunted, something of my normal humanity was not being nourished.

Additionally, I believe that the imperfections of my undeveloped self on the threshold of adulthood may be traced back to another contributing cause. Until my application to the Colonial Office I seem never to have taken any real initiative or to have decided for myself anything which was to affect the course of my life. Perhaps I would not be doing myself overmuch of an injustice were I to say that I can now see myself rather in the light of that Mulliner nephew, depicted by P.G.Wodehouse, whose girlfriend reported to him her aunt's characterisation of him as "a vapid and irreflective guffin totally lacking in resolution and purpose". Neither in going for a place at Worcester, nor in my decision to read Jurisprudence, do I seem to have exerted myself. So far as the first was concerned, the approach to the college appears to have been made on my behalf by Evans Prosser; and as for reading Law rather than, say, History, I seem merely to have drifted into that choice with scarcely any conscious cerebration. I certainly had no thought of making the law my career. (Mind you, in those days, as I was to discover after I had come up, no determinedly ambitious budding barrister would have taken a law degree before hieing themselves off to the Bar exams. The thrusters of whatever persuasion regarded their degrees as almost peripheral to their future careers - what counted was to make your mark, preferably in the Union; or in some other reputation-building sphere like OUDS or an undergraduate publication such as *Isis*.)

And so, as one to whom any thought of initiative had so far been alien, I spent those three final terms at Oxford. The requirements of the Devonshire course hardly called for much effort. To the pretty minimal extent that exertion was needed, I exerted myself. If the Selection Board had even half successfully done its job, there was no possibility of failing to satisfy the examiners that you had digested the content of the lectures and grasped the gist of the required reading.

**********

The arrival at Worcester as an ordinary undergraduate of the New Zealand test cricketer Martin Donnelly, who of course played for the University, rekindled my interest in the game which I played, but only for pleasure, on the delightful college ground. We were, I think, the only college lucky enough to have its playing fields inside its own grounds. I also continued with my squash; and was glad that I was given membership of the OU Squirrels - the University Squash Racquets Club, though the inter-university match hadn't yet been resumed. I was also elected a member of the Rhodes Club, membership of which was drawn from among Britain and the various Commonwealth countries - at that time Canada, Australia, New Zealand and South Africa, to which had recently been added India, Pakistan and Ceylon. Rhodes Club meetings always ended with the circulation of a 'loving cup', each member accepting this and passing it on with the words *"Die Weltbürger"*. How the wheel has come full circle in half a century.

**********

93

## Fledgling

During that year I met an Australian up at New College who had been in the Western Desert during the war. Through him I became interested in Arabic - not so much in the language itself as because its alphabet would provide me with the basic tools to read the old Turkish script which had been used for the language during the thousand years up to the generation immediately before mine (entirely unsuited though that virtually vowel-less script was to Turkish where vowel harmony is absolutely of the essence). I was extremely lucky to come upon and to be able to buy, cheaply, a rare copy in Thornton's in the Broad of the 1880 edition of the original 1856 Redhouse Ottoman-English dictionary, with the help of which I taught myself enough to be able later, from the Gold Coast, to correspond with my grandmother at the sort of prep school, "I am well, I hope you are well; it is very hot here", level of letter-writing. It could, I suppose, be said that in this way I was benefiting from that cross-fertilisation of academic disciplines at a university in which, more than by single-minded application to one's own subject, the true benefits of a university education consist. But I hardly saw things in just that light.

What I was involved in would seem to be a determined, but quite unfocused, search for something I must have felt I was missing - but of which I had only fitful feelings.

**********

After the Long Vacation at the end of the Trinity Term we were due to go to London for the last part of our course, which took up the last three months of 1948; and we would then head off for our respective postings. I decided to visit Cyprus for what was likely to be the last opportunity for a long time. That summer I went out by air on a scheduled route in a pre-jet age. It was the first time I had flown and the experience was exhilarating. That three-week holiday brought me to a point of resolution - in both senses of that word. I accepted for myself that the state of drift in which I existed couldn't just be allowed to continue uninfluenced by any action on my part. Cyprus was where I wanted to be and I now realised I wouldn't get there without willing it in earnest. Whether or not my will would prevail was another thing; but I would have to move in the matter. I realised that it would be foolish in the extreme to chuck the Gold Coast appointment without even going there (or indeed even finishing the Devonshire course). I would therefore return to England and continue along the road to which my uncle had directed me. But I now had it in my mind to make my application for transfer to Cyprus in the Colonial Service sooner than either he or I might have contemplated at the stage he gave his advice. In fact I decided I would do so at the end of my first tour - and leave the outcome to providence. I kept my own counsel and didn't even hint to my mother about my decision. Though 'decision' is too exact a word, and 'hopeful intention' would more accurately describe the outcome of my inner conflict.

***********

And so back to London. Living in 'bed and breakfast' digs, going to lectures at the LSE, and being instructed at the SOAS in Twi - the language spoken by the dominant people of the Gold Coast before the British arrived in the mid-nineteenth century and took the country after the three Ashanti Wars. (In one of these the British troops had been commanded by that Sir Garnet Wolseley who was shortly thereafter to head the peaceful takeover of Cyprus under treaty with the Ottoman Sultan before then going on to head the unsuccessful expedition to relieve Gordon in Khartoum in 1884-85.) Although Twi was spoken widely in the forested, central Ashanti country and, with variations, in the southern coastal area, the north of the country was largely Dagomba-speaking. Hausa was the lingua franca of the north as it was, much more widely, in Nigeria for which the great majority of us on the course were destined. They were therefore taught Hausa, as those posted to East African territories were taught the corresponding *lingua franca* of Swahili. Swahili and Hausa were relatively easy and those learning them were sufficiently proficient by the end of the three months to engage in very basic conversation - or rather to produce conversational phrases. Twi on the other hand is a 'tonal' language (a characteristic I believe it shares, if not to such a marked extent, with Chinese - and, I assume, with the other languages which go under that all-embracing name). Those of us learning Twi therefore made very much less headway; very little indeed in my case. The only Twi sentence which has survived with me after half a century (and I ask pardon for any

95

incorrectitude of any Twi-speaker who might conceivably read these words) is: *Kum apim, apim beba*, an Ashanti war-cry meaning "Kill a thousand and a thousand will come".

It was during these last few months in London that the two groups who had spent their respective first three terms of the Devonshire course separately at Oxford and Cambridge now came together. In London I met an engaging Wykehamist wartime Guardee whose posting was also to the Gold Coast. 'Engaging' because he was free of a solemn portentousness which seemed to hang over some of us - and indeed to be a part of a few. As I was to learn, my erstwhile colleague had a propensity to embroider a good story. On this occasion I took entirely *au pied de la lettre* an anecdote he told against himself. Walking down King's Parade at Cambridge he saw, coming towards him, an impressive looking African, and no less so by the fact that he was wearing a Brigade of Guards tie. The ex-Guardee fledgling colonial administrator, drawing himself up (and he was a large man), said, kindly but firmly, "I suppose you know you're wearing a Brigade tie?" To which the other replied, as firmly and kindly, "Yes; Grenadiers" (or whichever - I don't recall). He was the Kabaka of Uganda - more correctly, I think, of the Baganda people of that country. Known to his many friends as Freddy, the Kabaka was the hereditary king of his people; and, as it happened, he had indeed every right to his tie! (Deposed not so many years later, when the Governor of Uganda was the forceful and powerfully-willed Sir Andrew Cohen - a Deputy Under Secretary at the Colonial Office sent, unusually, to Uganda as Governor - poor Freddy Kabaka was, I believe, to end his days in sadly tragic penury in London after further tribulations following Uganda's emergence as an independent Commonwealth country.)

During our last few weeks in London we finished kitting ourselves out at the two main established tropical outfitters, who carried on a flourishing business. I patronised Griffith MacAllister. The Scottish name, in this colonial, imperial setting nowadays conjures up for me overtones, and resonates, as it evokes others such as Steel Brothers, Jardine Mathieson and many other famous, and once famous, names of traders and businessmen from the north Celtic parts of Britain. I see a kind of imaginary group portrait of faces receding into a faded past, back to the emergence, from the beginnings of the eighteenth century, of that empire, in whose last days, had we known it, we were then living; an empire which had essentially been founded on commerce. Not, in my view, was the growth of that new empire, which arose after the American Colonies achieved independence, a progress in which "trade followed the flag" - as some historians would have us believe. Quite the reverse. In the territories to become the new empire, which in 1948 was to have but a dozen or so more years of life, the first seeds had been sown by venturers pursuing profit in trade. The flag came later; in Africa just as it had done, much earlier in India. And in the process of empire-building in the 19th century, the Scots from the United Kingdom had played no small part. Whether in the lists of trading houses of India, of Burma, of Hong Kong and elsewhere, or those of the officers, on deck and in the engine room, of the ships which plied the empire routes; or in lists of club members; or on headstones in those far-off places - always there are Scottish names.

*There is a parable here, and a parallel between the part played in the growth of the British empire by a people from the mountainous outer marches of its homeland, and the not dissimilar relationship between the Turkish people (going back to the pre-Ottoman Seljuks) and their own peripheral highland neighbours, the Kurdish people. No historical comparison can ever be entirely apt. Yet, making allowance for all the huge changes and differences the world has witnessed in the last two hundred years, the stage in the development of relations between the Turkish and the Kurdish peoples has an almost disconcerting likeness, for me, to that between the English and the Scots in the late 18th century. What might not the benefits be to each if that which is most surely possible were to be achieved in fact (with the encouragement and help - rather than in the face of the obstruction and opposition - of third parties) through the recovery of that spirit of common purpose which has historically inspired both peoples? Until recent times that sense of solidarity had animated them both, from the days of the first crusades, when the Seljuk Turkish Sultan Nur ed-Din and his Kurdish commander Salah ed-Din (Saladin) had together resisted and driven out the invading Franks, until the battles after the 1914-1918 war when Kurd and Turk fought again to prevent the partition of their Anatolian homeland by the victorious allied powers.*

**Fledgling**

*A spirit of cooperative endeavour, freed from a blinkered negative tribalism and nationalism on both sides (the days of which are in any case already numbered - in Turkey as elsewhere) would show itself in constructive development for the mutual advantage of each; and fresh joint enterprise would bring to the lands in which they both live a prosperity in which they both would share and from which their neighbours and the world would also benefit.*

**\*\*\*\*\*\*\*\*\*\***

I have let my reflections carry me away from the direct account of my own story. And yet perhaps not so very far from it in truth.

# ~6~
# Yendi; Tamale; Accra

On a dark, foggy morning in January 1949 we steamed down the Mersey estuary on the *SS Accra*. A friend had given me Graham Greene's *The Heart of the Matter* to read on the boat. Perhaps it was kindly meant - to dissuade me from a career he judged ill-advised. The book and the day induced gloom. Not a particularly auspicious start. With recollections of that winter voyage in the Mediterranean in 1940 which had reduced me to reading fitfully on my bunk, I had resigned myself to succumbing again to seasickness, and especially so now with the prospect of the Irish Sea, the Western Approaches and the dread Bay of Biscay all looming ahead. The wish is supposed to be the father to the thought; and it seems that the dread is the mother of the fact. For a couple of days I could only ward off nausea by lying down. I can't recall how many days the voyage was due to take - or anyway before we had a stop at Las Palmas in the Canaries - but I decided that I really couldn't spend the rest of the time prostrate. I remembered that my brother had told me that Nelson was reputed to have been a pretty poor sailor, in being prone (if not supine) to seasickness, and that he too had found that when on watch - so that he *had* to carry out his duties - mind really did seem to get the better of matter. I accordingly stirred myself, got up on deck, and discovered to my great gratification that I was indeed capable of looking at the horizon slowly rising and falling above and below the ship's rail without such potently visible evidence of the heavy pitching and rolling affecting me.

The ship had its complement of "old Coasters", mainly mining engineers. One at least habitually laced his breakfast coffee with brandy, which bracing method of starting the day attracted no comment from anyone. My own, recollected, reaction at the time was simply a kind of perverse pleasure that I should have met in the flesh such a character out of a Conrad novel. There were tales of old Coasters of this kind helpfully showing "the young idea" the ropes by, for example, impressing upon them that quinine - one of the most bitter substances - was ineffective as a prophylactic against malaria unless the daily pill was well chewed before swallowing. That we were not so advised I uncharitably attribute simply to the fact that by the end of the war quinine had been replaced by mepacrine (which turned you a pale yellow). Paludrine was yet to come.

As I say, my reading about Graham Greene's fictional policeman Scobie hadn't been a very uplifting curtain-raiser to the career I was now beginning. That such careers were not unlimited in duration was of course accepted. At Oxford Margery Perham had in fact told us in her lectures that we should see ourselves as "scaffolding" in the building of the coming new independent countries of the empire; but the time-scale in which this scaffolding was to be dismantled was obviously thought then to be as long as our possible, even probable, career expectations - fifteen to twenty years. Odd now, looking back on it. Fifty was a normal retiring age from service in West Africa. None of us at least had any conception of the breathtaking speed we should all be travelling towards a world in which all the African dependencies would assume their positions as sovereign members of the successor organisation of the old League of Nations - the new United Nations Organisation, operating not, as before, from Geneva but, significantly and symbolically, from across the Atlantic in New York.

\*\*\*\*\*\*\*\*\*\*

The Gold Coast in 1949 consisted of four administrative divisions: the coast and its hinterland, which was the Colony proper; the central territory of Ashanti, with its Paramount Chief, the *Asantehene*; the Northern Territories; and British Togoland. The administration of each of the first three was under its own Chief Commissioner. Togoland was the western part of the old German Colony of Togo which, after the First World War, had been split by a central north-south boundary, the east going to the French as the new French Togo, and the west being tacked on to the Gold Coast. From 1920 to 1947 Togo had been

100

a League of Nations 'Mandate', and then a UN 'Trust Territory'. The British Trust Territory was divided between a 'north' and a 'south', each coming, respectively, under the administrative jurisdiction of the Chief Commissioner of the Northern Territories (CCNT) and of the Chief Commissioner of the Colony (CCC). All quite logical when you come to think of it.

Of arrival at Accra the capital, on the coast, travel to Kumasi in the Ashanti forests, and the journey north to the savannah country and the District headquarters of Yendi in the Northern Territories, I retain but fleeting memories. Dinner in Kumasi with the CCA was a full dress affair: gleaming silver, shining glasses, and service by the CCA's staff. The Oxford I had left had not been so magnificent. We cadets took leave of each other after engaging our own servants - in my case a cook and a 'small boy'. The latter was indeed no more than that, perhaps sixteen or seventeen years old. Sofu was his name; and to him I taught the alphabet - and how to write his name. My basic salary, without allowances, was £30 a month. The cook Salifu got £5, and Sofu £2.

Yendi was the seat of the Paramount Chief - the Ya Na - of the Dagomba tribe. The town had been the local administrative headquarters in the German colony of Togo. Since the headquarters of the British Northern Territories was Tamale, where the CCNT had his Residence, Yendi District, under its District Commissioner, was naturally subordinate to Tamale. The case with the Native Administration was the reverse; there were Dagomba Chiefs in the Northern Territories, including Tamale, who were of course subject to the Ya Na in Yendi. Not so very confusing really. Such were the doubtless inevitable intricacies resulting from the acquisition of colonial territories without 'natural' boundaries - as compared with an island like Cyprus bounded by the sea. (Yet just how much, or how little, of a 'boundary' that sea provided, later years were to demonstrate in exceptional ways.)

\*\*\*\*\*\*\*\*\*\*

My District Commissioner (DC) at Yendi was R.K. (Robert) Talbot, a middle-aged bachelor. The only other expatriate on the station was a

Scottish Water Department engineer, with a golden heart and one glass eye - 'Dead-eye' Dick Edmonston. On my first evening Robert Talbot took me for a walk round the station from his bungalow to the District Office down a tree-lined earth road (dating from German days, thirty years back), off which were Dead-eye's rather smaller one and, between the other two, my own two-roomed one. The latter two were thatched; Talbot's I don't recall. None of course had electricity or running water. During our walk we came up with, or passed, Dagombas, in ones or twos, from the small town half a mile or so distant. R.K.T. responded to the salutations they invariably gave. After several of these I thought it civil to respond too, and did so. Robert turned to me and memorably observed to his new, not quite twenty three year old Assistant DC, "I return the salutes on this station." This didn't affect our relationship, never all that close; I simply put it down to the way being a solitary 'bush DC' took someone in that position. Dead-eye on the other hand was a sort of father confessor. His wife was back in Scotland and he was clearly rather lonely, but he in no way repined. I had quite a few evenings talking and drinking with him, though his intake was far in excess of my capacity.

The morning after arrival R.K.T. introduced me to the office routine - and promptly handed over to me the duties of District Magistrate and Sub-Accountant. On assumption of these responsibilities - probably, but I don't remember, it was in connection with my magisterial functions - I had to take a formal oath, perhaps to administer the King's justice without fear or favour or some formula of that nature. Holy Writ was required, and I asked for a Koran, which was at once produced. Where it came from I didn't enquire; but a majority of the northern tribes were Moslem. These delegations of authority and responsibility to me were, I hope essentially as part of my training (or 'learning on the job'); but I suspect that in this way Talbot was also allowing himself more time for his own preference - district touring. Such touring was indeed the primary activity of the good DC, so as to be in close regular touch (but not too regular, or too close) with the Chiefs, and so as to supervise what was called the 'Native Administration' - the Chiefs having their own jurisdiction and responsibility in respect of Customary Law and Native Treasury. I was occasionally allowed to tour myself.

**\*\*\*\*\*\*\*\*\*\***

Arriving on tour at a village, one immediately called first on the local chief or sub-chief. Proceedings began with the usual round of formal courtesies and civil exchanges. Other conversation would - in my case - be through interpreters: Robert Talbot was fluent in Dagomba. Twi was practically of no use among these northern people, so the fact of mine being less than minimal was of no consequence. Either on arrival or departure - I forget which - the chief would give the visitor a 'dash', that is a gift, most usually of eggs or other foodstuffs such as fruit or vegetables. Custom's iron law meant that you could not refuse a 'dash'; but an equally rigid Colonial Service rule required that gifts could only be accepted if a return 'dash' were given. A frequent, and very acceptable, such return present was a dozen or so cartridges, which one therefore always carried (though I myself, despite my performance with the Selection Board, in fact had no gun of my own).

The official point of the visit on tour was to be available to hear any representations, and to convey in person any significant announcements. But the occasion was also used to check the various books and ledgers of the Native Administration Treasury in respect of receipts and disbursements on public works such as road building and maintenance. Roads were then all un-tarmaced, surfaces being the natural red laterite, which very quickly became corrugated. No-one seemed to know for sure just how this corrugation was caused; and one had to learn by trial and error to find the optimum speed - neither too slow nor too fast - to achieve the minimum bone-shaking. At that stage even the road from the Provincial capital Tamale to the south was only of this kind, though 'graded', and travel by car or 'pick-up' truck in the dry season meant that the traveller was very quickly shrouded in a red layer of dust covering both him and the contents of the vehicle. The days of the foot-trek had passed, but only recently, into history. I did once, but only once, make a visit to an outlying Native Authority by bicycle, having first sent my cook and small boy on ahead by 'pick-up'. I remember the very tall grass, through which what was not much more than a narrowish track ran, and my qualms as to what might be lurking on each side of the undergrowth. The north was technically lion and elephant country - but really only in the sense that these were not to be found at all in the forested south. For myself I never saw either.

Nor, if it came to that, snakes. Although there seem to be some creatures which are liable to induce horror and revulsion in nearly everyone, most people also seem to have an individual aversion to, and terror of, particular creatures - as Orwell so grimly recognised when he described the agonising fear of the rat endured by Winston Smith in Room 101. I have always been frightened of sharks, a fear which I think I can even trace back to the time I used to read in coloured comics of pirates making their captured enemies walk the plank. I can still see the illustrations showing the black fin cutting through the water alongside. But my aversion to snakes, which was nothing like my dread of sharks, I cannot account for. I wasn't particularly concerned about them in the daytime; indeed I was to learn that a snake is much more likely to be a good deal more frightened of you than you are to be scared of it. But at night-time, in the dark, the possibility of snakes was rarely out of my mind; and especially going out to the 'thunder-box', even with a 'Tilley' lamp, was not something I did with insouciance! It was Dead-eye who gave me the benefit of a theory to which he adhered. This held that snakes were somehow attracted to some people but not to others. One knew of this with cats of course; they seem to make a perversely deliberate bee-line for people who particularly recoil from their kind. I have witnessed this more than once; the cousin who disappointed her mother's matrimonial hopes for her (and for me) suffers from just such a cat phobia, and they do indeed seek her out with a view to rubbing up against her - to have her leaving the room at high speed calling for help. Dead-eye's theory had some evidence in support. While I never actually saw a live snake in Africa (much less in my compound) he claimed often to have done so, and indeed there were occasionally dead ones to be seen draped over branches in trees around his bungalow, dispatched by himself or his boys. It could of course conceivably be thought that some at least of these serpents might just have been attributable to the contents of the bottles which lay piled up empty at the back of his compound. (An unkind colleague had been heard to observe, quite unwarrantably, that "the trouble with the Water Department is that they don't drink enough of the stuff they don't produce".)

Dead-Eye's specific job in Yendi was, in fact, the construction of a catchment dam for irrigation purposes just outside the town; and a most effective piece of work it seemed to be. It created quite a lake, attracting many water fowl and other birds. It was there that I saw a bustard; and it was at Talbot's table that I first ate one; he, I am fairly sure I correctly remember, having shot it.

On one occasion Dead-eye invited me to go shooting with him. The method would not have commended itself or us to, still less have been received with any thing but severe disfavour by, the upholders of correctitude in the manner of pursuing game birds in Britain. Dead-Eye knew that there were quantities of guinea-fowl in the countryside around us and that, especially at the shank of the day, as the sun's heat diminishes and the fierce light begins to soften, these birds could be seen singly and in small groups at the verges of the track running through the bush. Along this track, therefore, we would take our turn to slowly drive the pick-up while the passenger would take periodic shots at the intended contents of the cooking pot. The gun, I believe, was not a shot-gun but a small calibre low-velocity 'rifle', though probably smooth-bore. That it didn't discharge shot, but a single small bullet was just as well. After getting a bird or two it was my turn to drive. A bird rose and flew across the line the pick-up was travelling; Dead-Eye followed its flight with the barrel and loosed off - missing the bird, but winging the truck's bonnet. Which is itself reasonable confirmation of my recollection that he wasn't using a shot-gun, or the engine would have got a discharge that would have put paid to it. The guinea-fowl tasted as delicious as the bustard; rather better, if anything.

\*\*\*\*\*\*\*\*\*\*\*

Thinking of those evenings with Dead-Eye brings back to me that most characteristic sound of the African night - the drumming. Across the short distance from the town of Yendi the night air was nearly always, as it now seems to me in memory, somehow caressed by the smoothly rhythmical beat of those drums. The art, and even more the science, of drumming was a mystery to me, and remains so. I knew that in the south, where the languages were 'tonal', drums could be used for communication. I believe I remember correctly being told that, at the time of the Boer War, news of particular battles would travel so quickly and over such great distances, right across Africa, where no other means of communication existed, that this could be explained only by the 'talking drums' being used. It could well have been so. I do not think that the drums which we would so often hear during the Yendi nights were 'speaking' in that sense. Talking drums involved the use, as I understand, of two distinct drums - one of a lower and the other of a higher pitch, to represent the intonations of the human voice speaking a tonal language. The drums in Yendi seemed not to have this quality - but who save an expert can tell?

***********

Two other things stand out in my memory of my time in Yendi. One is the Leper Station, as I think it was called, fairly nearby, outside the town. I visited this more than once; and I learned then that leprosy, dread though its reputation is, is certainly not infectious, nor by way of brief and superficial contact, particularly contagious. Indeed, while untreated it can be a horribly disfiguring and disabling disease, the widespread horror of it (deriving I suppose largely from bible stories and resonances of mediaeval histories with cries of "Unclean! Unclean!") was entirely unjustified. As we had no medical officer at Yendi, I can't call to mind what attention these poor people received or who administered it. I think there must have been a local medical orderly or dispenser, or somebody of that sort, supervised on periodic visits by an MO.

Nor do I remember from whom I received my shots of anti-rabies vaccine. I had come into contact with a dog which had shortly after shown symptoms of hydrophobia - a disease quite as horrendous as its reputation. If I remember correctly, the procedure in such a case was for the dog to be destroyed and the body at once dispatched, presumably to Tamale (but possibly to Accra), for tests to be carried out on its brain so as to determine whether or not it had indeed been rabid; and in the meantime anyone thought to have been at risk would begin a course of injections. These took place daily over a period of, I think, ten days to a fortnight. The syringe had a needle which to my inflamed imagination appeared to be about six inches long. In reality it was probably not more than around half that length, but it was quite long enough - it needed to be as the injection was required, I believe, to penetrate at least well into the stomach lining. Three or four days of this was quite enough for someone who averts his eyes even when getting an anti-flu jab. Ghastly though rabies is, I decided that the dog had at least not actually bitten me and, since I was reasonably sure that there was no broken skin with which the dog's saliva had come into contact, I was probably safe enough, even were the test on the dead dog to show it to have been rabid. I called off the injections. The test proved positive. But after a very apprehensive wait I was cleared of risk. And so, though it wasn't exactly a case of "the man recovered from the bite; the dog it was that died", at least the swift manner of its death wasn't the dreadful end it would have suffered had it been left to die in the agonies of hydrophobia.

\*\*\*\*\*\*\*\*\*\*

After six months in Yendi I was posted to Tamale as Secretary to the CCNT, although the post of Chief Commissioner was currently vacant and being filled, in an acting capacity, by the Assistant CC, with his job being temporarily carried out by the Senior DC. This latter was a white-moustached character with service in the north going back to the days, so he told me, when one of the tribes, the Konkomba, had the habit of using poisoned arrows, and being generally unruly. According to him, he had once had to take a punitive expedition against them for failure to pay their cattle tax. There certainly had been, by repute, some fairly eccentric officers around in the past. I was told of one CCNT who, some years back, had arrived to take up his new appointment to the post, after home leave in Britain, not by the normal route of a sea passage to Accra or Takoradi on the coast and then up to the north through the forest, but *via* the Mediterranean north-African coast and then southwards overland to his headquarters in Tamale.

As to whether another senior man of whom an anecdote was told, with much satisfaction by district officers, was an entire figment I never established. The story was certainly *ben trovato*, even if it might not have been wholly *vero*. An Assistant DC in an outlying sub-District was being inspected by by an Assistant CCNT. The visitor observed that the solid iron sub-District office safe, which held a sizeable imprest of cash, had only a single overnight guard, consisting of an 'escort policeman', a stalwart but illiterate body of men. The visiting fireman took exception to what he considered this slack and inadequate precautionary arrangement. Brushing aside attempts by his junior to explain and excuse himself, he insisted that the guard must be doubled. The sequel, as recounted, was predictable. The next morning there was no sign of guards - or safe. "Well," remonstrated the Assistant DC, "You wouldn't let me tell you. The safe was too heavy for only the one of them." Of another bush DC it was recounted that he had devised an ingeniously sure-fire way of seeing the end of unwelcome papers. Smearing such documents with honey or treacle ensured their being consumed by ants, even in a safe - if not always completely at least enough to be illegible.

My own duties were largely concerned with the administration of the headquarter offices. Among other things, this involved me in any ciphering and deciphering of messages from Accra at a time when the political atmosphere was beginning to warm up, owing to the activities of the Convention People's Party (CPP), the organisation which had been founded by Kwame Nkrumah, fairly recently returned from abroad. Typing of classified correspondence bearing on this aspect of things also fell to me to deal with. I had in addition magisterial duties in Tamale, mostly arising from cases of first instance; but I had to hear at least one case for determination whether or not there were grounds for committal to the Assizes in Accra. The case was one where the accused stood charged with murder, then a capital offence. There was in my opinion sufficient ground for the matter to be heard by the Assize Court, to which I therefore committed it with reasons stated. On a lighter note, also in connection with judiciary functions, I recount a piece of home-spun lore (essentially as a comment on attitudes which had not yet passed into history). This was that a sure test of whether or not a witness was telling the truth, was to watch his, or her, toes. If they wriggled, this was a clear sign of perjury. Naturally I gave no weight to this ingenious folk psychology; but I have to admit I would sometimes find my eyes straying downwards in curiosity.

As the CCNT's Secretary I also had some intermittent duties on the social side, such as invitations for luncheons and dinners, including the seating arrangements. There was an occasion when the guest list was such that I had two women sitting next to each other (or some similar *bêtise*). It was not till some months later that I heard a version of this which had me seating all the women on one side of the table and all the men on the other. I suspected that my ex-Guardee friend had had a hand in this rather overworked elaboration. It requires a real master to pull off an artistic exaggeration with literary justification and effect. Such as when G.B.Shaw vividly puts over the impression made on him by the performance on stage of a dancer, Vincenti. Returning home just after witnessing this he wrote his review:

"When I arrived at my door ... I found Fitzroy Square deserted ... The carriage-way round the circular railing presented such a magnificent hippodrome that I could not resist trying to go round just once in Vincenti's fashion. It proved frightfully difficult. After my fourteenth fall I was picked up by a policeman. 'What are you doing here?' he said, keeping fast hold of me 'I bin watching you for the last five minutes.' I explained, eloquently and enthusiastically. He hesitated a moment, and then said, 'Would you mind holding my helmet while I have a try? It don't look so hard.' Next moment his nose was buried in the macadam and his right knee was out through its torn garment. He got up bruised and bleeding, but resolute. 'I never was beaten yet,' he said; 'and I won't be beaten now. It was my coat that tripped me.' We both hung our coats on the railings, and went at it again. If each round of the square had been a round in a prize fight, we should have been less damaged and disfigured; but we persevered, and by four o'clock the policeman had just succeeded in getting round twice without a rest or a fall, when an inspector arrived and asked him bitterly whether that was his notion of fixed point duty. 'I allow it ain't fixed point,' said the constable, emboldened by his new accomplishment, 'but I'll lay half a sovereign you can't do it.' The inspector could not resist the temptation to try (I was whirling round before his eyes in the most fascinating manner); and he made rapid progress after half an hour or so. We were subsequently joined by an early postman and by a milkman, who unfortunately broke his leg and had to be carried to hospital by the other three. By that time I was quite exhausted, and could barely crawl into bed. It was perhaps a foolish scene; but nobody who has witnessed Vincenti's performance will feel surprised at it."

**Fledgling**

My period in Tamale was followed by a posting to the Secretariat in Accra. For the ambitious and able a Secretariat appointment, with all the chances of being 'noticed', was very much to be desired. In retrospect, however, I am tempted to think that three postings in a single tour were possibly susceptible of another construction. In *Some People* Harold Nicolson portrays a Diplomatic Service colleague just before the First World War. This man remarked to him, "I know I'm not very dashing or brilliant - but I swear my 'paragraph' in the Foreign Office List is longer than any other of my seniority." Nicolson continues: "I pulled the List towards me ... It read like a time-table ... It spoke of a series of intolerant chiefs stung successively to revolt." I wonder.

I was to have about another six months in the Secretariat. The work must have been monumentally boring as I can remember practically nothing of the things I was dealing with. Indeed straining now at my memory all I can call back is some faint idea of a project for stemming coast erosion somewhere by means of constructing 'groynes'; but just where has completely slipped my mind. It could have been near Keta (on the way towards Lome in French Togo) where my colleague, the suspect embroiderer of tales, was in charge of a sub-District, and with whom I once spent a weekend there. Otherwise work in Accra simply passed, if it didn't actually drag. Things outside, however, were beginning to simmer.

How far the CPP might be thought to have been able to foresee the consequences is a matter of opinion on which I wouldn't, especially at this distance in time, want to express a view, but demonstrations organised by them got out of hand and in Accra developed into a riot. The police intervened; two escort policemen were killed. Of the riot itself I saw nothing; it blew up very quickly and subsided as rapidly, as far as I can recall. The whole thing was in fact quite unexpected, being wholly out of character with the people who, if ebullient by temperament, were almost disciplined in their social behaviour and interactions; this perhaps being rooted in their tribal structures and hierarchies. The disturbances were possibly not unconnected with the

110

dislocations and discontents which came with, and also caused, the movement from the countryside to the towns, as also with the return of troops in the West African Frontier Force, who had served overseas in the war and on return had a different view of things than before. What tugs the strings of memory is the sight of the funeral procession of the two policemen, and even more the sound of Chopin's Funeral March - the middle melodic section - which, played by the police band, was the first time I had heard it orchestrated and not just as a piano piece. It was very moving.

Because of the climate, leave entitlement on the West Coast of Africa was more generous than in East Africa. I seem to recall that we in the Gold Coast earned around one week's home leave for each month of duty: one should bear in mind that we were scarcely out of the period when the West Coast still had the reputation of being "the white man's grave". Indeed, unless my imagination is becoming wholly unruly, the 'kit list' (or whatever it was called) issued by the Colonial Office still included, possibly only as 'advisory', a 'spine-pad' to ward off the effects of the sun's rays on the spinal column. (This strikes me nowadays as almost on a par with the outfitters guyed by P.G.Wodehouse in one of the Mulliner stories, whose salesmanship extended to trying to get whichever young Mulliner it was to include in his kit "this ointment - said to be excellent for alligator bites".) It was only a few years back that, from the Western Desert to the jungles of Burma, British troops had abandoned even pith helmets, and suffered no harmful results. No doubt it takes time for the administrative machine, more especially when other more pressing, not to say vital, calls are made on peoples' time in circumstances of war and its aftermath, to get on to such prosaic matters as amending clothing and equipment lists. I still have my black-japanned metal uniform case - but not the small hip-bath which could also be doubled for use as an additional receptacle for the 'carrying load' of a head-porter - as though we were still in the days of Livingstone.

**\*\*\*\*\*\*\*\*\*\***

To end this account of my time in the old Gold Coast I give a last impression: of the beach at Accra. This is brought to mind not just because the scene is captured in two or three of the very few photographs I still have of those days in my album, but particularly since it was there among the breakers in that sea that I partially overcame, without completely exorcising, my phobia of sharks. It was possible to enjoy surfing in a limited fashion on those breakers. To do so, however, involved swimming out with a board just outside the point where one could catch the breakers as they began to form. Sharks did not, so they said, come inside this line; but in any case, in my mind they might very well be just outside. I forced myself to swim out with my board to this imaginary, and mental, barrier, outside which I fearfully fantasised sharks gliding around - and turned in a rush, with immense relief, as I launched out back to the beach on the freshly swelling wave. Although as far as surfing went this was pretty tame stuff, for myself I felt I had achieved something in refusing to let my terror dictate to me. The dread of sharks remained, and still does, but I was now able to enjoy the Accra beach and its mild surfing with only a frisson as I approached the shark barrier.

*********

When the time arrived for my 'home' leave, I arranged with the Establishment Department to commute my entitlement to a passage to Britain into a cash equivalent and made my own way to Cyprus, travelling on a French boat from Takoradi, by way of Abidjan and Casablanca, to Marseilles. There I managed to get a berth on a Turkish ship which included Cyprus on its itinerary through the eastern Mediterranean. 'Berth', however, is a misleading way of putting it. The only passenger accommodation which had not been taken consisted in fact of two cabins, one port and one starboard, on the upper deck below the bridge - both described as *de luxe*. For this reason the crew must, I am sure, have had expectations of very handsome tips at the end of the voyage. They were too polite to do more than fail to hide completely their disappointment at their getting no more than the usual gratuities, which was all that I could produce; and I practically slunk off the ship at the end in deep chagrin.

*********

*And I can't resist going off at a tangent at the close of this part of my story.  Having just written "chagrin", I decided to check precisely what the dictionary definition is of this word.  It does indeed apparently correctly represent my feelings of disappointment and mortification; but I am intrigued to discover also that the word is stated to be derived "f. Turk. sagri [sic] rump of horse, prepared hide, SHAGREEN; sense by metaphor f. use of shagreen for friction."  One of the more notably implausible derivations to be found in dictionaries, as in other works - or so it seems to me. A horse's rump in Turkish is indeed 'sağrı' (with the 'ğ' silent and the preceding vowel lengthened, as in the Turkish food 'yoğurt'); but it is only in the last ten years or so, in the course of acquainting myself with old Turkish - for reasons I hope to come to later - that I learned the old Turkish word 'sayrı' meaning 'ill'; and this seems to me to provide at least as likely (or unlikely) a connection - in the sense of 'discomfiture' - as horses' rumps with the meaning of the French 'chagrin'.*

# PART IV : YOUNG BIRD

(1951-1959)

# ~7~
# Nicosia; Limassol; Nicosia

At the earliest opportunity after I had got to Nicosia I contacted the Secretariat and formally asked for a transfer to the Cyprus government from my post in the Gold Coast. Looking back now, I am astonished how I never seem to have contemplated what I should have done if my bid had failed. I simply do not recall what, at the time, I might have had in mind in that event. I appear indeed to have managed to put the thing right out of my mind while I decided to enjoy my leave in what I now definitely considered was, and was to remain, my own country. In retrospect I suppose that I was in that state of mind (I am disposed to say more accurately "of being") which is meant, and should be conveyed, by the word 'Moslem' (strictly *muslim*); for I had come to a decision, I had taken what action was within my means to accomplish, and the outcome was now in other hands than mine - in the hands of providence, of God. (A *muslim* being one whose will is 'God-surrendered').

It was very soon that I heard from Government House. The call was to an interview with the Governor, Sir Andrew Wright. I was not to know whether my application had gone straight to the Colonial Office in London and then been referred back to the Governor in Cyprus for his advice and recommendation (and indeed also to the Governor in Accra), or whether this interview was part of the initial procedure before Nicosia even passed my application to the Secretary of State for a decision. And I have no recollection of what the Governor and I talked about. I can, however, hardly have left him in any doubt at all that I did not see myself contentedly continuing into an indefinite future in the Gold Coast, and that my heart was in Cyprus - as was indeed the case. Although that interview had, so far as I now can judge

116

impressionistically, gone well, I could not feel completely comfortable as to the result, and certainly not confident. In all my life I never have been sure of an outcome until it has actually come about. Even after I had taken the Oxford Final Honours Schools examinations, in which my mind told me I had acquitted myself not dishonourably, I was still nervous until I saw the list posted up.

Not very long before the date I should have been due to make arrangements for a return to the Gold Coast - or, I suppose, to steel myself to resign if necessary - I had a telephone call from the Secretariat to say that my application had been accepted and my appointment to Cyprus approved. To my initial disappointment my posting was not to be to the capital Nicosia, but to one of the four other District Towns of Famagusta, Limassol, Larnaca and Paphos. I was to be Assistant District Commissioner in Limassol. Even with this minor regret at being posted away from Nicosia, I was nevertheless elated. I had obtained the thing my heart had longed for over the years. It was like wakening to the dawn of a new future, bright, unclouded and full of promise and hope. Sweet was it indeed in that dawn to be alive, and to be young was not very far short of "very heaven". So it seemed to me - and felt so - then.

**\*\*\*\*\*\*\*\*\*\***

While in Nicosia, before my transfer had come through, I had hardly moved outside the circle of my family and friends. Of contacts, social or otherwise, with Greeks I had none; nor was I aware of any such individual relations between Turks and Greeks. In fact I didn't know what, if any, personal relations there might exist between members of the two communities of the island. The residential Greek and Turkish quarters of Nicosia were quite separate; and even the shopping areas were largely apart, though becoming more intermingled towards their edges. The main such 'boundary' lay along the street which ran eastward into the town from the Paphos Gate at the western wall; and there was also the completely mixed intercommunal (though that word didn't feature in the vocabulary of that time) central municipal market just south of the main Mosque. Dry-cleaners were a new feature then (and come to think of it I'm not sure how common they were even in

England then); and there being no Turkish ones my mother patronised a Greek one not far off the main shopping street, which ran north from what was then called the *'Hadji Savva* opening' in the south of the town wall near the Bayraktar mosque. That street was the Ledra Street which, for those who would come to know Cyprus in the mid- and late-1950s, would have other, tragic and bitter memories and associations beyond those of just peaceful trade and commerce. Its name had not yet become "Murder Mile".

It was now, as the second half of the century opened, that I began to get a feeling - one might with justification say a faint whiff - of an unfamiliar unease in the air. I think I can best convey this by saying there was apprehension, even fear, in the atmosphere. Whether this was in fact something new, or whether merely that I myself was now becoming sensitive to something already there, I could not say. It was not pervasive in the strict meaning of the word as I did not come across it everywhere, nor always. But what I was now sensing was certainly nothing I had previously known.

The first, and very specific, experience I had of this was during a social call on my mother by a small group of half a dozen Turkish women. Among them was a stranger - and I believe the purpose of this particular call, which was otherwise the usual and frequent customary one between women - was to introduce this stranger to my mother. Although I had been on the point of leaving the house to go into the town, they, unusually, asked me to stay. (I was conscious anyway of being regarded as somewhat of a curiosity: someone who had spent most of his life outside the island - therefore also something of a stranger.) The visiting stranger was introduced to my mother and to me. She was a mother on the right side of middle age who had arrived on a visit to relatives in Cyprus, I think from Turkey. But I remember, and very clearly, that Rhodes was her actual home - as Cyprus was ours; and that she was full of misgivings about the future of the Turkish population of her island (of which at that time the Turks were about a third - a larger proportion than the Turkish population of Cyprus).

**\*\*\*\*\*\*\*\*\*\***

*Rhodes had, with the rest of the Dodecanese islands, and also Libya, been seized from Turkey by Italy in 1911, following the Italian attack on the Ottoman empire that year. With Italy's defeat in the Second World War, Rhodes had been handed to Greece. The enmity which has so often marked relations between Greece and Turkey had most recently culminated in the Greek adventure out of which modern Turkey had been born. At the time when relations between the two countries had been placed on a new footing after that war under the Treaty of Lausanne (barely twenty years before Rhodes had become part of Greece) there had been a huge exchange of populations from each side of the newly established borders between the two countries. Their respective leaders, Kemal Ataturk and Eleftherios Venizelos, arguably the only statesmen either has produced this century, had managed in the 1930s to establish at least a basis on which people of plain common sense, as much as of good will, could try to build a new relationship whereby their two neighbouring countries and peoples might come to realise that, if only for their mutual advantage, their common futures called imperatively for reconciliation. But Venizelos had died in 1936, and Ataturk in 1938. Then had come the calamities of the Second World War in which both countries had suffered, in Turkey's case more economically than politically. The war had brought an aftermath in which nationalist sentiment had again become prevalent, and soon even predominant. Instead of the creative ideas of moving forward in cooperation, which had animated the two pre-war leaders, there were now forged the necessary, but negative, bonds of mutual defence by which the members of NATO were joined. In defence against the threat of the Soviet Union, Turkey and Greece were allied with the other members of that organisation. But the spirit infusing the two eastern Mediterranean members was now not at all one of friendship - it was, rather, that epitomised in the Turkish proverb, "The shadow of the bear unites the fighting dogs". The atmosphere generated by Ataturk and Venizelos had evaporated. And so it was that, at the beginning of the 1950s, the Turks of Rhodes looked in desperate alarm to a future under the unfettered domination of the Greeks which had begun a bare couple of years earlier.*

**\*\*\*\*\*\*\*\*\*\***

119

By then other changes had also been taking place which, by the beginning of the 1950s, had ominous overtones for the Cyprus Turks too. Things had been happening of ill augury for anyone with political eyes to see or antennae to feel - things both inside the island and further afield. To take Cyprus first.

After the riots of 1931, such organs of central government as had previously operated with elected representatives had been abolished, and for the twenty years since then the island had been administered under a system of government which could be described as a benevolent autocracy. As far as the government's being benevolent is concerned, there may be some who would wish to cavil at the term; though not, I am disposed to believe, any who actually knew the place then - a very small number indeed now. While we do not today have the sort of inflamed propaganda that used to come out of Athens Radio in the middle of the 1950s, there are still those who portray the colonial administration in British Cyprus as tyrannous. I may myself, not entirely unreasonably, perhaps be thought to be *parti pris* in describing warmly the administration I was about to join. But I think it is for those who would dispute it to produce evidence in rebuttal which could stand up to dispassionate judgement, rather than to rely on plain assertion.

As for the British administration's having been autocratic, this is self-evident in the fact that every official of that administration was appointed. Yet even of these officials, by the end of the second World War, only a small handful were not Cypriot. The Governor was British, and the heads of most departments; and also the five District Commissioners and the High Court judges. But all other senior posts were held by people who came from the local population. These included all Presidents of District Courts and the District Judges, all Magistrates, Superintendents of Police, together with all district heads of the professional services such as Medical, Agricultural, Public Works, Forestry, Customs and the rest. And Assistants to the District Commissioners (essentially the Governor's representatives in the districts) were also now being appointed from the public.

That this administration, carried out by British, Greeks and Turks, was a highly efficient one and that it comprised people who (with one or two personal exceptions as may emerge in the course of these recollections) were concerned with the well-being of all, is not a proposition I have ever seen even attempted to be rebutted. In saying which I do not even exclude certain observations made by some serious journalists. One such, Christopher Hitchens, has referred to - and, in the modern jargon, "I kid you not" - "the gallows and the gibbet that made the United Kingdom famous in so many of her former possessions"! "An intemperate travesty" are the words which come at once to my mind. Were the author himself to ask my opinion in person, I imagine I would begin with "Well actually, I think 'drivel' is unduly flattering."

Although the central government of Cyprus through elected representatives had ceased in 1931, this was not the case in the six municipalities when I arrived in 1951. In 1943 legislation had been passed bringing back into existence in all six main towns, and in several of the larger villages, elections for mayors and council members. The result had done nothing to diminish, still less to dispel, Turkish apprehensions about the prospect and consequences of Greek domination. In those six towns the mayors were all Greek, and the Turks were in the situation of Churchill during the war, as reputedly described by himself, when he was asked by de Gaulle to influence the Bank of England in favour of a loan requested by the Free French government. *"Mais vous savez,"* he is alleged to have replied, *"moi, quand je suis devant la vieille dame de 'Threadneedle Street' je me trouve absolument impotent"*. And so were the Turks powerless and helpless in the face of Councils which merely overrode any opinion or argument opposed to that of the immovable majority Greek will. Frustration at the lack of redress over what was seen and felt by the Turkish councillors and public as conscious discrimination in the allocation of funds and services in the Turkish quarters, and for Turkish buildings and monuments anywhere, was heightened by the manner of some of the Greek councillors. There were some, on the left wing, who were prepared to act without regard to ethnic considerations, but distrust was such that many doubted whether even their aim was not so much the requirements of common justice as encouragement of cross-communal solidarity in furthering the ideological 'class struggle' - yet still in pursuance of enosis, as I had seen evinced by my "fellow traveller" on the *Ascania*.

**Young Bird**

And particular, specific ground for mistrust was amply provided by the right-wing mayor of Nicosia, Themistocles Dervis, whose deserved reputation was of a nationalist bigot. (I have only in the past month come on a minor, yet revealing, instance of how this bigotry operated. While clearing up some of my mother's effects I found among her papers a copy of a building permit given by the Nicosia municipality for the repair of a water tank in her garden. The form, dated October 1949, is wholly in Greek. By 1952 similar documentation among these papers is Greek on one side and Turkish on the other - at the instance, and intervention, of the central government.)

\*\*\*\*\*\*\*\*\*\*

*I have speculated to myself on Mayor Dervis's surname. The word has no Greek derivation but is, on the contrary, the Greek pronunciation of the Turkish word 'dervish', which is a not uncommon Turkish name. In fact a great-uncle of mine bore it. (His house in the Turkish half of Nicosia, since renovated as an example of the old Turkish domestic style of architecture, is now the Dervish Pasha museum.) Whether the mayor's openly expressed contempt for the Turks and his arrogance towards them, for which he was notorious, even among the British, might not have been compensating for some Turkish ancestry one can but surmise. The ugly phenomenon of displaying oneself as* plus royaliste *has been noted in the case of Nazis who later turned out to have had Jewish forbears. Whatever the reason, it was experience of men like Themistocles Dervis which was to play an important part in the way that Turkish mistrust, and fear, of the Greek leadership became focussed when twenty years later British rule was seen to be coming to an end - and afterwards when British rule ended.*

\*\*\*\*\*\*\*\*\*\*

Even more direct cause for apprehension on that score had recently been given. In 1947 the then Governor had, with Colonial Office approval, tried to break the constitutional log-jam. Without going into too much detail which would take me even further outside the scope of my own direct personal recollections, the proposals made by the British side had involved an elected Legislative Council in which the Greek members would have swamped the Turkish members by more

122

than double - even if they were to be joined with the (nominated) British members. In their obdurate pursuit of *enosis* and only *enosis* the Greek leadership had totally rejected these proposals (although the powerful AKEL communists had, despite a boycott called by the church, initially taken part in the Constitutional Assembly but had later withdrawn). This rejection by the Greeks of a constitution which the Turks considered would put their own community in the direst jeopardy was, not unnaturally, more than welcome to the Turkish side. But those constitutional proposals had been left open by the government in the expressed hope that the leaders of the Greek community would reconsider whether they might not be prepared to give such a constitution a trial.

Turkish disquiet was not lessened when the new Archbishop, the forty year old Makarios, organised a 'plebiscite'. This was carried out in every Greek church on the island by calling for signatures to be attached, openly, to a document demanding *enosis* by each member of every congregation following Sunday service. (The unregenerate British shop stewards of the era of Peter Sellers's film *I'm all right Jack* couldn't have produced anything better by way of intimidatory tactics.) The desired result of virtual unanimity was obtained, as was inevitable in such circumstances - even without the threatened sanction of excommunication for the recalcitrant.

In 1951 it was the very recent past which loomed in the minds of the Cyprus Turks as they anxiously peered at what might lie ahead. And two examples abroad gave especial cause for deep worry. 1947 had seen Britain's departure from the Indian sub-continent; and also from Palestine. In both cases the immediate consequence had been bitter fighting and violence between the two opposed peoples of those lands, leading to the most dreadful killings. And words of the ineffable Richard Crossman in 1948 had not gone unnoticed in Cyprus. In the large village of Kythrea (in Turkish *Değirmenlik*) a few miles north of Nicosia, he made a speech which included what can only be taken as a calculated incitement. He told the villagers there that the British never gave up a colony without the people forcing them out. And, for good measure, he later announced in the House of Commons that "the tragedy of the Middle East is that there is not a country whose people got their rights from the British without murder". Both India and Palestine were seen as evidence of Britain's readiness to throw in the towel when things got tough, and to leave it to the local people to sort things out for themselves. These events had made a sharp impact on a Cyprus which for twenty years had lived in a frozen political immobility - but still in peace, however static. And, as events were to show, fragile. The conclusions which the different sides in Cyprus - not excluding the government - were eventually to draw from these events I hope to describe. At that time the precedents of India and Palestine were to deepen the Turkish community's ever present suspicion and doubt as to the readiness and resolve of the government to resist the clamour for *enosis* being raised by the church in particular and the Greek political leadership generally.

It was in a Cyprus so politically and communally polarised that I began my duties: an island in which, conditioned by the church, the attitude of the Greek community to the Turkish was at best one of condescension, and at worst outright enmity if they judged that the less numerous population were getting above themselves.

**********

And yet I should be more than misleading and wrong if, in painting in this background to the island of my birth as it was in my twenty fifth year, I were at the outset to leave the impression that there were not individual cases of individual respect, even of friendship, between members of the two communities of the island. Generalisations have always to be qualified. But in Cyprus the very fact of *particulars* being necessary by way of individual qualification seems to me to accentuate the truth of the *general*: indeed in that island perhaps it is not paradoxical to say that it is not so much the exception, as the exceptions, which prove the rule.

**********

*Thirty years after this time a Greek Cypriot whom I did not know personally sent me a book in England which had just been published by her family firm. This was the account of a visit to Cyprus, more specifically to the capital Nicosia, in 1873, five years before the end of*

124

*Ottoman rule in the island, by an Archduke of the Habsburg dynasty. Its three-paragraph preface contained the (translated) sentence: "Turks, Greeks and Armenians, dwell intermingled, bitter enemies at heart, and united solely by their love for the land of their birth." In my letter of thanks for this book I said that I thought the Archduke's opinion, for which he had given no source nor authority, was misconceived and inexact. It was in my view not bitter enmity which had animated the people but rather mistrust and fear. Which is not to deny that these are emotions all too easily exploited, and transformed into 'bitter enmity', by those whose wish it is to do so. My view was not questioned by my correspondent.*

\*\*\*\*\*\*\*\*\*\*\*

The British, for a long time successfully, had tried after 1878 to hold the balance during the eighty years of their rule, but by the end hatred between the two communities, spawned of fear and mistrust, had remorselessly grown. The conclusion to which I was to be driven pretty soon after 1951 was that the Greeks and the Turks were not living together in Cyprus in any but the geographical sense. My impression was to grow that so far from living in 'toleration' one with the other, they rather 'tolerated' each other. The first seems to me to have a positive, a generous, sense; the second a negative, grudging - even a rancorous - one. That even the second may perhaps be the best we can hope for in a fallen world is an opinion not to be gainsaid in the face of what has since been done in the former Yugoslavia - where the maleficent involvement of the Serbian Orthodox Church has played its grim part. I do not believe that in 1873 the two peoples of Cyprus who constituted almost the whole population of the island were scarcely to be restrained from getting at each others' throats (as Archduke Salvator had, apparently, implied); but neither do I accept the view at the other extreme, that until 1974 (or 1963, or 1960, or 1955, or whatever other date is selected for political purposes) these peoples, separated by language and religion, were living in serene and unsullied amity and harmony (as is nowadays represented by those whose partisan interest in promoting a particular political thesis rests on that claim. A claim also sometimes advanced by others who are at least well-intentioned - but grievously misinformed). And there can, I think, be little doubt that, however one judges the relations between the two communities, the dragon seed of the coming harvest was sown when in October 1950 Makarios, at his enthronement as Archbishop, solemnly - and entirely gratuitously - swore: "I take the holy oath that I shall work for the birth of our national freedom and shall never waver from our policy of uniting Cyprus with Mother Greece." It was not "independence" but *enosis* which was the aim - from which he, the church, the Ethnarchy, and the Greek leadership as a whole indeed never wavered. And in the determination to secure that end the Turkish people of the island counted for nothing - as indeed nothing was done to conceal that attitude.

**********

Limassol, to which I came in the spring of 1951, was the town and district in which the Turkish population, proportionately to the Greeks, was much the smallest in the island - between an eighth and a ninth, as compared with the quarter to a fifth in Cyprus as a whole. My District Commissioner was an ex-RAF man recently arrived on the island. He gave an impression to me of being but half-hearted in his work, not particularly enjoying his duties or the place in which he was carrying them out. Not entirely different from my own attitude in the Gold Coast, I suppose. I subsequently was to learn that one of his children, or perhaps it was his wife, was not at all well and that Cyprus was not properly equipped to provide the care needed. (He very soon afterwards left Cyprus, and the Colonial Service.) It was the first time I was to learn directly the truth that one's demeanour is so often but a reflection and mere consequence of one's physical and mental state, or of those nearest and dearest to you. In fact that "Whether life is worth living depends on the liver" is not just a very neat - but regrettably untranslatable - pun.

The Cyprus district administration was, as to be expected, much more structured and dense than it had been in the Gold Coast. Each of the five districts (Kyrenia had for some time ceased to be a separate district and was administered from Nicosia) was divided into several *nahiyes*, of which there were four in Limassol District. Each of these 'sub-districts' was in the charge of an Assistant District Inspector (ADI) who was posted to live in its main village. His function was to get to

126

know thoroughly each village in his area and to maintain close liaison with the village headman (*muhtar*). Muhtars were appointed to these unpaid but locally prestigious posts. Where a village consisted of two communities, each had its own muhtar. The ADIs were directly subordinate to the District Inspector (DI) who lived in the district headquarter town, working from the Commissioner's Office. The DI was something like a sergeant-major or warrant officer, with the ADIs reporting to him in the first instance, rather as sergeants might in an army set-up. The parallel is not entirely apt since there were no 'other ranks' under the 'sergeants'' command. Nor does the comparison do full justice to the heavy personal responsibility, in exercising which the ADIs needed to prove and demonstrate their qualities of impartiality, reliability, honesty, trustworthiness, steadiness and constant dedication, not just to the service but to the public at large. It was from the ranks of the District Inspectorate that some local appointments began to be made to Assistant District Commissioner in the latter days of colonial rule.

Depending on how efficient the Commissioner's overall supervision was, effective control of the greater part of the district administration, and that in matters which directly concerned the villagers and affected their lives, could easily pass into the hands of the DI. And when an administration is hierarchical, the truth of the Turkish proverb is most apt: "The fish stinks from its head" - the rot sets in from the top. I was not exceptional in being fortunate in my experience of district administration, by serving under Commissioners who were on the whole men justifiably well-regarded. I never served under the only two exceptions who did indeed allow their districts - one was Nicosia - to become unduly under the influence of local subordinates. One of my Commissioners, however, was quite uniquely remarkable in combining devotion to the place, and to its peoples, with a dedicated high administrative ability. He has a special place in these recollections.

The members of the district administrative team in Limassol worked together in that spirit of cooperation based on mutual personal regard which animates a good organisation in which there is little consciousness of rank. There was also the same sense of pride in being part of a service which was known to stand in very high esteem among the people at large, and satisfaction in carrying out a worthwhile

127

job. Yiorgos ('George') Haralambous, the DI, was hardly a ball of fire, but his long service had given him wide experience, which he exercised in keeping the routine machine running smoothly. Our relationship was, to continue the analogy I have already made, something like that between the old sergeant-major, or even RSM, and the young officer newly joining the regiment. With him I went round the main villages, many of which were completely Greek; but our visits also included those few wholly Turkish villages in the west of Limassol towards Paphos District, where the Turkish population was, in contrast to the position in Limassol District, the proportionately highest in the island. I also made a point of visiting with him the very few mixed villages on the lower slopes of the central Troodos mountain range.

The disparity between the two communities economically was evident in Limassol District from the respective geographical situation of the Greek and Turkish villages. Limassol was the island's grape production centre; virtually all the vine-villages, on the southern slopes rising to the Troodos massif, were Greek. These were very prosperous, with their assured markets in the wine factories in the town itself. The few wholly Turkish villages were in the lower foothills south of the vineyards, and on the coastal belt in which carobs and low yield cereals were produced. It was not till several years later, largely through the efforts, organisational abilities, and entrepreneurial flair of a young Turk, Ramadan Cemil, the son-in-law of the Turkish *muhtar* of Episcopi, that commercial vegetable production on a large scale was introduced in Turkish areas and steady markets developed.

Among the Turkish villagers I sensed (and this was sometimes openly expressed to me) an air of gratification, and pride, that there was for the first time a number two to the Commissioner who was Turkish. In later years it has been claimed in some political quarters, and this has indeed gained a degree of currency, that the Turkish community did not get their due proportion of government expenditures. (The position in the municipalities I have referred to.) I must say that I have no recollection that in Limassol District it was ever represented to me by *muhtars* or villagers that as Turks they felt they were not getting their share of central government funds available to the District Commissioner for public works. If they looked to a prospect of any higher proportion by reason of my being the Assistant Commissioner, no such hope was ever expressed to me. But it might possibly have been implicit. What was very palpably the case was that they felt a vicarious or reflected sense of restored worth in an environment where they were almost swamped economically, and felt disparaged and despised by the very much larger community. (And I was aware of the risk of acquiring a sense of self-importance from the realisation that my fortuitous presence was the occasion for their feeling a sense of alleviation for their hurt.)

The appointment of a Turkish Assistant Commissioner may have served to nourish morale among the Turkish population of the district; but if it didn't of itself encourage, it certainly didn't inhibit the expression of that innate common sense and down-to-earth realism which so often marks the independent-minded, not least the villager. In one village Haralambous had been telling the *muhtar* about me. His account had mentioned that I had been to Oxford where I had obtained my 'diploma'. The substance of the conversation which had been, as usual, *coram publico*, was public property. When I was next in the village an old Turkish villager approached me and, after polite exchanges, observed, "So you have your diploma from the English university?" "Yes," said I. "My son," he replied, "don't forget that even a donkey has its piece of paper." The comment, indeed the pithy advice, I have never forgotten. It is for me an even more earthy version of "By their *fruits* ye shall know them", while also carrying the more direct message of warning against puffed-up pride. The very words in Turkish have, for me, ever since taken their place among the host of actual Turkish proverbs, of which this was not one; yet it surely ranks with them as being born, as all proverbs must surely be, in some phrase spontaneously coined for a particular occasion, but enduring as part of a living language because enshrining a truth. Proverbs are, after all, hardly a committee job, the outcome of a brainstorming session in an advertising agency, or the result of cogitation by publicity men in search of the 'sound-bite'. (The villager's remark was an allusion to the fact that in those days the sale of any animal was required by law to be supported by a document of title authenticated by the *muhtar* in his capacity of Certifying Officer - one of his many and varied functions.)

## Young Bird

My posting to Limassol, I had been told, was in the nature of an induction to become familiar with district administration machinery and procedures before I was brought back to Nicosia. Whether this would be to the Nicosia district administration or to the Secretariat was uncertain. So it made more sense, as a bachelor, to live as a permanent resident in a hotel rather than arrange separate accommodation. While the hotel was very convenient, it was also a bit claustrophobic as neither of the only two possible such hostelries - this was a long time before the rash of tourist hotels of the last two decades had sprung up - had anything like a comfortable sitting-room or indeed any public rooms beside the dining-room.

On weekends I would often drive to Nicosia to see my mother and, I'm afraid, unashamedly do justice to her cooking. Her house had a large garden and for the first time in my life I found enjoyment in gardening, although labouring in the garden would be nearer the mark. Replanting the long *dodonia* boundary hedge (killed in an exceptionally cold winter), and watering the orange trees and the flower garden with its many roses, was as relaxing, and the smell of the wet earth in the sunshine as refreshing, as in later years was the work of preparing and tending a garden bonfire with its comforting heat in a crisply cold English autumn. There was a sense of re-creation in gardening which I attribute, at least in part, to being able, as the P.G. Wodehouse character put it, to "put my mind into neutral". I was surprised that it used to irritate me when, quite a few years later in England, I first heard the ditty by, I believe, Kipling, though the sentiment could as likely be Newbolt's:

*Our England is a garden, and gardens are not made*
*By saying 'Oh, how beautiful' and sitting in the shade.*

The observation, though worthy, jarred with its seeming priggishness. Why not, I would feel captiously, do what you find, or want, to do in the garden and - just enjoy it?

**********

130

Early one Monday morning as I was driving back from Nicosia on the last stretch of the approach to Limassol, where the road from Yermasoyia came down to join the coastal road - then a completely rural unbuilt-up area, and I wonder what it is now - I saw an old *papaz*, a village priest, waiting. This was before hitch-hiking had become international, but he was clearly hoping for a lift. I stopped to ask if he was going into Limassol. He was, and I took him on board. My minimal Greek was up to that sort of enquiry; and also just about enough for very simple questions and answers. What has stayed in my memory of our rudimentary 'conversation' was, first, his air of guarded but polite reserve when, in response to his question, he heard that I was the *Voithos Dhikitis* ; but what struck me even more was his open bafflement on learning that this 'Assistant Commissioner' did not come from England as he assumed, but was from Cyprus, and Turkish. "*Alithia, Tourkos?*" ('Honestly, Turkish?'). I was reminded of the occasion some three or four years earlier, before I had gone to the Gold Coast, when I had just become a member of the (then) Royal Empire Society in Northumberland Avenue. I had been introduced in the entrance lobby to the Secretary, whose name I recall was Cust; and he had said *en passant* with, to my mind astonishing unawareness of his ill manners, "You don't look like a Turk". How, I asked him, did he expect me to look? Perhaps with a turban and scimitar? My response was perhaps excusable on the basis of (I believe) Oscar Wilde's definition of a gentleman as "one who is never *un*intentionally rude". Neither Cust nor the *papaz* were, I think, guilty of anything much beyond *gaucherie* in revealing a preconceived view of 'Turks'. That I was myself naive in being surprised by this was only later to be borne in on me.

\*\*\*\*\*\*\*\*\*\*

In the autumn of 1951 my posting to Nicosia came through. It was to the Secretariat. In a small colonial territory like Cyprus that central part of the government served in effect as the Governor's 'secretariat'. The Governor's residence, together with his private office staffed by a personal secretary and aide-de-camp, was Government House, about a mile south-west of the Paphos Gate. The Secretariat building was about halfway between the two. The head of the Secretariat, the

Colonial Secretary, was the direct channel of communication to and from the Governor. The handful of Senior Assistant Secretaries and Assistant Secretaries were effectively the Colonial Secretary's staff.

While I had been in Limassol a new Colonial Secretary had arrived in the island, directly from the Colonial Office in London. Such an appointment was, as I have remarked, unusual since the post of Colonial Secretary in dependencies would normally be filled from within the Unified Colonial Administrative Service which was entirely distinct from the London Colonial Office. The latter was one of the various Whitehall Departments of State which were staffed by successful candidates in the Competitive Examination for entry into the Home Civil Service. Cyprus's new Colonial Secretary had started his career in the Home Service in the Colonial Office, where he had, early on, been a private secretary to the Permanent Secretary, Sir Cosmo Parkinson (from whose recollections of his time in the Colonial Office I have already quoted). In that same book Sir Cosmo makes but a brief reference to his private secretary. He comments that "from 1937 to 1942 [I had] five [private secretaries] in all, which suggests that a year was about as long as any of them could stand"; and he adds, rather cryptically, "in fact the first, John Fletcher Cooke, was with me only a few months; whatever his motives, he then applied for transfer to the other side of the world." He concludes, "For those who followed, it was promotion in the Colonial Office." From Whitehall Fletcher Cooke had himself gone to Malaya. There he had been interned by the Japanese, surviving to return to London and the Colonial Office once more. And from there he came out to be number two in Cyprus. During my time in the Secretariat I saw him only once. He was to remain in the island about three years - just under, I think - and in that time the impression in general was of an ambitious man for whom Cyprus was but a staging post in his intended upward progress. In this he stood in sharp and direct contrast with his immediate deputy in the Secretariat, John Reddaway.

At practically the same time, before the war, as Fletcher Cooke had joined the Colonial Office, Reddaway had come to Cyprus in the Colonial Administrative Service. He had never left the island. He had married a Greek Cypriot, and had developed a deep affection not just for the island but for its people - both of its peoples. He spoke Greek, and wrote it rather better than a great many (some would say most) Greek Cypriots; and he also spoke and wrote a more than passable Turkish. He was a much respected, and by many a much loved, man. It was of John Reddaway that I was told by a Greek colleague in the Secretariat, "Mr Reddaway is good man - but very nervous!" I found this characterisation oddly unfitting to the man I was to have as my superior, tall and Viking-like in his appearance, complete with blond semi-drooping moustache. Only afterwards did it come home to me that by "nervous" my colleague had intended to convey not that Reddaway was a fearful, twitching neurasthenic, but simply that he had a short fuse. He was indeed liable to allow his disinclination to suffer a fool gladly to reveal itself, and either couldn't (or took no pains to) suppress his temper in openly venting his annoyance. For myself, I have found to my taste those in whom the flame of anger is fast ignited, but as quickly subsides and is extinguished - what in Turkish is called a 'straw flame'. Much more so than those people whose ire is, in fact, just as strong but coldly suppressed yet simmering, often in long-lasting and deep animosity - if not worse. With the first sort you know where you are - the relationship is entirely open, and indeed sincere. The other, in my experience, is more often than not quite the reverse, and continues to fester.

Secretariat work, at the level I was involved, does not now, forty years on - and more - readily bring to mind matters either sufficiently amusing or infuriating, or even just interesting enough, to warrant trying to recover anything seriously worth dredging or quarrying.

Outside the office I carried on with my attempts at self-taught Greek, practising my rudimentary spoken Greek in the 'market place' and in simple exchanges with Greek colleagues as opportunity served. For the written language I relied on phrase books and a pocket dictionary, this having been given to me by a fellow officer in the Secretariat - which I have recently discovered on my shelves with the donor's name still on the fly-leaf. (I believe the signature's owner has been a minister in the post colonial Greek Administration in the island.) It had been in the company of 'George' Haralambous, in Limassol, that I had first made a start in trying to learn Greek. It was in fact a requirement, on which rested one's salary increments, that one should show proficiency in at least the Lower Standard of Greek. Whether Greeks had similarly

133

to learn Turkish I cannot now, strangely enough, remember. I can only recall the odd one or two occasions when a Greek colleague spoke Turkish with me - at the sort of level of my Greek.

**\*\*\*\*\*\*\*\*\*\***

I took to hiring a horse, and would spend glorious hours once or twice a week out in what was then the countryside to the north and south west of Nicosia. Scarcely anything but open fields as far as Strovolos, as it was to *Orta Köy* and beyond. Occasionally I managed to get a ride on one of the horses at the Athalassa Agriculture Experimental Station to the south east of the town, cantering in a landscape of *mesa*-like flat-topped hillocks so very like that in which Indians and cowboys gallop in American Westerns. Those solitary rides, exhilarating and stimulating, come back to me nowadays every time I drive out to the airport at Ercan and see those same *mesas* out towards the southern horizon on the further side of the border-line between the Turkish and Greek sectors of the island.

**\*\*\*\*\*\*\*\*\*\***

It was during this time in Nicosia that an Armenian acquaintance, the son of one of the shopkeepers from whom my mother occasionally bought dress material, told me the joke then making the rounds among his friends. In an endeavour to get first hand information about life as it really was in the Armenian Socialist Soviet Republic, with a view to deciding whether or not to emigrate there, it had been arranged by an Armenian in Cyprus that a relative out there should send a chatty family letter with an accompanying photograph of the writer. If the picture were to show him standing up, this would signal that conditions were truly fine, and that they should come out to join him. If, however, he were sitting down, then on no account should they stir. The sequel is predictable. The letter and picture arrived. The relative was taking his ease, stretched out on a sofa. I don't remember whether there was any context to this comic way of conveying what things were like in the 1950s USSR generally and in Armenia in particular. In retrospect it does occur to me that it might, however vaguely, have been some kind of reflection of a degree of unease about the possible course of future developments in Cyprus.

As for myself, in unconsciously abiding by the injunction to take no thought for the morrow, my life was no doubt as idle as it was, for me, idyllic. To use the word I have since, over the years, heard uttered by more than one 'workaholic' - the most memorable such person I have heard voice it being the late Lord Reith, in his *Face to Face* television interview with John Freeman - I was not exactly 'stretched'. That didn't worry me. My days were sweet, passed as they were, if not in 'lotus land', as near as made no difference; and in "my own, my native land", where I had so longed to be. Fate had, I believed, been kind to me. To *us* indeed; for it was a great happiness for my mother to have one of her sons now actually in Cyprus, living with her in her own home. But the even tenor of those self-indulgent, even selfish, days was about to be jolted into a new sense of reality. And in a way which had never even crossed my mind.

\*\*\*\*\*\*\*\*\*\*

Immediately opposite us lived the Stones, still occupying the house which had been our own home seventeen years before. They had now been joined by their son Michael, demobbed and determined to make his life in Cyprus, but with no very clear idea of what he would do there. We used to see each other quite often. One day he appeared on the doorstep in the usual way. "Do you," he asked, "remember the Milner-Whites?" I said I did, and waited for him to come to the point. He held out a note he had just had through the post. It was from Lalage Milner-White. She and her father had come out to Cyprus as a respite from the English winter. In those days of post-war austerity and strict exchange control there was a severe restriction on the amount of sterling anyone could take out of Britain; but the limitation didn't apply to the 'sterling area,' which, broadly speaking, meant the Commonwealth and British dependencies. The Mediterranean alternatives were Gibraltar, Malta, and Cyprus, and the lot had fallen on Cyprus. From what I later was to gather, the connection between Cyprus and the old East Allington rectory contingent hadn't registered when father and daughter had decided on this winter break in the Mediterranean. Lalage was then living with her father in England.

Their pre-war home in Devon, like the village of East Allington, had been in the area which was totally evacuated in the war for use by

135

the Allied forces to train with live ammunition for the coming D-Day assault on the Normandy beaches. This was the period vividly portrayed by Leslie Thomas in his book *The Magic Army*. It is a long time since I read that book, and I don't recall whether he refers to the obelisk put up on the beach at Slapton which pays tribute to that civilian evacuation in some such terms as 'the great willingness which the people of the South Hams showed in giving up their homes, etc.' I fear that this, too, was a case of the wish being the father of the thought! (I have since writing the above had the chance to check the actual text of the inscription on that obelisk. It reads in part:

*" This Monument was presented by the United States Army Authorities to the people of the South Hams who so generously left their houses with their lands to provide a battle practice area for the successful assault on Normandy in June 1944 ...")*

After the war the Milner-White home, Sheplegh, had been sold and the family had moved to Sussex. Lalage's mother had died there some two and a half years earlier.

The Milner-Whites hadn't known it when they had made their arrangements in England through Thomas Cook's, or whoever, but in those days the Dome Hotel in Kyrenia had for some years been pretty much of a sort of residential home patronised during the winter months largely by that soon almost extinct genus, retired members of the old ICS and other overseas services - or rather, more often by their relicts. Oppressed by this less than lively society Lalage looked for some outside interest. At a time when there was no such organised facility in the island, she managed to hire a car through one of the hotel waiters, and she and her father spent a few days sight-seeing. The unchanging loveliness of the thirteenth-century abbey of Bellapais was as it is today - but with none of the later development along the road leading to the village from the coast. After seeing all there was to see in Kyrenia and round about, father and daughter set out, with Lalage driving, on a trip to Nicosia. Up in the pass through the Kyrenia hills, where there were then hair-pin bends, there was a loud bang as a tyre punctured, and the car veered off towards the drop. Lalage managed to correct the swerve and stop the car. As she got out to investigate, the second front tyre also retired hurt - this time with a long hissing, dying, gasp. Rescue was not too long in coming, and the two were given a lift into Nicosia, from where they telephoned the Dome and left the matter in the hands of the hotel.

It was while Lalage and her father had been stranded at the roadside that they learned of the death of King George V. Waiting up in the pass for a car travelling in the direction of Nicosia, they saw one coming towards them, but from the other direction, heading for Kyrenia. The driver stopped and announced to the obviously English stranded couple, "Your king has died." (When Lalage told me this, a long time afterwards, I was reminded of my mother's having recalled that when the announcement had been made of the engagement of the then Princess Elizabeth to the then Prince Philip of Greece, a Greek Cypriot - someone who I believe worked with her in the Red Cross - had jubilantly talked about "*O Filipos mas*" - 'Our Philip').

It had only been after exhausting the not very abundant diversions as were then available to a young girl and her retired father in Cyprus during the winter, that the bulb lit up in Lalage's mind: there had been those boys at the East Allington rectory who had come from Cyprus. The only surname she could remember was Michael Stone's. She looked this up in the telephone directory; there was only one entry under the name - in what was in any case a pretty slim volume in those days. Her note to Michael was to suggest a meeting at the Dome. I was a bit nettled that the note hadn't been addressed to me, but I agreed to go with Michael. I hadn't forgotten the pig-tailed Lalage. Michael had a friend, the Greek assistant or deputy Government Printer; and the three of us, all bachelors, would sometimes meet at such watering holes as 'Charlie's Bar'. We invited him to join us for tea at the Dome with Lalage. And so, sadly symbolising what in 1952 was still possible, the first guests Lalage received in Cyprus were these three young men - an Englishman, accompanied by a Turk on one side and a Greek on the other. The Greek member of that trio has since died. The Englishman and the Turk now between them straddle their seventieth years. When they too are gone there will be few left who will be able to recall that Cyprus of their young adulthood which the men of ambition, hatred and violence were so soon to destroy.

## Young Bird

**********

The effect on me of the first sight of Lalage since her early teenage years calls, I suppose, for treatment by either a Mills and Boon author, or Barbara Cartland - not that I have actually read any of these writers' works. For myself, I simply knew then that I must not lose this girl. Put like that it sounds as egoistic a reaction as I suppose it was - but that is how I remember my feelings to have been. And it seems not to be too far from an accurate judgement of my state of mind and heart at the time, as I am very sure that nothing else would have galvanised me. I had to move very quickly. Lalage and her father were due to leave in about ten days for a fortnight's visit to Jerusalem; and they would not have all that much more than the same sort of period back in Cyprus before they finally left to return to England.

Quite where I took Lalage during those few weeks I have but faint recollections. I remember an evening at a 'cabaret' called the Chanticleer; a dance at the English Club in Nicosia; and an evening of Scottish Dancing at the similar club in Kyrenia. This alone is a measure of how smitten I was. My dancing of any kind was not exactly elegant; indeed the term much favoured, I believe, by schoolmasters for termly reports, ' barely adequate', would have been complimentary. And as for Scottish Dancing, I knew no more of it than I could glean from watching and trying to learn and follow. The man who was to be my brother-in-law - not Lalage's brother, she only having two sisters - was to tell me of his own experience in not dissimilar circumstances when he found himself pirouetting - though a Scotsman would have my guts for so describing it - opposite another man, to be informed curtly - if not venomously - "You set to a woman, Sir; not to a man !" What, indeed, will a man not do to secure the woman of his heart?

This not being a romantic novel, I will refer only very cursorily to the course of the subsequent emotional switchback on which I travelled over the next month: the increasingly anxious fortnight waiting for Lalage's visit to Jerusalem to end; the mixed feelings on her return - delight at seeing her, apprehension, even trepidation, at the prospect of renewing the pursuit; determination to carry on all the same. The hackneyed call, "Nothing venture, nothing gain", emerged from somewhere inside me, and even from my Higher School Cert. set book there came to my aid Lady Macbeth's taunt to her husband to "screw your courage to the sticking place .... and [you'll] not fail". There followed more meetings with Lalage and an excursion or two. And then - on the slopes of Troodos where I had followed her, though I couldn't ski - my eventual proposal. This arrived so suddenly, indeed so abruptly, that it surprised me - as Lalage tells me it did her. It wasn't accepted - but nor was it rejected. The long days of uncertainty passed in gloom and despondency at what the outcome would be in the brief time left before father and daughter departed. And then, as abruptly as the proposal, totally unannounced and unexpected, Lalage arrived one morning at my office in the Secretariat building. And we were engaged.

Most oddly, on this occasion, although indeed what I had longed for had come to pass, I do not remember that I was now filled with that sense of elation and ultimate well-being and "all's right with world" which I had known at previous moments of realising and obtaining something ardently desired. There was not this time the feeling of a decisive break with the past, of a new future of unbroken, unclouded happiness. I suppose that I must have unconsciously known this time that I would be taking on great responsibilities, and that the earlier entirely selfish satisfactions of getting my degree, and of being accepted for the Colonial Service, were of a very different order from the deep happiness which came in knowing that I was to be married, as I looked to a life with Lalage.

The responsibilities I would now be taking on were not something I had consciously considered, but mentally unformed though they were, such thoughts hovered, as it were, largely unknown at the back of my mind. Charitably regarded, it was perhaps in a more detached and conscious awareness of the practical aspects of being engaged and married (concerning which the newly engaged is himself too paradisially happy to focus on) which impelled a bachelor colleague in the Secretariat, an Englishman some ten years or so my senior, to produce shortly afterwards a never-to-be-forgotten, jewelled, sentiment. "How," he asked me one morning on the verandah off which our offices opened, "How does it feel to be engaged? I sometimes think it must be rather like putting up a minute, and wishing you could recall it." I assured him I wasn't, as yet, having any such second thoughts.

139

**Young Bird**

From the vantage point at which I now stand I suppose I could say, using the term which was first coined in Cyprus, that I had taken the first step into a kind of 'Green Line' zone, on the other side of which lay adulthood.

\*\*\*\*\*\*\*\*\*\*\*

For the remaining days of their Cyprus visit Lalage and her father now moved from Kyrenia to Nicosia, from the Dome to the Ledra Palace. That mock-Venetian building was, despite its style, reasonably congruous with the local buildings as these were in the early 1950s, with which it harmonised in its use of Cyprus golden sandstone. It had only been put up within the previous couple of years, standing between mother's house and the ramparts of the old town to the east. The boundary of the hotel's large garden marched with the rear border of mother's, but with the wide unbuilt space of the two gardens - mother's being full of fruit-bearing trees - and surrounding cypresses and eucalyptus, we were hardly conscious of the new addition to the still scarcely developed western outskirts of walled Nicosia. The Ledra Palace was to play more than once its part in the sad tale of the island when the campaigners for *enosis* made their violent bids to achieve their ends - even (indeed especially) after independence in 1960, in contempt of the constitution of the new Republic and of international treaties. But now, at the beginning of the 1950s, it was nothing more than the newest hotel in the island, and the only one in the capital of any pretensions. For Lalage and me its position couldn't have been more convenient. Father and daughter could walk the few hundred yards from the hotel entrance facing the town and, skirting our garden, come round to the front of our house. Here the widow and the widower met for the first time. And so did my mother and Lalage. The last time my future father-in-law had seen me had been more than fifteen years before, when I had been at the less than prepossessing pre-pubescent stage.

My mother had of course been delighted when I had broken the news to her that Lalage and I were engaged. Her prospective daughter-in-law very much confirmed her in her conviction that providence had dealt kindly with her. In her view her son had, on this vital point, shown the most impeccable, and immaculate, judgement. She was also charmed by her future *dünür*. (There is no equivalent word in English to give the meaning of the relationship between the parents of a bride and groom: 'relation-in-law' is both imprecise and inelegant.) My own assessment would be that, in her eyes, Rudolph Milner-White would perfectly have exemplified the idea, now seemingly outmoded, of the 'gentleman'. At the start of Noel Annan's panoramic survey *Our Age*, in which he portrays that type of Englishman whom it was the aim of the 19th century public schools to produce, he shows how it came about that those of his 'age' became disenchanted and disillusioned by this "insufferable ideal"; to the point where he and his contemporaries rejected both the image and the values it symbolised (or, at the very least, the manner in which those values were sought to be transmitted). In mother's case, the man who was now presented to her was the embodiment of the sort of qualities which she and her husband believed invested the best kind of Englishman - a gentleman such as, I think, they believed themselves to have been fortunate to have met in the late 1920s. It was not surprising that mother should have been more than just pleased that the daughter of a man like Rudolph Milner-White was to be married to her younger son.

\*\*\*\*\*\*\*\*\*\*\*

*To go off at a tangent - but only slightly. It is an odd fact that there was once a synonymous Turkish word which served the same function as the English word 'gentleman' - 'Efendi'. Like 'Pasha' and 'Bey' it was used generally as an honorific or title, added after the name; but separately it also denoted a person of virtuous qualities and high character: Çok efendi adam - as one might say 'A perfect gentleman'. In both languages the words have, perhaps significantly, acquired a rather archaic tinge - more's the pity. But there is also something of an ironic aspect to the Turkish word. Not many Turks nowadays seem to be aware that the word 'efendi' is, derivatively, Greek. Its origin is the Byzantine word, from which English also gets its 'authentic' - denoting a quality which should transcend chauvinistic sentiment. It is a commentary on the times that if something admirable these days has its origin (Greek or Turkish) correctly attributed to one side, it at once loses its virtue for, or becomes a cause of offence to, the other*

*side. Like the correct use of the terms 'Turkish coffee' and 'yoğurt'.*
*Instead of finding denial of these kinds of fact by the "other side"*
*merely risible - which at one level is all that it is - I am made both*
*depressed and angry when I recollect the depth of blind, nationalist*
*antipathy which the denial signals, and perpetuates.*

**********

To come to my own feelings towards my future father-in-law. These
were of admiration and gratitude. Here was a man, far from robust,
who comes out for a holiday to escape an English winter. Instead of
returning to his home refreshed and strengthened, he is confronted
with the news that he is, in a matter of months, going to lose his dearly
loved daughter, who has been his stay since his wife died. And to a
Turk. (It was very shortly after this that a cousin - after school in
England, like me, and indeed after commissioned service in the Rifle
Brigade - had his engagement to an English girl so strongly opposed
by her parents that it was broken off.) But Milner-White was in truth
a gentleman. In both senses of the word. Gentle he was - even mild -
by temperament, to an extent that no-one would have imagined from
his bearing and manner that for a quarter of a century he had been one
of the rulers of British India. And a gentleman he was in that other
sense into which the word's meaning evolved: from 'chivalrous' ( in
the connotation of a mediaeval knight: yet who could have been less
'gentle-manly' than the thugs who rampaged through Europe and the
Near East on their 'crusades' - save the mark?) to one who is 'courteous'
(in the sense of behaviour befitting a 'courtier': and what could be
further removed from a genuine politeness than the mannered etiquette
of the royal courts?). True regard for feelings shows itself in sincere
respect for the other. Lalage's father bore the immediate prospect of
the loss of his daughter, to someone not of his faith, and who lived
three thousand miles away, with immense dignity and - I do not hesitate
to say it - forbearance. And in doing so he demonstrated his love for
his daughter. To me he showed great kindness. Not in that form of
'bonhomie' which the French also so well characterise as *fausse*, nor
in a kind of fatherly condescension or toleration; not even in telling
me of his intention to help his daughter financially, or seeking any
such reassurance from me. He treated me in fact simply as someone

142

worthy of marrying his daughter. If Britain can continue to produce people such as him, it may be possible for the coming generations to see their country stand high in the estimation of others. Peace be on him.

**\*\*\*\*\*\*\*\*\*\***

I took the leave I was due; and we were married in London in the autumn. The ceremony was in Caxton Hall Registry Office - it was not then possible for a Moslem and a Christian to marry in a church in England. Among the few guests at the registry office was Lalage's paternal uncle. It would be an injustice both to his memory and to this attempt to record my perceptions as they have developed over the years, were I not to mention my regard for the plain decency and humanity of Eric Milner-White (then the Dean of York, after having been Dean of King's, Cambridge, re-originator of the King's Carol Service, and devout High Anglican) in the way he, too, welcomed me as the husband of his favourite niece, without even the scintilla of a hint that the welcome was in the slightest degree qualified - or merely dictated by politeness.

We had a splendid wedding reception at Lalage's home - to the evident, though courteous and polite, curiosity of her Sussex friends and neighbours about this foreigner with whom she had decided to link her fate. Of the occasion my memory is slightly blurred. I recall beginning my speech to the effect: "I asked Lalage just now how I might address you; and in particular whether I could begin with 'Friends!...' She told me that I could not. So - just in order to make the point - as early as possible - that I do not intend to be ruled by my wife: Friends! I am, as you can imagine, very happy today ...." Whether taken charitably as a feeble attempt at waggishness - which fortunately it was by my audience - or as bombast, the nearly forty-five years of our life together have demonstrated the falsity of the claim I then made.

We drove off, in a car which was a present from Lalage's father. Our destination was Naples, where we would catch the *Filippo Grimani* on which to sail to Cyprus. We bed and breakfasted through France and beyond, and since continental breakfasts were followed by the simplest of *al fresco* mid-day snacks of bread, cheese and tomatoes, accompanied by local wine, we needed a reasonable evening meal. Driving under the influence of that rough wine on a pretty empty stomach would today be properly regarded as reprehensibly stupid, and criminal. But it was not so then. If I look for additional justification I call in aid that traffic in those early 1950s was still extraordinarily sparse; we really did have the country roads very largely to ourselves. We skirted large towns and cities - both to avoid urban driving and to reduce hotel bills. In Geneva I went down with a bad cold. (I have since been surprised to discover that not a few others have also succumbed to this and to other ailments on their honeymoons. I don't know if it tends to support the validity of the maxim that 'misery loves company', but this knowledge has served to soften the recollection of my own discomfiture at that time.)

We crossed from Switzerland into Italy over the Mont Cenis Pass. Our sense of adventure - shades of Hannibal and his elephants, even if that wasn't in fact his route - was only partially dimmed by the fact that on their side of the frontier post the Italian officials were happily devoting their energies to a sort of six-a-side game of football in the middle of the main route into their country. To be delayed on one's journey not by over-punctilious and zealous, or officious and even offensive, officialdom but by such charmingly carefree and indifferent guardians was, then, not at all vexatious; rather it was a pleasing embroidery to the overall pattern of our journey. Nowadays this cavalier attitude would, I fear, be more likely to run the risk of censorious deprecation over the laxness at border crossings boding ill for the security of travellers and countries against the atrocities of the terrorist. In just the same way do I now, as an air traveller, feel my safety is put at hazard when passenger baggage checks seem to be too perfunctory; whereas not so many years ago I would have fumed at the tedium, the intrusion, and even the waste of time which such searches involve. So much are we now conscious of the dreadful extent to which drugs and terrorism influence and affect us all, however indirectly.

Italy in those days, not far short of half a century ago, was almost completely empty of tourists. We avoided the northern cities and driving down the western coastal road, made for Tuscany. Of Pisa, Florence and Siena what can one say that has not been worked to death

144

in a thousand books?  But let today's reader picture an Uffizi where two young people could wander through gallery after gallery only occasionally encountering someone else; a Ponte Vecchio and its approach roads along the Arno uncrowded and unhurried; a Campo at Siena looking almost as it might have done in Dante's day; and the uncluttered surroundings of the Cathedral, Baptistry and Leaning Tower at Pisa - picture these and you will have a glimpse of a joy in solitude and peace which now is lost to a more crowded and hectic age.  That we were so favoured by fortune was only dimly apparent to us then; but as I now look back I am indeed conscious of what we have to be thankful for.  And all along the way we travelled we could spend a night at any hostelry which took our fancy, within the limits of our purse - and this even though we only had sterling when, in those days, the dollar was called "almighty", and was the currency everyone longed to possess.

As we got further south, through the Roman Campagna, the roads began to show signs of the war years in the shape of intermittent shell-craters.  (In London, too, at this time there were the unrepaired remains of bombed houses still to be seen - quite a few in the part of Kensington where Lalage's sister lived near Holland House, which had itself been reduced by fire-bombs to a wreck, its library gutted.)  We reached Naples a week too early - the exact day the *Filippo Grimani* was to sail being a slightly movable feast; but this was also due to a habit I have still not been able to shake off - getting to railway stations, ports and airports in much more than good time.  In which respect Lalage has generally compensated for this by arriving only just in the nick of time.  (I have always liked to believe that it is a sign of a fated marriage that the partners do somehow balance out in these odd kinds of ways.  So far I haven't been let down by one test:  I have never yet met a married couple where *both* partners are bad sailors.  Either both of them will be immune to seasickness, or if one suffers in this way it always seems to happen that the spouse will be able to stand up to anything a sea can produce.  And this is so with us.)

Rather than spend the week in Naples we decided to drive round the bay to Sorrento.  (The song of that name was in those post-war years almost as well-known and popular as  'Lilli Marlene' - the one coming from our erstwhile German foes, and the other from the Italian

145

ones!)  We chose a hotel the cost of which for the week was well within our budget - in sharp contrast with the time I had taken the berth on the Turkish ship on my return from the Gold Coast - and found ourselves allocated to a huge bedroom *en suite* with a massive marble bathroom.  A fittingly impressive base from which to go out on visits to the places where once the Emperor Tiberius was reputed to have indulged himself - though, as with so much of received historical wisdom, I have always tended to the view that Tiberius has suffered from one-sided versions of events. These excursions naturally included the remains of Pompeii after its brilliance and luxury had ended in a Sodom and Gomorrah-like cataclysm.  The renowned obscene murals were for me then an acute embarrassment; in fact I'm almost sure we didn't see them - I certainly have no recollection of them.  We also made trips to the islands of Ischia and Capri.  The latter was where Gracie Fields then lived, for most of the year anyway I believe, and for our generation the place had strong evocations with the soupily romantic and widely popular song of the pre-war years, "Twas on the isle of Capri that I found her."  The island had also been the home of the writer Axel Munthe, now I suppose almost forgotten - like his once renowned autobiography, *The Story of San Michele*.

Our route to Cyprus took us through the Straits of Messina with the view of Mount Aetna  which had caught the imagination of my great-grandfather Beligh as he had sailed in the opposite direction from Alexandria to Europe eighty three years earlier, and through the Corinth Canal.  Our voyage ended at Limassol.

We stopped on the eastern outskirts of the town where there was a petrol pump - not to 'fill up'; in those days we bought petrol by the gallon in Cyprus according to requirements. The attendant, or owner, told me that I was going to be the Assistant Commissioner there again. And when I got to Nicosia this advance notification from that distinctly original source was duly confirmed officially.  Very Cyprus - of that period.

# ~8~

# Limassol; London; Nicosia

There was once a man so sensitive that no-one could tell how he would react to the most anodyne or innocent remark. Were you to greet him with a cheerful "What a lovely sunny day!", he might be liable to go "pale and tense" - and possibly "clench his fists till the knuckles stood out white under the strain" - because he would be reminded that "it was on just such a lovely sunny day that his wife had run away with the chauffeur". This imaginary character was introduced into a piece of dialogue by P.G.Wodehouse in order to make comically, indeed farcically, a point which needed emphasis. I take him as a paradigm for that equally hypersensitive being, the Greek or Turkish Cypriot, whenever their common homeland is a subject of discussion - particularly political discussion. We are inclined to see ourselves as having right entirely on our side, to regard anyone who might even hint that the other side could conceivably have a point as clear proof of prejudice on the part of a person who must be an unmitigated enemy of their own side - and an equally unprincipled protagonist of their opponents'. Perhaps we from Cyprus (and, indeed, from the two mainland countries of Turkey and Greece as well) are in this not really so very different from the great ruck of humanity at large. But, from my own observation, those whose origins are Greek or Turkish do seem to have a similarity, in this regard at least, to that other community of which a friend said to me, and not so long ago, "We Jews are like other people - only more so".

For rather less than the next ten years my life was to turn pretty much on the fate of the island of my birth. For rather more than a like period it was then to be almost wholly detached from the island. And then there was to come a time when I would again be engaged with the

147

place, but in ways quite unforeseen, nor even quite comprehended; so that I was to be unsure how far Cyprus was of me - or I of it.

I do not believe it to be true that "man's love is of his life a part - 'tis woman's whole existence". The idea that the depth of emotional attachment, sexual or otherwise, is determined entirely by gender seems to me to be at the very least highly open to question. Nor does it appear to me that its strength is unvaried over time. My love affair with Cyprus became dangerously close to its being my whole existence when, as it were in exile from it, I had dreamed of the place of which I had had but tantalisingly brief experiences. The reality, as it always is, was to be something different.

I hope I may be able to call back from memory, unsupported as it is by contemporary diaries or notes, something of what I saw, heard, thought and felt in those days before, and after, EOKA terrorism wrought dramatic changes to the island. Everyone concerned and involved must judge for themselves whether those changes have been to the happiness of the people of the island - or whether the very reverse. My attempts to recall and record those years (especially from 1952 to 1960 when, in that latter year, a sovereign state of Cyprus came into being in a sequence of events, of which *pars minissima fui*), will be made without consciously wanting to tread on any corns; but also in full readiness to do just that if it seems the only way I can remove the pressure of another's foot from mine or someone else's. What I should like to be able to do is to enable someone today to see, hear and feel what I and my wife were then seeing, hearing, and feeling. In embarking on this attempt I shall not try to minimise possible offence. Any other considerations apart, trying to do so would, it seems to me, be as futile an endeavour as to hope to avoid wounding the feelings of the man who lost his wife to his chauffeur. One simply cannot know what truth or perception might be likely to affront or hurt someone's sensitivities when the subject is Cyprus - especially if it is someone's birthplace.

Cyprus, like Greece is blessed - or cursed, depending on one's judgement of its consequences - by that peculiar phenomenon 'philhellenism'. In one of his many percipient essays George Orwell looks at what he calls 'transferred nationalism'. Those who adopt the cause of some country not their own do not simply become ardent advocates; they make that advocacy so much a part of their being, almost one might say their souls, that they not infrequently run the risk, and not seldom succumb to it, of the cause becoming their very reason for existing. In that state they can find themselves defending absolutely anything 'their' side maintains, oblivious of the facts. Like the MP on the Government benches at the time of the Boer War. When an Opposition Member pointed out that the number of Boers claimed to have been killed in all the separate official communiqués added up to more than the total of the Boer people, the outraged Government supporter rose to his feet and hurled the accusation "Cad!" across the gangway.

This personal account may perhaps come to the way I believe the slender possibilities of some kind of accommodation over Cyprus have constantly been stultified through the baneful influence which philhellenism has, directly or indirectly, exerted. But for the present it is relevant to recall what was in 1952, when Lalage and I came back to Cyprus, still very much in the future - a conversation I had with John Reddaway in the mid-1980s not long before his death. I had mentioned to him, what I had never touched on during the time of our service during British rule in the island. These were my thoughts about what I saw as the deleterious political results produced by philhellenes. He remonstrated, "But, you know, I'm a philhellene." I replied that to my way of thinking he was no more what he said he was, in the sense I strongly deprecated - indeed resented - than a 'nationalist' was a 'patriot'. A philhellene, in his sense, was properly, I would have said, someone who had esteem for the culture which had emerged from the city states of the pre-Christian centuries; someone who was detached in recognising also the gross imperfections of those political organisms; both the blemishes which were inherent (like an economy based on slave labour, treatment of women as chattels, and racial arrogance), and those which were derivative (in their common human failure to live by such universal validities as individual great men had propounded). Reddaway's 'philhellenism' did not, I suggested, allow his esteem for that past to be degraded into motivating a biassed political stance, with a blind adherence to the Greek side in any matter where they were protagonists, in the way that was far too often demonstrated by other 'philhellenes'. The result was to delude Greeks into believing themselves to be the favourite children (as they very often become the "spoilt darlings") of Europe; and in consequence they are encouraged into excesses which prevent them making a more realistic assessment of what practical support they could actually expect on any particular issue. And this belief stood in the way of their seeing through, and abandoning, their wilder fantasies. The 'philhellene' I meant - in whose ranks I could never imagine him, Reddaway - was the kind who carried idolatry to the point where, like some of the less lovable Greek political and church leadership, they seemed to be incapable of recognising that there was no more of a nexus between Plato and Papandreou, or between Menander and Mercouri, than there was between Marcus Aurelius and Mussolini. (He understood the British people I was alluding to.) Let John Reddaway then, *pax cineribus*, bear honourably that designation which he claimed for himself - and which others have so grievously dishonoured, to the harm, the despoilment, and the grief of so many.

**********

It was to John Reddaway that I reported as his new assistant in Limassol in the autumn of 1952. His first act was to offer Lalage and me the use of the Commissioner's small 'rest house' at Platres in the mountains below Troodos until we were able to find, for rent, a house in Limassol town. This courtesy and consideration was typical of the man previously described to me as "nervous". We found a two-bedroomed bungalow off the sea-front and close to the football stadium, and were soon settled in.

Our life was very domestic. At home Lalage, with a daily Turkish 'help', made great strides in running our home, which included shopping in the market and, though never previously having had to cook, very quickly coping with meals. In this she had the benefit of guidance from my mother when we visited her in Nicosia, as we tended to do on many weekends. The late autumn and winter months were not especially conducive to outdoor recreation in Limassol. Skiing was very primitive on Troodos, and neither of us were anyway much interested in that sport. We managed to get in some riding on the Akrotiri peninsula, on horses lent to us by the Jewish manager of the plantations at Fassouri, but this was only a very occasional pleasure in the winter. In the warmer days of the new year, which heralded the spring we had some lovely rides on the peninsula, following the shore of the salt lake, in and around which flocked clouds of pink flamingos. This was still half a dozen years before the new airfield and RAF station had been built, totally changing, and ruining, Akrotiri.

Our weekend visits to Nicosia were not only to visit mother, but also to try to find some social life, mostly with the members of my extended family. There was a dearth of social activity in Limassol itself. And looking back I find this lack puzzling. I do not remember that at the time we were conscious of this absence as an actual deprivation. It may have been that in those early days of our marriage we were well content as newly-weds, as well as temperamentally, to be very much in each other's company. There could have been another more objective factor at play.

While it is no doubt true that generalisations are likely to be misleading, it could I think be said that certain peoples have a tendency, at least, to share some characteristics which distinguish many of them from most others. While most Greeks tend to incline towards a 'bonhomous' sort of 'hail fellow-well met' approach, the generality of Turks are more likely - and I would say they resemble many British in this - to be reserved. The former are more likely to make the first approach; the latter to expect a first approach to be made. This sweeping observation is demonstrably not borne out in Turkey where, in the rural areas, the stranger is still virtually in the position of a 'traveller', but then the tradition there of responsibility for hospitality to the traveller and stranger is still very much alive. Before the evolution of the language in the last generation the Turkish word for 'guest', *misafir*, was derivatively the same as 'one on a journey'. But in Cyprus, where, for the last three generations, travelling has hardly been an arduous business, and where the 'foreigner' has long ceased to be much of a curiosity or a novelty, welcoming the stranger seems no more to be a feature of social relations, as far as the towns are concerned anyway.

In any event, as between the Greek and the Turkish communities there was certainly no less cleavage than I had first become aware of in Nicosia. Here, in Limassol, they also lived in their separate quarters of the town, the small Turkish quarter being on the western edge, at the far opposite side where, with the help of our office staff, we had found our rented house only a short walk from the Commissioner's official house near to the stadium. (From where in the early mornings of Greece's national holidays we would hear the sounds of the speeches and general clamour; and into which, in the full heat of mid-summer in 1974, the Greeks were to herd all the Turkish men of the area.) Our landlord, though we never met him in that capacity, turned out to be the Solicitor General, Criton Tornaritis, who was later to play a leading Greek Cypriot part in the discussions on, and the drafting of, the constitution with which Cyprus was to become an independent republic in 1960.

There were, in the 1950s, no institutions in Limassol, or other places that I knew of, which could have served to bring together people from the two communities. Save to the extent that commercial or other mutual business interest might bring individuals into contact (and in this commercially thriving town, where the Greeks were so heavily preponderant and economically dominant, there wasn't a great deal of that kind of contact) the Greeks and the Turks appeared to be pretty well self-contained, to be leading two very much isolated, indeed virtually insulated, existences. I do seem now to recall having felt some surprise, near to resentment, that we had had no kind of approach, certainly nothing in the nature of an invitation, from any of the three Lanitis brothers. They were among the leading Limassol business people, with expanding interests in a range of enterprises - not least at that time having the concession for production and sale of the newly introduced Coca-Cola, the signs for which were becoming ubiquitous. The elder Lanitis had been to Oxford (rather before my time) and I would no doubt have been naive had I thought that this connection might have led to some hospitality from him to the newly arrived married couple.

There were of course the 'cabarets', some more reputable than others, as is to be expected with such institutions. These provided opportunities for anyone with the fairly inexpensive price of admittance to have a meal and a drink and to dance to the music of a local band and - the main attraction of the place - to view cabaret turns, the female members of which were largely drawn from the eastern Mediterranean and from Hungary. But these cabarets were not places where one met people; you went there together with your existing friends. And so did Lalage and I. Our companions were usually two Turkish couples; one, the rising young businessman already mentioned with his wife, and another married couple, he being a dentist. We met, too, a very agreeable young Captain in the Royal Engineers who was Adjutant to the battalion stationed at Polemedhia, then a separate village some three miles north of the town. He turned out to be vaguely related to Lalage. With him and his wife we enlarged our circle of friends.

\*\*\*\*\*\*\*\*\*\*\*

There had just been established at Polemedhia an odd set-up called the Near East Arab Broadcasting Station (NEABS). Its exact status was obscure and the nature of its broadcasts, all in Arabic, enigmatic. The Director and half a dozen senior staff were British, and the rest Arab - mostly Palestinian. It was pretty clearly some kind of propaganda unit and equally obviously run under the auspices of the British government. I introduce the NEABS into these recollections of my life because through it Lalage and I were able to broaden our knowledge of people by meeting, and making friends with, Palestinian Arabs, of whom there were many on its staff. But having brought the NEABS into this story, it would be appropriate to round off its own saga by recording what happened, a few years later, after we ourselves had recently left for Nicosia. Its Director, Ralph Poston, took a vehement personal stand at the time of the Suez crisis when the British and French forces landed in Egypt - in collusion with the Israelis, though that was not known then, however deeply suspected by some, and strongly denied officially. The British public divided over the issue, much more evenly - though no less fiercely - than during the pre-war days of appeasement generally and Munich in particular. Poston was passionately of the camp which opposed Eden's adventurism, based, as he and many others judged, on a totally false analogy being drawn between Nasser and Hitler less than twenty years earlier, and a complete misreading of the extent and the nature of what was actually happening in Egypt and the Arab world. Holding strongly to his convictions Poston threw up his post - in circumstances which had him placed in custody, or house arrest, for a few days - and departed with his wife and four small children back to a Britain which had no job for him. The rest of the story is not part of mine, though we maintained sporadic contact. In course of time he was ordained into the ministry of the Anglican church; and before he died he accepted Islam.

\*\*\*\*\*\*\*\*\*\*

*And recollecting Ralph Poston brings to my mind an episode in the life of another Englishman of the immediately preceding generation, of whom I knew absolutely nothing at the time. Marmaduke Pickthall was born in 1875, the son of a Suffolk rector. From Harrow he failed to get into the Levant Consular Service. Through a family church contact he went out to Palestine in his mid-twenties with the chaplain to the Anglican Bishop in Jerusalem. For a couple of years he wandered about Syria (the Ottoman province of which Palestine was then a part). He later wrote: "In all my previous life I had not seen any happy people." In the city of Damascus his enthusiasm expanded and he sought to embrace Islam. He was dissuaded by the Sheykh el Ulema of the Great Mosque: "Wait until you are older and have again seen your native land. You are alone among us. So are our sons alone among the Christians. God knows how I should feel if any Christian teacher dealt with a son of mine otherwise than as I now deal with you." Pickthall took the old man's advice. It was not until more than twenty years later in England that he made his public affirmation of his Moslem faith. Twelve years later still, in 1930, his translation of the Koran was published. As, strictly speaking, the original Arabic of the Koran cannot be 'translated' he entitled his work 'The Meaning of the Glorious Koran'. I believe it has never since been out of print.*

\*\*\*\*\*\*\*\*\*\*

Not long after my second posting to Limassol a new Governor arrived in Cyprus. This was Sir Robert Armitage, who had latterly been Financial Secretary in the Gold Coast. I was rung up one day by the keen and eager editor of the English language newspaper, the *Cyprus Mail*. He said he believed I knew Armitage from his previous appointment. I replied cagily, and truthfully, that a young Cadet Administrative Officer, as I had been there, was not likely to be on

154

even nodding acquaintance with the number three of the administration and a member of the Executive Council in a large colony like the Gold Coast. But, insinuated the voice on the other end of the line, I surely could tell him something about our new Governor? I replied that Armitage was very good-looking! I was in fact being objectively truthful in side-stepping my questioner in this way - at the same time mischievously comparing him mentally to the disadvantage of Fletcher Cooke, for whom that description scarcely applied. I can't now recall whether the report as it duly appeared in the paper (either attributably or otherwise) contained this rivetingly interesting information about the features of our new Excellency. If it did, it certainly didn't do me any good - nor any harm - so far as one can judge.

This new appointment was probably made as part of a fresh strategy in face of the determined and adamantine refusal of the Cyprus church leadership under Makarios, with the increasingly militant 'Ethnarchy Office' which he had created, to allow his flock to have any dealings with the government machine. Armitage's arrival was shortly afterwards followed by a new law which gave powers to set up in villages, at the discretion of the District Commissioners, 'Improvement Boards' with elected members. The idea was gradually to introduce to the village people the concept and the practice of self-administration, on the analogy of the municipalities in the towns. The process was to be gradual, both by way of pilot Boards (not that that term was in currency then) to test the scheme out on a village by village basis, but also because of the very practical consideration that funds would not have allowed of the widespread introduction of the project. These funds in the first instance very largely came from the central government in Nicosia but, so far as I remember, derived from allocations from London under what was then a new method of development finance for all colonial territories inaugurated by the Colonial Development and Welfare Act.

In a territory not so politically charged as Cyprus - which was not really, in the classic sense, a colony at all (but rather a strategic staging post, and a *place d'armes*) - the underlying concept was admirable. And even in Cyprus there were tangible benefits in the villages where Boards were set up and operated. But non-cooperation remained an article of faith with the politically powerful and hostile church, and there never were real grounds for thinking that out of these bodies would grow any genuine feeling for self-government, still less anything likely to lead to a desire for self-rule. (Any such hope, it seems to me, could, not too unkindly, be seen as paralleled by some of the old-fashioned type of Missionary endeavour which looked to conversion being produced by material, secular, benefits). Only the most ill-informed rosy optimism could have thought that there was the slightest chance that the unabating campaign of antagonism to the government waged by Makarios and all the other Greek political leaders for *'enosis and only enosis'* could be checked or curbed, much less directed into cooperation for practical purposes of economic amelioration and development for the benefit of the people through this, or any other, financial means. I doubt that many in Nicosia entertained such unrealistic expectations. Certainly Reddaway, and those remaining few who had long experience of the place, based on personal knowledge of, and friendship with, many of those in both communities, harboured no illusions on that score.

But this didn't lessen our willingness in Limassol to put an effort into the new structures, which we saw as being worthwhile and useful in their own right, without being deluded that political benefits, or 'spin-offs' in the later jargon, were likely to flow. And in the Turkish villages I was more than glad that their inhabitants, who had no inhibition about taking advantage of the financial benefits from this, albeit very limited, exercise in 'village democracy', should reap where others were not prepared to to plough and sow.

\*\*\*\*\*\*\*\*\*\*\*

Among the District Commissioner's duties which Reddaway was glad to pass over to me were those which fell to him in his capacity as Marriage Officer. There was a Marriage Officers Law which made provision for civil marriages to be conducted between parties who either did not wish to be married in a religious ceremony, or could not be because the religious authorities concerned would not countenance it in their particular case. The precise reasons are no longer in my memory. What *does* linger is the legal content of the relevant legislation. Under the provisions of the Marriage Officers Law the

District Commissioner was *ex officio* the Marriage Officer for his district. Under the quite separate, and comprehensive, Interpretation Law 'District Commissioner' was defined to include 'Assistant District Commissioner'. (Though not in the terms of the legendary legal draftsman who produced a like provision in a Bill that "For the purposes of this Act 'man' embraces 'woman' "). It therefore appeared to John Reddaway to be entirely within his powers for him, by administrative action, to devolve his functions in that capacity to his Assistant. And I, too, could see no fault in so reading these two statutes in conjunction. Two couples, over a period, were thus made man and wife by me. To no-one's dissatisfaction. Or so we thought. How this administrative devolution, or delegation, of authority came to the notice of the authorities in Nicosia I do not know, but the combined wisdom of Fletcher Cooke and the Attorney-General, Stelios Pavlides, concluded that my appointment as Marriage Officer required to be gazetted *retrospectively* in the Cyprus Gazette. I recall that when we were told of this decision my reaction was to hope fervently, for their own sakes, that the parties to these two nuptial ceremonies would not read the Gazette - a statistically minimal possibility - and so realise that for at least a period of time they had been 'living in sin'. This was, as I was later to discover, the fate of the very proper couples in J.B.Priestley's comedy *When we are Married*. I never heard that our couples ever went through that - then humiliating - experience.

\*\*\*\*\*\*\*\*\*\*

Not the least among Reddaway's acquaintances from the Greek community in Limassol was Costas Partassides, the communist mayor of the town. His tenure of that office came to an end when he went to prison. This was shortly before my arrival in Limassol. The Gilbertian episode was the outcome of a sequence of events which he clearly engineered to produce precisely that result. He achieved a short spell in gaol for defying the government. This never did any harm to a politician's prospects in a colonial territory; and where, as in Cyprus - and contrary to the lucubrations of Christopher Hitchens *et hoc genus* - the territory is ruled by a benevolently mild government, nor is any particular hardship suffered. Costas Partassides's incarceration came about when he decided that the name-plate of one of the town's main

157

streets (and the one most in the public eye, being the sea-front) constituted an affront no longer to be tolerated. He had a point - up to a point! The name in question was that of Herbert Richmond Palmer, who had been the Governor who replaced Storrs when the latter, and his residence, had come to grief in the 1931 riots. For twenty years the name-plates on the sea-front had stood - to general indifference from the populace and passers-by. And so too had others - not only in Limassol - which bore, in the three official languages, the names of past notabilities and 'worthies' (or not, depending on the point of view), Greek, Turkish and British. The individual's place in history was looked on with favour, or with a more than jaundiced eye, according as the person was thought to have advanced, or betrayed, the particular community's cause. (Admiral Codrington, for example, whose name appeared on a prominent street in Nicosia, was the man who, in 1827, had done a 'Pearl Harbour' by attacking and severely damaging the Turkish fleet at Navarino during the Greek War of Independence - without warning, and when Britain was in fact neutral and at peace with the Ottoman empire.) But in 1952 the mayor of Limassol judged the time opportune to remove the objectionable name-plate in his town and replace it with '28 October', this being the date of the Greek rejection of Mussolini's ultimatum to them in 1940 - known as *Ochi* ('No') Day. Partassides well knew that since 1931 an Order in Council required changes of street names to be approved by the Governor. He was instructed to replace the new name-plates; and when he naturally (or anyway predictably) refused, the job was carried out by the government. Down they came again the following day; and the government took the matter to court. Failing to comply with the court's order, the recalcitrant, but doubtless pleased and gratified, mayor was committed to gaol for contempt. Where he stayed for a brief period until Mr Hitchens's viciously tyrannical government's Supreme Court judged him to have 'purged' his contempt. Meanwhile the Municipality was 'put into commission', which meant that the functions of the elected Mayor and Council were carried out by a commission chaired by the Commissioner, assisted by two nominated citizens of Limassol, one Greek and one Turkish.

\*\*\*\*\*\*\*\*\*\*

It was in this capacity, as mayor *ad interim*, that Reddaway decided to take official cognisance of the fact, which was undoubted to a detached and objective witness to whom the relevant information and detail was available, that the Turkish community had over the years received but scant attention from the municipality's coffers. (It was also the case that, as the smaller and poorer community, they had contributed much less than the Greek community to the revenues - though that might not be thought to be a consideration, in a normal and dispassionate administration, for distributing or allocating expenditure.) Having first decided that this discrimination needed to be recognised, and the recognition expressed in a practical way going beyond a mere gesture, Reddaway broached the subject with me. I took counsel with my Turkish friends and we suggested that a fitting way to compensate the community for past neglect would be by providing a building which could be used for social purposes and as a community centre - a sort of club house but open to all. In Turkey a whole network of *Halk Evi*'s (People's Houses) had gradually been developed over the past few decades where they had been instruments in the hands of the Republic's single-party government in developing the literacy campaign which had gone hand in hand with the extension in the use of the new alphabet in the Latin script. There was no such requirement in Cyprus, but *Halk Evi*'s in the island would provide a place for lectures, meetings, plays and readings, and generally be a focus for a population which had virtually nothing beyond the coffee-house. As it happened, only a couple of years earlier the first general elections under a multi-party system in Turkey had resulted in the defeat of the party which had been Ataturk's, and the peaceful transfer of power to the new Democrat Party, with the *Halk Evi*'s beginning to fall out of favour with the new government in Turkey, which saw them as, in effect, organs of the Opposition. They thus began to acquire a reputation in Turkey for involvement in party politics. But in Cyprus they had no such tinge and the concept remained merely cultural. As I remember, a site was provided by the *Evcaf* Office ; and a building was erected by the municipality.

\*\*\*\*\*\*\*\*\*\*

**Young Bird**

1953 was the year of the Coronation. In Limassol this provided a set-piece colonial occasion, of which the high point was a visit by a Royal Navy ship (was it *HMS Devonshire*, or *HMS Bermuda?*) with its contingent of Marines, including band. The main formal and ceremonial function was the reading of the Proclamation of Accession by the District Commissioner from a dais on the sea-front, followed by an inspection and march past by the Naval and Marine detachments, together with the Police. The occasion was fortunately not demeaned in any way by evidences of Greek nationalistic fervour, which was entirely absent; still less by demonstrations, which the Ethnarchy and Makarios presumably deemed would be counter-productive. (Unlike the occasion of the Queen's visit in 1993, for the Commonwealth Heads of Government meeting in the island, which was marred by hooliganism that resulted in unseemly demonstrations and the shattering of the royal Rolls-Royce windscreen.) Indeed in 1953 the official entertainments in the evening, which included a Grand Ball, were fully attended. More than fully in fact, because some notable *enosis* advocates communicated their dissatisfaction at not having received invitations and, when these were belatedly provided, duly made an appearance.

One particular picture that remains firmly in my mind's eye is of the young Marine officer standing in front of his contingent, the bright early morning light glinting on the sea, at the inspection of the ceremonial parade. He had been with us at a party the previous evening, where he had enjoyed himself overwell. A long thin youth, he stood there in gleaming whites, drawn sword held firmly before him at the salute, his height accentuated by his pith helmet topped by a brass spike as he swayed back and forward like an animated metronome. A performance if not admirable, at least worthy of admiration for maintaining both composure and verticality.

**\*\*\*\*\*\*\*\*\*\***

My Greek preliminary oral examination was now due, and I saw the way to deploy for this purpose the interestingly unusual activities of that year. In preparing for the Coronation celebrations much work had been done to decorate the streets with coloured lighting as well as bunting; and a particularly effective touch had been produced by the

PWD District Engineer, a Greek Cypriot. The town's large drum-like water supply tank was visible a long way off, standing as it did on its lofty supports. The DE conceived, and carried out with electric light bulbs, its transformation into a night-time jewelled crown, which shone above the town to general admiration. Coronation year had also seen the elections to the dozen or so (if my memory correctly serves) of the villages which we had selected for the establishment of the new Improvement Boards. By boning up on the somewhat esoteric vocabulary which these events embraced, I conceived the idea of diverting the fairly rudimentary conversation that my *viva voce* Greek exam would entail into topics where I should be able to demonstrate my knowledge of such abstruse matters as 'street-decorations', 'illuminations', 'proclamation', 'ballot-box', 'voting list' and the like. (Not a single one of which I could today produce in Greek.) And so I played it. But I also demonstrated on what weak foundations was based my knowledge of Greek. For one member of the examining panel enquired of me, so I recall, *Apo pou isthe, kyrie?* (Where are you from, sir?). My reply was to the effect that my family was from Nicosia but that I was born - *eghenithika*- in Famagusta. Or rather that was what I thought I had said. In, fact confusing the active with the passive of the verb, I had actually informed the panel that "I gave birth - *eghenisa* - in Famagusta." My having occasioned them considerable mirth no doubt contributed to their decision to let me through. (Which calls to mind the story - equally true as it happens - of the man who was taking his oral in Swahili in Uganda. He was asked how he would request someone to 'come here'. Just about up to this, he produced the correct phrase. "And how would you ask someone to 'go there'"? enquired the examiner. He pondered the problem, which tested his acumen, as well as his knowledge, to the limit. "I would go over there," he eventually replied, "and ask him to come here." He didn't pass.)

***********

And all the time the campaign by the Greek leadership for "*enosis* and only *enosis*" continued in full vigour. The Archbishop's Ethnarchy had now also focused their attention even more on the schools which, under British rule, were entirely independent in their administration and their syllabus. Even without the specific fomenting of nationalist fervour through the Ethnarchy's youth organisations, which boiled over at every celebration of the Greek state's national holidays, it is not difficult to imagine the effect, in forming the attitudes of the Greek Cypriot youth towards their Turkish co-habitants of the island, wrought by the use in the Greek Cypriot elementary schools and especially in the 'gymnasia', or secondary schools, of the precise textbooks which were used in the schools of Greece where Greek history was traditionally portrayed in terms where nothing good, but rather everything obnoxious, in regard to Turks *tout court*, was the staple. What history, so-called, has done in the past to exacerbate the relations between the Protestants and the Catholics of Ireland it has done in at least equally baneful measure to the peoples of Cyprus. And in both places religion (in its most debased and corrupt outward manifestation) has also played its dire and horrendous role. It is painful - yet necessary - at least to point to that aspect.

And if I am to be truthful to what are, after all, my recollections I cannot pass over one scene which stands clearly in my memory: minor though it may be thought to be it left a bitter taste. In the summer months Cyprus had open air cinemas, as the heat in a pre-air conditioning age made indoor cinemas impossible. Lalage and I were at one of these performances. I have no idea now what the film was, but probably a Hollywood 'epic'-type production with grand scenic effects and the like. In one scene there was shown a large congregation of Moslem worshippers at prayer. When they prostrated themselves, in the formal ritual, an absolute howl - there is no other word - of derision broke out from the largely Greek Cypriot audience. In its unpremeditated, unorganised, expression of ill-will and contempt this was disturbing. One could not but ask oneself what kind of deep-seated, indoctrinated passions of hostility were being given expression in such a spontaneous outburst? And by whom it had been engendered?

It cannot be sufficiently emphasised that the call by the church and the leadership was always for 'union with Greece'; it was never for 'independence'. It is, of course, undeniable that the mere fact of colonial status, of 'dependency', is scarcely congenial and will be felt by independent spirits as galling. But the protagonists of political change in the island never for a moment sought a sovereign independent statehood, nor ever wavered in their inflexible aim of bringing Cyprus as an entirely integral part into the Greek state. Practical considerations didn't enter into it. Whether or not in material terms the inhabitants of the island - by which they meant the Greek inhabitants - would be better off under British rule or under enosis was quite beside the point. The issue was always held out as essentially a 'holy' one - not surprisingly, though distastefully, since it was primarily propagated by the church. Both through its political office the Ethnarchy, and in the more directly ecclesiastical structures of the monastery, the diocese, and the town and village church, Greek Cypriots were regularly and fervently called by their priests to their duty to 'mother Greece'.

The point needs no labouring to see that the idea of becoming citizens of a state which held them in open contumely was, to put it mildly, rather less than welcome to the Cyprus Turks, for whom their existing status as 'citizens of the United Kingdom and Colonies' under British rule was infinitely preferable. That this was the view of the matter taken by their Turkish co-habitants of the island was abundantly clear to the Greek side generally; but so far from doing anything to try to allay or moderate Turkish apprehensions, Makarios and those he led simply ignored and discounted the feelings of the Turkish people of the island whose fate (so long as it was thought possible to regard them variously, and variably, with indifference and disdain) was to them of no consequence.

*Twenty years further down the road down which Makarios took his flock - and dragged others - through the desolation of the years of EOKA terrorism and their aftermath, a member of a Greek Cypriot body called 'The Cyprus Research Centre' was to write, in a book entitled 'Peaceful Co-existence in Cyprus': "The very fact that the present book, whatever its value, has been written only in 1976-77 instead of some sixty or eighty or at least thirty years ago, points to our belated realisation of the crucial importance of systematic knowledge of our Turkish neighbours, their problems, mentality, origins and relations with us. This delay has been fatal for the inter-ethnic developments in the island." The final sentence is, to say the least, scarcely drawing it mild. Yet the sentiments are to be warmly welcomed. Twenty more years down that same road, they could still be a guide, for Cyprus and the two neighbouring mainland countries.*

**Young Bird**

*But I fear it would now represent the triumph of hope over experience.*

***********

For another eighteen months or so after the Coronation Cyprus was to continue at peace, a place of outward delight to Lalage and me. It would have been difficult in 1953 to imagine - as we certainly did not - that so soon, from among the essentially decent and kindly people of this enchanting island, there would come those initial few who would begin the era of violence and murder which was to embroil, and corrupt, many others in their brutalities in the pursuit of what they had been taught to believe were sanctified ends. Naive we may have been; but perhaps no more so than Metternich, who, a hundred years earlier, had wryly to confess to his surprise at the political line taken by 'Pio Nono': "I never bargained for a liberal Pope!" That a Greek Orthodox Archbishop could, and probably would, behave in the mode of a mediaeval political prelate through methods of intrigue and violence was something one might bargain for; but that the Greek people of Cyprus at large should become a fertile field for the poisonous seed to germinate and flourish was not something I had ever envisaged. And yet, in retrospect, the brutalities of what was then the recent civil war in Greece, employing murder, destruction and intimidation (including the kidnapping, for ideological indoctrination, of children) had been a harbinger and a portent, had we known it. And indeed it was in that civil war that the future EOKA leader, Grivas, was to earn his spurs as - and I choose my adjectives carefully and exactly - an unsavoury extreme right-wing fascist fanatic. We see the type now in Mladic, Karadzic and Milosevic in Bosnia and in Serbia.

***********

At the beginning of September in 1953 Lalage went into the Limassol General Hospital, where she gave birth to our first child, a boy. She was under the care of the Greek Cypriot District MO. A week or so before there had been an extremely severe earthquake in the Ionian Islands. When I visited Lalage at the hospital before the birth, the sun would set each evening in a western sky awesomely crimson; and this

164

continued in the days after the child was born. I do not now remember whether it was at exactly this time that people began to attribute this magical, yet frightening, intensity of the unusually red sky, as the sun sank during those evenings, to dust particles raised far away over in the west by the Ionian Islands' disaster. But, precursor or not, a week after the birth of our son the Paphos earthquake struck.

The main shock was felt at about six in the morning - late enough for most village folk to have left their houses for the fields and so, fortunately, there were not many lives lost. It was alarming to think what the death toll might have been had the quake come, say, an hour earlier. The shock was also felt in Limassol - my bed shook in our single-storey house, and I knew at once what it must be. There was no damage at all in the house, or all around. I went at once to the hospital before going on to the office.

\*\*\*\*\*\*\*\*\*\*

At the hospital I discovered that in the first-floor room where Lalage was, there had been falls of plaster from the ceiling - one right over the corner where the baby's cot was; but he had been taken out of the room and hadn't by then been brought in for his morning feed.

\*\*\*\*\*\*\*\*\*\*

In the office I got reports from our ADI in the western side of our District nearest to Paphos District, and from the police. From these a picture emerged of the scale of damage in that westernmost District where, or near where, the epicentre seemed to have been and where aftershocks were continuing. Limassol District had been scarcely affected. An Earthquake Reconstruction Committee was at once formed. Reddaway was appointed to chair this, and I became the secretary - and was posted temporarily to Paphos. Members were drawn from the PWD, the Antiquities Department and the new Social Welfare Department. The clear first objective was to obtain and distribute tents and blankets to shelter those whose houses had been made uninhabitable (and of course those very many others who were too frightened to spend the night inside even undamaged buildings).

165

## Young Bird

But vitally important too was the need to carry out an immediate survey of damage so as to be able to assess the scale of assistance needed to rehabilitate the maximum number of houses, so that people could return before the onset of winter. For those whose houses were beyond repair a simple unit was designed for construction locally by the PWD, and under contract, which was based on prefabricated reinforced concrete columns, to be erected on site by being set into a pyramid-like base poured on the spot. The curtain walls, using the rubble of the old, could be filled in by the villagers themselves - most of whom were well able to carry out such work with this traditional building material of these western parts of the island. The government would provide prefabricated doors and windows, also roofing material of rafters and corrugated asbestos which were already in production at the Amiandos mines (up in the mountains near the school I had gone to twenty years earlier but long since closed). For the many buildings damaged but repairable a system was devised to make provision of the necessary amounts of sand and cement, with small cash grants, to the individual owners. In the case of Paphos town, where such owners were not accustomed to being their own masons, it was decided that monetary compensation was the most sensible way of getting repairs carried out. Not unexpectedly the politicians took this - to them possibly heaven-sent - opportunity to denigrate these efforts to cope with an emergency; and by calling for everything - including the impossible - to be done by the government, blunted the spirit of of self-help and so delayed unnecessarily the work of reconstruction. Nevertheless the work continued. After three months the Committee's job was finished. I returned to Limassol, where Lalage had been helped with the baby by my mother, who had also been with her for the birth.

***********

In late January of the following year Lalage's father, accompanied by the middle of his three daughters, who had taken Lalage's place at home with him, came out to visit us and to see his new grandson. But *en route* Ursula sent us a telegram from the ship. Rudolph Milner-White had suffered a stroke. They disembarked at Port Said and he was taken to hospital in Cairo. It was quite possible that he could be dying. I got compassionate leave. Mother took charge of the four

166

month old baby. By plane and train Lalage and I reached Cairo. After a day or two her father's condition stabilised and we were able to arrange a passage for him and Ursula to Cyprus; and we flew back. In hospital in Cyprus we took our son to see, and be seen by, his only grandfather. Did either consciously know the other? My father-in-law died a week later, a year younger than I am today. He is buried in the English Cemetery at Polemidhia; his gravestone, a single slab bearing his name, with that of his wife (buried in Sussex) and, in Latin, "I have lifted up mine eyes ..." (Why is this opening line of Psalm 121 translated in the prayer-book as 'I *will* lift up...' ? I have often wondered.) When we left Limassol later, on my transfer to Nicosia, one of the clerks in our office, who was himself from Polemidhia, volunteered always to keep an eye on the grave and the pepper tree we planted at its head. Which he did even after the upheavals following 1963. Since the separation of the populations in 1974 he has lived with his family as one of the Turkish refugees from the South resettled in the North. (Within the last few years we have been sent photographs of the grave. One was from Michael Stone, who still lives in southern Nicosia. The other was from a Greek Cypriot I shall call Zach. We met him, with his wife, at our son's wedding nearly twelve years ago, she having been a great friend of our new daughter-in-law at university. It was strange thus to meet a Greek Cypriot for the first time in a quarter of a century. We are now good friends; as are his and my son's children).

\*\*\*\*\*\*\*\*\*\*

A new Commissioner was now posted to Limassol. He arrived from Nigeria where, on transfer to Cyprus, he had just handed over to my brother, who had been appointed to that colony some three years previously. Considering the immense size of Nigeria - by far the largest of the British colonies - it was an astonishing coincidence that of all the districts there it should have been Ham Ramsay's which my brother should have taken over, and that I should have been his Assistant when he took up his duties in Cyprus. His transfer there, I was to learn afterwards, had been influenced by the effect of the Nigerian climate on his wife's health. They were a very likeable and conscientious couple. I soon came to know him as a man who, if not the most

167

imaginative, was one of the utmost principle and integrity; someone who would take his responsibilities with great seriousness - for whom the word 'duty' (though I never heard him use it) would be paramount. In this latter regard his character was similar to what I remembered of my father - though Ham Ramsay was barely ten years older than me. Both were, to use terms which ring oddly old-fashioned in my ears today, upright and honourable.

\*\*\*\*\*\*\*\*\*\*\*

It was, as I remember it, about the spring of 1954 that I began to hear from the ADIs rumours of explosives being talked of in some of the villages of our district. This was of course reported to central government, and to the local police. The Superintendent in Limassol was a Greek Cypriot, Hasabis. There was now in the air a rising awareness - nothing specific, but a sense - of something foreboding. In our house our Turkish daily 'help' began openly to voice her fear of, and hostility to, 'the Greeks' - something which, from her, Lalage and I recall as new and disconcertingly unpleasant. I had come across complaints about certain individual Greeks being less than impartial in regard to specific decisions and issues where it was felt that communal bias had operated. And where the government was not directly involved, as for example in municipal matters, there was as I have already mentioned much dissatisfaction. But it was new in our experience to hear bitterness openly expressed in an unrelated way about the general untrustworthiness of *Rumlar* (Greeks) as such. This kind of thing was certainly being reflected in the local Turkish press; but to a great extent this was regarded as a counter-weight, indeed a direct reaction, to the daily pro-*enosis* clamour of the local Greek newspapers.

\*\*\*\*\*\*\*\*\*\*\*

And then came the incident of the Greek *caique 'Ayios Yiorghios'*. This small vessel was intercepted unloading dynamite and small arms on a beach in Paphos District. The tension now rose sharply. After this there could be no question but that some organised violence was being premeditated and planned.

**\*\*\*\*\*\*\*\*\*\***

There followed demonstrations in Greek schools throughout the island, which not infrequently took to the streets. The general background was the decision of the Greek government in Athens to try to bring the question of Cyprus before the United Nations. That aspect is no direct part of my own story. What is, however, very germane indeed is the tense emotional atmosphere in the island, which was (and must deliberately have been) brought to a pitch of fervour that was bound to lead to trouble. By January 1955 Athens Radio had reached the point of virtual direct incitement, likely, and no doubt intended, to bring youths out on to the streets in the towns of Cyprus: "We must use the language the colonial powers understand - the language used by the Jews and the Mau Mau, the language of blood, sabotage and dynamite." The invitation of Richard Crossman ten years earlier was being accepted and acted upon in Athens - at second hand. But it was very much at first hand that the invitation was being warmly embraced on the island. As was very soon to be public knowledge, Makarios had already made his arrangements and dispositions with the disaffected, disappointed, and prematurely retired Greek army colonel Grivas. That man had been born in the village of Trikomo in the Famagusta District of Cyprus, but his adult life had been spent in Greece where, in the army, his reputation was that of a brutally extreme right-wing nationalist. (I cannot forbear to observe the sadly ironic parallel of that other right-wing extremist retired colonel, Turkesh, who was also born in Cyprus, but spent his adulthood in Turkey.)

*I have, as an aside, sometimes pondered on the odd phenomenon that in the supposed 'melting pot' of the United States where, instead of nationalist fervour being somehow dissipated and dispelled into the atmosphere, the chauvinistic passion of the emigré, notably among the American Greeks and Armenians, seems to take on a particularly virulent form - to say nothing of the American Irish. "Absence," it would seem "makes the heart grow fonder" indeed, and sometimes in very ugly forms. Perhaps my own attachment to Cyprus has something of this in it - but I should like to think that if so it is defensive, and*

169

*without my wishing ill - certainly not harm - to 'the other': 'patriotism' rather than 'nationalism'? I hope so anyway.*

Makarios knew full well the character and nature of the man with whom he allied himself in setting up the organisation which was now to reveal itself in Cyprus - EOKA, sworn to fight to achieve *enosis* without any compunction. The oath (to my mind as blasphemous as it is sacrilegious) sworn by both Makarios and Grivas with each of the other ten members of the Committee formed in Athens in 1953, which gave birth to the idea out of which EOKA sprang, began: "I swear in the name of the Holy and Consubstantial and Indivisible Trinity ..."; and ended "...And I shall obey blindly the relevant orders given to me."

Whether it was late in 1954 or early in 1955 is no longer in my mind, but within about a year of Ham Ramsay's arrival in Limassol we were faced with a huge and violent demonstration in the town. I do not even remember what was the immediate occasion for it - though in a sense by now that was immaterial, the proximate cause being the fanaticism whipped up by Athens from abroad, together with the incitements of Makarios's Ethnarchy and its sponsored youth organisations on the spot. The police were quite unable to control the mob. The military were called in - "in aid of the civil power", to use the official phraseology. It was in fact a detachment from either the 40th or 45th Marine Commandos, but no matter - and Ramsay himself went down to the scene personally. He asked me to take post at the central Limassol police station, about half a mile distant, with which he would try to maintain contact, and from where I would be able to report on the situation to Nicosia. The Riot Act was read. This is not a figure of speech; riot drill requires the strictest adherence to detailed procedures, and these include the reading of a precise text, translated into the vernacular, calling on the rioters to disperse under pain of being fired upon. If on the third repetition of this warning the crowd has not done so, a single shot is fired on express command. Contrary to what I have sometimes heard is thought to be the case, this is not over the rioters' heads - which can be calculated to inflame - but at a single individual who is identified as a main instigator. And this was done. A man fell. The mob scattered. The man did not die. There was no further mob violence in Limassol. (I can still recall the sound

170

of the disapproving consternation in Fletcher Cooke's voice over the telephone when I told him from the police station what had happened.)

\*\*\*\*\*\*\*\*\*\*\*

April the first, 1955. I was rung at our house very early, at about dawn, as I recall. I don't now remember whether the call was from the town ADI or the police. In the light of what I was subsequently to gather about our Police Superintendent, the message could indeed have come from that source, if only as a cover. There had been explosions at each of the two police sub-stations in Limassol, one at either end of what was then the almost undeveloped by-pass round the north of the town. I arranged at once with Hasabis to inspect the damage together. It turned out to be only minor at each location. These two incidents were seemingly Limassol's share of what was an island-wide signal of the start of the EOKA campaign. No great damage was in fact caused anywhere in this first opening shot. The significance was in the demonstration by an established organisation of their ability to carry out this sort of operation. And very soon to mount personal attacks also - intended both to harm and to intimidate. And not long after to kill in cold-blooded murder.

It would imbalance this attempt to record the memories of my life, if I were now to try launching into a detailed survey of the events which, beginning with those explosions of April 1955, culminated in the establishment of the Republic of Cyprus in 1960. (Though 'culminate' is a singularly inapt term to use in view of what the birth of that republic was, itself, to bring in its train. That republic, that independent State, was in fact, as will be seen, never more than, nor ever intended by Makarios and the others of his camp to be, anything but a brief halting point on the broad highway to *enosis*.) And in any case such an attempt by me now would not be possible, writing forty years later, without ever having kept a diary or a journal, or indeed any notes. What I hope I am able to do is to draw a broad picture of the way the terrorist campaign affected the Turkish people in general, and me and my family in particular, in shaping the future course of our lives.

As to the nature of the terror campaign, it should properly be remembered that all this was happening at a time before we were to become inured to what is nowadays virtually endemic throughout the world. We, and I include myself in this, have also to bear in mind that the nature of the violence was far less 'sophisticated' then than it later was to become, for example in the British Isles - to look no further. This was before the days of 'semtex' and the highly technical explosive devices we have since come to regard as 'normal' with the IRA, ETA, HAMAS, PKK, and the rest. But violent death is still the same bereavement and tragedy, however, and by whom, it is perpetrated; and intimidation is still the same base and cowardly tactic, whether used by the ideologue or by the psychopath (where these may be different).

The timed explosive device under your car had not appeared in Cyprus then; and the first 'bombs' were pretty gimcrack. We had a couple thrown at our house at night, only the first of which exploded - and that to no great effect. The second, some time later, we discovered the following day in a flower-bed under our bedroom window. Our 'help' saw a piece of piping there and we got the army to remove and detonate it. It was a very amateur job, activated by lighting a fuse like a wick and lobbing it at the target. The fuse must have gone out in flight or on impact with the ground - or possibly simply failed. Yet it was, to say the least, decidedly unpleasant to know that there were people around who were in the business of delivering this kind of message. Compared with what, until recently, was going on in Northern Ireland and the British mainland, in Spain, in south eastern Turkey, and elsewhere, this sort of thing was small scale, however measured.

But the appalling consequence was the utter destruction of whatever small residual belief might yet have existed, within the two communities, that living together on the island was still possible. It is a truism that when trouble strikes one knows who are one's friends. In Cyprus the grim result of EOKA's activities (and again I would emphasise that this was being carried out under the auspices of the church) was that you could not now know who might not be your deadly enemy - who it was who might have you, literally as well as metaphorically, in their sights. In effect personal trust between Greek and Turk, where it existed, virtually disappeared. (I have to say at this

172

point that I was distinctly uncomfortable, to put it no more strongly, that the Personal Secretary to the successive Limassol District Commissioners was, throughout my time in the district, the niece of a prominent member of the Archbishop's entourage in the shape of the ultranationalistic Ethnarchy Council.) This total breakdown of trust is a dreadful thing. Just how insidious it is cannot be conveyed. Not by me at any rate. It can only be experienced.

\*\*\*\*\*\*\*\*\*\*

Right from the start EOKA's targets included members of their own community as well. They shot dead our young town ADI while his wife was in hospital having given birth to their son. One never could know what was the motive in selecting a particular victim. In this case it was quite possibly straight intimidation - *pour encourager les autres* - by the murder of a loyal young member of the district administration. And by such methods a small group of dedicated extremists managed effectively to cow their people into preventing them giving away the terrorists' identities. For however widespread might have been the indoctrinated support for the *idea* of *enosis*, I didn't believe it to be in the nature of *most* of the ordinary people actively to lend themselves to despicable terrorism, nor to give willing comfort to those who dispensed it.

\*\*\*\*\*\*\*\*\*\*

But hand in hand with the demoralisation, even degradation, of their own community came the other direct and ineluctable consequence of this vicious resort by Makarios to the methods of gangsterism: the strengthening of the will of the Turkish community and of their resolve to look now for their support not only to the British government but across the forty miles of sea which separated them from Turkey. It was at this time that I heard for the first time the saying *"Türkün dostu Türktür,"* the literal translation of which is 'A Turk's friend is a Turk'. But, just as in English, this can be taken two ways: 'The person who is a friend to a Turk is himself/herself a Turk' - is, as it were, an honorary Turk. But it can also be understood, and meant, in the sense that 'A

173

Turk can count only on a Turk as a friend'. The attitude that is given expression by this latter sense of the phrase now took hold among the Turks of Cyprus. There had not, even before, been lacking those who had always taken the starker view of things - a view which some might qualify as paranoid. (Though, if so, I have to confess that, as may emerge before I manage to finish these recollections, such a qualification is valid, in the Cyprus context, to precisely the same degree as in the ironic disclaimer "Just because I'm paranoid doesn't mean they're not out to get me" - the validity of which was for the Cyprus Turks to be proved by events.)

**********

And now other developments, too, began to erode Turkish Cypriot feelings of confidence that they could rely on the British to resist the Greek side's persistence. In parallel with the counter measures to terrorism introduced by the new Governor, Field Marshal Sir John Harding, efforts were renewed by the Secretary of State in London, in consultation with the Cyprus administration, to attempt to secure some advance towards constitutional self-rule in the island. As with every past venture in this direction, this one also was to come to nothing. The rock on which all such moves had foundered was still in place: the rigid, unmoving, Ethnarchy's inflexible insistence on "*enosis* and only *enosis*". "Let not the best become the enemy of the good" is a wise saying in this world of imperfection. "The best" is scarcely how a Turk would define enosis as the fate for Cyprus and for his people; but that was how it was regarded by the Archbishop and, seemingly, by the majority of the community whose guide, spiritual and political, he was. In stubbornly insisting on his 'ideal' as an immediate objective he jettisoned the possibility (many would say the probability) of his achieving his aim over time, through his rejection of constitutional offers and advances which the Turkish side would have been powerless to resist, and which they saw as inevitably leading to that same *enosis*, which was for them their doom.

In 1956 Lord Radcliffe was appointed to come out to Cyprus as a "Constitutional Commissioner" to make proposals for the introduction of elected representational self-government in the island. (He had, nine years previously, demarcated the boundary between the new states of India and Pakistan, following which the largely Moslem-populated Princely State of Kashmir had ended up as wholly in India.) The Archbishop had been thought by some to have been sensing a change in the British government's attitude to the island - believing that they might now be willing to be rid of their responsibilities there - and he appeared to judge that he could help them to implement what he took to be their intention. He had therefore agreed in late 1955 to talks with the Governor. These once more broke down - this time on the Archbishop's insistence, to which the Governor refused to yield, that responsibility for internal security should rest with the elected local government under any new constitution. (The *chutzpah* of this, from an archbishop - God save the mark - who was even then responsible for the mayhem of the EOKA campaign which was still under way, takes some beating.) Despite the collapse of these talks in Nicosia Lord Radcliffe still came out.

He announced that he was willing to receive written or oral submissions (in private if so desired), and these were forthcoming from many quarters - though not from the Ethnarchy. The Cyprus Turkish leadership naturally made its views abundantly clear. Among other views Radcliffe heard those of the communist ex-mayor of Limassol, Partassides. (These, and who shall blame him, were given by him at a private meeting arranged in the home of a third party, an Englishman.) I also asked for, and was given, permission to tell Lord Radcliffe what I thought. I saw him for certainly less than half an hour. What I said I do not recall. But it could only have been on the lines that any constitution which procured for the Turkish people of the island no more than paper assurances of 'minority rights' and, in particular, did not have some mechanism which *built in* safeguards to prevent a future unilateral adhesion of Cyprus to Greece would, in my judgement, have no long life. By 1956 the issue had begun to involve public opinion in Turkey; and I told him, as anecdotal evidence to this effect, of a recent episode there. Lalage and I had taken a short local leave in Istanbul, never having been to Turkey before. (Though a member of the Unified Service I was only entitled to a passage to England on alternate leaves.) A taxi-driver in Istanbul, understanding from my accent that I was from Cyprus, had refused to accept a fare - remarkable in any country from a taxi-driver - and had fulminated against the 'dirty dog'. This was a punning description, *pis köpek*, to signify the 'bishop', *piskopos*, the Turkish word, taken from the Greek, for the holder of that office.

In the event the Radcliffe proposals contained an internal inconsistency. These recognised that "Everyone knows that Cyprus is not homogeneous". Radcliffe went further: "The influences which make for separation between the communities are strong - religion, language, education, tradition and custom. [He didn't include in his list of "influences" the pernicious consequences of EOKA's murderous activities]. They are reflected by separate quarters for Greek and Turk: in the country by Turkish villages and Greek villages. On the other hand there is only a weak supply of unifying elements which would make for a general consciousness that all communities are Cypriot communities." But in a later, and crucially vital, passage Radcliffe dismissed the "claim put to me on behalf of the Turkish Cypriot community [for representation to be shared as equal partners with the Greek Cypriot community]. If I do not accept it *I do not think* [my italics] that it is out of any lack of respect for the misgivings that lie behind it ...... *either* it is consistent with the principles of a constitution based on liberal and democratic conceptions that political power should be balanced in this way, *or* no other means than the creation of such political equilibrium will be effective to protect the essential interests of the community from oppression by the weight of the majority. *I do not feel that I can stand firmly on either of these propositions*" (My italics). As later events were to demonstrate in the most devastating fashion, even the eventual provision of a constitution rooted in power-sharing, deriving from the principle of co-partnership, and structured to provide for this, was not to be proof against the concealed intention - later to be made horribly clear - of the majority to dismantle the constitution. And this for the precise purpose of destroying "the essential interests of the [Turkish] community", by removing the parts of that legal instrument which stood in their way, and by openly violating the provisions which expressly excluded both *enosis* and *taksim*. (This latter was 'partition', which by now, in 1956, had become the rallying cry of the Turkish side. As a counter to the incessant *"enosis kai monon enosis"* - 'enosis and only *enosis*' - the Turkish response had become *"Ya taksim ya ölüm"* - 'Either partition or death'.)

\*\*\*\*\*\*\*\*\*\*

Such was the dreadful climate of animosity, mistrust, fear and hatred (if indeed these latter two are not but different aspects of the same contagion) which had engulfed the island. And in that atmosphere Lalage and I now had anxiously to consider what future there was for us and our child in this new Cyprus. Our feelings were at one. It is idle for me now to speculate whether I might not have viewed things differently had I been unmarried and without having to think of a family. I *was*, and I *did* have to. We were both coming to the conclusion that whatever the future held for us, it was scarcely likely to be in a Cyprus where the two communities were being violently driven into themselves, and inflamed against each other in seemingly inescapable violence and counter violence.

\*\*\*\*\*\*\*\*\*\*

And then fate took a hand. My father's elder brother, the ex-judge from the Gold Coast, had, just before Lalage and I had got married, sold an area of land just to the north of Nicosia, which had become very valuable because of its potential for development. This had been the property of my late grandmother, the Mufti's wife, and had been inherited by her children. My brother and I had our equal shares in our father's inheritance from this land. At the time of our marriage Lalage and I had told her youngest, married, sister (the erstwhile 'brains of the family') that we would love to be able to buy a house in London near to theirs, as an investment and a possible future home. Now, three years later, out of the blue, we got a letter from her. There was an executor's sale of a house within walking distance of them, at a price we could just manage. What, asked Lalage's sister, was our decision? We made up our minds within the hour. Astonished at our own decisiveness, we telegraphed: "Please buy." In a matter of a week or so the sale was concluded, or as near as made no difference; and we knew we had a place of our own in London. But without a job in England? We made the further decision in a spirit of rashness which from any considered point of view must be thought to verge on madness. I resigned; and we made our arrangements to leave the island. Sir John and Lady Harding were kind and considerate enough to give us a

177

small, domestic farewell lunch. Early in 1957, in trepidation and hope, yet (in my case) with a heavy and burdened heart, we left.

\*\*\*\*\*\*\*\*\*\*

The next chapter of our life, in England, was significant - and not least by the gift of our second child, a much wished-for girl, who was born to us, in our own house, during this period. The arrival of our daughter was to be the only unalloyed joy we were to know in the coming months.

\*\*\*\*\*\*\*\*\*\*

Our time there was, indeed, to be rather in the nature of the 'short, sharp, shock' to be advocated for the country's delinquent youth some twenty years later by the benign Willie Whitelaw in Mrs Thatcher's first government. Short it was - only about eighteen months in London. Sharp, and a shock - in the dramatic impact of being jobless with a family; and a realisation pretty soon borne in on me that, in the job market, a foreign name was a grave disability.

\*\*\*\*\*\*\*\*\*\*

We were put up by Lalage's sister and husband in their house, which they owned with Ursula and which, as PGs, we now shared with them and their two small sons, while our own house was made habitable. The work included turning the basement into a self-contained flat (which, as will be seen, had its own, unforeseen, purpose in our story) for letting, so as to provide us with some income while I job-hunted. And a pretty dispiriting business I found that to be. Even then, before 'Commonwealth immigration' was seen as a problem of dire proportions - and indeed as it was to become, in political terms anyway, in the 1960s - an applicant for a job bearing a distinctly un-English name had a hard time of it. In commerce, in business, in local government - there seemed no prospect even of an interview. (I suppose in fairness it could have been that someone aiming to start at the bottom at the age of thirty-one wouldn't have been too well regarded in any event; and I had no other prospect save the bottom rung of a ladder.) After I can't recall how many months I eventually found work in a small printing firm. The *idea* of printing rather appealed to me, and I enjoyed learning about print processes and type-faces and that sort of thing. However, the craft of that trade was not something one could come in to from the outside - much less at my age. I was engaged on the sales side, and I was soon to discover that I was temperamentally not enough of an extrovert, go-getting type to make any sort of a success in that area - much less to enjoy it. Yet I was grateful that we now at least had an earned income.

**********

*I must get this down while it is still fresh with me. I had broken off to go for my daily walk, with the recollection of those days gloomily in my mind. I had stepped out of our small, snug flat right opposite the great west front of Salisbury cathedral, today the first of March, thirty eight years after that first experience in London as a father of a family. It is a bitingly cold day, yet the sky is both blue and full of slow-moving clouds bringing long intervals of bright sunshine. By the river I saw a duck accompanied by twelve tiny ducklings, who couldn't have been more than a day or two out of the egg. In the river and alongside in the meadow swam or waddled every sort of river bird - ducks of many kinds, geese, swans and their cygnets (as large as their parents but distinguishable by the brown flecks in their feathers), coots and moorhens. And on the magnolia trees colour breaking out from the tips of masses of buds. And overhead two pairs of swans flying slowly, low. At Harnham mill many more had gathered on the mill-pond by the bridge. Into my mind came the verse of the Turkish mystic, poet of the Unity of Existence and Being:*

This is a secret treasure, hid - what do Sufis seek to find?
Upon our lake, contentedly, sport water-fowl of *every* kind.

*The thought that those words of Yunus Emre written seven hundred years ago, and three thousand miles away, should resonate in me, today, here where three hundred years ago the English mystic George Herbert was the Vicar of Bemerton just down the road, is one of those*

179

**Young Bird**

*rare moments of perceived but undirected joy.*

**********

Whether I could, or would, have stuck it out as a print salesman must be very doubtful. I think it unlikely. But, as things turned out, my resolution was not put to the test. My sales area included the districts of Westminster and Victoria, and in Victoria Street was the modest office which the colonial Cyprus government maintained for its UK representative - I forget now his exact designation. I occasionally called on the then incumbent, who happened to be one of our slight acquaintances from Limassol days. He was a Greek Cypriot businessman, married to an English woman, who (possibly because he was regarded as insufficiently 'nationalist' by EOKA) had been appointed to the London office on contract. (It would, I think, have been from him I learnt also that a Greek Cypriot colleague of mine in the administration, married as it happened to a Scottish nurse, had under direct threat from EOKA resigned and been appointed on a temporary basis to the Information Department of the Commonwealth Relations Office in Whitehall.)

The sequence of events in my case is now hazy in my memory; but I remember that in conversation with the Cyprus government representative I was given more than an impression that great changes were afoot on the Cyprus front, both as regards the security situation and also in the political field. The exact details would not be germane, if indeed I could recall them; but the overall tenor was quite dramatic. On the security front it was clear that EOKA was more than contained - it had been penetrated and its offensive capacity was on the point of being broken. Politically there had been a switch from the die-hard pursuit of *enosis* to calls for 'independence'. In making this change Makarios had presumably been influenced by the representations of the British Labour Opposition (among whose proponents was Barbara Castle, who's acquaintance I was to make - so to speak - a few years on) which saw, or claimed to see, Cyprus as but one more simple case of a colonial territory seeking its future as a self-governing, independent, sovereign new member of the Commonwealth, and of the family of nations - an attitude with which the open objective of submerging

Cyprus into the Greek state would hardly sit comfortably. Mrs Castle's subsequent words in the Commons in October 1958 make an interesting contrast with those of Makarios a month earlier, though the latter were not to be known publicly till afterwards. She told Parliament, "The Archbishop cannot go on endlessly offering compromise after compromise, only to get snub after snub and insult after insult"- truly the demagogue in full flow. Makarios meanwhile had, in fact, revealed the truth in a letter to Grivas: *he* explained that his "proposal to Barbara Castle, though appearing to be a concession, constituted a tactic which the situation imposed". The later behaviour of Makarios was to make blindingly clear how he had become convinced that the terminal destination of *enosis* was only to be reached via the Clapham Junction of 'independence'. The ramifications and Byzantine complexity involved in analysing the course of events which followed are far beyond the scope of this personal narrative. But the security and political changes which had been taking place, as I understood them at that time - and depressed as I now was in England - seemed to put a new complexion on the possibilities through which there might just conceivably be a part for me in the coming developments.

And I was now hearing from Reddaway, through the Cyprus London Office, that the administration in Cyprus would be glad were I to return. But to what? For myself I was sufficiently disillusioned in England, and intrigued enough from what I was hearing, to be prepared to see whether, with an end to violence - the situation was not entirely unlike that in the initial stages of the cease-fire by the IRA which is in force as I write this today - there could be a genuine attempt by the leaders of the communities to make a go of a new order in the island, if that could be achieved. I was not optimistic. But I was prepared to test on the spot how things might be likely to work out: whether genuine independence was conceivably something the Greeks might show by their actions they wished to embrace, and if so what would be the possibilities of fashioning an accommodation between the two communities in a unique modern state which would preclude one side overwhelming the other and in due course obliterating it - as had happened to the Turks in Rhodes and Crete. Lalage, resignedly, and courageously, agreed with me to return on this venturesome and chancy basis.

## Young Bird

\*\*\*\*\*\*\*\*\*\*

In the spring of 1958 I went out to Cyprus. Lalage, with the children, followed some weeks later, having managed to let our London house, furnished, to American tenants. I meanwhile had obtained possession, as tenant of my uncle, who was now in Hong Kong, of the old house in Nicosia (our home in the old Froebel school days) which he had now inherited from grandmother. There we came to live - opposite my mother, who continued to live on her own in her house backing on to the Ledra Palace hotel.

\*\*\*\*\*\*\*\*\*\*

I was now again in the Secretariat under John Reddaway, who had become in effect the Colonial Secretary (though under the new Emergency structures brought in by Harding he was now designated Administrative Secretary). I was also separately appointed as the Clerk of the Governor's Executive Council.

A few months earlier, in December 1957 - the month after our daughter was born - a new Governor had been appointed. This was Sir Hugh Foot - the father of the now well-known Paul, and brother of Michael - and the rest. Much was to happen over the next two years; but the essence of the story can be told quite shortly. For some six months the island was to be quiet - no killings or violence. In that respect the parallel with the current Irish situation continued. The similarity of the two situations lay in the fact that the men of violence may have put away their weapons and munitions, but they had not surrendered them. Indeed in the Cyprus case, unlike the Irish one, there had been no formal declaration of an end to violence - not even under some cagily worded formula.

But by far the greatest portent for the future as I saw it, compared with the position in the island since I had left it some eighteen months before, was the change which now occurred on the international scene and the possibility of this being reflected in the island.

\*\*\*\*\*\*\*\*\*\*

Foot had arrived with a new outline plan, which he had sold to the Colonial Office in London. The details of that plan are not so important as the fact that by now all concerned (except possibly the Archbishop himself) seemed well aware that there was now no conceivable chance of achieving any kind of settlement, much less a lasting one, without the full and open support of the Turkish, as well as the Greek, government. The fact had to be faced that, in the later jargon of such inter-ethnic and national conflicts, there was a Turkish 'dimension' to Cyprus, as well as the previous and continuing Greek one.

The Turkish proverb says: "If your opponent is an ant, treat him as though he were an elephant." Hitherto over the Cyprus issue the Greeks had reversed this *mot*: they had chosen to see the Turkish elephant as being in the position of an ant - to be ignored or brushed aside as insignificant. But now, especially since the Radcliffe proposals, the Turkish government too had become uneasy and apprehensive. Those proposals may have been abortive but they had seemed to carry a hint that for this first time Britain might be seriously tempted to 'do a Palestine'. Cyprus was not, as Palestine had been, a UN Trust Territory over which Britain had not technically exercised sovereignty, but it was not necessarily less likely that she might withdraw from this 'colonial' island, in just the same way as she had relinquished her 'trusteeship' responsibility in Palestine, were she to judge this to be in her own best interests (the criterion, after all, on which every state ultimately makes its foreign policy decisions). So long as Britain stood as a safeguard against Cyprus's becoming a part of Greece, Turkey for her part was content to leave to her the burden of coping with Cyprus and the Archbishop. But were that safeguard to vanish, then Turkey's own best interests dictated that the island, a mere forty miles from her southern shore and controlling the approaches to Iskenderun and Mersin, should not pass into the hands of a state, Greece, which, for all that it was a fellow member of NATO was no more friendly towards her, to put it dispassionately, than the two fellow-Commonwealth members, India and Pakistan, who had been in a virtual state of armed hostility ever since their creation, were towards each other. Turkey's interest in the matter was far from being merely the well-being, even the survival as such, of the Turkish people of the island. The crucial issue for Turkey was her strategic position, which determined her national security. It is by no means out of place to emphasise this aspect here - it is directly relevant to the way things were to work out and to affect the lives of those whose story I am trying to tell. And it is especially relevant to point to this dimension of the matter now, more than twenty years after that year - 1974 - which so many people today seem to imagine was Turkey's first interest and involvement with Cyprus this century.

The 'Foot Plan' was, in effect, but one more scheme for introducing self-government without making an effort or attempt to grasp the nettle of where any self-government might, indeed would be likely to, lead. And *enosis* as such was in no way excluded (though nor for that matter was *taksim.*) Serious demonstrations now broke out in the Turkish quarter of Nicosia. Ominous in itself, this reaction to the 'Foot Plan' was made more so by the strong implication that the Turkish Resistance Organisation (TMT), which had come into existence as a counter to EOKA, had evolved into a well-controlled body capable of acting in a concerted fashion. EOKA, too, resumed its operations; and very soon Cyprus was to witness the worst excesses of any period. There seemed no chance of the Greek and Turkish governments playing a part in moderating the passions of their communities on the island - if anything rather the reverse.

At this critical juncture the Macmillan government in London now took the initiative. A statement to Parliament in June included for the first time amongst the express aims of the British government "to achieve a permanent settlement acceptable to the two communities in the island and to the Greek and Turkish governments." This was official acknowledgement of both the Greek *and* the Turkish 'dimensions'; and this was underlined by a public invitation to each of the two governments "to appoint a representative to cooperate with the Governor." From the Turkish-Cypriot point of view the most momentous departure was in the introductory part of the statement to Parliament - to the effect that the British government's "new policy represents an adventure in partnership - partnership between the communities in the Island and also between the Governments of the United Kingdom, Greece and Turkey."

It was to be six more months before the dramatic breakthrough came in December 1958. And in that period fighting continued between the two communities - indeed reached terrible proportions. So much so that even the Prime Ministers of Greece and Turkey now called on their communities to end what was on the verge of becoming outright war. It was in this climate that things suddenly and most dramatically changed. I still clearly remember Foot coming in to begin a meeting of the Ex.Co. and announcing that the Foreign Ministers of Greece and Turkey, Averoff and Zorlu, had met and worked out the outline of a settlement (which was soon to be endorsed by their two governments, and then formally agreed by all three governments in London in February, 1959). The true nature and complexity of Cyprus had finally been acknowledged and acted upon by these three directly concerned governments. It was not, *pace* Barbara Castle, a simple issue of a single people exercising a right to self-determination, nor of a territory colonised by the metropolitan power now moving, in simple order, through the usual processes of internal self-government to its emergence as a homogeneous sovereign state. The status of Cyprus was conditioned by an intensely complex and intricate set of factors, and was deeply enmeshed in a history in which religion, in its most maleficent manifestations, had - to use this word in its truly literal sense - bedevilled things.

\*\*\*\*\*\*\*\*\*\*

And now it remained to see if, having recognised the reality, all the parties had the genuine wish and the will to make the proposed 'partnership' work. Within the island two developments now proceeded *pari passu*. The first was concerned with the normal day to day governance of the island - however one might then construe normality. And, concurrently, work proceeded on the task of delineating in detail the principles and, in consonance with these, the drafting of the legal instruments with which Cyprus was now to shed its 'colonial' status and join the family of nations.

I was involved only in the first of these activities. The second was the function of a series of 'Joint Committees', the membership of which was drawn not just from the two communities of the island but also, significantly, from specialists in constitutional law in Greece and

Turkey. The Cyprus members naturally included, amongst others, the Solicitor General, Criton Tornaritis (that landlord of our first married home in Limassol, not all that long ago, though it seemed a generation past, so much had the scene, and the very air of the island, changed from that at the beginning of the same decade).

When Foot had brought to Ex. Co. the news of the outcome of that momentous meeting between the Turkish and Greek Foreign Ministers, he had added that HMG would have no difficulty in accepting whatever those two governments were to agree between themselves as to the future of Cyprus. Despite what has subsequently been claimed by the partisans of the different sides, what is incontrovertible is not only that the essence, and much of the content, of the eventual Zurich and London accords received the signed agreements of all the three governments in 1959 but, and as importantly, that the detailed formulations embodying all this were the joint endeavours of the most senior officials of the island's two communities, supported by experts from the two 'mother' countries, specifically provided for the purpose by those two outside governments. There was no question of these detailed arrangements having been foisted on the peoples of Cyprus by outsiders, without they themselves having played a direct part in the working out of those details. The huge question of course remained: how genuine was the 'agreement' in Athens, in Ankara, and - most vitally - in the archbishopric in Nicosia? So far as Lalage and I were concerned, this was indeed the crucial question.

\*\*\*\*\*\*\*\*\*\*

It was in the context of the 'on-going' conduct of the island's internal administration that my feelings, my fears, as to what the future held for the people of the island, and for us, began to crystallise into an ever-increasing despondency and foreboding.

\*\*\*\*\*\*\*\*\*\*

There is contemporary evidence of my extreme pessimism at that time. This evidence I have remembered, and got out, to remind myself of it. At the back of my copy of Gunnis's *Historic Cyprus*, which I have

186

mentioned before, there is a map showing all the villages of the island. Some time in 1959 I had used a system to make clearly visible the distribution of the island's population as between the Greeks and the Turks: a dot represented ten inhabitants - blue for Greeks and red for Turks. I see that I didn't actually succeed in completing the whole map; but even on the basis of what the south-western part of the island revealed I had tentatively pencilled in several possible lines of a conceivable partition of Cyprus intended as a division which would produce a separation with the *least worst* likely dislocation of populations who might be likely to want to move to areas under their majority control. I had not then envisaged an actual agreed transfer of populations, as had followed the end of the fighting between Turkey and Greece in Anatolia in the early twenties. And I had never even remotely thought that violent expulsions would ever become deliberate acts of policy, as we have since seen in what was once Yugoslavia. I suppose I must have been thinking, at worst, of the way whole populations had moved across the 'Radcliffe boundary' between the new states of India and Pakistan a bare dozen years earlier, acting under the dreadful impulse of fear. The line of separation which I had pencilled in more than thirty-five years ago - and fifteen years before the attempt by the Greeks to achieve (through a violent *coup* in 1974) that *enosis* which was frustrated by the action of the Turkish government - show that the one I thought preferable, on the criterion I have described, was almost the same as the one which now divides Cyprus between the Greek south and the Turkish north. The only difference is that my line does not include on the Turkish side the salient running southwards to the east of Nicosia and the area contiguous with the UK Sovereign Base Area of Dhekelia. The map at the back of that book has never been seen by anyone but Lalage and myself.

It was not that, in those days of 1959, I believed the constitutional framework (which was largely public knowledge) was *on paper* in any way inadequate. Very much the contrary. The solid foundation of the new republic was to be the clearly accepted principle of a partnership between the two peoples, inside and outside the island; and this was the best of all auguries for a new era in their relations between populations whose well-being demands that they should build their futures in true cooperation, and not in enmity - much less in duplicity. From the Turkish point of view the soundest of safeguards

187

against some fanatic - and there will always be such who detest the very idea of peaceful accommodation - trying to upset these delicate arrangements, lay in the new republic's birth being underwritten by a tripartite Treaty of Guarantee signed by Britain, Greece and Turkey. Any reservations or doubts about the future should, in theory, have been allayed, if not completely dissipated, by these carefully constructed arrangements, painstakingly crafted by the Greek Cypriots and Turkish Cypriots with the full support and assistance of the two mainland governments. Why, therefore, was I becoming more and more filled with hopelessness and fear for the future when this theoretically best of all possible compromises appeared to have evolved out of the ghastly enmities of the past?

\*\*\*\*\*\*\*\*\*\*

It is hard to think myself back to that time. It is, rather, impossible. And in any case the attempt would be as pointless as it would be fruitless. For it comes to me ever more strongly that the course of my life has been determined not so very much by carefully reasoned decisions on my part. If it has not been fate which has ruled me (and I am far from convinced that such 'fate', or providence, is not a reality - though operating in ways I cannot even begin to grasp), my life seems to have been governed, in no small part, less by decisions I have taken through reasoning things out than by my acting ultimately on impulse - by a kind of feeling, or sense, that a particular action is called for.

I have a photograph which shows a group of men sitting round the outside of a horse-shoe shaped table. This was taken by the Information Department at the first meeting of an expanded Executive Council in the summer or early autumn of 1959. The body was a sort of extra-constitutional organ which served as an interim 'Council of Ministers' under the chairmanship of the Governor. Its members consisted of Makarios, Dr Kuchuk - the leader of the Turkish Cypriots - together with half a dozen Greek Cypriots and half that number of Turkish Cypriots. This body's weekly meetings were intended as an apprenticeship in their future responsibilities for those who were to be, respectively, President and Vice-President of the new Republic, and the holders of the various portfolios in the coming government.

188

The outcome of the elections due, at that stage, to be held in January 1960, was already taken to be a foregone conclusion. Hardly surprisingly. It might even be considered as an entirely natural consequence of the years through which the people had lived. That the new constitution was to provide for a Greek President and a Turkish Vice-President was of course known. It therefore made sense that the coming holders of these two offices should, in advance, select their ministers so that they might make a start in gaining some practical experience in government.

Two Secretaries served this 'council'; one Greek and one Turkish. I was the latter. Week by week I saw regularly all its members. And at close quarters - the chamber where meetings took place was barely fifteen feet wide and about twenty-five long. My desk was only slightly more than an arm's length behind and to the right of Makarios. Foot had him on his right, with Kuchuk on his other side. Two of the future Greek ministers were known EOKA terrorists. One, the prospective Minister of the Interior, was some ten years into the future to engineer an unsuccessful assassination of his President - and Archbishop - at a time when the Greek community was violently split between extreme rightist, rightist, and leftist supporters of *enosis*. He was himself successfully assassinated shortly after his own failed attempt.

**********

Continuous close proximity with people of this kidney worked its effect. It was borne in on me, and not too gradually, that an island ruled by such as these would be absolutely unendurable.

**********

It is only too easy to slip into the sanctimonious language of the prig. We are all touched by evil. And, even proverbially, people's individual proclivities for ill, our own particular propensities, seem quite often to embody an affinity to a larger group. 'Honour among thieves'; and in the Turkish, 'A crow doesn't peck out another crow's eyes'. Even so, and however priggish it may appear, I can only say that, in retrospective remembrance, I felt myself to be not just without a part in this

189

'collective', but in a very palpable way as utterly apart from it. "Evil", as a word, is to my mind not one which can usefully be used to define humans collectively as a way of conveying any very precise meaning. But that word does have a place in the language as it is commonly used. It comes to my tongue now when I call to mind that bearded figure bearing the title of Archbishop. Perhaps, in less theological language than is implied in the use of 'evil', I can convey the effect his presence had on me by saying only that he, especially, came over as baleful, baneful and utterly noxious. I should need a thesaurus to search for words which might better serve to make known the revulsion he produced in me then. Inside that chamber I felt the sinister air of an intolerable malevolence.

At these meetings there was a complete absence of even the slightest evidence from Makarios (and little enough from his colleagues) in word or demeanour, to suggest an intention sincerely to work in true cooperation, much less in partnership, with the Turkish side. There was no sign even of respect for their separate existence. I was left in no doubt at all upon the crucial point. On assuming office the President of the Republic, would be required to swear to uphold its constitution, including those provisions which excluded *enosis* (as well of course as *taksim*).

There had always been an inherent contradiction between such a Presidential oath and the one Makarios had, quite gratuitously, sworn on becoming Archbishop ten years before. One or other of these oaths he could not avoid having to forswear (a dilemma he could have avoided simply by eschewing political office and merely remaining Archbishop - a course he did not choose to take). The question, for, me was simple: on which of his two oaths would he decide to perjure himself - as perjure himself he infallibly must. Watching him - he hardly ever opened his mouth - at those weekly meetings, I *knew,* if not exactly instinctively, perhaps instinctually, which oath would be the occasion for him to dishonour his sworn word. The oath he would jettison would be his Presidential one to maintain and preserve a Republic founded on co-partnership and guaranteed by international treaty.

At school, seventeen years earlier, I had had imprinted on my sixteen year-old mind words from *Hamlet,* which I had then taken with no more seriousness than I had the famously bathetic "Exit pursued by a bear" in *A Winter's Tale*. Now, as I looked on Makarios as the weeks passed, I understood, precisely - and not just mentally - the depths of Hamlet's coldly perceptive, "Meet it is I set it down, that one may smile, and smile, and be a villain." The republic about to be born would, I concluded, very soon succumb to Makarios's solicitous care. In the terms of the Turkish proverb, from such a 'head' the Cyprus republican 'fish' must inevitably, and all too soon, begin to 'stink' - and that abominably. And end in the decay of corruption.

\*\*\*\*\*\*\*\*\*\*

I told Foot that Lalage and I found it impossible to contemplate the prospect of living, and of bringing up our children, in this poisonous atmosphere. And I said, too, that I was convinced that the new Cyprus was doomed: Makarios would sooner or later bring about the destruction of the carefully worked out constitutional provisions which stood in the way of his being able to neutralise the Turks and so secure his goal of *enosis*. I therefore wished to leave before the republic even came into existence. He was good enough to try to dissuade me; but accepted that I was not to be moved. He did not rebut what I had said. Refute it he could not.

\*\*\*\*\*\*\*\*\*\*

And so, at the beginning of January 1960, embarking on a new life, we left Cyprus for the second time - intending never to see it again. Mother stayed.

# PART V : TAKING FLIGHT

(1960-1980)

# ~9~
# London; Ottawa

Writing today it comes to me that, over the past few years, I have seen on television at least half a dozen well-known people (as it happens most of them politicians) standing before the cameras, and putting on as brave a face as they can manage, as they make a clean breast of their affair with a mistress whom they have decided to discard. And, so far as is in my memory, the scene is nearly always shot with the betrayed wife standing beside her husband, giving him her support - either in words or, more often, in dignified silence. This scene is before me now, with some pain. Presumably this swims up out of my unconscious because my inner self perceives here some parallel with my own situation when Lalage and I made the decision finally to cut adrift from Cyprus. In truth the decision had been mine, and Lalage's part had been to sustain me with her support - a support more than willingly given. For I too had in effect determined to ditch a mistress. My infatuation with Cyprus - and the thing was little, if at all, less than just that - throughout the whole of our seven years of marriage must have been for Lalage as though her husband was carrying on a wretched love affair - even if it wasn't with another woman.

The end of patience is salvation. So the Turkish proverb has it. And so it now seemed to be. We looked towards a future in which our life together would reveal new meanings in England, after I had severed my bonds with a Cyprus for which I had once conceived such a deep attachment. Just as when a man abandons the human mistress he once thought he had loved above all else, when the separation from Cyprus came it needed no judicial or formal procedures. The analogy is, after all, not with a divorce. It was, in the end, essentially a matter of judgement - and will. And what ultimately weighs heaviest in the balance is the realisation that the family - wife and children - come first. That was certainly how it was with us: a judgement of what

194

would be for the best for us all. For myself it seems to me now that once again an outcome was finally being determined not so much by cold reasoning as by my feelings in the matter. Judged in this way there was no shadow of doubt that the decision was the right one - though it was clouded with anxiety as, without a job, I looked to the future.

My attitude towards the mistress was, however, less clearly defined. The sense of having betrayed a woman must inevitably bring terrible pain - perhaps even tear the betrayer apart. My betrayal - if it was truly to be considered in that light - did not bring me such grief. Yet I had to contend with a sense that I could properly be open at least to reproach, or at least recrimination. I count myself fortunate that at no time did anyone ever cause me to know that bitter taste.

***********

In London we were again put up (I had almost said 'put up with') by our forbearing relations, since our own house was still let. It suited our tenants, as indeed it also suited us, that they should remain in occupation until the coming December, still nearly a year away. With nine children (four each from their previous spouses, and one new arrival) they didn't want the upheaval of a search for another tenancy - a proceeding which would have been likely to be protracted - before they were due to return to America. And we needed the income produced by the furnished letting of our house.

It was now that fortune smiled on us, bringing a double benediction. We, too, needed to rent somewhere to live as a family; and our finances nowhere near stretched to this, the rent from our own house being essentially our means of sustenance. The incumbent of the parish church was about to vacate the living. The vicarage was a comfortable Victorian house, more or less midway between our house and Lalage's sisters' where we were living. The church council decided that during the coming interregnum, rather than leave the premises unoccupied they would let the first floor as a flat (the upper floor already being let). We were very lucky in getting it at a very affordable rent - though our tenancy was precarious, as it would only last until a new vicar was appointed. (As it turned out the new appointment wasn't made until just after our tenants had let us have our own house back.)

During the months that we lived in the vicarage flat there were to be sporadic visits from the departed vicar's relatives who came to take now this, now that piece of furniture which was to go to them. The vicar was good enough to arrange for these occasions in consultation with us so that we didn't actually have to face chairs, tables or beds being whisked out from under us; but all the same these visitations, bringing something of the atmosphere of the the bailiff's men in a pantomime, did rather heighten the sensation of instability which hung over our new life in England. But by the end of the year we were at least safely back in our own home. And even before then the black cloud of real uncertainty and foreboding about earning a living no longer hung over us. For providence's second great gift had also arrived.

While we were still living in the flat, I got a message from the Commonwealth Relations Office. (This, with its acronym of CRO - and not to be confused with the Criminal Records Office as has, on rare occasions, happened - was the Whitehall Department concerned with United Kingdom relations with independent commonwealth countries, corresponding to the Foreign Office's similar responsibility towards foreign countries.) I had been recommended by the Governor in Cyprus - where the government was still the pre-independence colonial administration - for interview.

In fact I had three successive interviews, the last being with the Under-Secretary, Head of Establishment. The atmosphere was cordial, even friendly. What was being considered was my suitability for an appointment as a temporary, unestablished, Assistant Principal with a view to my going for the Competitive Examination at an early date. At which of these interviews it was I do not now recall, but one of my interlocutors observed, "You know, Mr Faiz, your name would be a problem for us." At that moment it did not - perhaps fortunately - enter my mind that my erstwhile colleague in Cyprus, with the resoundingly Greek name of "Papadopoulos", had seemingly not presented to the CRO a corresponding difficulty - even admitting that his first name had been transmogrified from 'Achilevs' to 'Achilles'. But even had that parallel occurred to me then, I rather doubt that I would have made the acerbic point to my interviewer. And it was not till several years later that I was to become aware of a Permanent Secretary at the Foreign Office - its most senior official - who rejoiced in the somewhat less than Anglo-Saxon surname of Caccia; and also to learn of another luminary of the same Department of State, who was to become British Ambassador to Japan, under the name of Cortazzi. As it happened, with the experience of my job-hunting in England those few years earlier, I had already been allowing my mind to dwell on the idea of changing my name. Having now determined to make my home in England for good and to bring up my children here, it was at least arguable that there was little point in maintaining the gratuitous impediment of an exotic name. With the additional spur of the ungracious comment - indeed the implied warning - of the CRO official, I now resolved to anglicise my name. I did so, by deed poll, and in the simplest manner possible - with the substitution of an 'r' for the final 'z'. The single letter change had the advantage that I did not need to alter my signature, since its last letter was in any case capable of being read either way. So it was that I joined the CRO as A.S. Fair.

I hadn't needed to consider the expedient which had reputedly been canvassed, a generation earlier, of the son of the once famous 'Mr Five per cent'. Nubar Gulbenkian was the son of the multi-millionaire Armenian oil tycoon whose wealth derived from his share in the oil concession - granted by the Ottoman Sultan Abdul Hamid over the fields which became the Iraq Petroleum Company - in the largely non-Arab part of what is now Iraq, retained by Britain within that new state's borders when it was created after the 1914-18 War. The younger Gulbenkian, educated at Harrow, and a keen social rider to hounds, had a decidedly un-English appearance, heightened as it was by his Assyrian-style spade beard. Added to which he is said to have liked to appear, even on horseback, sporting a wholly uncustomary exotic button-hole. So foreign did he look indeed, that when a friend suggested he anglicise his name - as it might be to 'Gullibanks' - the latter is said to have replied that he would first need to change his name to something else, like 'Robinson'. "For," he observed, "if I were to be introduced to anyone as 'Gullibanks', the inevitable response would be: 'Oh! And what was it before that?'" My outward form at least hadn't called for such a double subterfuge.

The period of waiting for the CRO's decision after my interviews seemed to last an age. Was it as much as a couple of months before I heard? Immense was our relief when a letter arrived from Whitehall to tell me that I had been accepted. My rank was to be the lowest in the Administrative Class - an Assistant Principal, normally the grade of an applicant who comes in straight from the university, on probation. In my case, not having entered through the Competitive Examination, I was taken on by way of temporary appointment to the 'unestablished' staff. Whether there was then, or has been since, another *Temporary* Assistant Principal I have no idea; but it would be a good deal less than accurate if I were to say that, at the age of thirty-four, even in such a capacity, it was merely happiness which I felt in joining the CRO. It needs little effort for me today to recapture the great sense of peace, of entering calm waters after being buffeted by the tempest outside the harbour wall, when I knew that I had been appointed.

However, in order to make the move from a temporary appointment to join the permanent establishment of the Office I would have to compete in the usual entry examination. This was not the one for normal first entry into the service. An 'over age' exam had been introduced, which attracted the candidature, amongst others, of an increasing number of people whose careers in the Colonial Service were coming to an end earlier than had been anticipated. This was the time of Harold Macmillan's 'wind of change' speech in South Africa (still then a member of the Commonwealth). The number of ex-colonies, especially in Africa, joining the ranks of the independent members of the Commonwealth was rapidly growing. As the Whitehall Department dealing with the United Kingdom's relations with these new independent Commonwealth countries, the CRO also needed to augment its own staff. Some came from a contracting Colonial Office; but the way was opened for a small number from outside Whitehall by way of competitive examination.

I had one, unsuccessful, attempt at this examination which consisted of a three-part selection process. The first stage was a written exam lasting, I think, a full day. I remember that a part of this was a long essay on a small choice of subjects, and that I chose to deal with the issue which was then a topic of much controversy - the Penguin publication of *Lady Chatterley's Lover*. My treatment of this I have

198

forgotten; but I suspect it was in the nature of 'on the one hand ... yet, on the other...' The written paper was followed by a three-day series of tests, interviews, mock committee meetings, and similar. Lastly there was the interview before the full Selection Board. It was at this hurdle that I fell. It may have been some six months or so later that I appeared before the Selection Board a second time: same chairman, different members - as the chairman was kind enough, quite jovially, to tell me as I took my seat. (Apart from the chairman I would certainly not have recognised any of what, to my exaggerated imagination, seemed to be about two dozen intimidating characters now facing me.) When I had presented myself to my first Board, my morale had been stiffened by the knowledge of my having just successfully taken the fences of the first two stages of the competition; and the very fact of my being on the staff of the C.R.O., even if unestablished, had also no doubt helped to bolster me. Yet I had been nervous. And I suspect that I had overcompensated for this by adopting a false air of confidence, which probably conveyed an impression of one rather too full of himself. So while I remember almost nothing of the substance of either of my appearances before these two Selection Boards, I do recall being rather more subdued at the second one. Whether or not this change of demeanour, to something closer to a natural manner, played any important part in the outcome I cannot know. But this time I passed.

It is, proverbially, better to travel hopefully than to arrive. I had not - consciously anyway - been embarked on a journey, or had thought of myself as travelling. Yet I now felt myself as having arrived. Quite where, or what, I had reached I only now try to establish in my mind as I look back today - at twice the age I was then. I had attained a haven. My wife and I were now in our own home. My employment was secure in a job to which I felt I was suited, in a country of which I had fond memories going back to my childhood. We could look forward to a future which would enable us to bring up our own children in a stable and secure atmosphere so utterly different from that which we had left behind and which I dreaded would, sooner or later, bring tragedy on the land of my birth - a country I no longer regarded as my own. It was, I think, not so much joy, or even happiness, which filled me; rather I was overwhelmed with thankfulness, with gratitude. It would be plain truth - I couldn't call it 'simple' truth - to say I was conscious of the meaning of the word 'blessing': at least in the way it was once used in what is now the seemingly outmoded saying "count your blessings". Much of this could I suppose be in the nature of what was conveyed by something an Armenian woman had once said to my mother, as she was to tell me a number of years later when she too came to live in London. The actual words, in Turkish, have an aural impact, through assonance, which is lost in translation: *Doğduğun yer değil, doyduğun yer vatandır* 'Not where you are born, but where you are replete is your homeland'.

But what is it to be replete? Perhaps it is the sensation of completeness - but in the grosser mode of completion to excess. Not in fact just satisfaction, but rather satiety - over-satisfaction. Yet in my case my feelings were somehow clouded by a sense not of satiety but, oddly, of something missing - of *in*completeness. I am reminded of a colleague with whom I shared a room in the CRO. Not infrequently, as we would be descending the staircase to the main door at the end of the day, he would suddenly stop - pondering whether or not he had locked his safe. He would then go all the way back, to find - more often than not - that his safe had been secure all the time. What moved him to act in this way was, to use his own phrase, *un sentiment d'incomplitude*. My own sense, or feeling, of incompleteness was something different, the nature of which I was only to discover and understand many years afterwards.

There is a passage in Harry Williams's book *The True Wilderness* where he is discussing the nature of pagan society in the early Roman Empire: "In the ancient world, social and religious life were inextricably interwoven. Religion was not thought of as a private matter ... at the meal libations would be offered to the gods and if you were there it would be next to impossible for you not to participate in the ceremony. Imagine today a person who thought blood sports wicked cooped up in a house-party assembled for shooting, and you can get an idea of what it meant to be a Christian in a pagan society. *You were a complete outsider*" (my italics). Those words were written in 1965 (but I was not to read them for another twenty years). At that period we were still living when Christianity - at least the Church of England - was not, as compared with Islam, generally conceived as being "inextricably interwoven" with day-to-day life. Nor, however, was it then so marginalised as it has since become. It was still the case that the generality of the people of this country - or so it seemed to me - in some way cohered, and felt themselves to *belong*, almost palpably, to a society or body in some way 'Christian'. Certainly such had been the England I had known during my experience of it up to that point. It was an England in which the non-Christian was by no means 'one of us'. I still sensed myself not as being a part *of*, but apart *from*. And I wanted to belong. In a different context, and to make a separate point, Harry Williams goes on to say that people often "seek to save their life [through a blind adherence] not because after examination and trial they have found orthodoxy true but because it gives them an immediate protection, like a mother's arms, and saves them from the danger of standing [in a religious context] on their own feet. *But by seeking to save their life they really lose it*" (my italics).

Feeling now that in my new life I needed really to *belong*, completely, I decided to take the final step. I resolved to join Lalage in her membership of the Anglican community. The vicar was an understanding man. I told him that I found powerfully attractive the teaching of the great man, the great prophet, whose words had come to us in the three synoptic gospels; but that I could not in honesty say that I accepted - if indeed I understood - the credal formularies, and the dogmas, which were enshrined in Christianity. These were beyond me. I was in two minds even whether Elizabeth the First's formulation was merely evasive or an expression of agnostic faith when, of the Communion, she said: "His the word, he spake it; his the bread, he brake it; and what that word doth make it - that I receive and take it." But in that latter spirit - and letting my heart not my head decide - I made my act of will.

\*\*\*\*\*\*\*\*\*\*

Out of the mists of the past there comes to me a memory - a recollection of a line of sophistry intended to make a logical, or possibly philosophical, point the exact nature of which now eludes me:

"How many hairs on the upper lip constitute a moustache?" Does one hair? Obviously not. One on either side? Just as evidently, no again. Then, two hairs on each side? And so on by successive

201

increases. "But clearly at some point the totality of hairs does indeed constitute a moustache, doesn't it? Why, yes - but what is the line on one side of which is the state of *'moustache existent'* and on the other the contrary state of *'moustache non-existent'* ?"

Whatever it was that this process of reasoning was intended to illuminate, it comes to me now as I reflect on my state of mind as it was those many years ago when, in deep contentment and thankfulness, we lived in London.

If that elusive thing *happiness* can be said to come into being - to have objective existence - I suppose it might perhaps be defined as a state of contentment born of the realisation that all the things have been attained which a person may have consciously and reasonably desired. To believe that life has really no more to offer. By this subjective, and selfish, yardstick I was, in my thirty-fifth year, very happy indeed. But over the next fifteen years or so a process was to take place which was to bring me to the knowledge that if, as Edith Cavell was reported to have discovered before her execution as a spy in the first World War, "patriotism is not enough", this was equally true of happiness - at any rate in the way in which I had conceived it to be. And I was also to learn that just as what is not a moustache moves imperceptively to become what quite definitely *is* one, so also does the state of seeming happiness transmute into complacency as one moves not across a boundary line but rather through a terrain like the misnamed "Green Line "in Cyprus, which is in reality a strip of territory, wider or narrower at different points, separating the two parts of the island. Between the one and the other there is a state of unreal being.

In Cyprus I had foolishly thought I had found "Shangri-la", an earthly paradise. Inevitably, and properly, that fantasy had been dispelled. Direct and prolonged experience of the place had shown me how false was the idealised picture I had created in my mind. Reality had replaced myth to take its rightful place. I was yet to learn, again through experience, that other truth - that life itself is in its essence constant change. Even to look for stability will lead inescapably to disappointment - and worse. Just so will a deliberate seeking after happiness. It has seemed to me that happiness does not come with stability but with the capacity to find peace in adjusting to the inescapable mutability of the human condition. The constancy which we generally all yearn for is there, but it is to be found in the flux of our lives and those of others - and in ways unthought. It was to be nearly twenty years before I was to come across, and feel the truth of, what a late 18th century Turkish poet had expressed:

*Life's skill in this subsists - to find our happiness in this world's pain;*
*So come Creation's sufferings and joys - to go, and come, again.*

This it seems to me is what Yeats is giving us, but in direr language, with his "foul rag and bone shop of the heart". What I had longed for in coming to England from Cyprus was happiness in a stable society. And that, I believe, we surely found, according to our understanding at that time. But stability is relative not only to place but to the pace of the ineluctable change and development which is kneaded into the very matter of all human societies and institutions. I had yet to learn for myself that where there is no dynamism there is death.

We were living in the the Britain of the Macmillan years. It is fashionable to mock, either as political chicanery or bland complacency, or indeed as blind obtuseness, the claim then made that during those years the people of this country had "never had it so good". But when due allowance is made for the need to qualify broad generalities, it does seem to me as I look back that, by and large, the people of Britain at that time did indeed have much more reason to be satisfied with their way of life, by comparison both with the lot of the generations which had just been left behind and indeed with that of my fellow citizens today in these islands. And for none do I think this is more true than for the young. As the father of a young family in the early sixties I viewed the future with eager expectation; and as the years unfolded there seemed to be very good reason to hope that the coming generation of young people had before them the prospect of a better society, a better world. There was hope in the air. And there was money in the pockets of the young - as was to be seen in the way the burgeoning advertising industry aimed its campaigns, for the first time, at this new moneyed market.

## Taking Flight

But I veer away now from seeming to be embarking on an *Anatomy of Britain* in the mode of Anthony Sampson. This is not an attempt at a grand panorama of an era such as that produced in drama form in Noel Coward's *Cavalcade*, nor as magisterially presented in Noel Annan's detailed survey *Our Age*. I am trying simply to give an account of one person's memories over a lifetime of seventy years. And yet, as I look back to marshal my formless thoughts about my life over the past thirty and more years I am forced to the recognition, more and more, that it is misleading, if not impossible, to tell a personal story in isolation from the general changes of an evolving society. The changes through which we were to live were stressful. Not only in Britain but practically everywhere people are, as we approach the end of the 20th century, witnessing a profoundly different world from that of a generation ago. Each of us who has lived through those times will make his or her own judgement of what the impact has been on them. The changes which affected me will, I hope, emerge as I try to continue with my story.

The pattern of our lives was mundane: the very antithesis of the Chinese curse "May you live in interesting times". I, like scores of thousands of other young professionals, fathers of families, travelled daily to and from work - in my case going to Whitehall, by bus or underground as the whim took me - in the role of breadwinner. (And how archaic the word, and the very concept, now seems - even to me.) Lalage, also in the manner of the time, ran the home, took our young seven year old son to and from the local junior school, and looked after our three year old daughter (soon to be helped in all this by a series of - what was, as yet, a new institution - *au pair* girls. And extremely lucky we were with these). I'm not sure now whether in 1960 people still worked on Saturday mornings, but even before the arrival at about that time of the five-day working week, the British 'weekend', devoted to hobbies and domesticity, was a strong feature of nearly everyone's life. We took great advantage of the many opportunities London affords for the pleasure, and instruction, of children (and of parents): the Science Museum, the Victoria and Albert Museum, Kensington Gardens - unchanged as it seemed from my infancy - Hyde Park, Holland Park, with the newly built Commonwealth Institute (unkindly likened to 'the Tokyo Municipal Baths'), Kew Gardens. The list is almost endless. You may characterise our existence according to your own viewpoint: conventional, complacent, bourgeois, or just boring? Or possibly simply delightfully domestic. That, I imagine, is how we would have judged it, had we in fact given the matter any thought. Actually we didn't - and that can be taken as the measure of our contentment. We seem to have lived in, and for, the moment. We had no great apprehensions as to the future. The road ahead seemed to me to be mapped out.

We were of course reminded from time to time of the nuclear age, and there were many who saw this in apocalyptic terms. The Aldermarston Marches were annual events, and the Campaign for Nuclear Disarmament (CND) had a wide membership. I did not myself share the prevalent fears about a possible - even a likely - nuclear holocaust. Not because I had analysed the likely course of future developments and had reached a more sanguine conclusion about what might be the outcome. I feel fairly sure that what determined my attitude, which was almost one of indifference, was the realisation that we had just left behind us a very real short-term danger in Cyprus threatening our future in an extremely direct and personal way, and that, by comparison with that, the risk of nuclear catastrophe was far too remote, both in time and statistically, to worry about. The position was rather like that of the young and healthy towards death. That the danger we had felt the Turks faced in Cyprus was indeed only too real, and even imminent, was to be confirmed a couple of years later in 1963 - as I shall tell. And today, thirty years later still, it might be argued that what brought the nuclear arms race between the West and the Soviet Empire to an end was, paradoxically, the economic burden which that race imposed on the latter's economy, which proved structurally, and essentially, wholly inadequate to compete with its economically far more powerful rival. But we, in the first years of our life in Britain, anyway had other things which caused us anxious thought.

In buying our house three years earlier, sight unseen while we were still in Cyprus, we had, as I say, acted impulsively and even imprudently. It was large, and the outgoings were burdensome. No doubt for that reason it had been relatively inexpensive to acquire. Another reason was that it was on the 'wrong' side of the Addison Road which was a sort of boundary between Kensington and

Hammersmith. (So much so that when giving our address in a shop in Kensington High Street I was, at least once, asked "That's W8, isn't it?"; and I would find myself prefacing my reply - as with that to the formulaic enquiry about one's school - "Well, actually...", since our postal address was the much less socially desirable W14. How things have changed since then in this regard also!) But to return. I had misgivings about whether we might not have bitten off more than we could chew in owning our house. Having moved back in we had lost the income from our tenants' rent. We needed to increase our income, and we let the lowest floor, a semi-basement at the front with access to the garden at the back, as a furnished flat. This we made self-contained by removing the stairs leading down from our hall, and closing up the gap left in the ceiling. Over the next couple of years we had two or three young tenants. One of these was a certain Hanbury-Tenison, who I think must have been the Robin Hanbury-Tenison since become well known as explorer, author, and broadcaster, and the President of Survival International, which he co-founded. How many are the ships we pass in the night - often without even recognising their lights as those of another vessel.

It was at this time that my brother, having transferred within the Colonial Administrative Service from Nigeria to the Legal Service in Zanzibar (at that time a separate colony, but subsequently merged with Tanganyika to form the new Commonwealth country of Tanzania) also decided to live in Britain. He came to London and having, unlike me, become a barrister after leaving Oxford and before going to Africa, now applied, successfully, for appointment in the Legal Department of one of the Whitehall ministries. Which one I don't recall, but it was the same one to which that other barrister, Robin Day, much surely feel a heavy debt of gratitude. For in rejecting his similar, but earlier, application, they opened the door through which he then passed to travel down the road which eventually led to his becoming the archetypal British television pundit. My brother started by living in rented rooms in London, but we were able to prevail on him to become the tenant of our flat when it next fell vacant.

***********

It was not until I had been working there for quite a few months that I realised that the Commonwealth Relations Office was very far from being an old established feature of the Whitehall scene. It was a comparatively new accretion, which had only come into existence after India and Pakistan had emerged as independent Commonwealth countries. Until then responsibility for pre-partition India in Whitehall (the London end, as it were, of the *Raj*) had rested with the India Office under the Secretary of State for India. This arrangement went back to the demise of the old East India Company following what is traditionally called the 'Indian Mutiny' and the proclamation of Queen Victoria as Empress of India - to a large extent as a counter to the Czar's acquisition of large territories in Moslem Central Asia, Turkestan. In 1931, under the Statute of Westminster, Canada, Australia, New Zealand, and South Africa had ceased to be colonial territories and each attained the newly created status of 'Dominion' (of the Crown, to be understood). That is, independent sovereignty, but with recognition of the Sovereign of the United Kingdom as their Sovereign too. Responsibility in Whitehall for these new sovereign states lay with a new Dominions Office under a Secretary of State for the Dominions. The CRO itself was but the amalgamation of what by the 1950s had become the redundant two Departments of State dealing separately with India and with the Dominions. All very simple and logical. When I joined it, the CRO was only about ten years old.

Apart from Sir Cosmo Parkinson's slim volume *The Colonial Office from Within*, referred to earlier, I do not know of any account in the nature of memoirs of those days by a member of the civil service in Whitehall. This doesn't surprise me. I would not attribute this reticence, or even reluctance, to what might perhaps be thought to be the obvious reason - the notorious Official Secrets Act. I suppose it could be said that there was a kind of general culture which operated to keep separate the doings of the office from the outer world, so that it didn't impinge on one's social life outside. But this wasn't, I would think, in any way peculiar to civil servants in these Departments. Rather, I would imagine, it was an attitude common to professional people in all walks of life at that time. A more likely inhibition from embarking on a public description of the day to day activities of a Whitehall Department of State would be that they were not exactly redolent with dramatic or even comic - much less cosmic - interest. This might be thought to be an odd observation in the light of the very popular series *Yes, Minister*. But that portrayal, more in the nature of satire than reality, had to do with machinations in the highest reaches of the service; and the *dramatis personae* at that level were most unlikely themselves to expatiate on their experiences. For myself it was only towards the end of my time that I rose to become, and then for a few years only, even a head of department, an Assistant Secretary - I hope not in accordance with the iron and inflexible *Peter Principle*, which dictates that one is always promoted to the level of one's incompetence. At that less rarefied height the propensity, or at any rate the occasion, for Gargantuan clashes (like that of "mastodons bellowing at each other across the primeval swamp" - to quote P.G. Wodehouse again) hardly arose. I cannot even recall any such colleague as the one who was reputed to have been seen striding purposefully along the corridor. Asked where he was going he replied, "I'm off to have a flaming row with X." "What about?" enquired the other, to receive the reply, "I haven't decided yet." Incidents of 'human interest' are more likely to happen when one's work brings one into direct contact with members of the public; and that contact was non-existent in a ministry dealing essentially with government to government relations.

The department of the CRO in which I worked was the South Asia Department, dealing with India, Pakistan and Ceylon. My own work at that stage was interesting but not over-demanding, and was concerned more with relations between the Office and British High Commissions abroad than with other Whitehall ministries at home. However, the departure of the French from their erstwhile colonies of French Indo-China (Vietnam, Laos and Cambodia) had involved the setting up of three International Control Commissions there, and as their tripartite membership was appointed respectively from Canada and India as well as from Poland we did have dealings with our opposite numbers in the Foreign Office. This sort of overlapping between the 'geographical' departments of the two Offices was to play its part when it was decided a few years later that the FO and the CRO should be amalgamated to form the new Foreign and Commonwealth Office (FCO), which is still in being. So also is the anomaly by which the United Kingdom continues to be represented in foreign countries by Embassies, but by High Commissions in Commonwealth countries. The nicely subtle reason for this is worth a passing glance.

Strictly speaking, an Ambassador is not sent to another country as the representative of the current British government. He, or she, is appointed to the foreign Head of State as the personal representative of the Sovereign. (Or, as was nicely put in Tudor Elizabethan English by Sir Henry Wotton, to produce the neat pun: "An ambassador is an honest man sent to lie abroad for the good of his country".) In those Commonwealth countries which are still monarchical (for example Canada, Australia and New Zealand) the Sovereign of the United Kingdom is their Sovereign too - though in a separate personal capacity. The resident Head of State in such Commonwealth countries is the Governor-General. He, or she, is also the Sovereign's representative in that country. It would be absurd for the Queen of the United Kingdom of Great Britain to appoint an ambassador to herself to represent herself in such another of her domains, where she has in any case another representative. So the British diplomatic representatives in such Commonwealth countries (and, *vice versa*, those of such countries in Britain) are High Commissioners; and instead of Embassies there are High Commissions. This, too, is perfectly plain and simple - if you need to think about it. Not so clear is why in Commonwealth countries which are republics, and where therefore this fine consideration does not apply, the same requirement of High Commissioners rather than Ambassadors is thought to be relevant. Charitably, one could say this was only another instance of that otherwise admirable British way of allowing things to develop without dislocating change - to be kind, one could say 'organically'. If, however, one were to be blunt, one would have to regard this particular development as being haphazard and, because based on a false view of the actual nature of the relationship between these countries, likely to lead to harmful policies. It is sometimes better that things should be allowed, 'naturally' and 'organically', to atrophy and wither away instead of being kept "officiously alive". The concept of Republican "Commonwealth" countries sharing the Queen as "Head of the Commonwealth" is, in my opinion, one such thing which were better in oblivion.

There was another historical relic involving the CRO. Her Majesty's Embassy in Dublin was not, as you might expect, within the purview of the FO, but came within that of the CRO. I have never gone into the detailed history of that anomaly, which was only tidied up when the FCO came into being with the merger of the two Offices.

But briefly, the Irish Treaty of 1922 had created the Irish Free State, and as its status was somewhat analogous to that of the Dominions of that time, it had also been brought into the Dominions Office's field of responsibility. This arrangement continued even after the Free State had evolved to become Eire and then the Republic of Ireland. That was still the position when I had joined the CRO. Whereby hangs a tale I was told, which was not at all apocryphal.

A routine procedure was operated in the CRO by which the Head of a British Diplomatic Mission which reported to it would regularly produce what I think I correctly remember were called "Personality Notes" on their *chers collègues* (there were then no *chères*) who were serving in the same capital to which they were accredited. These notes were informal and candid pen-portraits. Everything about the subject was included which would enable personal relations to be conducted in an atmosphere of harmony, sweetness and light. Some things would speak for themselves, such as any foods which should not be served . But the Notes would also cover any marked likes and dislikes, any propensities not to be encouraged, any quirks of temperament or domestic circumstances requiring particular delicacy, and so on. The description aimed, in short, to bring the subject vividly to life in the mind of the reader before meeting in person. These reports were sent by the originating Mission to the relevant geographical department in the CRO in London. There they were scrutinised before being reproduced as a "Print", and then periodically circulated as Confidential documents. The distribution list included the Heads of British Missions abroad in the capitals of the countries whose Head of Mission was the subject of the Personality Note in question. Came a day when a batch of these printed, confidential, personal and very revealing sketches was misdirected. Instead of being dispatched, centrally from the CRO, to the relevant *British* Posts abroad as intended, they were sent by mistake to the *London* Diplomatic Missions of the countries whose diplomat was the subject of the particular Personality Note. Among those Missions who received such an unsolicited character-sketch of a fellow member of their own Diplomatic Service was the Irish Embassy in London. Luckily the error was detected very quickly in the CRO, where the Heads of the geographical departments concerned (very concerned indeed) got on to the telephone immediately to ask their opposite numbers in the London High Commissions and the Irish Embassy to return the envelopes unopened. The Irish had been rather quicker off the mark than the others, and when the telephone call came through the Head of Chancery's response was, "I'm so glad you rang. The First Secretary's just brought me what was in the envelope - and we've been discussing what the devil we should do with it!"

It was not very long before I cast off from the shores of Whitehall and found myself in the diplomatic sea. Overseas postings were, of course, in the nature of things for members of the CRO, just as they were for members of the FO. They were indeed welcome for the variety of life which they brought, as well for the improvement in one's finances which came with the allowances accompanying overseas service. For Lalage and me they were more in the nature of the proverbial fly in the ointment - or, in the Turkish equivalent, the thorn which he who loves a rose has to bear. As a family we had rather had our fill of living abroad, yet service in an overseas mission was likely to comprise at least half of one's career. Not so very far in the past the situation had been quite different, and only about a generation or so back the Diplomatic Service had been separately recruited from the staff of the Foreign Office, with very little interchange between the two - not unlike the separation between the old Colonial Office staff and members of the Colonial Service. Lalage and I were, therefore, resigned to the prospect of being resident abroad for periods of three or four years at a time. The dozen or so Commonwealth countries we might have been sent to ranged between the "old" ones of Canada, Australia and New Zealand (South Africa had just withdrawn - not expelled, as nowadays seems sometimes to be thought); the two new members of the Indian "sub-continent" India and Pakistan; Ceylon; Malaysia in the Far East; and the newly emergent countries of Africa and the Caribbean. When my posting was due Lalage was ill and had had to spend time in hospital, followed by a period of recuperation. The Office was considerate enough to defer my overseas appointment, which was to have been to the recently opened High Commission in Port of Spain, Trinidad and Tobago. That country's climate is in fact tropical, being rather closer to a geographical appendage to the equatorial north of the South American continent than it is to being a Caribbean island. My actual posting came about half a year later, and this time it was as one of two First Secretaries (Political) in the High Commission in Ottawa.

211

**Taking Flight**

Lalage and our five year old daughter were booked to cross the Atlantic and steam up the Saint Lawrence to Montreal in the late autumn on one of the Cunarders which still made that passage in the sixties. Before sailing she had to arrange to let our house, fully furnished (less the downstairs flat which providentially, as will be seen, was still occupied by my brother). Our son was by now a boarder of two year's standing at a prep school in the country and would be coming out for his three annual holidays, two of the air passages being paid by the Office and the other by us. Officers on overseas postings also received an allowance towards the cost of school fees, which ceased during home postings. As my presence in Ottawa was required before all these arrangements could be made, I flew out in the early autumn just as the glorious colours of the early Canadian "Fall" were beginning to appear.

**\*\*\*\*\*\*\*\*\*\***

It would be verging on the impertinent even to try to paint a picture of the vast and diverse country which is Canada after but a single posting. Yet I can attempt at least to recall the impressions which it left with me.

While, with the help of the Office, I looked for a house to rent, I used to walk to and from the High Commission about a mile or so from the hotel where I lived. This practice was regarded as distinctly eccentric by the Ottawans, though not looked on as quite so odd as the habit of my predecessor (as it happens, a Foreign Office man) who, I was told, would do the same thing even as the cold of the approaching winter was in the air - and with no more protection than a scarf and gloves. Not something to be attempted after the winter had really arrived. Lovely as the Canadian winter was to the eye, and invigorating in its crisp dryness, the air could be positively dangerous with the prospect of frostbite, especially when the "wind factor" was added.

There was an overall feeling of strangeness in being in a place where there seemed to be scarcely any visible evidence of human activity going back much more than a century. (There are, of course, large chunks of urban England of which now, thirty years later, much the same could be said - with a rather different significance.) We had

212

a sensation of being in a very youthful place, a feeling difficult, if not impossible, to relate to anything specific. And this aspect perhaps contributed to the children's enjoyment of their time there. They revelled in the atmosphere of openness and space - and not only in the physical aspects. In retrospect I think that we were sensing that this was somehow a young person's country; a place for those who were not yet set in their ways. Refreshing, but needing a little adjustment for those no longer in their first youth.

Ideas of what is old can often be relative. The palpable embodiment of the historical past of the capital, Ottawa, was to be seen in the dignified buildings crowning the bluff above the river on Parliament Hill. Yet these were only more or less contemporary with Oxford's late mid-Victorian Science Museum. Ottawa was at this time entering a period of rapid development, and the British High Commission was, within a year of our arrival, to move from the rather homely building on its site above the river bank at Earnscliffe to premises downtown in one of the very few multi-storey blocks which were rising opposite the Centre for the Performing Arts, then nearing completion. (Earnscliffe remained as the High Commissioner's residence.) We were, I think, fortunate to have known the Ottawa of those days. It still had an air, to us at any rate, which carried evocations of its original existence as a logging camp on a tributary of the great Saint Lawrence; indeed the very smell of the pulp mills, almost aromatic, would occasionally waft over the town. (What was for us part of Ottawa's attraction and charm - that it had not yet lost its early character - was viewed in quite a different light by the Air Marshal who had leased our London house. To him, or his wife, it was "a hick town". *À chacun son goût*). The site had been carefully chosen for the capital of the new Federation, which had been born in 1867, as being on the boundary between the Provinces of Ontario (British) and Quebec (French) in recognition of these two national dimensions of the country, but without favouring either.

Canada at this period had a rather special, indeed a unique, position internationally. The dependent territories of the European colonial powers, especially those of Britain and France, had been almost racing each other in their rush to independent sovereign statehood and membership of the United Nations Organisation, then barely fifteen

213

years old. Canada was a large country which was both a member of the wealthy West and yet carried no stigma of an imperial past. As such it could attract, as indeed it did, the respect of these newly independent members of what came to be called the "Third World" - those countries which were neither of the capitalist West nor the communist East (in the over simplistic and imprecise terminology of that time). Because of Canada's being seen in this light, these Third World countries made every effort to maintain a diplomatic mission in Ottawa. Where such a country was unable to do this it made a point of giving the head of its mission in Washington, or of its mission at the United Nations headquarters in New York, dual accreditation in the Canadian capital as well. It could not be said that the great majority of such Ambassadors, or High Commissioners, accredited to the Governor General in Ottawa, were exactly overworked in that place. Second perhaps to the various missions at the UN in New York in those days, the best models of the diplomat as "cookie pusher", to use the American term, were probably to be found in the somewhat overcrowded diplomatic set in Ottawa. Agreeable as they generally were individually it was certainly difficult to think that the nature of their relations with the Canadian government was such as to require their engaging in full-time activity.

For official entertainment, provided at home, the number of guests tended to be rather swollen, and the staff for these occasions were engaged from outside through, as far as I recall, an agency. Such cocktails and receptions were so frequent, and so many of those attending were those present each time, that it was hardly surprising that the outside staff who were also making many of the same rounds became so familiar with the tastes of the individual guests that they were able to serve them their drinks without first asking.

Diagonally opposite our house was the residence of the Ambassador (or possibly Minister - I'm not sure at what level his country was represented in Canada, Embassy or Legation) of a small South American country. He tended not to shave when the call of duty didn't require him to leave the confines of his house. In this cavalier preference for comfortable ease over propriety he had my personal sympathy, but his attitude was in sharp contrast to that of his wife who was always a model of elegance. Very much an Anglophile, it was in

214

his house at a very small and informal drinks party that I heard of an episode illustrating one reason for this - his admiration for English *sang froid*. I don't now remember whether it was he or a colleague of his, but the person concerned was at the time his country's consular representative in, I think, Liverpool - anyway a northern city. There he had decided to take lessons in horsemanship. His instructor had very rightly given great emphasis to the need to acquire a "good seat" and, for that purpose, to ensure the correct positioning of the rider's legs at the different "paces" of the horse. On one occasion when they were out cantering, his mount suddenly took off out of control and bolted. The only reaction from the instructor was a calm and unemotional "Heels *down*, Mr Sanchez, heels *down!*" By such means are genuine feelings of respect and admiration engendered between people of different countries, quite as much as by formal and official contacts. ·

There was one rather unusual way in which the fact of Canada's being a member of the Commonwealth impinged on the British High Commission's work. The particular importance of the relations between the United Kingdom and the United States not unnaturally involved a large amount of diplomatic and inter-governmental activity. This brought about quite frequent British visits to Washington at ministerial level. It would have been taken amiss by the Canadian government if a senior British minister were to make the transatlantic journey to the US capital, not so far to the south, without calling also at the Canadian capital. How much more was this the case when the visitor was the Prime Minister. And so it was that during my first winter in Ottawa we had a visit by the then PM, Sir Alec Douglas Home (having renounced his peerage to become the Queen's First Minister). He was accompanied by Lady Home, and also by Sir Burke Trend, the Secretary to the Cabinet, with the usual entourage. After meetings in Ottawa the party was due to go on to Washington, via Toronto, where they were to stay the night after having attended a function there . At Toronto it was discovered that the Cabinet Secretary's overnight luggage had by-passed him and gone on to Washington. Arrangements were made to provide substitutes for the essential missing articles. So far as the articles of clothing were concerned neither I nor the other First Secretary could have provided the wherewithal - he being six foot seven in height, and I but five foot six.

## Taking Flight

It was at the beginning of that same winter that the (was it the fourth or the fifth?) United States President, was assassinated. It seems to have become a tradition to recall where you were when you heard of the death of President Kennedy in Dallas on that November afternoon. I was in my office at Earnscliffe when I was given the news by the Information Office of the High Commission. I have to say that while I was naturally shocked by the violently sudden death of the American head of state, I was in no way conscious that some awesome and epoch-making event had taken place, nor that this was some peculiarly tragic end to a supremely gifted young statesman from whom much could still be expected - which was the tenor and burden of so much of the comment which was to follow the tragedy. Nor has all that has since been produced in hyper-eulogistic vein, of the Camelot variety, about the man who was the youngest President of his country, done anything to make me believe that an extension of his presidency into the period when that high office was held by his own Vice-President would have been productive of any changes for the better, to the benefit of either the West or of the world. Assiduous, expensive, and concerted media presentation by image makers - and not infrequently by image breakers - is something I have only been conscious of from my middle years on; and I see no evidence that this meretriciousness is on the wane. Perhaps this is nothing new in human affairs, but the means for engaging in it are greatly increasing. The hope would seem to lie not in attempts at control (which would itself be pregnant with even greater evil or harm) but in growing awareness of what is going on. And I think I am not over-optimistic in seeing that there are at least some signs of a growing spirit of healthy scepticism on the part of the public.

In Ottawa I found myself being drawn into reflecting on the functions of diplomatic missions in reporting on political events. My time there coincided with the hotly debated issue of the Canadian flag, as well as with one of the periods when the argument over the status of the largely French-speaking province of Quebec effervesced. After much debate in the Canadian parliament, whose sessions I followed with interest from the diplomatic gallery, the former question was resolved to virtually everyone's satisfaction while I was still in Canada, by the acceptance of the red maple-leaf centred red and white flag which replaced the previous ensign with its quartered union jack. The London *Times* of those days had a resident correspondent in

216

Canada. He had been in the country many years and had made a wide range of friends, acquaintances and contacts. It came to me that there was often little value in producing thoughtful 'political despatches' for circulation in Whitehall (or not, as the case might be), when well-established foreign correspondents could cover - as indeed they did - the same ground perfectly adequately in their sound reports to their widely read national newspapers at home.

The vexed question of Quebec's status is still alive - indeed seemingly even more vigorous today. It remains an issue whether or not that province should secede from the Federation. The topic was warm enough in the early sixties, even before the visit to Quebec by President de Gaulle some few years afterwards when he mischievously stirred the pot with his resounding public call *"Vive le Québec libre!"* from a balcony in Quebec City. Behaviour scarcely becoming a statesman from, still less the head of state of, a friendly nation. In the case of the similar mischief-making by Madame Mitterand in more recent years, it has at least only been the *wife* of the French President of the day who has acted in helping foment dissension in Turkey by giving encouragement to the minority PKK terrorist organisation, funded and nurtured by the Syrian regime, and supported by the Greek authorities. Which is not to say that there has not been dispersed resentment felt among some Kurds over past treatment they received from the Turkish authorities, and from individual oafish Turks. Just as there were like feelings in Quebec by those who felt it deeply when their culture and language were slighted by similar Canadians. For example, when some vulgarian non-French-speaking Canadian would shout "Talk white!" at Quebecois conversing in their own language amongst themselves - as I was told would occasionally happen, not so far in the past.

"Parity of esteem" was the term used to express what was felt, not infrequently, to be lacking in Canada. And without doubt the same applied in Turkey. In which country does it not? Instances can be multiplied, but to not much constructive purpose. Perhaps the best advice is the biblical admonition to look at the beam in one's own eye - before concerning oneself with someone else's. How many people know that, within the lifetime of some of us, Welsh children in their own land were made to wear accusing placards round their necks if they were heard to speak their own tongue while in school? It seems to me that when third parties decide to involve themselves in other countries' problems having to do with cultural diversity, they would do well to ask themselves, when they hear of other people on the receiving end of treatment of which they disapprove, how best their own feelings of sympathy might be given expression constructively - in action which could make for reconciliation, and help to heal rifts, rather than to deepen and widen these in ways which then find outlets in violence and savagery.

**\*\*\*\*\*\*\*\*\*\***

In the last week of December 1963 we heard on the wireless that fighting had broken out in Cyprus. My feelings were mixed: bitter impotence at being so far away and cut off, as I thought, from events; and smouldering fury that what I had feared was likely, sooner or later, to be Cyprus's doom - but which, deep down, I must have hoped against hope would not be visited on it - had now come to pass. It had happened much more quickly, and far more ferociously, than I would have imagined even in my worst moments.

Initially we could, naturally, have no knowledge of the details, but it was clear enough very early on that the centre of the trouble was in the capital, Nicosia, where of course my mother was still living in her house behind the Ledra Palace hotel. Very soon, too, the Ledra Palace itself began to feature in news reports and not, as might have been imagined, simply as the headquarters and watering hole of the press corps (as it had been only a few years back in the days of EOKA terrorism). This time the hotel was a Greek redoubt from which they fired into the Turkish areas through a wide arc.

**\*\*\*\*\*\*\*\*\*\***

*What was happening - worse and much more ominous even than the actual fighting - we were only to learn about some years later. The Greek operation was executed under a coldly calculated programme deliberately intended to overawe, and indeed to neutralise, the Turks so as to intimidate them into leaving the island. "Neutralise" is the word used by Angelos Vlachos, a Greek diplomat who was the Greek Consul-General in Cyprus during the days of EOKA, in his book* Ten Years of Cyprus, *when he is describing Makarios's aim in 1962. I did not know in 1963 of the recent tortuous clandestine scheming by Makarios, and his colleagues in villainy, to undermine the Cyprus Republic, which had come into existence three years earlier - as a member of the Commonwealth, one needs to remind oneself. Nor was I even aware of their inflammatory pro-*enosis *speeches during those years, in shameless violation of the Constitutional provisions prohibiting any activity promoting* enosis *directly or indirectly, provisions which Britain was treaty-bound to uphold and guarantee. A particularly vicious public utterance had been a speech on 2 September 1962 which could scarcely have gone unnoticed by the British High Commission in Nicosia - as it had certainly not been by the Turkish population. The Archbishop told the villagers of Panayia (which, ironically - to use a mild word - means "All Holy", being the customary designation of Mary the mother of Jesus): "Until this small Turkish community that forms part of the Turkish race which has been the terrible enemy of Hellenism is expelled, the duties of the heroes of EOKA cannot be considered as terminated." The vile words "ethnic cleansing" were not to affront, and sully, the world for another thirty years, but the pernicious thing itself was the openly proclaimed objective of the Greek politicians of Cyprus voiced through the mouth of the Orthodox Archbishop of the island, who was also its President at the time he made that atrocious statement. It was also to transpire that they had even produced, in black and white, their programme to achieve this aim - the infamous* Akritas Plan. *This, when discovered, was circulated to the UN Security Council and General Assembly in 1978. It has never been disclaimed by the Greek side. The details are out of place here; but they are revealing of how to set about producing an ethnically 'pure' state without actually driving out the ethnically 'unclean' population,* en masse *in the later Serbian mode.*

**********

But all this was, as I have said, unknown to me in December 1963. My only concern at the time was my mother's safety. I asked my

219

Deputy High Commissioner if the official channels of communication from Ottawa to the British High Commission in Nicosia, *via* London, could be used to establish her situation, and as necessary, help to get her out to London if that was what she wanted. This in fact was done. She joined my brother in his small flat, having abandoned her home and possessions. That home, in the so-called 'Green Line', was in due course taken over by the UN for occupation by officers of the peace-keeping force, with payment of rent to the local 'government' - that is to say to the administration which had been usurped by the Greek Cypriots - from which my mother never saw a penny. But she was safe. It seemed to me then that when she had closed her front door in Nicosia behind her our connection with Cyprus had finally been severed.

\*\*\*\*\*\*\*\*\*\*\*

Halfway through our tour of duty in Canada the report of the Plowden Committee was published in London. Their terms of reference had, broadly, been to examine the responsibilities and operations of British diplomatic missions abroad and make recommendations for their reorganisation so as to put them into a position the better to carry out their functions in the best interests of the United Kingdom, having regard to Britain's changed position in the second half of the century. Generally speaking, the Committee concluded that much greater emphasis should be be given to activities aimed at stimulating and expanding Britain's overseas trade and commerce. Among the practical measures which the Committee recommended was the amalgamation of the staff of all diplomatic missions abroad into a new combined Diplomatic Service, with common terms and conditions of service, irrespective of which Home Ministry the individual members belonged to. For there were Ministries in London other than the FO and the CRO which provided staff for these diplomatic missions abroad - for example the Board of Trade (as I think I am right in thinking it was then still called, under a President of the Board of Trade). In the Ottawa High Commission, for example, there was a large Commercial Section under a Minister (Commercial) who ranked with the Deputy High Commissioner.

The Plowden Committee had, as I believe, shied away from recommending the logical step that the FO and the CRO should cease to remain separate Departments of State and should immediately be merged under a single Secretary of State. (This was in fact to happen not so very long afterwards.) Their recommendation for a unified Diplomatic Service was, however, at once accepted by the government; and since the terms of service of the CRO members of that new body were held to have been altered for the worse, those members were given the right to choose whether or not to opt to join the new service. I never bothered to establish in what respect our terms of service were regarded as being more adverse than before. Or, if I did, I have now forgotten the particulars of how our conditions were judged to have deteriorated. Possibly these might have been thought to have consisted in, for example, a liability which had not previously existed, to serve in such disagreeable places as Vietnam and the other newly independent countries of what had been French Indo-China, or in similar countries that had formerly been parts of French West Africa; but it seems more likely that it might have been thought that such a consideration would apply in the case of the countries behind the 'iron curtain' in Eastern Europe. They would certainly have been regarded as distinctly insalubrious by Lalage and me. But whatever had been the basis of distinguishing between members of the FO and of the CRO in this regard, we found ourselves with the options of my electing to continue as we were, but within the new Diplomatic Service, or to leave and become part of the Home Civil Service.

I am pretty sure that even while we were in Canada, we must have known that there was a strong possibility - if not indeed more of a probability - that, were I to opt out of joining the Diplomatic Service, I should be offered an appointment in the Ministry of Overseas Development (the ODM as it was to be abbreviated, to differentiate it from the Ministry of Defence). This new Ministry had been created, headed by a Minister with Cabinet rank, by the Labour government which had come to power in the recent general election after thirteen years in opposition. I could have known very little about the detailed remit of this new Ministry but it was pretty evident that, as the arm of government concerned with development aid to the 'Third World', it would be very likely to focus largely on those countries which had been UK dependencies and that they would receive the greater proportion of Britain's aid programme - as in fact turned out to be the case. It seemed therefore a logical, even natural, progression that my career having evolved from one in the Colonial Service, and then moved into the realms of Britain's largely political relations with the same countries after they had achieved independent status, should continue into the area of Britain's aid relationship with those countries which were undeveloped (a word which very soon was dropped to give place to "developing"). But even without this superficially logical neatness Lalage and I had no hesitation in deciding that the option should be exercised in favour of leaving the diplomatic life. Neither the undeniable financial advantage of that life, nor what an outsider - and not a few insiders - might regard as the glamour of the diplomatic round, as compared with the hum-drum and prosaic existence to be expected as a civil servant in Britain, counted for much when set against the immense attraction for us of being able to live a settled life without the prospect of having regularly to up sticks. We wanted at last to be able to put down deep roots, and now that providence had put the possibility in our hands it seemed foolish, indeed churlish, to refuse it. We didn't. Gratefully we accepted it. I formally exercised my option to leave the diplomatic life.

**********

Our mid-tour leave was due in the summer of 1965. Knowing now that we should not be seeing out the normal full tour of duty we decided to use this three or four weeks' period to see, in the short time we had, something more of the vastnesses of Canada. Some colleagues used their local leaves to travel south of the border to tour through the American states. We had preferred to see what we could of Canada itself, and had been drawn to the grandeur of the rivers, lakes and forests which were easily accessible from Ottawa. Lalage's two younger sisters had been evacuated to Canada during the war. They had lived with a Canadian family in Montreal who had virtually been foster parents to them. This family had a summer place on the St. Lawrence at Fernbank, near Brockville, to which they very hospitably invited us; and we were able to spend a couple of happy weekends at that lovely spot. In the spring-time we also visited Niagara Falls, on the Canadian side. And there we did at least set foot on American soil, which you could do at the mid-point of the bridge over the river forming the international boundary. I have no memory of any formalities that might have been required to do this.

But we had really been bitten, or smitten, by the magnificence of the Canadian wilds when, through the kindness of an Ottawa family, we had been able to spend our local annual leave the previous summer, while our son was also out with us, at the Petawawa Fish and Game Club. This was right out in the forest, some sixty or eighty miles beyond Ottawa, so far as I recall, in the Algonquin to the north. Log cabins, and a cook-house, just inshore from a series of lakes in which you could fish, or canoe, or go on longer *voyages*, and go on trips in a small boat fitted with an outboard. Paths through the forest were "trail-blazed" by markings on trees, and you were advised not to venture off these tracks from which it was only to easy to lose yourself. The place was of course bliss for the children. Not even the occasional presence of a water-snake or two, which weren't poisonous anyway, could spoil the really lovely lake-water swimming. The call of the 'loon', a sort of cormorant-like bird of the forest lakes, belling out in the morning and evening will, I imagine, stay for ever in the memory of anyone who has heard it, hauntingly evocative of those wonderful wildernesses.

The summer of 1965 was the last one before our time in Canada was to come to an end. We decided to spend a fortnight in the Rockies at Lake Louise. It was to be a once-in-a-lifetime opportunity, taking the inside of a week travelling there and back, on one of the two great Canadian trans-continental railways. I think we had booked on the Canadian National and not the Canadian Pacific. The train journey was a fitting climax to our two-year stay in that magnificent land. Transatlantic, yet not American; British and French, yet not European; wealthy, yet not arrogantly so. This is how I think of Canada. We were, as we entered on our early middle age, probably just past the point where we could have contemplated spending the rest of our lives there (which we never in fact ever thought of doing). But we could sense how powerfully it could have stirred the imagination of those who might have looked out from Britain in search of a place where immigrants would hope to find those opportunities which an ageing Europe seemed less and less likely to be able to provide as the century advanced. Canada was at this time keenly seeking such immigrants. I am reminded of this by a postcard we bought with a fine view of the Parliament Buildings. This is subtitled: 'Send postcard for further information and free illustrated literature to Assistant Superintendent of Emigration, 111-112 Charing Cross Road, London SW1.'

I have earlier in these reminiscences remarked on how I seemed, at different times in my youth in England, to be living in an environment which was almost caught in a time warp. There were one or two instances of this sensation in Canada too. Church attendance seemed enveloped by a sort of air of 'properness', more even than of conventionality, which carried me back to the days of the Rectory at East Allington in the thirties - itself palpably different from the atmosphere of church in London at the beginning of the sixties, though I am hard put to it in trying to be specific. One such piece of evidence in Canada was that women in church always wore hats of the kind I would have associated with an occasion such as a garden party, and - unless my memory is playing me false - invariably with gloves. I remember that a book, of the character of kindly admonition, criticism and stimulus, came out in Canada at this time bearing the title *The Comfortable Pew*.

Which recalls to me three separate memories which come neatly together in my mind. At some time when I was in Cyprus, and I think before we were married, a cousin of mine who was not a practising Moslem once told me that he did not take kindly to the ritual of the formal prayers of Islam, which involve very precise reverential postures and, indeed, prostrations. He was of the opinion that we would do better to have "seats" as they did in churches. (I think that at the time I simply said that this sort of church furniture was, I believed, a relative innovation, and that the interiors of the great cathedrals of the West certainly had remained empty of such 'furnishings', like mosque interiors, until fairly recent times.) To the extent that my cousin's opinion was the expression of a scarcely perceived objection to having to humble himself in prayer, he was of a like mind with an Anglican cleric I was to hear on British television not so many years later, who told his audience that he could never accommodate himself to a religion which would require of him that he should abase himself in prostration to the ground. Which conjures up the third of my recollections. And this one struck me so forcibly at the time that I made a note of it. In a

224

book published by the S P C K there is the intriguing sentence: "It is to be regretted that some, though not all, of the Christian communities in Muslim lands are becoming like the pew-bound West, and as they tend to lose their freedom of expression in worship lose with it the help of prostration so eloquent of lowly adoration."

Our family journey across Canada from Ottawa to the Rockies took us through the vast prairies, the boundless skies above meeting the encircling horizon of the flat immensities around us on every side, as though we were travelling through a terrestrial sea with the railway track behind us as the dead-straight wake of our earthly vessel running on and on, seemingly to the end of the world itself. And as other ships might break the solitude of the oceans, here such interruptions came with the appearance from time to time of the lofty grain silos or 'elevators' heralding the harbour towns of these cereal seas, where our vessel took on fuel: Regina, Moose Jaw, Medicine Hat, Calgary. Then, to return to reality, the foothills of the great far western ranges began to appear and the train climbed and climbed, passing through tunnels, sometimes looping on itself so sharply that as we emerged we could see from the forward observation car the rear of the train disappearing into the tunnel entrance behind.

It is tempting to draw facile parallels. However when, more than twenty years later, I was to see from a soviet aeroplane the huge plains of Kazakhstan (still at that time a part of the Soviet Empire) the sight did indeed evoke in me something which was recognisably the same sort of feeling as I had known when travelling through the Canadian prairies. What, after all, are the steppes but the prairies by another name, the same thing with a different label? It would no doubt be fanciful to suppose that I was experiencing some kind of atavistic affinity, which linked me to the land-locked continental fastnesses girdled by snow-capped mountains out of which some part of my dimly remote ancestors could once have come some fifty generations or so earlier, and yet that powerful attraction of those huge spaces - lands, waters and skies - was undeniable.

*********

It was many years after those Canadian days, and shortly after my visit

225

to Central Asia, that I made one of those fascinatingly inconsequential discoveries which, though wholly unconnected with factual truth or reality, yet have strong personal resonances. I believe it is the case that the Asian land mass was, not so far distant in the history of the world, one with the northern American continent. There is, so far as I know, no etymological connection between the languages of the original inhabitants of what are now two quite separate continents, or of those who are their scattered descendants today. The piece of serendipity which was revealed to me was contained in a postcard sent to Lalage from an American friend. This showed the resting place in America of the old London Bridge, dismantled and shipped across the Atlantic to be reassembled there. The site was a lake, or the arm of a lake; and its name was Havasu. And *hava* and *su* have the meaning, in Turkish, of 'air' and 'water' respectively. A pleasing coincidence.

\*\*\*\*\*\*\*\*\*\*

We hadn't yet completed two years in Canada when we made our journey back from the Rockies to Ottawa. Quickly though those months in the country had passed, they still represented something rather more than a third of our daughter's age. In that time she had given evidence of something she and I seem to share - what I might call a certain quality of being impressionable. This can be taken as a possible disadvantage, in suggesting a tendency to be overmuch influenced by the people and the things around you. To be unduly impressionable is, doubtless, not to be recommended, as it might perhaps be thought to make you rather too easily prone to fall under what the law knows as another's 'undue influence'. (The case of Lord Crewe comes to mind. Or was it Lord Derby? Anyway the peer who, in the First World War, was caustically and contemptuously likened by the viper-tongued Lloyd George to a cushion because "he carries the impression of the last person who has sat on him".) But to be impressionable in a moderate way ought, I believe, be accounted to someone as a virtue (or at least as a compensation for such disadvantage as it brings), suggesting as it does a natural inclination towards empathy, to having a sense of fellow-feeling. Advantage or not, this tendency to impressionability showed itself in me linguistically when I was at East Allington. I very soon developed the Devonshire way of speech, which had little if anything to do with the rectory itself. I remember how surprised I was when I first saw the word 'blooming' in print. Until then I had mentally seen it as 'blimmin' - which is how I, and others I had heard, would pronounce it in, as it might be, the choicely dismissive description of someone as a "blimmin idjit".

In the case of our daughter she had in a very short time acquired the Canadian, if not indeed the 'Ottawa valley', accent. (Even to the extent of that particular vowel content by which, if by nothing else, a Canadian is still revealed to me: the diphthong 'ou' (as in 'out') which always has a hint, and mostly much more than that, of an 'oo' (as in 'boot'), which seems to me to carry traces of the Scottish lineage which is the heritage of so many of the original 'British' population of the country. I only have to hear a voice, in what is loosely called an 'American' accent, say the word 'about' to know that the speaker comes from north of the 49th parallel.) We were at a table right at the end of the restaurant-car of the train next to the door into the kitchen. The waiter had just finished putting down our plates in front of us when our daughter observed - *apropos* what exactly quite slips my mind - that something was "jolly good". I suppose it was the combination of, and contrast with, the Canadian intonation and the most un-Canadian expression of appreciative pleasure which touched the spot with the waiter. He stiffened, and one could see the muscles of his mouth and cheeks tighten as he made the effort to control himself. He disappeared like a shot behind the dividing doorway from the other side of which we heard him bursting out delightedly to his fellows: "She said 'Jolly good'! 'Jolly good'!"

Looking at the matter another way, it still seems very odd to me that anyone can live for any time in a strange country without this having the slightest impact on them linguistically. I wonder how far wrong I am in feeling that this is, to an extent, the result of some inner lack of sympathy, some unconscious resistance even, to any real involvement with the place.

**\*\*\*\*\*\*\*\*\*\***

Forty and more years ago cinemas in England would sometimes show short travelogue films before the main item of the programme. The commentary of these films would invariably end with what were, even then, a hackneyed few sentences in the nature of "... And so, as the sun slowly sinks in the West, we take our reluctant farewell of ...", while onto the screen was projected a suitably striking view in illustration of the spoken sentiments. At the beginning of these reminiscences I have said, of our garden at Chitterne, that the view from the house towards the church was almost ridiculously picturesque. Even with the recollection of those near to banal travelogue films in my mind I am willing that a comparably picturesque scene should serve as the last image of Canada as we knew it thirty years ago - a picture unchanged, I imagine, today. A sun blood-red and a flight of birds silhouetted against it; summer snows on the peaks of mountains, pink before they lose all colour as the last light of day fades completely; the waters mirroring from the dying sun a gleaming streak into, across, and out of which a canoe is silently paddled. And a perfect moon rising in its turn to give its light to the earth.

# ~10~
# London; Beirut;
# Jordan; London

*Quand je regarde mon derrière, je vois qu'il est divisé en deux parties.*
In England, in the days of my youth, the word 'derrière' had passed
into the language, as a preferred euphemism adopted by the delicately
nurtured, in mentioning a person's bottom. Hence the above French
pronouncement's featuring in a joke of that time. Like so many good
jokes this one was fathered onto more than one alleged progenitor. I
have heard it recounted as having been solemnly made, to French
audiences, both by Churchill (whose peculiar form of Anglo-Gallic
might be thought to give plausibility to his being, in truth, its author),
and also supposedly by an earnest English spokesman for some
salvationist group. In each case the speaker is represented as intending
to convey that when he looks back over his past he sees it as separated
into two distinct parts - by some vitally significant, or determining,
event. For my part, as I look back at the person I was in my fortieth
year, on our return to Britain towards the end of 1965, I find myself
remembering this old anecdote, not because in my case I see a life
divided in any such dramatic fashion. What I do see, now, is a *person*
divided - indeed two people. Not, as it were, having changed from the
one into the other across a line in time; but because the one, entirely
unconsciously, carried the other within himself. How that perception
of myself came to me over a span of years will, I hope, emerge in the
course of this account.

There was, all the same, the more obvious duality between my
working life and my home life. These, with no very deliberate intent,
I managed to keep pretty well compartmentalised after taking up my
appointment in the ODM, even more than I had been able to do

229

previously when in the CRO, where there had been a certain amount of mixing socially with members of High Commissions in London. Official social occasions virtually ceased with our return from Canada; but a couple of such functions have remained in my memory.

The first which comes to mind involved my only brush, to date, with the police. We had had an invitation to a reception at the New Zealand High Commission, which was now at their new building at the foot of the Haymarket. We drove there from Kensington, since our destination provided its own, underground, parking. At the end of the party we started back in the car but hadn't reached the western end of Piccadilly before a police car came up, overtook us, and drew up in front. A policeman walked over, and I wound down my window to enquire what was up. He asked me politely to show him my driving licence. I replied equally politely that I didn't keep it in the car. Well, what about some other means of identification? Again I couldn't produce any. Showing some signs of exasperation the constable asked if I would please tell him my car registration number. I hardly ever drove the car myself since, as I have said, I habitually travelled to and from the office by public transport. My inability to provide this detail clearly aroused the officer's liveliest suspicion. I now expected that the breathalyser - newly introduced by Barbara Castle, who had since become Transport Minister - would be produced. Instead the policeman gave me a cold look, and observed "I suppose you know you're driving without lights?" (What had happened was that, emerging from the quite unaccustomed lighted underground car-park I had blithely driven off into the lighted streets.) "I'm most frightfully sorry, officer!" I said in my most grovellingly apologetic manner - and stretched out my hand to switch on. Only to discover that I couldn't find the light switch on the dash-board. Lalage kindly leaned forward and pressed the switch. I drew away - under the cold gaze of the constabulary.

The other such official social occasion was quite different. In the first place it was only I - not Lalage - who was invited. Secondly the venue was within walking distance, somewhere in the vicinity of the top of the Earl's Court Road. A First or Second Secretary at the Soviet Embassy had requested the pleasure of my company at a small cocktail party at his home. My name must, presumably, have come out of a previous Diplomatic List. We were required to notify the office of any contacts with Soviet or Iron Curtain diplomats. When I did so I was told to report after the event. There was in fact nothing of substance to report: no attempt to 'pump' me, or seduce me - in any of the various meanings of the word - as was understood to be the usual *modus operandi*. I wondered indeed why I was on the guest list. But I was left with one impression, which I hope (and think) I did report. This was the air of inspissated sombreness, almost gloom. It was around Christmas time; and along my route as I walked to the place I passed windows with undrawn curtains beyond which were decorations and lighted trees. The complete absence of these at the cocktail party heightened the contrast of atmosphere; but the joylessness of the place was palpable enough. I positively felt sorry for these beings from a different world

\*\*\*\*\*\*\*\*\*\*\*

The staff of the newly established Ministry of Overseas Development came, in general, from an increasingly attenuated Colonial Office, from the Treasury, and from the Foreign Office. A wholly new, and non-'Whitehall', component was a team of economists. Not that the generic term is geographically apt to describe us in the ODM, since our home was not Whitehall itself but in a brand new manifestation, at the Buckingham Palace end of Victoria Street, of a rapidly developing tower-block London. Out of my window on the fifth floor - out of eight - I could survey a vista over Stag Place containing not a single building erected before the sixties.

I discovered that the Minister in charge of this Department was Barbara Castle, and that the Permanent Secretary was Sir Andrew Cohen. Both have already featured in earlier pages of this account. As could be inferred from the previous references to them, I did not feel anything like empathy for them personally, and especially not for the Labour politician, whose involvement in Cyprus had, in my view, been nothing if not deleterious. I had never met either before; nor was I to meet them for some time. When I did it was to be but briefly; in the case of each of them, only once and then on matters of such insignificance that neither occasion stays in my memory. In Mrs Castle's case I remember only that it was a committee meeting she

231

chaired. The couple were known - hardly surprisingly given the huge bulk and pachyderm quality of the junior member of the duo - as 'the Elephant and Castle'. In the case of the senior member it might have been some intended allusion to a certain impregnability about her, especially in argument, which gave point to emphasising her likeness to a crenellated fortification. An anecdote I heard in a pub towards the end of the war about a Polish fighter pilot in the RAF came to me. Together with British colleagues three such Poles are at a bar where one is explaining that he has no children because, as he says, his wife is inconceivable. "No," replies one of his Polish friends, "you mean she is *unbearable*." The other one interjects to make the ultimate correction. "What you are wanting to say is - 'she is **impregnable**'. All three qualifications could be said to be applicable, in the correct and not misintended sense, to the redoubtable redhead who set up and first headed the ODM. Sir Andrew Cohen, as I suppose I might have expected from my recollection of the part he had played in the removal of the young Kabaka of Uganda, reminded me more of one of Bernard Levin's witticisms when twisting certain lawyers' names to fit their alleged activities or characteristics. As, for example, 'Sir Shortly Floor-Cross' parodying the name of Sir Hartly Shawcross, who had moved from the Labour to the Conservative benches in the House of Commons. In like manner he transformed the name of the reputedly overbearing Sir Reginald Manningham-Buller, who nevertheless managed to reach the Woolsack, into 'Sir Bullying Manner'. A sobriquet which could have been thought no less inappropriate for the man who was to be the first civil service head of the ODM.

Something should, I think, be said about the Ministry in which I was to spend the rest of my salaried working life.

The original idea of organised development aid to the poorer countries of the world stemmed from several sources. One of these was the experience of the international organisations created in the immediate post-war years as the machinery by which assistance was channelled for the reconstruction of the war-torn countries of Europe. There was the International Bank for Reconstruction and Development (the IBRD) with its specifically financial, and also supervisory, subsidiary - the International Monetary Fund (the IMF). Similarly originally confined to Europe was the OEEC (Organisation for

European Economic Cooperation). The United Nations Organisation, too, had set up, among its numerous Specialised Agencies, the UN Development Programme (the UNDP) as the organ for giving world-wide 'Technical Assistance', that is aid other than in the form of finance by way of loans or grants, through the provision of 'experts' in a whole range of work. Now, some ten years after the IBRD's creation, there grew from it a subsidiary which provided extremely 'soft' loans to poor countries, for example interest-free loans repayable over forty years and carrying a ten year amortization-free period. This was the IDA - the International Development Agency - funded by the wealthier members of the IBRD. About the same time the OEEC became transmuted into the OECD - the Organisation for Economic Cooperation and Development - which now had its own specialist 'agency' in the form of its Development Assistance Committee (DAC) to provide a forum, outside the UN, for coordination and cooperation on aid matters between, essentially the same rich 'donor' countries of the world: the USA, Canada, and Japan now became non-European DAC members.

Bilateral aid programmes were also being developed separately by several countries, in the main for helping those territories which had until very recently been their own dependencies and which were now among the ranks of independent sovereign states. But it was not only the erstwhile 'metropolitan' countries, like Britain, France and Holland, who were entering this field; the United States also established its AID - the Agency for International Development. And West Germany, too, had set up its agency for this purpose - but I'm afraid I've forgotten its name, my German being non-existent. (My ignorance of German was only minimally rectified - actually possibly extended - by my being made the recipient of an anecdote by the man who was to become my Deputy Under Secretary towards the end of my service. Fluent in German, an extremely competent, unpompous and amiable Yorkshireman, he was one of the original component of the ODM, who had come in from the now defunct Colonial Office, where he had been since his first entry. According to him, there had once been an assassination attempt on a tribal chief in what had been South West Africa when it was a German colony, before the First World War. The incident had been reported telegraphically: *Hotentoten Potentaten Attentäter Attentat*. It then transpiring that the intended victim was

233

actually the ruler's aunt, a correction was issued: *Hotentoten Potentaten Tante Attentäter Attentat*. My apologies to any German who might conceivably ever come across this.)

On achieving power after thirteen years in opposition, for only the second time ever with a clear Parliamentary majority, the British Labour party had decided that they were in a position to introduce on the inter-governmental front something comparable to the domestic system of 'welfare', or at any rate something informed by the same principles implied in the desire to "close the gap between the rich and the poor", which had animated their own overall domestic policies. The crucial principle - or anyway one of the essential such principles - was that the aid programme was an entirely government-to-government business. We were not supposed to interfere in a sovereign country's internal affairs. And yet there was a plain requirement for some kind of 'vetting' of ideas put forward by a 'recipient' country to a 'donor' country to determine the objective of taxpayers' money funded out of the UK Aid Programme - and a clear need to establish some control over its disbursement. The attempt to square this particular circle was to run like a kind of *obbligato* through aid policy and practice.

The concept of development aid, so it seemed to me, had come into being largely as an ideal without the practical details having been worked out. The intention, I suppose, had always been to sort out the practicalities *ex post* in the course of applying the principles which would determine whether a perceived need really existed and whether, and how, it might be addressed. This as a general rule would not, I think, be entirely unreasonable. Indeed I would imagine that without first adopting some such position few things aimed at ameliorating existing ills in any field would ever get done. Yet there was also a very strong element in the ministry which would not have recognised this as the real spur to activity but which, rather, regarded development aid as some kind of almost inherently warranted - virtually theological - corpus, and those who administered it as something in the nature of acolytes with no function in the formulation of its doctrines and dogmas. The expounders of this morality, the guardians of this theology and doctrine, were the Development Economists.

Much paper has been covered in the discussion of the theories which have variously been propounded about this arcane science of development economy. Indeed at that time a whole school of economic theory was being developed, with university faculties devoted to its study and elaboration. And at one stage it seemed to me that there was an attempt being made, perhaps unwittingly, to engender in the lay practitioners of aid an undue attitude of deference and respect for this branch of knowledge, which was in danger of becoming comparable to that which I was to discover was accorded in the Soviet Union to "our engineers". These soviet scientists seemed to be adulated as the custodians of an infallible method of resolving all difficulties in their sphere of specialisation, and so vouchsafing a happy existence to humankind. (I was to hear this kind of eulogistic talk from our Russian Intourist guide in Samarkand, *apropos* the irrigation system of the cottonfields of Uzbekistan in the countryside all around, and this a bare five years before the horrors of what was to be called the "desertification" of the Aral Sea, in consequence of the over-extraction of its waters, was to feature on our television screens.)

It would be of no relevance to my attempt to produce some internal coherence to this part of my recollections were I to devote time trying even to summarise the different development aid theories which, often pretty promptly, were to supersede each other as the current orthodoxies. Examples are the 'trickle down' theory which, in the manner of the Soviet centralised economic planning methodology, concentrated on huge major capital projects in the expectation that the wealth generated would seep down to the population at large; and the contrary idea that aid should be focussed on small local activities directly related to the needs of the rural inhabitants. From the concept of "small is beautiful" was born the vision of "Intermediate Technology" as the appropriate way by which the economies of the "developing countries" were to be galvanised. And so on. In the event however what could be said, in the jargon of the decade, was that "pragmatism ruled; OK?" I fairly soon found myself empathising with those who were becoming disenchanted with orthodoxies and who preferred to look for solutions in the light of their understanding of what the situation seemed to call for, irrespective of pre-ordained doctrine. I realised as I advanced into middle age that I was increasingly out of sympathy with the doctrinaire, and with perceptions which separated things into 'either ... or ...', instead of trying to see the possibility, perhaps, of 'both ... and ...'. Nor was this true only of my working life.

Another basic principle of our aid programme was that it should not be used for the provision of military equipment. To refuse aid directly for this purpose was one thing. But how to ensure that aid for promoting the overall social and economic development of a country didn't result in a portion of the increased revenues thus generated for the local budget being used to fund items not considered proper for financing directly from overseas aid was something else. After all, wasn't the 'recipient' country a sovereign state entitled to make disbursements from its budget as it saw fit? It would again not serve the purpose of this personal story to go into the ways in which, over time, this sort of clash of interests was sought to be resolved. (On the face of it, as reported in the media, the famous Pergau dam episode of recent years - and more than fifteen years after my retirement - seems but a new manifestation of this recurrent problem of reconciling the desires and objectives of 'donor' and 'recipient' countries.)

There was, too, the continual - almost continuous - dialogue on the nature of the relationship between aid and trade. The opposing arguments on either side of this debate were, in part, a reflection of the different political attitudes and doctrines of the Labour and Conservative parties. The former held that aid to developing countries was self-justified, and that the content and administration of the aid programme was a matter of detached and autonomous policy. On the other hand the Conservative party took the view that aid was no more and no less than an aspect of the overall relations between countries - was, in short, but another tool in the armoury of foreign policy. That being so, when the Conservatives came to power in 1970, they abolished the ODM as a separate Ministry with a Cabinet Minister at its head. Instead they gave responsibility for overseas development aid to the Secretary of State for Foreign Affairs, with day to day administration entrusted to the supervision and control of an FCO Minister. We thus became the Foreign and Commonwealth Office (Overseas Development Administration) - FCO(ODA) for short - ODA for even shorter. The alternation between ODM and ODA has continued ever since in accordance with the political complexion of the party in power. In my time (I left during Mrs Thatcher's first term of office) this change had made little practical difference except that, with political objectives in view, a degree of flexibility under the ODA label probably needed rather less theoretical justification or excuse than might be the case

236

under the ODM one. But in practical terms that distinction would have been fine at best.

The departments of the ministry were, in broad terms, divided between the geographical and the functional. The former dealt with specific countries or groups of countries; and the latter were either the source of expertise in different aspects of aid evaluation, or dealt with relations with individual bodies or organisations, or were concerned with servicing the aid programme and with general policy including, for example, its overall size and its apportionment between multilateral and bilateral aid projects and between particular recipients. I spent the last fifteen years of my paid working life (apart from two short interludes) in the ODM, the ODA, once more the ODM, and then finally the ODA again. Just as my first Labour Minister had been the formidable Barbara Castle, so my last one was that determined lady Judith Hart of the same party.

With the exception of the two short spells outside the ODA I worked during this period in four departments: International; Middle East and Mediterranean; Education; and Crown Agents and Private Investment. Until my last four years, when I became a head of department, at the grade of Assistant Secretary, I was what was known as a 'desk officer', normally one of two or three such officers working to a departmental head and supported in turn by two or three executive officers. Each of the departments in which I served warrants a brief comment or two.

International Department dealt with the IDA and with DAC; but also with bilateral contacts with other donor countries. Among my very first jobs (working, naturally, under my Assistant Secretary) was briefing Mrs Castle for visits from the Dutch, and the German, Aid Ministers. My impressions were twofold. First that the Minister was just as much, if not indeed more, reliant on, and ready to receive advice or briefing from, the economists (who had all been brought in by the Labour administration). Second, that the inter-ministerial visits were as much concerned with boosting the image of this new thing, 'development aid', in the public mind as they were with actual matters of substance. But if I were right in so thinking, there would not seem to be anything very peculiar in that, since all high level gatherings, whether domestic or international - and not least when at the 'summit' - appear to be at least as much occasions for presentation and publicity as they are of substance. I doubt that it would be far from the truth to say that the higher the level, the greater the 'hype', and the less concrete achievement produced directly from the meeting. I hope I am not being jaundiced. It may perhaps be a risk of advancing years that one takes a rather more sceptical look at what one sees, but the relatively recent prominence, these last ten years or so, of those unlovely phenomena the 'image maker' and the 'spin doctor' doesn't lead me to believe that I am simply recording subjective disenchantment.

Involvement with DAC and, when I was in Education Department, with UNESCO, brought me into contact with the wonderful world of international gatherings. Both these bodies had their headquarters in Paris. The first being, as already indicated, a committee of the 'donors club', the OECD, member countries were represented at working level by staff from those countries' diplomatic missions in the French capital. The United Nations Education Scientific and Cultural Organisation, however, was one of the United Nations's Specialised Agencies, with membership open to every member country of that organisation - a right of which each one availed itself - and many had their own specific representation with offices in Paris. Members of UNESCO's Executive Board (the senior working level below periodical ministerial gatherings) were ostensibly elected *ad personam*, in recognition of their theoretical independence of their governments. This in no way stood in the path of their being nominated by those respective governments. Nor was any incongruity seen in members from totalitarian countries (and not only those from communist states) being put forward by such regimes for Board membership, as supposedly 'independent' of them.

Since they did not attend meetings as government representatives, Board Members received payment, from the UNESCO budget, on a *per diem* basis with corresponding allowances of various sorts, not excluding entertainment. When meetings of other inter-governmental bodies, DAC for example, were attended by civil servants from Whitehall they travelled out and back, stayed at hotels, and paid for their meals out of a daily subsistence allowance paid for by their ministries at the normal British civil service rate - which was very properly modest. By contrast the allowances paid by UNESCO to their Board members were handsome indeed. This I learned fortuitously. I was with the UK Board member at a UNESCO meeting lasting several days. He was an Under Secretary in charge of the Division of the ODM under whom Education Department, with several others, came. He was also the UK representative at the UN Food and Agriculture Organisation (FAO), whose meetings took place at its headquarters in Rome. The UNESCO and FAO meetings overlapped by one day. For the final day of the former meeting I was left as the *ad hoc* acting UK Board member. In that capacity I was given by one of the UNESCO staff an envelope containing the Board member's *per diem* allowance. The amount is no longer within my memory, and even if it were there would be no meaning in the franc figure today against the present sterling/franc conversion rate. But I still do carry the memory of the surprise I felt when I opened the envelope and saw what a single day's allowance was.

UNESCO's revenues derived entirely from the contributions made by its member states. The method of arriving at its annual budget was scarcely conducive to economy. Every member state would put in bids for spending; some process of evaluation, and horse-trading, was then undertaken by the generously salaried Director-General and his staff, and this yielded an itemised 'expenditure' side of the coming year's budget. The total sum was then apportioned among the members on the basis of their relative wealth as measured by their Gross National Product to yield the required 'revenue'. It doesn't need a great deal of perception to see that this methodology inevitably yielded a budget swollen by bids and expectations from those governments who would be paying very little indeed of the cost of implementation. Its questionable financial management apart, the whole organisation also degenerated into a forum of unseemly political acrimony. Which perhaps ought not to have surprised anyone who had some knowledge of that *furor academicus* which has not been too rare in places having to do with education and culture - even when national interests and politics are not added to the cauldron. (After I had ceased to be involved, however minimally, with its affairs, disenchantment with UNESCO reached the point where Britain actually decided to withdraw its membership, as I believe did the United States also.)

The only time I was in a department responsible for direct UK bilateral aid to individual countries was when I was in Middle East and Mediterranean Department. In fact I served there twice. The first time was in the late sixties, after my initial posting to International Department. In this geographical department I was concerned with aid to the countries of the Near East and Arabian peninsula. As far as Arabia was concerned, recipients included the Gulf States of Abu Dhabi, Dubai, Sharjah, Ras al Khaimah, Fujairah, etc. These being the separate small sheikhdoms which now comprise the fabulously wealthy Federation known as the United Arab Emirates, one might well ask what the UK aid programme had to do in that part of the world. The reason, as so often, was to be found in the history of British involvement in the area. A lengthy historical digression on this point is out of place in what is my own story. But, in very short summary, Britain had assumed the role of responsibility for the defence and foreign relations of these small sheikhdoms in the course of the 19th century as part of her strategy of safeguarding the route to India. This relationship was embodied in treaties with the various sheikhs, in consequence of which their countries were known as the Trucial States. In each of the main ones there was a resident British 'Political Adviser', performing the same pro-consular function - albeit as a much lesser fish in a vastly smaller pond - as had for example Baring (later Lord Cromer) in Egypt at the time of General Gordon and into the early years of the present century. British policy in the Gulf was now essentially concerned with keeping relations sweet, to counter possible influences inimical to British interests. In a few years the discovery of enormous quantities of petroleum was to make the area wholly inappropriate to receive development aid, but at this time there was scope for that form of aid I have already mentioned - the provision of specialist personnel by way of 'technical assistance'. But the main recipient country of UK aid within the responsibility of my section of Middle East and Mediterranean Department was the Kingdom of Jordan, which was indeed a developing country. It was a classic example of an area where both development aid theory and political expediency merged without any principles clashing too seriously. To Jordan we provided both capital aid (in the form of modest development aid loans) as well as technical assistance.

It was the practice in the ministry for desk officers and heads of departments to visit, soon after appointment, the main territories for which they were responsible, in order to acquaint themselves on the ground with the work they were financing. I went out on such a 'familiarisation tour' around Easter of 1967. The tour began and ended with the customary couple of days' call on the Middle East Development Division in Beirut. This MEDD was a sort of overseas offshoot of the ODM itself, headed by a member of the ministry with head of department rank and with a staff consisting of an economist, an engineer, and two or three other specialists whom I don't now remember. The Division's function was, broadly, to lead in identifying aid projects and to help with their appraisal for suitability for aid financing, as well as to keep an eye on the course of implementation of approved projects. (There were later to be further Development Divisions set up for other regions, including the Caribbean and South East Asia.)

Beirut had not then been reduced to the virtual heap of rubble it was soon to become. I was to get a faint glimpse of what lay under the surface of the prosperity of what was still the bolthole of the super-affluent from the countries of the area. The head of Dev Div, as it was called, gave a luncheon party to which I was invited. All the other guests were Lebanese of the sort to be expected at such a gathering, businessmen, professionals, academics and so forth. Conversation flowed, but I remember nothing of it. Until, that is, it turned to my visits which, after those to the several Trucial States, to Bahrein, and to Muscat, had ended with the most extended of these - in Jordan.

I mentioned that I had taken the opportunity of an inspection of an electricity project we were funding at Zerqa, north of the capital at Amman to visit the famous Roman site of Jerash, and that I had there encountered, for the first time, the PLO. Someone had come up to me and waved me away from taking a photograph in a particular direction, and the member of the British Embassy in Amman who was accompanying me had told me that he was informed that the man was a PLO member. This casual introduction by me of the Palestine 'dimension' produced an intemperate and vehement attack on the Palestinians. I confined myself to expressing the wish that a resolution could be found to the conflicting interests of the parties to the dispute over what had been Palestine, which I hoped would be based on justice - without which there seemed no prospect of a lasting peace. But the very word "justice", as having any applicability to the Palestinians, was but petrol on the flames. An altogether astonishingly unexpected virulence was this - which I was to recall when, years afterwards, the news broke of the Lebanese Maronite Falangist massacres of the entire population of the Sabra and Chatilla refugee camps, following the Israeli seizure of south Lebanon. I can only assume that some, if not all, the guests at that luncheon party were sympathisers, if not actually members, of the Falange. Again, it being no part of my own story, I avoid a diversion into any but the briefest mention of the fact that the independent state of Lebanon was the creation of the French after the First World War, with the deliberate aim of producing a Christian majority country in the almost wholly Moslem Middle East - with not entirely unpredictable results. But at this point I am reminded of an aspect of the post-Ottoman Middle East, which does in fact impinge on my family and me.

***********

*Both on that familiarisation tour, and often since, I have found myself thinking of the terrible fate of those Arabs who once lived in that area which was the district of Palestine, then a part of the Ottoman province of Syria. Would they conceivably consider that what befell them, as the direct result of their ambitions and of the frequently contradictory ones of the victorious Western European powers after 1918, had been preferable to their position before that? I have previously remarked that no one takes kindly to being ruled by a foreign country, and the cry for independence would surely have been heard sooner or later from the political leaders of the major Arab regions of the Ottoman empire. But the manipulation of local political objectives by outside powers had produced infinitely worse, for those Palestinian Arabs, than that which their leaders had sought to replace.*

*King Hussein of Jordan is the great grandson of the Hussein who was the Sherif of Mecca and the Hejaz during and after the First World War. Instead of the Sherif becoming the sovereign of a new independent Arab kingdom, as he had been promised by Britain, it turned out that those who had during that war encouraged, and paid, him to take the British side against his Ottoman suzerain were, after it, unable to prevent his being expelled from his ancestral tribal lands in the Arabian peninsula by the rival Saudis. He then came to live in exile in the British Crown Colony of Cyprus. The Mufti of the place was, as I have told, my paternal grandfather; and the Governor was that Sir Ronald Storrs who had previously been Oriental Secretary in Cairo during the World War, and the Military Governor of Jerusalem in the early years after it. He could scarcely have been ignorant that the promises made to Sherif Hussein during the war by his chief in Cairo, Sir Henry MacMahon, were not reconcilable with the agreement reached around the same time by the British emissary Mark Sykes with his opposite number the Frenchman Georges Picot. Was Storrs abashed one wonders? In exile in Cyprus the Sherif, who spoke perfect Turkish, often met the Mufti, who spoke perfect Arabic. I wish I knew what the latter thought of the former, and both of them of the man now the Governor!*

*That recollection brings to me another memory, this time of the year 1935, my first year at Ellesmere. I see myself being introduced - at a Speech Day, I think - by the headmaster to someone named Sir Ronald Storrs. I do not know that he has been the Governor of Cyprus - or if I was told this it couldn't have registered. The death of "Lawrence of Arabia" was referred to by Storrs. The exact context I cannot remember; but it was that year, as I was to know later, that Lawrence had been killed in a motor-cycle accident. The name of Lawrence, or indeed any of his pseudonyms, would have meant nothing at all to me when Storrs spoke to me of him. When I think of the incident now, sixty years later exactly, I am in no doubt that he was being crass to an extraordinary degree; but I am left wondering whether that crassness lay more in his stupidity - in thinking that a nine year old would have had the remotest idea of whom he was talking about - than in the insensitivity implied in his even bringing up a topic which would hardly have been expected to be congenial to a young Turkish boy, assuming he might be thought to have known anything about the man. But what staggers me much more today is that he could have been so obtusely lacking in plain good manners as to have made no mention whatsoever of his acquaintance with my grandfather, or indeed my father, to whom he owed his skin, if not his existence, at the time of the Greek riots in Cyprus a bare four years previously. For my mind is completely blank of any such mention. But of course one's recollections can be treacherous. If in fact he did mention my father, then I apologise to his memory.*

***********

There were, as I have said, a couple of times when I was briefly posted away from the ODM - or rather from the ODA, since it was the Conservatives who were in power under Edward Heath on both occasions. On the second such occasion I found myself in the Foreign and Commonwealth Office.

In the FCO it was customary for a head of department to have an 'Assistant'. To be appointed to such a post was not a promotion, rather it was something in the nature of recognition that one might be in line for possible promotion. There was in the FCO a department, Far East and Pacific if I correctly recall its title, whose responsibilities included the residual colonial dependencies in the Pacific, like the Solomons and the Gilbert and Ellice Islands. To this department I was appointed as 'Assistant', at an age when the ambitious would certainly have thought themselves 'passed over' in terms of career prospects. Whether or not it was in direct consequence of this sort of halfway house to promotion to Assistant Secretary rank I don't have a very clear idea, but I do remember round about this time being surprised at feeling discomfited when others younger than myself were becoming  heads of departments in the ODA. Some there were who clearly were 'high fliers' and due for rapid advancement. And, at any rate theoretically, I should have felt no pang either when others I thought no more able than myself also went up the ladder. After all I was, in my own estimation, not keen to be promoted. I had sat lightly to the idea of promotion, as I was both content with my lot and not particularly keen to assume the greater responsibility which came with the job of head of a department. And I hadn't made any secret of my attitude. (Nor did I find the obvious 'pushers' congenial.)

Yet clearly there was something in me which was not that indifferent detachment, that calm contentment with what fate had apportioned for me, which I had rather smugly and arrogantly thought to be my genuine attitude. Was it the case that I was sensing something of being 'unfulfilled'? I doubt it. At the time I think I genuinely did not want to be  promoted, even to the not very lofty height of Assistant Secretary.

244

And certainly today, too, I recoil when I hear anyone express a longing to be "stretched", or "challenged". (The memory of the late Lord Reith's *'Face to Face'* interview by John Freeman on television, which I have already mentioned, comes to me again as one of the most extreme instances of this.) So far as I can judge at this distance, I suspect that there was, in my reaction to other people's promotions, little that was positive, and that I was being influenced much more by some such negative and unattractive impulse as mere envy. And, as I see it now, my resistance to promotion was in fact being motored much less by indifference than it was by a deep-seated lack of self-reliance. However, I suppose there could just have been something else at work. I remembered that when I had appeared before the Civil Service Selection Board we candidates had been told, at a very early stage, if not at the very beginning, of the three-day process, that we were being judged for our potential to make the grade 'at least' to Assistant Secretary. Not to make that grade would therefore mean that one had not justified the original assessment of one's potential. I suspect that I was unconsciously coming to the realisation that were I in fact to retire without reaching the expected minimum level, I should have to face myself in retirement as a failure. I have said that I had remembered what we had been told at the CSSB. That reminder came in a very specific way - during the first of my postings away from the ODA.

In the early seventies I was again at the CSSB. Not this time as a candidate, but seconded for about six months to serve as a member, in the capacity - not entirely accurately termed - of 'observer'. The process of assessing candidates who had successfully negotiated the first stage in the selection process - the written examination - involved their having to face, over three days, a three-member panel of examiners at the CSSB offices in London, doing the sort of things I have already described when narrating my own experiences as a candidate. These panels comprised a chairman, a psychologist, and the so-called 'observer'. (It happened that during my stint of half a year at the CSSB there was a woman psychologist and the remainder of the panel were all men; but how far this was a representative proportion of the whole I have no idea.) Each team received, at the end of every week, its detailed list of the candidates who were to appear before them the following week, when they were to conduct the various exercises and tests I have already touched on. Apart from the group 'exercises' each candidate was separately interviewed by each member of the panel, and these interviews were followed by joint assessments. The entire process was very systematised and thorough.

The panel members operated as a team throughout the days of selection, but each one had their own particular function. The chairman, who was generally a retired senior civil servant or ambassador, brought to bear the weight of experience in judging the candidate as a whole and in forming an opinion on his or her potentialities. The psychologist's role I suppose would be self-evident, but essentially it was to form a view on the candidate's balance and capacity to hold up against pressures - to withstand what is now called 'stress'. As for the 'observer' his, or her, job was to look at the candidate's intellectual capacity - judged by reference to a range of abilities. It is not the requirements of the Official Secrets Act which stand in the way of my listing these various mental qualities and their parameters which one sought to establish - I don't even know whether that Act is still in operation in the full vigour it once had. It is that I simply do not now recall the details, except that they included such things as 'intellectual penetration' - how far and how readily the candidate was able to get to the root of a problem by distinguishing the relevant from the peripheral. Some of the things the observer was looking out for naturally also came within the psychologist's range of interests. As, for example, how far the candidate was capable of flexibility rather than sticking stubbornly to a pre-judged position.

I, also, learned many things from my experience at the CSSB. For example that I had myself been lucky to have been selected in my attempts to pass into the Home Civil Service in the first place. The standards were extremely high; the processes were very rigorous; the examiners were concerned to be absolutely fair. I must have known this vaguely when I had been a candidate, but it was another thing to see the thing in operation and to take the responsibilities of judging others oneself. At the risk of seeming to be straining after the flippantly epigrammatic, I have to say that I did in fact, and not infrequently, ponder whether, had I been a candidate appearing before myself, I would have passed myself. (In writing which, that salutary and humbling question now comes into my mind which I once remember reading - was it Malcolm Muggeridge who posed it? - "Would God pass, if set an examination in theology?") As, I imagine, with any selection process, our candidates invariably fell into three pretty clear categories. There were the tiny minority who were plainly going to be successful - barring some quite dreadful and unforeseeable *contretemps*. There were those at the other end of the spectrum, equally few in number, by whom one was astounded that they had ever managed to reach this second stage of the selection process, and who would seem to be doomed to inevitable disappointment at that stage. And there were those, the proportionately huge mass in the middle, whose fate must seemingly hang by the thinnest of threads, so great was the calibre of them all, and so immensely difficult the task of differentiating between them. It was now, in working as part of the CSSB system, that I learned that those candidates who went forward to the third and final stage of the selection process - the interview by the Selection Board (at which, as a candidate, I thought I had come a cropper on my first attempt) - did not necessarily do so on a firm recommendation from the CSSB to the Board. In other words appearance before the Board did not, for some, mean that they had 'passed' at the CSSB stage: they might merely have been sent on to the Board as a borderline candidate *in case* the Board might think them just suitable, and push them across the line. And, after having seen the system in operation from within, I am not being over-modest in thinking I was probably one who, on my first appearance before the Board, had reached them in just that way - and had not been so pushed. And might well have been so pushed on my next appearance.

One of the observer's jobs was to welcome each new batch of candidates in words, which one virtually memorised, intended to put them at their ease in as informal and friendly an atmosphere as possible. The rubric called for some such encouraging words as that they should bear in mind that they constituted some statistically very small percentage - I forget the exact figure - of the population at large, so that they could regard their mere presence for these three days of the selection process as evidence of their high attainment. And either at this preliminary induction, or some other point in the proceedings - I do not recall exactly - they were told that we would be looking for people who, as I have said, had "at least" Assistant Secretary potential. For this, if for no other reason, I was gratified when, in the year of the

Queen's Silver Jubilee, I was promoted to Assistant Secretary in the ODM.

My appointment was to the Crown Agents and Private Investment Department, the primary job of which was to sweep up after the Crown Agents *imbroglio* of the late sixties and early seventies. The matter is still sufficiently recent history for the mess, by which the then colossal losses of around £80,000,000 were incurred, not to have been completely forgotten. Setting out this body's full title - 'the Crown Agents [CAA in *acronym*] for the *Colonies*' - points to the reason why on earth an Aid Ministry should have been in any way involved. The CAA's function had historically been to act as agents in the UK, mainly in the purchasing field, for individual British colonial governments. Large sums of money were in total involved. As the colonial empire faded into history, the Colonial Office's various functions were gradually sloughed off to different Ministries - CRO, FCO, and Treasury. The successor states of the Colonies, the new independent Commonwealth countries, continued to use the CAA's services. The Colonial Office's residual responsibilities for the Crown Agents had, in due course, devolved onto the ODM.

In a very British evolutionary way the CAA themselves had, over the years, "just growed" - Topsy fashion - into a complete anomaly with, unbelievably, no actual legal existence, despite having launched out into the perilous seas of the property market and secondary banking, using funds which had been deposited with them by their 'principals' - the colonial and, later, their successor sovereign, independent governments. No conscious assessment had ever been carried out of the CAA's relative benefits and disadvantages - nor even any judgement made of the need for their very *raison d'être*. (The situation in that regard being not entirely dissimilar to that of the other oddity the Commonwealth itself.) To sort this out, to define the CAA's functions, and to give them a legal, statutory, existence, occupied the department for a couple of years (while, *pari passu*, the Tribunal of Enquiry went into the history of the whole affair). Much of the work of framing the requirements for the Parliamentary Draftsman and the passage of the resultant legislation through Parliament was done by an extremely able young desk officer, a woman, in the department. I left it largely to her discretion how far she wished to refer matters to me, and confined

248

myself to supervision, in its broadest sense. Not entirely unlike the 'Alan Brown Touch' I have mentioned in connection with my Oxford tutor's method. In administration this is known as 'delegation' - and is usually accounted as a virtue. I am doubtful that it was so construed by the desk officer.

The Minister, Judith Hart, took a personal interest in the progress of the Crown Agents Bill, which had not passed all its stages by the time the Callaghan government lost its Commons vote of confidence in the middle of 1979. Had we failed to get it through before Parliament was dissolved for the general election, the Bill would have lapsed. But we managed to get it into a list of uncontentious measures and it went through all its stages, and received Royal Assent in time. An anxious time. Several months' work was still needed to complete all the subsidiary legislation required to regulate in detail the new statutory Crown Agents' operations, and to set the date when the Act should come into operation, the 1st of January, 1980. After that necessary work was finished, early in the new year I asked formally for a transfer to some other department more closely involved with what might be considered the normal functions of a development aid ministry.

A greater contrast between Sir Peter Preston, my last Permanent Secretary, and Sir Andrew Cohen, my first, could not be imagined. In physical form, as in manner, they were poles apart - could in fact have come from different planets. I was surprised when Sir Peter, asking me to see him, made the point that I deserved a change from the affairs of the Crown Agents; and I was both surprised and pleased when he offered me the department in which I had served as a desk officer. Would I, he asked me, find it embarrassing to be the head of Middle East and Mediterranean Department? I said that it wouldn't - if it didn't embarrass him. He was in fact delicately alluding to the fact that outside those in Establishment Department he, at least, knew that A.S.Fair was the A.S.Faiz of the old Colonial Service and hailed from the island for whose aid relations with the UK (minimal though they were) the Department in question was also responsible. I made the point, however, that I would not make any familiarisation, nor any other official, visit to Cyprus but would leave this to the desk officer concerned, for whose work I would of course be responsible.

Much had happened in Cyprus since my mother had fled in 1963.

## Taking Flight

Just what that was  will form part of my story as I turn now to what concerns my domestic life after our return from Canada in the autumn of 1965.

**\*\*\*\*\*\*\*\*\*\***

Back in our house in Addison Crescent we had begun a life of blissful contentment.  As a family we had not just picked up the threads from the days before Canada.  We were now firmly rooted in England.  Not only was I in a job which did not require regular extended postings abroad with separation from our son (and the possibility of the same applying in the case of our daughter), but with my mother now seemingly a permanent exile from her country, having no prospect of ever being able to return to her own house, I felt that somehow fate itself had conspired to confirm the rightness of our original decision to make our own future in this country.  It was not just the British citizen, I thought, but the Englishman, who was now entirely at home.  Symbolically we bought a puppy - a delightful young beagle, whom we called Snoopy.  Hardly an original name nowadays for a dog of that breed, but it was not in fact one particularly well known at that time in an England into which the doings of 'Peanuts' - the 'Charlie Brown' strip cartoon characters - had only just begun to penetrate.  In Canada the world of those small folk had featured daily in the newspaper and had been very popular.  Our Snoopy was our visible and much loved link with our time in the senior British Dominion, as well as the expression of our hope that the days of our wandering were over.

Both children were very happy at their schools; our son in his last year at his boarding prep school; and our daughter back at Queen's Gate, also among the same friends and teachers she had known before Canada - but where she now had to unlearn the handwriting she had been required to use across the Atlantic.  Both son and daughter were to be successful when the time came for them to bid for their entrances to Westminster, and to Godolphin and Latimer.  It was an added bonus that to each of these they could go, respectively, as a weekly-boarder and as a day-girl.

Holidays we spent at home except for my annual couple of weeks' leave and very occasionally an Easter break in the country. As a kind of substitute for Cyprus we tried Malta for one summer leave; but, although it shared the Mediterranean setting, there was not even the most nebulous flavour of the unique quality of that other, larger Mediterranean island we had known. Yet we liked Malta well enough to make it our regular summer holiday haunt for three consecutive years. Up on the northern shore of the main island, across the channel from Gozo, and away from the urban areas we passed our days by, and in, the water, where even I learned to water-ski to make up for not having learned the snow version in Cyprus and during two winters in Canada. Before then we had spent one summer leave each in Scotland and in Ireland. The latter holiday was near Wexford, in a family house being run as a hotel. Its name was Bargy Castle. One of the two sons of the family was a wholly unexceptional lad who sometimes would strum his guitar, to himself, after dinner. He has since become the famous Chris de Burgh.

The time was to come when first our son and then our daughter felt that they had grown too old for holidaying with their parents; and we were to understand that the days of thinking automatically in terms of the family as a unit were drawing to an end. An entirely natural process of course which, indeed, if it does not happen, is very likely to have harmful consequences. But this otherwise very desirable evolution - though it naturally hurt at the time - in the personal development of the individual members of any family was taking place during a period which had especially fraught, and to many of us perilous, overtones.

\*\*\*\*\*\*\*\*\*\*

'Grass',' pot', marijuana, flower power, Ché Guevara, the Red Brigade, the Isle of Wight festival, Tim O'Leary, 'drop out', 'hang out', 'sit in', 'squat'. These words, with scores of others, and the changing attitudes they represented, came in like a surging flood as our children left their childhood to venture into the world of adulthood.

\*\*\*\*\*\*\*\*\*\*

251

## Taking Flight

Parents, in every age of the world's history, have presumably looked on in some trepidation at this stage of their lives and of those they have brought into the world. The myriad aspects of the clash between the generations, the inevitable urge to question and to resist authority, have provided themes for chroniclers, poets and prophets back to the earliest mists of recorded time. And perhaps there has never been a generation in which parents concerned for their children have not thought that the times in which they were living were particularly, and perhaps even perversely, out of joint. All the same I strongly suspect that future generations might well look back to the age which opened with the 'swinging sixties' as uniquely disturbing - in the plainest and least pejorative - sense of that word. I look back over, literally, a complete generation: the years during which each of our children have married, with wonderful partners, and have made us happy grandparents to five grandchildren, three boys and two girls - all exceptionally lovely and lovable. Super families. (I would say that, wouldn't I? But it is from others that I have heard that last adjective.) The passage of the intervening years have brought the usual anxieties and sorrows, in the causes of which every one of us has a share. But it is a most wonderful blessing for each of us to know a love and a trust for the other, born, so I believe, of an openness developed through a continuing growth in respect for that other as a person in their own right. More I do not believe anyone has the right to hope for; still less to expect. I am profoundly grateful.

And not least because I learned through my relations with my children, as well as with my wife, that rigidity of attitudes and opinions can be pregnant of great harm; not to other people only, but to oneself. There was the character in one of his many anecdotes, recounted by the Hon Galahad Threepwood, who observed sadly to him one day, "Between you and me, Gally, I suppose I'm one of those fellows my father always warned me against." This now strikes me as a good deal more healthy an attitude, in its regretful tone, than the one expressed by the self-righteous man held up as a warning in the parable of Jesus: "Lord, I thank you I am not as other men." Though I have no memory of telling my children, in terms, what I expected them to be, or to become, and so by inference of "warning" them against any specific types - this was, of course, before today's dire necessity of cautioning even the youngest against the perils they might face from some strangers

252

- I must certainly have conveyed this indirectly in my general attitudes. That each of them has turned out to be their own self, rather than a bogus simulacrum, modelled upon some kind of desirable 'type', is I am sure as great a fulfilment for them as it is for us, their parents, a deep and eternal satisfaction.

\*\*\*\*\*\*\*\*\*\*

At some time towards the end of the sixties I suddenly became aware that the house we were living in was worth a very great deal of money. My neighbour, who had bought his house after we had returned from Canada, mentioned one day, entirely *en passant*, what he had paid for it. I was astounded at the figure, which was more than five - though less than ten - times what we had paid for ours rather under ten years earlier. This information I found very unsettling. I have mentioned how I had once been apprehensive that our house might turn out to have been too large for us to cope with; and although, financially speaking, that consideration did not now weigh to anything like the same extent I continued to be rather conscious that it was a bit *au dessus de ma gare*. Yet providence had seen to it that the accommodation it provided was just what was required to enable my brother to give a home to my mother after she had lost hers in Cyprus. They continued to live in the garden flat below us in their own self-contained home, from which they could easily visit us, as we could them. (I remember that it was in their flat we all saw on television the historic victory by Britain against Germany in the European Cup. But it was generally our daughter, four years younger than her brother, who regularly watched the television with her grandmother.)

The realisation now that we were sitting on what was a fortune started a train of thought. Or rather this began to crystallise day dreams which Lalage and I had been indulging in even while we had been in Cyprus - that one distant day we might be able to retire to some spot in the depths of the English countryside, such as we both had memories of from our childhood in Devon. Almost as a routine we now began to skim through the country house advertisements in the Sunday paper.

\*\*\*\*\*\*\*\*\*\*

Unsettled by the knowledge of our house's value, I was at this time also getting more and more unsettled in my feelings about the Church. If I try to express these succinctly, I think I would say that I found myself much more in sympathy with what I understood of the person of Jesus than I was with the formulations and the institutions of the Church as such. Put another way, I would not, I think, be far out in saying that I liked individual Christians, but not the body of them as represented by this or that particular group manifestation, and especially not what passed as 'Christendom'. At this point there was nothing of my Turkish background at play here; there were many cradle Anglicans who were also floundering. In the terms of the book which had come out in Canada those few years back, "the pew" was ceasing to be very "comfortable". I may illustrate my position as I now see it by reference to one of the Charlie Brown strip cartoons in the Canadian newspaper that I have mentioned. The rather repellent little girl Lucy had set up a small booth, like a Punch and Judy stall, from which she operated as a psycho-analyst, with a notice announcing the fact, and that her fee was 5 cents a go. Charlie Brown tells her that he too intends to take up this line of business. Lucy rebuffs him with "You can't become a psycho-analyst; you don't love humanity!" "I do too love humanity," responds poor Charlie, "It's *people* I can't stand!" *Mutatis mutandis*, it was the reverse of this - though less categorically and not so all-embracingly stated - which would be a truer expression of my developing position. I tended to like the people, not the Church.

**\*\*\*\*\*\*\*\*\*\***

The Church of England was at this time engaged in talks on the possibility of an Anglican-Methodist rapprochement. These discussions had failed to reach a conclusive result at Synod level, and the matter had been left to be pursued experimentally at parish (Anglican) and district (Methodist) level. Our parish was one of the very few which the authorities had agreed should be allowed to see how far it might be possible to carry things forward. We used to have a regular series of evening meetings in the church hall (actually a modest sized vestibule to the nave) at which questions of general interest were discussed by a visiting speaker and a three- or four-member panel of parishioners: a sort of non-political 'Any Questions' or 'Moral Maze'. To one such meeting came a certain William Kyle. He was a Methodist Minister whose responsibilities involved overseeing several of the local Methodist districts. Quite separately, and on his own, but with the full knowledge of his own hierarchy, he had just begun to set up the extremely modest beginnings of what was to become the Westminster Pastoral Foundation. The name came from the headquarters building of English Methodism, Central Hall Westminster, in which Bill Kyle had been allowed the use of half a dozen small underground rooms. He told us about his work and his hopes for its development. 'Counselling' was his subject that evening, and it needed some explanation. The name was misleading since 'counsellors' did not give counsel, or advice; rather they listened. This is not the place to expound on what has since become a recognised means of providing help and filling a widely felt deep need for many thousands of people. It is enough to say here that after we had listened to Bill Kyle I remarked to Lalage that I thought this might be something for her. And so it turned out. She became one of the first students in the embryo set-up which came to birth underground - in more than one sense - a quarter of a century ago; and in the profession of counselling she has found her personal fulfilment.

**\*\*\*\*\*\*\*\*\*\***

Towards the end of the sixties, whose developments troubled so many who had known a Britain before the social and economic fault-lines of those years seemed to be endangering historical foundations, my brother had been debating with himself whether it made much sense for him to continue living in Britain. He had not married, and had no responsibility for a family. His way of life was simple and undemanding of more than a very minimal income. Why, therefore, should he not make his home in a Cyprus of blue skies and old memories? When his annual leave came up he spent a couple of weeks in Nicosia reconnoitring. He returned with his mind made up. Despite the beleaguered situation of the Turkish population, with the Greeks effectively controlling the government machine ever since the fighting which had broken out in December 1963, and though the Turkish community was virtually pinned into their several enclaves, it was possible for a Turk to live in the Turkish part of Nicosia, the largest such enclave, even under economic blockade. He made arrangements to sell a piece of his property there and to buy a small bachelor flat on the ground floor of a newly built apartment block. This was a quarter of a mile or so north of the barrels marking the northern boundary of that strip of land called, misleadingly, the 'Green Line', in which mother's house was still occupied by the the UNFICYP forces - a hundred yards beyond which were the barrels marking its southern boundary and the beginning of the Greek side of the town at that point. By 1973 my brother was in a position to make his move. He did so in the course of that year.

**\*\*\*\*\*\*\*\*\*\***

Meanwhile what was to be our *Annus Mirabilis* was lying in wait. 1974 was politically momentous as the year which, just as unexpectedly as 1970 had brought victory to the Conservatives under his leadership, was to witness Edward Heath's failed attempt to convince the electorate that they should continue to entrust his party with power. The Heath Conservatives' humiliation in the face of the over-mighty trade unions was followed in turn by the dismissal of the Callaghan Labour Party. Their electoral defeat in 1979 inaugurated the Thatcher years, when the Conservatives came in with widespread support for what was in effect a programme of Gladstonian Free Trade Liberalism, combined with the nearest a British public would accept to a reversion to 19th century control of trade union activity seen as being "in restraint of trade".

But in characterising 1974 as a year full of wonder - a year to be marvelled at - I am thinking of it much more narrowly, in personal terms, as being a climacteric in its consequences for me and our family. Although at the time, and in its short term aftermath, it was much more truly *horribilis* than *mirabilis* yet, viewed against the backdrop of the years which were to follow, I can see it as having been closer to the latter than to the former - pregnant with richness in the way our lives were to develop.

**\*\*\*\*\*\*\*\*\*\***

I cannot recapture in detail the way in which the public mood moved during that year - from euphoria to foreboding doom about the fate of the country's economy, and indeed about the future of Western capitalism. Feeling myself back to that time, it comes to me as though the country were showing the symptoms of an individual manic depressive. The processes by which economic inflation took hold and gathered pace in a way never before experienced in Britain in living memory, and without our even being fully conscious of what was really going on, is astonishing when I think back on it. We personally were, no doubt, far from being alone in our ignorance and naivety about the forces at work and the way the sophisticated players in the market place were using these to their personal advantage. Property speculation, one of the areas in which the Crown Agents had thought to make colossal profits, but in which they were to come to grief with huge losses to the taxpayer, was thought to be the royal road to wealth. But I will try to bring the thing within the compass of our own family story.

I have mentioned how, after we had learned that the value of our home had more than quintupled in less than ten years since we had bought it, Lalage and I had taken to flipping through the Sunday newspapers' property advertisements for houses in the country. We were not doing much more than fantasising about what we might do when I were to retire - in some fifteen years time, as it then seemed. Scanning the estate agents' country advertisement pages inevitably drew our attention to the London property pages as well. By the early 1970s it seemed that, certainly for our part of London, house prices were rising much faster compared with those in fairly remote rural areas such as we had been contemplating as the place of our dream retirement home. The idea of actually being able to retire early began to assume the dimensions of possibility, even reality. We were, without realising it, being seduced into becoming property speculators. Nor, it seems now, were we alone in this. As it turned out we weren't even in a particularly small minority.

At the time my brother had gone to live in Cyprus in 1973 our son also had decided that he wanted to set up independently, and had moved out to a flat with friends. This left Lalage and me with our teenage daughter occupying our very large house, with my mother alone in the

257

flat down below.  Without our giving any really detailed thought to arrangements in a possible new home, the house advertisements seemed to suggest that there was plenty of scope for comfortably adjusting to the circumstances of a move to the country if we were able to judge that to be financially sound.  (It was at that time, as I recall it, that the term "granny flat" first entered the language.)

\*\*\*\*\*\*\*\*\*\*\*

Our daughter had meanwhile achieved excellent O Levels, but was finding her single-sex day school too confining.  In her first A Level year she realised she had made a wrong choice of subjects.  To make a change would not only mean losing a year but also finding herself in a class in which all the girls would be her juniors when hitherto the reverse had been the case.  She wanted to begin a new A Level year at a new school. We were fortunate in getting a place at a mixed boarding school in Somerset, where she settled in quickly and successfully, happy in her work and with her new friends.  Her old ones, especially ones she had known since her first junior school days in London before going to Canada, she still met during her holidays.

In the summer of 1973, still in our Addison Crescent home, she had come on a fortnight's riding holiday in Andalucia with Lalage and me.  A wonderful experience which we look back to with most fond memories.  For myself, my first - and only - sight of the Alhambra at Granada gave me a startling new understanding of the purity and grace of the 13th and 14th century flowering of  Islamic architecture in a Moslem state where the three monotheistic faiths had once flourished in a tolerance ignored in any of the modern histories of which I then had any knowledge.  And yet 'History' - though admittedly focussed on 18th and 19th century English and European - had been my main subject for Higher School Certificate thirty years earlier.

\*\*\*\*\*\*\*\*\*\*\*

It was also in 1973, only about half a dozen years after we had learned from our neighbour of the huge increase in the value of our house from what we had paid for it in 1957, that our neighbour on the other

258

side told us that he was hoping to sell his place for a figure which was by then very much more than ten times our house's value about fifteen years earlier. More significantly, the sum was very comfortably in excess of what was an almost talismanic figure of £100,000. At that time this was real wealth - I suppose about equivalent to winning around half a million pounds on today's national lottery. We had also been getting unsolicited letters from estate agents for some little while. Early in 1974 we decided to respond to such an approach from the most well-known of these.

*In one of his hilarious short stories about the impecunious, but ever hopeful, rogue Stanley Featherstonehaugh Ukridge, P.G. Wodehouse has the man outlining his latest scheme for settling on easy street. He had just met up again with a friend who had, literally, struck oil in America. Ukridge persuades him that he should buy "a house in the country with a decent bit of shooting" and that the matter should be entrusted to him, Ukridge. 'I said "Leave it entirely in my hands, old horse. I'll see you're treated right." So he told me to go ahead, and I went to Farmingdons, the house-agent blokes in Cavendish Square. Had a chat with the manager. Very decent old bird with moth-eaten whiskers. I said I'd got a millionaire looking for a house in the country. "Find him one, laddie," I said, "and we split the commish." He said, "Right-o," and any day now I expect to hear he's dug up something suitable. Well, you can see for yourself what that's going to mean. These house-agent fellows take it as a personal affront if a client gets away from them with anything except a collar-stud and the clothes he stands up in, and I'm in halves. Reason it out, my boy, reason it out.'*

The above gross parody of estate agents' scheme of operating dates from seventy years ago. Their image over the past twenty years still remains rather less than flattering. We put ourselves in their hands and took their advice to go for a sale in the spring of 1974. The house remained on the market for the rest of the year. Scarcely anyone showed any interest. When, after the normal advertisements in the usual way, we were advised to have an auction with a glossy, expensive, brochure we took this advice too. The auction was in the autumn. The reserve price was not reached. We should, I suppose, have taken the house off the market at that stage. But we were novices in a game in which those whose business was the sale and purchase of properties had their own agenda. We allowed our home to remain for sale - in a continuing, and increasing, state of apprehension and anxiety at what was happening in the property market. Had we but been aware of it, the slump was already upon us, and those who were not constrained to sell would have been well advised to defer decisions until the air was clearer. As it happened, this slump was to be followed before the end of the decade by a strong recovery - culminating indeed in the even more lunatic rise in house values which was to end in the South Sea Bubble of the early and mid-1980s, with its attendant tragic phenomenon, never before seen, of 'negative equity'. That at least we were spared. But we did sell our home - at a price which did not yield the hoped-for result of retirement to the country. We bought another house in London - less expensive, less spacious, and very much less pleasant. From there I continued with my job. My mother, as I shall tell, was now no longer living with us.

**********

How we can deceive ourselves. In my case, it seems to me that I was wholly ignorant of the effect on my teenage daughter, and even on my son, of my own fermenting inner uncertainties - my haverings over religion, over career expectations, over who and what exactly I was. These irresolutions, although rarely, if ever, openly expressed as such must clearly have been a most unsettling cumulative influence on her, which would have seriously added to the difficulties of any child, particularly a teenage girl, at any time. So it seems to me now. And not least the most recent indecisions over selling our home. I have since learned that our own doubts and uncertainties act most insidiously on those close to us. Indeed the closer the ties of affection, the greater seemingly is the infection. Not only through some inner, psychic, way of transference, which I can only dimly sense to be so, but - and this I believe I can see quite clearly looking back - because the very closeness and intimacy (which we can sometimes identify with love, though it seems to me to be merely a small aspect of it) can paradoxically serve to stand in the way of open expression and interchange, and so actually impede understanding. Somehow I must have assumed that in the family we each in some way *knew* the others' hopes, fears and anxieties by a sort of osmosis, without having to talk about them.

260

I have earlier castigated what I have considered to be Sir Ronald Storrs's crassness in terms of his stupidity and insensitivity when he visited Ellesmere in 1935. I can now see that I was as much open to a similar charge of obtuseness at the time of my children's adolescence.

The year 1974, as horrible as it was later to be seen as marvellous, dragged on. My mother had been growing restive about how her bachelor elder son was faring on his own in Cyprus after more than a year. In the summer she packed for a short visit. She had been absent more than ten years - much the longest time she had ever been away from the island. At the end of June she flew out to visit my brother in his small bachelor flat.

Rather less than three weeks later, on the 15th of July, came the news of a bloody armed *coup* by the extreme right-wing Greek Cypriots, in concert with the military regime in Athens, against the Makarios administration in the island. The first accounts claimed that Makarios had been killed. Nicos Sampson, it was announced, had been set up as "President of Cyprus".

\*\*\*\*\*\*\*\*\*\*

*This man had been the leading killer member of EOKA in the 1950s, when he was known to have been personally responsible for a number of murders in Nicosia. He was particularly notorious for boasting about the number of Turks he had himself killed in the winter of 1963-64, at the time my mother had fled her home.*

\*\*\*\*\*\*\*\*\*\*

The course of events then may be summarised very briefly. Though the details were only to emerge during the weeks which followed I was myself able at the time, fortuitously, to keep track rather more closely of what was happening on the ground. The *coup* had been carried out while I was doing my stint in the FCO and my department was physically close to the central FCO 'incident room' - as I think it was called - where incoming information was collated and mapped. I got permission to visit this room from time to time and could follow on the wall-map the course of the fighting after Turkey had intervened.

## Taking Flight

**\*\*\*\*\*\*\*\*\*\***

*Within hours of the Greek coup in the island it was to transpire that Makarios had managed to escape from the 'Presidential Palace' (which I took to be the old Government House, the site of the previous building, burned to the ground during the 1931 Greek riots, from which Sir Ronald Storrs had been taken to safety by my father). It also emerged in the months after the 1974 coup that the Sampson conspirators had been intending, with the Athens government, to declare the union of Cyprus with Greece. But with the failure of the assassination attempt on Makarios, the conspirators dithered. With the Turkish intervention five days after the coup, the Athens government fell. As soon as Ankara had learned of the Cyprus/Athens coup, the Turkish government had moved very quickly on a matter vital to Turkey's national security (as had been recognised in the Treaties which had brought Cyprus into existence as an independent republic in 1960). That same day the matter had been brought before the NATO Council. The following day the Turkish Prime Minister - the only socialist one, as it happens, that Turkey has had to date - flew to London to urge the British government to fulfil its obligations as a guarantor of the Cyprus Constitution and Accords under the 1960 Treaties. He warned that if Britain did not so act, in conjunction with Turkey the second guarantor, to frustrate this armed attempt - with the connivance of the forsworn third guarantor, Greece - to bring about the internationally outlawed enosis, then Turkey would exercise her treaty right to move unilaterally. The British government, in office a bare four months, far from vacillating in turn, as the Greek conspirators had done, decisively reached its conclusion: they would not adhere to, but would renege on, their treaty obligations.*

*The Turkish Prime Minister told Harold Wilson, and the Foreign Secretary James Callaghan, that Turkey would exercise her Treaty right.*

On 20th July, five days after the armed coup on the island, Turkey landed troops on the northern coast of Cyprus four miles west of Kyrenia, and at the same time dropped paratroops into the northern outskirts of Nicosia, both to secure the vital road between the capital and the north coast and to resist attacks on the Turkish population of the capital. The rest is history - though seemingly little known, or anyway remembered, in Britain these days.

\*\*\*\*\*\*\*\*\*\*

It was the lines of fighting around Nicosia, traced on the wall-map in the FCO incident room, which I was able to follow. The centres of fiercest engagement, in which heavily armed units from Greece were involved, were the airport a few miles to the west of the capital, and the vicinity of the Ledra Palace hotel which was a major Greek strong-point. When the cease-fire came in a few days the airport was left in no-man's land. So, too, was the Ledra Palace - and my mother's house. There, a bare fifty yards southward of the barrels marking the present northern boundary of the 'Green Line', it still stands today - deserted, dilapidated, desolate.

\*\*\*\*\*\*\*\*\*\*

The effect on me of the news of the Cyprus *coup* was unsurprising, predictable even: much the same emotions as had stirred me when, eleven years before, I had heard in Ottawa of the fighting in Nicosia. Although I had, in my own judgement, completely severed my connection with the place, fate had so arranged matters that, as in 1963 so again in 1974, my mother was once more caught up in the fighting - and this time so too was my brother. It was therefore not surprising that I should have experienced anger and apprehension. And coupled with fear for their safety I felt, again, fury at the Greek treachery which had once more visited violence and killing on the people of the island by those inflamed with a nationalist ideology which seemed to me then, twenty years ago, as much a perversion of true patriotism as idolatry is of religion. It seems so even more today when we have the detestable proofs of this before us in the consequences of Milosevic, Karadjic, Mladjic and the rest.

\*\*\*\*\*\*\*\*\*\*

## Taking Flight

And yet there was in my reaction to the news of the Turkish intervention on 20th July 1974 that which was to me wholly unpredictable and astonishing. I experienced an overwhelming sense of what I think I can only describe as a huge release of tension. I remember actually saying aloud, "Thank God; at last!" Whatever else I might have meant by this, it was abundantly clear that I was recognising in myself something quite beyond any pretence or role-playing - a reality deeply and genuinely felt. At the moment itself, and for some considerable time into the future, I took this to be an uprising of an inner self, long-denied and deliberately suppressed, a 'Turkishness', however inchoate and ill-defined. That there was indeed such a strong component in whatever revealed itself in a spontaneous reactive outburst is undeniable. It was, however, to lead to a new discernment of what 'Turkishness' was, or could be. Not simply yet another manifestation of that corrosive and destructive nationalism, narrow and exclusive, arrogant and self-righteous, as had evoked such loathing in me when clothed in Greek habiliments, and was to become for me almost as repellent when I was, if only very rarely, to see it in Turkish garb. (More so, perhaps, in the latter case when it subjectively was to appear as a debasement of a thing one loves: truly the Roman was right who said, "The corruption of the best is the worst".) What the long-delayed salvation of the Cyprus Turks in the summer of 1974 was to lead me to was the discovery of something positive, constructive - and universal. But not at once.

**\*\*\*\*\*\*\*\*\*\***

By 1975 we were no longer in our much loved Addison Crescent home. It had been the previous November which had suddenly brought a firm offer for our house - the first since we had agreed to put it up for sale way back in the spring and after the nugatory and expensive auction in the autumn. In ignorance, and apprehension that this might be the only opportunity to realise this large capital asset, with the market now clearly falling rapidly, we had decided to accept the offer. Yet again I had allowed impulse - and this time a very negative one, arising from fear rather than hope - to determine a decision. Even more than when I had resolved to abandon Cyprus, I think I could now make a more than cogent debating case that the decision, in both cases, was

264

'wrong'. But as things were to turn out, I could argue even more strongly to the contrary. Again experience has worked to enable me this time to understand the essential truth of what I once had simply accepted: that "there's nothing either good or ill but thinking makes it so". As I write now, I can recall vividly the distress and desolation we felt after we realised that we had sacrificed our home. Not for nothing have people bracketed that experience with the trauma of those other separations through divorce and bereavement. And yet I can now also see that many wonderful and enriching circumstances of our family are traceable to that sale more than twenty years ago - for all the more direct sadnesses it also caused at the time. For myself, the sense of guilt in feeling that I had made a disastrous mistake - not measured just financially but in the effect it had on those I loved most nearly - weighed so heavily on me that I must have been not far short of a state of clinical depression. As I then felt it, Lalage, I, and our daughter seemed to exist in a sort of inescapable limbo: in London still, but not where we had been so happy for so many years; I soldiering on in the ODM, but my heart even less than before in what I was doing; Lalage continuing in the home and with her training in pastoral counselling; and our daughter, too, bearing up bravely - though it was wrenchingly obvious how keenly she felt the hurt of losing her home, the house in which she had been born. Though he was then living away from us we now know that our son, too, was affected.

**********

Life went on, dreary and dispirited. But not entirely without hope.

**********

Our son pursued his independent way of life. But this way was not simply that of the 'drop out', in the pejorative sense that was implied in the minds of people like us at that time - or at any rate of people like me, set in our own ways and distrustful of the other's. Though he had taken excellent A levels he had opted, in the way of the high-spirited of the times, not to go to university. With no settled and pre-planned 'career' in mind, he lived "taking no thought for the morrow", though not otherwise quite like the lilies of the field; for he certainly toiled (in order to earn) - and no doubt occasionally also spun. In a whole range of occupations he travelled by himself the road to genuine self-reliance, and indeed self-respect, which I myself had never reached at the same age.

At school our daughter continued to do well all round. From the very first we had chanced upon an odd and inconsequential link with the place, which had somehow seemed to be of good augury. When we had first driven her down we had been astonished to discover not only that one of the masters was the man who had been the deputy head of the old NEABS station at Limassol, but that another turned out to be Ham Ramsay - whose Assistant Commissioner I had been in Limassol twenty years before. At the time of the riot there, which I have described, our daughter's birth was still three years into the future, but the huge coincidence of our fortuitous meeting again, and my being able to introduce her to this man from her father's past, had seemed in a mysterious way to give a significance, and even a validity, to her new beginning at this boarding school. At that school she had amply justified her original wish to make the move from London. So well did she acquit herself that she was a couple of years later to be a candidate for Cambridge. We knew that statistically the chances of success were at extremely long odds for a girl wanting to read English Literature there, since that School was hugely oversubscribed by such candidates. At her *viva* she was asked what she read for her own pleasure. I still think that if she had answered by bringing P.G. Wodehouse in she could - perhaps would - have got her nose in under the wire. Not simply because it would have been just as true as her actual reply, in relation to the 'classics' of the English literary canon, as by reason of the possibility of her establishing a personal rapport with one of her interviewers. Such are the niceties of the interview technique. But, as so often, out of disappointments come uncovenanted happinesses. It was in the course of her encounter with Cambridge that she met a fellow candidate who has remained one of her closest friends, graduating with her from Exeter, and becoming her chief bridesmaid.

Meanwhile, returning once from visiting her at school, we had decided to travel back to London by taking a minor route over Salisbury

266

Plain so that we could have a look at a house which we had seen advertised in the papers the previous week-end. The village was Chitterne, isolated in a tree-fringed hollow on the southern edge of the plain. The house was in grounds completely walled to give seclusion, yet right in the village with the church on the other side of the southern boundary wall. The main part of the building, facing south, was very early 19th century Georgian, having been added to the original cottage of half-timbered Wiltshire cob. The first floor provided a ready built 'granny flat'. (This was still before we had sold the Addison Crescent house and my mother was still living in her flat there.) The Chitterne house was ideal - except that the price was quite beyond our pocket, reflecting the fact that the grounds included a sizeable stable block with acreage to match. We therefore put The Grange out of our minds.

\*\*\*\*\*\*\*\*\*\*\*

For the summer holidays of her A Level year our daughter was invited to stay with an old friend from our Cyprus days when he had been on the staff of the Political Officer, Middle East Forces. Now in the mid-1970s he was the British Ambassador in Libya, where Colonel Ghaddafi had but recently taken power. While she was having this first holiday abroad away from her parents, Lalage and I took it into our heads to go ourselves for a fortnight's holiday to Turkey.

\*\*\*\*\*\*\*\*\*\*\*

Apart from the short trip to Istanbul rather more than twenty years earlier (where I had had the conversation with the taxi-driver which had provided me with an illustration of the point I had made during my brief talk with Lord Radcliffe a couple of years later), we had never been to Turkey before. This time we went as 'package' tourists, travelling by way of what was then a fairly recent innovation - a 'two-centre holiday'. We were booked for a week in Istanbul, followed by a week on the southern coast (almost opposite Cyprus) at Alanya.

# PART VI : THE SEARCH STARTS

(1976-1980)

# ~11~
# Istanbul; Alanya;
# Antalya; Chitterne

It was on this holiday in Turkey that I found myself for the first time consciously trying to balance the Turk and the Englishman within me. Or was it the Englishman and the Turk? To the extent that I was in truth conscious that this was happening I was in the same measure reluctant and uncomfortable. It was not a matter of being aware of an unresolved choice so much as being burdened by a sense of unfulfilment, or unrealisation. Words allegedly spoken by Winston Churchill in his latter days as Prime Minister are apposite. When a new Member whom he did not know came into the Commons smoking room, the great man asked of his cronies the person's identity. "Oh, that's Bossom," remarked one. "Bossom! Bossom!" came a growl from Churchill, "Neither one damn thing, nor the other!"

During our fortnight in Turkey I passed, both with our fellow tourists and with the Turks we met, as the person named in my passport: a seeming Englishman, born in Cyprus. Though I had no need to resort to outright lies, I felt the heavy weight of the Roman aphorism that *suppressio veri suggestio falsi est*. My position, I explained when asked, was that I had been keenly interested in things Turkish since my schooldays, and afterwards especially in the Turkish language; I had served for many years in Cyprus during the period of the British Administration; I had greatly improved my Turkish there, acquiring both fluency and a marked Cyprus accent (which was then as distinct from mainland Turkish as the Cyprus Greek accent and dialect was from that of Greece); I had left the island with the end of British rule, and had never been back since. Not a word untrue - and yet how misleading. I imagine I was concerned mainly to avoid letting myself

270

in for the sort of discussions about the situation in Cyprus which would have been likely to result from Turkish interlocutors' knowing that they were talking to a fellow Turk from that island.

And so it was that Lalage and I moved about in the Turkey of the mid-1970s merely as members of one of the small groups of package tourists who were then beginning to appear on the scene. They had come in the wake, as it were, of the earlier bands of 'hippies' who had been visiting the country for some years, many of them in transit to lands further east. These were still in evidence, mostly congregating in the vicinity of the great early 17th century mosque of Sultan Ahmed, now more generally known to foreign visitors as the Blue Mosque because of its gloriously tiled interior. In those earlier days of tourism even the magnificent imperial mosques and the other 'sights' such as the old palace of *Top Kapı* (so called by reason of its lofty entrance arch, the Cannon Gate) were but sparsely visited by organised groups of tourists. The British in particular were only newly discovering the country as a popular resort. A decade and more earlier the first wave of 20th century travellers had been their spearhead. But these had been the more moneyed and independent visitors to the land. Rose Macaulay's novel *The Towers of Trebizond* depicts these kinds of people rather loftily passing through a country of whose inhabitants they seem practically unaware; as though for them the place had not really been in existence, but had in some manner been in abeyance since before the time the Moslem Turks had arrived nearly a thousand years earlier with the appearance of the Seljuks in Anatolia in 1071. It was about ten years after this holiday in Turkey that I came across a book which had been published about five years before our visit. *Discovering Turkey* by Andrew Mango was one of the few such books I have read of which the author is deeply versed in the country, its history and its language. The writer makes, most strikingly, the point I have touched on. In his Introduction he remarks:

> '*Without the appreciation of the Turkishness of Turkey, enjoyment of the many other good things that the country has to offer can be marred by an incomprehension which all too easily turns to irritation. There are, it is true, travellers who succeed in shutting out Turks from Turkey, and many classical itineraries have been*

271

*written in which the country has been treated as a museum, with
the Turks receiving an occasional and often unfavourable notice
as keepers of a vast treasure-house. But this approach will not
commend itself to the sensitive traveller who will rightly see in it
the sign of intellectual blindness.'*

The core of this sort of view of the Turkish people could possibly be
succinctly expressed as consisting of seeing them as entirely marginal
- exotic at best and, at worst, barbarous: in one word, as 'other'. In
another, as inferior; not exactly in the sense of Kipling's "lesser breeds
without the law" whom the British had once ruled, because the Turks
of Turkey never had been so ruled, but rather as a people who might
have been more fortunate had they come under that tutelage. Some
there were who had respect for the Turks as a people who had also,
like them, experienced (had, one might say, suffered) an imperial past.
But of that vehement and vicious anti-Turkish attitude which had
informed a section of the British public in the second half of the 19th
century (inflamed by a misinformed and supposedly religiously inspired
hostility to the foremost of the Islamic powers of the time), there was
no trace of which we were personally aware during our couple of weeks
in the country in 1976. Hardly surprising really, since entrenched
Turkophobes were unlikely to want to find themselves amongst Turkish
people in Turkey.

**\*\*\*\*\*\*\*\*\*\***

*Among those at the East Allington rectory had been a boy whom I was
later to know again at Oxford, where he read Classics. He was to tell
me that when he had been wondering what to do after taking his degree
I had suggested that he might pursue some research in Cyprus. I had
completely forgotten this conversation but, as he was to remind me,
many years later, it had set him on a course which had led to his
Doctorate and eventually to becoming head of the British School in
Athens and a pillar of the archaeological establishment. We kept in
fairly tenuous touch over the years, he and his wife spending a night
with us every year when they were on leave from Greece. After dinner
one evening he showed me some papers about a fund-raising*

272

*programme by his institution. One name featured prominently among the sponsors; and I had to tell my friend that had he deliberately tried to predispose me against contributing he couldn't have done better. I explained. This Englishman had appeared quite recently on television to allege gratuitously a parallel, which was for me as tasteless as it was spurious, between Argentina's lawless attempt to annex the Falklands and Turkey's exercise of her treaty rights to foil the lawless Greek attempt to annex Cyprus in 1974. I had taken extreme exception to this, and had written to tell him so, in no uncertain terms. (When I wrote, quite seperately, some time afterwards to his Greek Cypriot wife to thank her for the present of a book, I began by telling her of my previous letter to her husband, so that things should be entirely open. In reply she asked me to "excuse my husband's remarks," on the grounds that "he is above all a diplomat ... and a Greek scholar." Though admiring her loyalty to her husband in seeking - as he himself had not sought - to write in extenuation, I couldn't help reflecting to myself that her otherwise laudable attempt to justify the unjustifiable seemed a neat example of what in Turkish is known as "the excuse worse than the offence."!)*

*But even for those to whom the Turks were simply exotically 'other' it is hard to know in just what, for them, that 'otherness' consisted. Different people shared this kind of attitude in various degrees depending mainly on how far their opinions had been coloured (I had as well said 'tarnished') by bias towards the 'Hellenic' rather than the 'Roman' aspects of the Classical past - one could say by a 'Greek' as distinct from a 'Trojan' predilection - and even more by how much of a 'Christian' atmosphere they might have been exposed to, and to which aspect of that most varied and multi-faceted faith.*

*None of us is free of these kinds of bias. For myself, I have sought to find my way through the morass by seeing a distinction - or trying to - between 'bias' and 'prejudice'. It has come to me that every human is inescapably subject to bias, in the precise meaning of the word. We are all weighted in favour of one direction or another, through upbringing. What is important is not to deny the fact and claim a non-existent impartiality, but to discover and identify the bias - and seek to counter it so far as is humanly possible. Prejudice on the other hand is, in its exact sense, to arrive at a judgement in advance of the facts, and to be unwilling (even unable) to alter the prejudged view after being presented with countervailing facts and arguments. If we are all ineluctably biassed, we do not have to be prejudiced, however difficult it is to overcome that state of mind. It has been said that "the advantage of a classical education is that it enables you to despise the wealth which it prevents you from earning". However true, or false, that may be, it is surely hardly contestable that it predisposes many to prejudice in any matter which involves those whom they are brought up to see as the present-day heirs of the ancient classical world.*

*As an instance, there is the case of that same old friend of my boyhood whom I have just mentioned. At my own dinner table in London he once remarked that he could "never forgive the Arabs (or was it "the Moslems"?) for their destruction of the great library of Alexandria". He had in mind the arrival in Alexandria of the Arabs within ten years of the death of the Prophet Mohammed and the legendary burning of the contents of the renowned library there by the Caliph Omar. This was an episode on which I, too, had been brought up - but since then I had, and quite recently, been enlightened by having bought a book following a television series by an American, Carl Sagan. There I had been intrigued to read:*

'The last scientist who worked in the Library [of Alexandria] was a mathematician, astronomer, physicist and the head of the Neoplatonic school of philosophy - an extraordinary range of accomplishments for any individual in any age. Her name was Hypatia. She was born in Alexandria in 370 AD. ... The Alexandria of Hypatia's time was a city under grave strain. ... The growing Christian Church was consolidating its power and attempting to eradicate pagan influence and culture. Hypatia stood at the epicentre of these mighty social forces. Cyril, the Archbishop of Alexandria, despised her because of her close friendship with the Roman governor, and because she was a symbol of learning and science which was largely identified by the early Church with paganism. In great personal danger, she continued to teach and publish until, in the year 415, she was set upon by a fanatical mob of Cyril's parishioners. They dragged her from her chariot, tore off her clothes, and, armed with abalone shells, flayed her flesh from her bones.  Her remains were burned, her works obliterated, her name forgotten.  Cyril was made a saint.'

*The paragraph in the book immediately preceding this passage ends with the following sentence:*

'When, at long last, the mob came to burn the Library down, there was nobody to stop them.'

*The Moslem Caliph had reached Alexandria barely a decade after the Prophet had died in 632AD.  The destruction of the great Alexandrian library of classical antiquity is traditionally, therefore, alleged to have been carried out by the Moslems two hundred and fifty years after it had been put to the flames by the Christian crowd.  By a nice irony it is after almost that precise span of years, following the ransacking and looting of the city of Constantinople by the Crusaders in 1204, that the armies of the Turkish Sultan Mehmed the Conqueror are even today repeatedly stated to have done just that when they took the city in 1453 - although by the time they captured the city the ancient treasures of Byzantium had long since been pillaged and scattered throughout Europe among the Frankish looters' heirs and successors!  My friend Hector had the grace to acknowledge the fact, in place of the fiction that he had hitherto taken as history - as indeed had I, with my English upbringing, until then.*

*At the risk of piling Pelion on Ossa, I recall one other instance of self-education which enabled me at around that same time to put in another word in season.  The* Sunday Times, *in the days when I used to read it, carried a column by a man who had been at Oxford during my time, and in the same college as myself.  One day Godfrey Smith made some animadversion in his column to the treatment of the Jews throughout history which seemed to tar the Turks with whatever brush it was that he had, otherwise, quite properly applied.  (The details are, I fear, no longer with me.)  I wrote to point out that throughout the long history of the Ottoman state the Turks were, so far as I knew, unique among the countries of Europe in never having oppressed, certainly never having persecuted, the Jews.  In fact when the Jews had been given the choice of expulsion from Spain or compulsory conversion to Christianity in 1497, the then Ottoman Sultan Bayezit had received them all into his dominions with the reputed words, "What a foolish monarch is this Ferdinand who impoverishes his realm of such subjects, to the enrichment of mine!" (As indeed the Ottoman Empire was to be so enriched with the great influx of the Sephardic Jews into such cities as Salonica, where they amounted to a third of the population.) I am happy to record that Godfrey Smith too, to his honour, wrote to say that he had not known this, and to express thanks for the information.*

***********

As I have said, at the time of our Turkish visit in 1976 I, too, shared much of the mind-set of my contemporaries in the educational establishments of this country of those years. It was only intermittently that I was to manage to re-educate myself, in a sporadic and unstructured fashion, about the Turkish people and their place in history, and so to form a rather more balanced and coherent view than the one which had emerged from an English upbringing and environment. And, if it comes to that, than the one which I was later to learn some Turks, too, seemed to have derived from their history books, to judge from what has sometimes been said to me by them, and from what I have once or twice read in Turkish books. But more of that, I hope, later. Meanwhile what comes to me now is something which I was only to read for the first time in the early 1980s when my daughter gave me a copy of *The Letters of Lady Mary Wortley Montagu*. I have just looked up her letter of 10 April, 1718, when she was the wife of the British Ambassador to the Ottoman Court. Refuting the alleged destruction by the Turks of classical remains in their capital city she mentions some statues and observes:

*All the Figures have their heads on, and I cannot forbear from reflecting again on the Impudence of Authors who all say they have not, but I dare swear the greatest part of them never saw them, but took the report from the Greeks, who resist with incredible fortitude the conviction of their own eyes whenever they have invented Lyes to the Dishonnour of their Enemys.*

276

\*\*\*\*\*\*\*\*\*\*\*

In the summer of 1976 then, Lalage and I took in the sights of old Istanbul, the city encompassed by the walls of Byzantium on the west, the waters of the Golden Horn to the north, the head of the Sea of Marmara to the south, and the Bosphorus to the east. The hotel we were in was actually on the Üsküdar side of the Bosphorus, the 'Scutari' of Florence Nightingale in the Crimean War. From that hotel we looked out due west across the water over to the unsurpassed view of the *Top Kapı*'s outlines and the march of minarets stretching along the hills. An unforgettable panorama at all times, and never more so than against the light of the setting sun.

A less picturesque aspect of the hotel came from its being close to the lorry 'park' at the ferry terminal on that side of the Bosphorus. (This was before the great vehicular bridge had been built across that waterway to link the Balkan with the Anatolian sides.) The view over to Istanbul was not impeded because of this 'park' since the hotel was up the hillside, sufficiently overhanging the terminal for one to look out over it and the road without a sight of what was just underneath. But the presence of these huge trans-continental TIRs was made known to us all in the hotel by reason of its patronage by their British drivers. A most interesting bunch. Not entirely unlike 20th century versions of their 16th century forbears, the sea-captains of those times who voyaged in the then often uncharted and largely unfrequented seas in vessels which would by no means have dwarfed these latter-day massive wheeled land ships. (I think I correctly remembered from my childhood model-making days that Drake's *Golden Hind* had not been much more than twice the weight of Columbus's 50 ton *Santa Maria*.) The TIR drivers had tales of having to light fires under their lorries to unfreeze after winter night-stops on the high plateaux and other outlandish points on their routes right across and far beyond Turkey. Embellished, more than likely, but these tales certainly carried a savour of their 'voyages'. It was, however, the hotel's notice-board which communicated both the ingenuity and enterprise of these new age 'merchant venturers', as well as their tribulations. As, for example, such notices as they pinned up to enquire of their colleagues: "Can anyone take on," say, a dozen crates of this or that, "for delivery to" such and such a place. Or another conveying the sad tidings of so and so's incarceration in, as it might be, Teheran, for whatever it was by which he had fallen foul of the authorities, with the signatories' message of best wishes and hopes for his speedy release from prison. I wish I had taken note of the exact wording of such missives in the nature of minor documentary echoes of an era.

***********

A personal memory I take with me from a city which has something for everyone. Lalage and I had got off the ferry one morning after breakfast and were walking up from the Galata bridge, starting off in the general direction of the Blue Mosque through narrow streets beyond the old Spice Market and the *Valide* Mosque. Down a side street we saw another small mosque and decided to look at it. We went into the colonnaded outer courtyard, empty but for an old man sweeping it clean. He motioned to us to enter the mosque. The man left us. It was a jewel. Perfectly proportioned, exquisitely tiled, it breathed peace, and prayer though nobody else was there. We felt we wanted to stay awhile, and sat down inside at the foot of the back wall by the entrance facing the *mihrab*, the apse-like prayer niche before which the imam stands with his back to the worshippers as he leads congregational prayer. It was as though there were a silent, invisible, congregation present. When we left the man was outside in the courtyard. He bowed us out, his hand over his heart. I returned the salutation. We had been in the late 16th century *Rüstem Pasha* Mosque. Many are the splendid and inspiring buildings which Istanbul contains, to evoke wonder and admiration at the devotion, the artistry, and the craft which brought them into being; but, for me, none are so infused as this gem with the spirit of those who over the centuries prayed in the place.

***********

After our week in the old imperial capital we flew south-east, to the domains of the predecessors of the Ottomans, the Seljuk Turks. We landed at Antalya, from where we were taken by bus in the dark along the coast to Alanya some eighty or ninety miles further east. Our hotel was one of the only two newish little hotels in almost open country rather under a mile out of the town itself and also on the coast. The area was then almost untouched by tourism, in fact at that time it seemed as if foreigners who visited the place did so mostly as passengers to what was one of the spots on the itinerary of their small liners cruising in Turkey's western and southern waters. We tended to treat our hotel mainly as a headquarters for sightseeing in Alanya itself and for well-organised expeditions for our party to classical sites in the neighbourhood, like Side, Aspendus, and Perge, as well as trips for *alfresco* meals at places like the Manavgat waterfalls or cascades, and in the foothills of the great Taurus mountains rising up to the central Anatolian plateau.

The hotel was mostly patronised by Turks. The place had its own swimming pool, and when not out on excursions we spent most of our time in and around this pool. On one occasion there were next to us a mother and father keeping an eye on their son of about five or six who was splashing about in the water. I don't recall exactly whether it was to admonish him for boisterousness, or whether the time had come for them to go in to eat, but I heard the father call out to the boy, by name, to come out. The name was 'Emre'.

*********

*It so happened that when, some twenty years and more before, I had been systematically brushing up my written Turkish, I had used a particular 'Reader' which had included four verses from a poem by a 13th century Turkish 'minstrel' named Yunus Emre. The Reader, which I still have, does in fact mention in a footnote (as I now see) that the writer was a* Sufi, *a mystic, but it seems that this hadn't registered with me at that time, and I had taken the words in their direct sense as a love poem, without perceiving that they were actually allegorical, just as the Song of Songs in the Bible is, of the soul's passionate longing and love for the Divine. The first and the last of these four verses had stuck in my memory over the years. In translation they read:*

Engulfed by fire of Love I walk blood-hued for all the world to see,
No more is mind nor mindlessness - come, see what Love has made of me.

279

Poor Yunus I, now wholly spent, from head to foot my body rent,
Far, far, from Friendship's lands now sent - come, see what Love
has made of me.

\*\*\*\*\*\*\*\*\*\*\*

Now, when I heard the father call out to his child in the pool, I idly
asked him whether he had by any chance named his son after the poet
(the name being to me, in my ignorance, very uncommon). He nodded;
and I, moved by I know not what, recited the words of the final verse
in the original Turkish. The father looked amazed and was curious to
know from this odd Englishman, as he thought, where I learned what
I had just quoted. I told him; and also who I was, in the unforthcoming
and devious terms I have already mentioned. In the resulting brief
conversation it emerged that he was a bank inspector taking a break in
Alanya, and that we were due to return to England at the end of our
week, flying from Antalya to Istanbul for the London connection. We
parted with mutual good wishes.

Our return journey from Alanya to Antalya a few days later was to
have involved our being collected by bus from the hotel in the very
early morning - in fact well before dawn. Our small party hung around
outside the hotel entrance in the dark while nothing happened, until
the local 'courier' (or, perhaps, 'representative' - he wasn't in fact to
accompany the party to the airport, at least a couple of hours' journey
away to the west) established, or realised, that no bus was going to
turn up. With an efficiency and dispatch which could only be admired
and commended, he rustled up three or four taxis with, at that hour,
the necessary load of petrol in each for the journey and with drivers
instructed to get our group to Antalya in time for our flight. The driver
of our taxi batted along the coast road, but it was only as the rising sun
behind us gradually began to bring visibility that I became conscious
of just how fast we were travelling. I spoke up from behind: *Geç
olsun da güç olmasın* (the equivalent of the English 'better late than
never' - literally 'let it be late rather than difficult'). He grunted in
apparent agreement, but the pace didn't slacken at all. I then called to
mind the more powerful and vivid English, 'Better twenty minutes
late in this world than twenty years too early in the next', and

280

beseechingly produced a Turkish rendition. This time he responded - his shoulders heaved in a spasm of Ted Heath-like silent laughter - and the speed relaxed. (The relaxation being, however, rather in the nature of that in the account I heard many years ago on the Jack Benny Show when his servant Rochester is telling how he once thought he had encountered a ghost. Streaking off at top speed, he soon realises that the ghost has now apparently vanished. At which, he explains, he was so relieved that he "slowed down to a sprint".) We got to Antalya in one piece. Luckily the airport was on the eastern outskirts and we drove straight to it without having to go through the town.

We rushed in, the aeroplane on the tarmac. Our departure formalities were briskly completed; and as we hurried to the terminal exit there we saw young Emre's father waiting - for us. He came forward and handed me a parcel which I took to be something in the nature of a box of Turkish Delight. Taken aback at seeing him there at such an hour - indeed at all - and in the turmoil of the hurried departure, I fear I was only on the polite side of perfunctoriness in thanking him for his kindness in coming to see us off, and for his present. It was after we had taken off that the packet I had been given seemed not to feel quite like a box of confectionery. Nor, indeed, was it when I had unwrapped it. It was in fact a very handsomely bound volume entitled *Yunus Emre ve Tasavvuf* (Yunus Emre and Mysticism). The book was to be seminal for my personal development; but the seeds were to be dormant for several years yet.

**\*\*\*\*\*\*\*\*\*\***

In the autumn of that year we accompanied our daughter to her school at the beginning of term. On our return to London we broke the journey in Salisbury. And there in an estate agent's window we saw the picture of a house for sale. It was, again, that of The Grange at Chitterne. But now, two years after we had viewed it and had abandoned the possibility of buying the place, it was only the main house that was being offered. The detached stable block and a great part of the grounds had been sold separately, and what was now for sale was of a manageable size. We learned that the price had more than proportionately come down to reflect the time that had elapsed while it had been on the market, and the agents advised us that we could probably get it for even less than the asking price. Back in London we eventually decided to put in a bid. And after some hesitancy the owner accepted our offer.

**\*\*\*\*\*\*\*\*\*\***

It was as I moved from my fiftieth to my fifty-first year that I had taken this decision, rooted in my deeply felt wish to find fulfilment as I thought (or perhaps it was really some kind of release I was looking for), in having a place in the depths of the English countryside, against the possibility of retirement as soon as I might be able to do so. It was an escapist dream which I shared those days with a very great many people, as I am sure the newspapers, magazines, and other records of the time would confirm. In my case I suspect that, beyond whatever was the prevailing general mood, there was an empty personal hope of being able to recapture a lost childhood world, a world not so much passed forever into the mists of time, as one which had never actually existed save in the longings of a heart which must have felt that it hadn't ever really known a home. Sententious as the recognition most surely is, its truth is not on that account any the less. And what the heart dictates has its own validity - and a claim at least to be heeded.

However the hard reality remained. We had to recognise that retirement to the Wiltshire countryside was simply beyond the bounds of possibility for another eight or nine years. And meanwhile we would only be able to keep The Grange going, on a sort of care and maintenance basis, as a weekend place and holiday home. Once again we had embarked on a risky venture. It fairly soon became clear (and more particularly after the place had been left unlived in for a Wiltshire winter) that to go on in this way would cumulatively make the house uninhabitable before we could realistically hope to make it our permanent home. Nor could I have commuted daily to London from Chitterne, itself half an hour by road to Salisbury with an hour and a half's rail journey on to Waterloo. However, weekly commuting, even if onerous, was still feasible; though I had to work hard at convincing myself of this - I had been spoiled by my years of being able to live and work in central London, when practically all my colleagues faced tedious and trying, not to say tiring, railway journeys, many on ancient

282

and uncomfortable rolling-stock. My erstwhile room mate in the old CRO (he who at the end of the day would sense that "feeling of incompleteness") used to travel up from the depths of Kent where, in winter, it was not unusual to be snow-bound. We therefore concluded that, as soon as the prospects of selling our London house, to which we felt no great attraction, looked reasonable, we would dispose of it. Chitterne would be our home where Lalage would live all the time; and I would find myself bachelor 'digs' as near to the office as I could, while I lived the life of a weekly commuter for the indefinite future. While we waited for a purchaser a year and a half of anxiety was to pass. It was a worrying time in any case as I was now in the throes of the attempt to sort out the Crown Agents *imbroglio*.

But then we got an offer out of the blue for our London house (from a Lebanese Maronite as it happened). And by another huge stroke of luck, or providential dispensation, I simultaneously learned (interestingly from a Methodist minister who was in touch with our local church through the Anglican/Methodist 'experiment' which was in operation) that the widow of a very senior BBC executive, who lived in a mansion block of flats almost next door to the house we were selling, let rooms on a bed-and-breakfast basis - and had a room vacant. Things fell neatly into place, and the transition could hardly have been smoother. By the summer of 1978 we were residents of Chitterne - Lalage full-time, I from Friday night to very early Monday morning. Our daughter had her own room and bathroom; and our son came to stay periodically.

\*\*\*\*\*\*\*\*\*\*

The village itself was exceptionally warm and welcoming. But we also had an entirely unexpected introduction to the place. A few months after we had bought The Grange we ran into a young barrister in London who was a member of the Parish Council there. He remarked that he had heard we had bought a house in Chitterne. Astonished, I asked how he had learned this since, I said, no-one knew of it except our immediate family. His reply was that there was certainly one other person who knew - the person who had sold to us; and he had been their neighbour in the village. It turned out that our London

283

acquaintance was the son-in-law of the owner of the 'big house' in Chitterne, a fact of which we had until that moment been completely ignorant.

However, after this auspicious introduction, I very nearly put my foot in it the winter of the year we eventually moved in. There was some kind of 'bring and buy' sale one Saturday evening in the Village Hall. Lalage and I went to this. At one point I found myself talking to an elegant personage who I supposed might possibly be a service officer in civilian dress. He enquired, in friendly fashion, whether I was enjoying myself in the village. In a spirit of flippancy which sometimes comes over me - as also some others I'm told, though they perhaps are better able to guard against giving expression to it - I said that I was sure I would be very happy there. "For," I said, "I share the view of the Earl of Ickenham" - at which point a slightly pop-eyed and unbelieving look spread over his face, as of one who had not made the acquaintance of that fictional peer from the pages of P.G. Wodehouse - "who," I continued, "always used to say that he thought the ideal existence was to have plenty of tobacco, and be cut by the county." I was in a short time to discover that I had in fact been talking to someone who virtually personified the county, in that corner of it. So it wasn't surprising that his reaction at the time was rather less than cordial - though perfectly polite. But he took it in good part when I explained the quotation; and that I meant to signify merely that I tended to lead a fairly quiet social life.

***********

So well ensconced were we that, for our first summer, we were able to have my mother and brother over to come and spend a couple of months with us as a break from the heat of that season in Cyprus and, just as much, from the life they were living in Nicosia. The Turkish community's position was now infinitely better than it had been up until July 1974, before the Turkish army had arrived. They were physically secure in life and limb, and free from that even more insidiously debilitating sense of being swamped by a larger community who very often looked on them at best as but an unwanted segment of humanity - and at worst as a cancerous growth. But the Turks were nevertheless still, after 1974, oppressed by the feeling of being boxed-in; and of course in my mother's case she had been living in the cramped circumstances of a small bachelor flat for four years. To be able to relax in a roomy house with a spacious garden; to see again her grandchildren; to meet and talk with new people in the village - all this was revivifying for her. And for us all.

I will try to lighten the atmosphere of my, albeit perfectly accurate, description in the preceding paragraph of the pernicious consequences of the Greek people's conditioned perception of their Turkish neighbours, by illustrating the way in which this would sometimes reveal itself. My sister-in-law last year lent me Colin Thubron's book *Journey into Cyprus*. This, published in 1975, is an account of the writer's walks around the island during 1972. (I have to admit that he largely forfeited my sympathy before I had even begun to read his account, when I saw in the final paragraph of his half-page Preface: *"The nervous cohabitation* [between the two communities] *which I witnessed in 1972 was, I now realise, the island's **halcyon** time."* (my emphasis). For whom, I asked myself (thinking of the Turkish people of the place generally, and my mother in particular), did this insensitive ass choose so to describe the island at that time? But I ploughed through the book; and found it in myself to forgive him what I now choose to regard as his initial lapse, when after a hundred and seventy seven pages I came upon the following delightful example of the mind-set which, by years of indoctrination, the Greek church, educationists, and political leaders had managed to produce in their flock. Thubron is describing his visit to the very village of Değirmenlik where, twenty four years earlier, Richard Crossman had, as I have told, made that criminally inflammatory speech. *"I had,"* writes Thubron, *"come into the village with ideas of cauliflower cheese pie and white sauce, baked cauliflowers, pickled cauliflowers - only to find that it was Sunday and no vegetable shop was open."* A misunderstanding occurs through Thubron's use of a word for the vegetable which the villagers don't know - but he doesn't explain why this is so.

*"'Cauliflowers?' the miller repeated. He looked blank.*
*"Yes," I pleaded. "Kunupidhi."*
*"We don't have them. I've never heard of them. Perhaps you can get them in Nicosia."*

285

## The Search Starts

*Later I stopped an old woman.  "Cauliflowers ..." she said suspiciously.  "There aren't any.  The Turks killed them."*
*"But they aren't people ..."*
*She said quickly: "They were pulled down.  Demolished."*
*"They're vegetables," I said firmly.*
*She wiped a dirty sleeve over her mouth as if to speak better, then answered with finality: "The Turks ate them".*

\*\*\*\*\*\*\*\*\*\*\*

It was from this time, after my mother and brother had returned to Nicosia in the autumn of 1978 and when, with the end of that season, I was free from work in the garden at Chitterne, that I began to devote time during weekends to reading about Turkey as a country, with a distinct history and way of life, evolving over the centuries. I was fortunate that Warminster, some half a dozen miles away, possessed an unusually  excellent bookshop which I found very helpful for this purpose.  Over the next five years or so I made myself relatively knowledgeable on different aspects of Turkey's past, and in particular familiarised myself with her architectural heritage. (The comparison implied in the use of the word 'relatively' is in no sense with those for whom these matters are a subject of specialist study; rather it is by reference to the previous state of ignorance in which I was shrouded, like most of those who had shared my upbringing. "In the kingdom of the blind the one-eyed is king".)

\*\*\*\*\*\*\*\*\*\*\*

I have told of the defeat of the Labour government in 1979 (which had put in hazard the Bill to regularise the status and functions of the Crown Agents, though by co-operation between the government and the opposition the necessary legislation had been carried quickly through all its stages in time for the Royal Assent before Parliament was dissolved that year).  In 1980, during my third year in the grade of Assistant Secretary, and now serving as Head of Middle East and Mediterranean Department, Whitehall was swiftly to feel the direct impact of one aspect of the radicalism which embued the Thatcher Conservative government.  Whether or not the exercise was conducted

286

to embrace all Ministries simultaneously in one fell swoop, or was only carried out selectively for some, I do not now recall, but the ODM, now once again the FCO(ODA), was required to carry out an urgent and radical appraisal of its policies, functions and objectives, together with a detailed assessment of the establishment and staffing levels needed to fulfil those responsibilities. By the early summer the ODA had completed this task. The result was to show that we carried an excess of five posts in the Assistant Secretary grade. Those of that grade who were in their last five years or so before retirement age were asked if they would wish to volunteer for early retirement. I did so. As well as I can remember, there were rather more than five volunteers, and I was the youngest. I most fervently hoped that I would be among the five who would be selected.

**********

By now a full twenty years had passed since I had left Cyprus with my family, metaphorically shaking its dust from my shoes. With the immense changes which had come about in the last five and a half years since Turkey had intervened, having been able to talk at length with my mother and brother during their visit to us, and carrying the vivid recollection of what I had felt within myself at the time I had heard of their deliverance in July 1974, I now knew for sure that the idea of trying to insulate myself from the place completely and for ever was not just futile but, in an indefinable way, what I can only try to express as being somehow "unhealthy". Not for myself only, but also for my children. I decided in 1980 that I would spend my summer leave entitlement that year in North Cyprus (which had not yet become the Turkish Republic of Northern Cyprus). I had of course already established that, contrary to the misleading picture that had been put out and was widely believed, the north was neither beset by Turkish soldiery (tourist brochures of Cyprus which I saw in the Warminster bookshop carried maps which showed the north of the island imprinted in red: "Under Turkish Military Occupation"), nor was it totally cut off from communication with the outside world (much as certain parties would dearly have wished it to have been). I asked my son and daughter whether they would like to spend a fortnight's holiday there as package tourists together with Lalage and me. They were very happy to do so.

## The Search Starts

In the event the four of us were joined by one each of their friends who, within four years, were to be their spouses. I need say no more of our stay in North Cyprus than that it was an emotional return; and an illuminating experience.

\*\*\*\*\*\*\*\*\*\*\*

On return to England in early September I found that the ODA was nearing the end of its discussions with the Civil Service Department about the volunteers for early retirement. I was told I should for the moment go back home and take what would probably be a short period of "gardening leave" - an expression I had never before heard. Within a couple of weeks - though it seemed a good deal longer - I was telephoned by our Minister's Private Secretary to tell me that my application for early retirement had been accepted. And so it was that I was able to retire; rather more than five years from the normal retirement age and with my fully earned pension. Despite all my admonitions to myself in the light of those other times in my life when I had again been granted (and perhaps earned) what I had ardently sought, I still found it hard this time not to feel that now I truly had found, or been vouchsafed, my final heart's desire. And certainly as the weeks and months passed, it really seemed so.

# PART VII : JOURNEYING

(1981-1996)

# ~12~

# Chitterne; Edirne; Istanbul
# Konya; Istanbul; Bursa

My time in retirement was now divided mainly between work in the garden and making a beginning with a first serious try at a plain English prose translation of the verses in my Yunus Emre book. Life now could not have been more different from the one I had lived as a London civil servant. But the effect of that difference was only to emerge at the end of the first year.

During those intervening months the aspect of the changed way of living of which I was most aware, and which I very gratefully enjoyed, was that I was no longer the prisoner of a clock, wound up and set by others. This was an independence I had experienced only once before - when I had been at the university; but even then the sense of freedom had been constrained. As an undergraduate I had been extremely impecunious; and even during my last year on the Devonshire Course, when I was free of money anxieties, the prospect of the Gold Coast had tended to bring a sense of constriction, rather in the manner of "shades of the prison-house began to fall around the growing boy". But now in Chitterne I was not only financially secure (if by no means affluent), I was entirely my own master: what I chose to do, as much as when I chose to do it, seemed to be limited only by my own freedom of will. I was, so I thought, "the master of my fate ... the captain of my soul". This freedom seemed not to pall.

Admittedly the work of translation was intellectually taxing, so my mind was not being left to atrophy. It was in any case a mental activity which, by contrast with that which had occupied my official time at the Ministry, was wholly agreeable and becoming more and more enjoyable as I got immersed in it. Before settling down on a daily and systematic basis with the Yunus translation, I had bought the entire set of Anthony Powell's *Dance to the Music of Time*. These volumes both relaxed my mind and also served the equivalent mental function of whatever it is that wine-tasters use to clear the palate before taking a sip. I could broach the contents of the 13th century Turkish poems and roll them around my mind with a fuller appreciation when it had first been cleared by tasting the flavour of 20th century English. (I fear that having written that, it looks like a promising candidate for 'Pseud's Corner' in *Private Eye*. But it is nevertheless true.) In the garden I went at things hammer and tongs, thinking that bouts of heavy exercise - digging, raking, hoeing, chopping, sawing, log-splitting, leaf-raking, - could not but be healthful for the body, as it seemed also to be salutary and effective in stimulating the mind.

I continued happily, indeed euphorically, in a state of mind during these months of retirement when I clearly remember thinking - and more than once - how fortunate I was by comparison with those unlucky ones for whom leaving their working days behind them was, as advice columns in the papers suggested, pregnant with risk. Their lot, it appeared, was at best to experience the anxieties that came with a sharp drop in income, and at worst to suffer a drear and deadly monotonous drag of days which they could find nothing to fill, while burdened with a terrifying feeling that they no longer had any value in society. The received wisdom was that, for these, their first year of retirement in such a frame of mind carried at least the possibility of a heart attack. I believed myself to be far removed from such unhappy people.

In the event my own heart attack came just less than a week from the first anniversary of the day I had heard the glad tidings of my early retirement.

\*\*\*\*\*\*\*\*\*\*

Whether the change I now experienced was that "wonderful" concentration of the mind which, according to the great Doctor Johnson, is brought about by the imminent prospect of death, I cannot truthfully say. Nor am I altogether sure that I can realistically link the way my life was now to develop to this sudden and stark reminder of my mortality, and of the tenuous hold we all have on our lives. The only direct connection I can make comes from the recollection of one thing that happened in hospital. I was, I am pretty sure, still in the intensive care unit when I had to complete some form or other which included a question about the patient's religion. If only to avoid having to affirm adherence to one or other of the only two formal religions of which I had any knowledge (and from both of which I felt pretty much separated) it came into my mind to answer "Sufi"; and this I wrote down. No-one enquired what I meant. Had they asked me to elucidate, or to be more specific, I could only have said "Moslem". I had, though only intermittently, been pondering for some little time what in fact it meant, in anything but the most superficial way, to be either a Moslem or a Christian. There was nothing I knew of my parents' faith to which I could not have given my unqualified assent; whereas, in the credal and doctrinal position of Christianity there were fundamental aspects to which, in the last extremity, I could not in honesty adhere. (I had also grown cold to that religious body after experiencing the practical application, in Cyprus, by its leaders there, of their professed faith - without this being repudiated by its leaders here, or anywhere else. Rather than feeling that kinship or brotherhood which is supposed to mark its members, I was increasingly filled with disenchantment - and revulsion). And yet, while I was able, in all conscience, to affirm, "I witness that there is no Divinity save God, and Mohammed is his messenger" (*Esheddu en la ilahe il'allah ve esheddu en muhammeden resul allah* - which is all that is required of the person who wishes to join the community of Islam) it was not yet that I was to be able to know of the essence of that faith, which would make itself felt in both heart and head.

***********

I was back at home by the end of the year. My convalescence required me to walk each day; first just by way of strolling in the garden where I had previously toiled, and then increasingly briskly for a couple of miles. Depending on how I felt and the state of the weather, this meant a walk of more or less three quarters of an hour. Such walking had, of course, been my routine, to and from the bus stop at the beginning and the end of my working day in London for many years. The abrupt cessation in retirement of this well-established rhythm of my life could well have had a major part in contributing to the onset of my heart attack. These daily walks have remained my almost unbroken routine ever since. All sudden, sharp exercise had then, and now, to be avoided. But apart from these changes, and my daily pill, my outward life continued as it had been before I had gone into hospital.

\*\*\*\*\*\*\*\*\*\*

One day in the Warminster bookshop the proprietor took down from a shelf a book he said he thought I might perhaps find interesting. It was a translation from the Turkish, carrying the English title *The Unveiling of Love* and subtitled *Sufism and the Remembrance of God*. The bookseller presented it to me as a gift, on the apologetic, and ingenuous, grounds that the copy was defective, having been produced with eight pages left blank by the printer. The book's original had been written by the current Sheykh of the Halveti-Jerrahi Order of Sufis. I read this gift of a specifically Sufi book, by a man living seven centuries after Yunus Emre (whose words had also come to me as a gift), with an increasing sense that here was something for which I had unknowingly been searching - perhaps since my childhood. The second of these books drew me back to the first one, with a new understanding of the deeper layers of meaning contained in Yunus's verses. And I began to feel that one day I might manage, mainly for my wife and children, to go beyond a mere prose translation and to put into English verse the 13th century mystic's message. At this stage, as I recollect it, two passages in particular struck me. The first had resonances with Jesus's saying that he had "come not to destroy the Law but to fulfil it". Yunus's words, in reference to the similar seeming conflict in Islam between the spirit and the letter of the 'Law' (the formal obligations of religion), were, as I was later to render them:

> *The Law as combless honey is, the Way as butter well refined;*
> *But why for Friendship's sake may these two not in sweetness be combined?*

(Where 'Friend' is used by Sufis as signifying God). Yunus's second call resonated with me at the very personal level, in a poem in which he is addressing himself:

## Journeying

*Why take the distant journey when the Friend within myself I see?*

But while I now first began to glimpse the prospect of the existence of an inner way, I still travelled the outer journey. And this was to include another visit to Turkey.

**\*\*\*\*\*\*\*\*\*\***

We flew to Istanbul the following summer. This time I would not dissemble, but would travel as what I was - a Cyprus Turk who had lived for many years in England, both before and after working in Cyprus until the British had left. And on this occasion Lalage and I made our own arrangements, to enable us to see, inside three weeks, the three towns outside Istanbul which especially interested me as having marked catalytic changes in the historical development of the Turkish state: Konya, Bursa, and Edirne. The first had been the capital of the pre-Ottoman 12th and 13th century Seljuk dynasty, during which Yunus Emre had lived (as also had his near contemporary Jelal ed-Din Rumi, in memory of whom was founded the Mevlevi Order of Sufis, often called the 'Whirling Dervishes' outside Turkey, by reason of the outer form of their ceremonial). The second city, Bursa, was the first capital of the nascent Ottoman dynasty in the early 14th century. The third, Edirne, was the first capital on the Balkan side of the Bosphorus after the Ottomans crossed the water in the mid 14th century. All three places contained marvellous architectural treasures from these, and later, times. We planned our itinerary centred on Istanbul from which we could travel out, radially in turn, to spend three days or so in each of the other provincial centres, returning for a few days at a time to visit places of interest there too, but mainly to rest at our 'headquarters', in the decayed comfort of the old Pera Palas hotel. This has since been restored to its first glory when it had been built, towards the end of the 19th century, as the terminal 'Grand Hotel' for travellers on the original, and real, Orient Express; but we were lucky to be able to see it - and indeed to afford it - before its restoration, while it was still in the last stages of being the sort of spacious, shabby genteel place with which I have always felt an affinity. A place not very different, in that regard, from the hotel in Sorrento on our honeymoon, though a good deal less opulent.

Our holiday was all we could have wished, and more - in ways unforeseen. The architectural wonders of which I had been given a foretaste in the books I had boned up on were emphatically not belied by the reality, either in Istanbul or in the three provincial towns. But I need not elaborate on these; in the last twenty years since our visit many books, and not merely tourist guides, direct those interested to the most important of the historic buildings from the country's last half millennium. In any event this is an attempt at a personal story rather than a sporadic travelogue, even though places on tourist routes inescapably feature in my account.

\*\*\*\*\*\*\*\*\*\*\*

A minor setback occurred on the first of our provincial visits. We had allowed for two full days in Edirne. On arrival by bus from Istanbul we went to the hotel I had earmarked from the brochure provided by the tourist section of the Turkish Embassy in London. The proprietor (or manager - I was never very sure which he was), a retired lieutenant-colonel, was embarrassed to have to tell us that on the following day, our first full day, there was to be a country-wide population census, and that this was always carried out under curfew: tourists and visitors included, everyone had to remain indoors and off the streets between certain hours from early morning to late afternoon. A pity, I thought irritably, that we hadn't been told of this imminent curfew when we had registered on first arrival at the Pera Palas the day before we left for Edirne. So much for my carefully planned, and tight, schedule of visits to places I had itemised. When I told the Edirne hotel manager he said he would look into the matter. In a little while he reported that, from his enquiries, it would be alright if on the census day we were to take ourselves off on foot (all but a couple of the major mosques were in the centre of the town, close to the hotel), but we should carry our passports just in case.

It was an odd experience wandering next morning through the deserted streets. Enquiring heads stuck out of windows; some only silently inquisitive, but many giving expression to their owners' curiosity in friendly banter about where we were from and what we were doing. We were able to see quite a lot of the exterior of the greatest mosques and old caravanserais (one of which had been converted into an attractive looking cloistered and colonnaded hotel) while we strolled around for about an hour - until a car pulled up and we were asked by a policeman to explain ourselves. Having done so, and shown our passports, we were allowed to resume our saunter. But within the hour another representative of authority drove up. This time we were simply told we should be indoors until the curfew ended. Unwisely, as seen in retrospect, I explained how we came to be out on the street and added that we had been allowed to continue by one of their colleagues only a short while ago. We were directed, sternly and with no banter, to return to our hotel at once. The hotel manager was apologetic. To make amends he arranged to take us around in his car the next day to visit the interiors of the two major mosques within the town I particularly wanted to see, as well as several places of interest in what were now outlying areas well beyond it.

For the town had shrunk very much since the days of its greatness, especially during the 19th century when it had been captured, occupied, and despoiled several times. First by the Russians in 1829, and then by the Greeks and Bulgarians in 1912; retaken by the Turks in 1913, it was seized and occupied by the Greeks in 1918 until their defeat in 1922 and its return, with the rest of eastern Thrace, as part of the new Turkish Republic, under the Treaty of Lausanne the next year. Even now, in 1982, Edirne still had very much the feel of a frontier town - which indeed geographically it was, being only a matter of miles from the Bulgarian and Greek borders - though that sensation had no doubt been fortuitously accentuated by the deserted streets on the day of the curfew. Yet its glory had not wholly departed. That glory was still supremely symbolised by the masterpiece of the 16th century architect Sinan, 'the Great', whose life spanned two reigns: those of Suleyman (known to his contemporaries in western Europe as "the Magnificent" but to his countrymen as Kanunî - 'the Lawgiver') and of his successor, Selim the Second. It was in the latter's reign that Sinan produced his incomparable work, the *Selimiye* Mosque in Edirne.

\*\*\*\*\*\*\*\*\*\*

Returning to Istanbul, we allowed ourselves a complete change, to relax and gird ourselves for the next stage due to begin in a couple of days. This was to be to Konya, a full day's fatiguing bus journey away to the south east across the Anatolian plateau. We decided to take a leisurely day trip up the Bosphorus as far as the entrance to the Black Sea at its northern end, stopping at various spots before our return to the Pera Palas. During this little excursion we fell into conversation with a German couple. From them we learned of a shop in the booksellers quarter behind the Bayezit mosque and next to one of the entrances to the great Covered Bazaar in Istanbul. The man said he thought we might find it an interesting place without being very specific as to why. Lalage and I spent the next morning going around the old imperial palace of Top Kapı.

It was only after lunch that we thought to take up the Germans' suggestion of a visit to the bookshop. What I had gathered, from my reading, to have once been an area of narrow streets (rather, so I had imagined, like those in the old Nicosia 'within the walls') - the place of the *sahhaflar*, 'book-dealers' - had in fact been modernised into what would nowadays be called a 'mall' or 'arcade'. A great variety of shops selling all manner of books and prints fronted onto a square in a completely pedestrian precinct. After some enquiry we traced the shop we took to be the one the German had told us of. It looked in no way different from its neighbours. We went in.

There was no one in the place except for a young man in charge. I can't remember whether we first looked around the shelves; my first memory is of the three of us sitting and talking. Of "cabbages and kings": of England, of Cyprus, of India - where Lalage had been born; but in no case about anything 'deep', or even serious - our conversation was, rather, general discussion about places and people. In the course of this my interest in Yunus Emre came up. Our host got up, walked over to a shelf and, in a scene which seemed to be a replay of one that I had witnessed recently, took down a book. He told us that the owner of the shop was the Sheykh of a Sufi Order, that a book of his had been published in English translation, and that he would like me to have this original Turkish text of that book. He handed it to me. I was surprised when I saw that the name of the Turkish book's author was the same as that of the writer of the book I had been given in

Warminster. But the Turkish book's title was different from that of the English one. In translation it would have read: *The Path of Love - The Way of Union* [*with the Beloved*, to be understood]; yet skimming it I suddenly realised that, here in Istanbul, I had just been given as a present the very book which, in English translation, I had also received as a gift a mere matter of weeks earlier, and a couple of thousand miles away, in Warminster. I was now dumbfounded. As who wouldn't have been? I told our new acquaintance of this almost unbelievable coincidence and said that I would now have the great pleasure of being able, on my return to England, to use the Sheykh's original to complete in English manuscript the eight blank pages in my copy there. (Which indeed I have since done).

The Sheykh himself was not in the shop on the day of our visit, it being the day when, each week, a *Zikr* was held by all the followers of the *Tarikat*, at which any who were not members could also be welcomed. That ceremony, or celebration, varying in form within the different Sufi Orders, is essentially a ritual of the 'remembrance' of God by way of 'recollection' through invocation of particular Names, or Attributes, of the Divinity. We were invited to attend that evening's *Zikr*. After having spent an hour or so back at the hotel resting, we returned to the bookshop at the hour we had been bidden. A man was there waiting to drive us to the meeting place. This was only about a quarter of an hour's drive away. There, before the *Zikr*, people had gathered and were sitting and chatting quite informally; and we were introduced entirely naturally and without any ceremony. Very shortly afterwards the Sheykh arrived; and he invited us to join him at the evening meal before the *Zikr*. Out in the garden there was a simple table at which the Sheykh took his place at the head and we were among a dozen and more who were seated on either side of him, facing each other. The majority of us were foreigners.

The Sheykh was a bulky, strongly built, man in his sixties, rather above medium height, with grizzled grey hair, unbearded but moustached. His appearance suggested he might have been (though the preface to the Turkish original of his book was to reveal that this was not the case) a retired military man: almost severe in countenance, however not at all stern - indeed with an occasional half-humorous look about his eyes; a person weighty, but without self-importance, and entirely unpompous. A man one felt who had great experience of people of all sorts and conditions; someone one could trust; far removed from such as we have become familiar with over the decades, from press, radio and television, who as religious leaders have so often fallen victim to that seemingly 'occupational' risk of self-inflation.

The table talk was mainly in English, occasional translation being provided by one of the senior *murids* ('novice', 'follower'). Towards the end of the meal someone asked how we might share a bowl of peaches, too few for each of us to have one. The Sheykh replied by asking, in turn, how the questioner would like the peaches to be shared out, "According to God's, or to human, apportionment?" "According to God's," was the response. The Sheykh cut up one or two peaches and, without comment, handed out parts to some, undivided whole fruit to others - and some got none.

**\*\*\*\*\*\*\*\*\*\***

*I have put down this account of the episode just as it was in my memory at the time I write it now, more than twelve years after the event. But, as will be seen shortly, Lalage had, within days of it happening, written down what is clearly the accurate version of the detail. And yet the difference in that detail in no way alters the nub or the essence of what had happened, and the point of what the Sheykh had done. (It occurs to me that here is an illustration of the possible way in which outwardly disparate descriptions of what is supposed to be the same event by different evangelists in the separate gospels could as well have been honest accounts as deliberate elaborations or distortions.)*

**\*\*\*\*\*\*\*\*\*\***

We rose from the table as the *ezan* was heard, calling to the evening prayer. I asked where I might go for the ritual ablution which I needed to make before the prayer and went out with several other men. When I returned I found that Lalage had gone off with the other women. In the prayer-hall the women and the men sat separately, on either side of a lattice-work screen. After the prayers, which had of course been led by him, the Sheykh turned to face the congregation, all in the position of the concluding prayer - kneeling, but sitting on your heels. Comfortable if you are used to it. Not, if you are not.

*Zikr*, as I have said, is a means of recollecting the presence of God by invocation. There are, naturally, very many such invocations and each *Tarikat* adopts its own preferred way of doing this. On this occasion we followed the Sheykh in his Order's *Zikr* by repeating, slowly, the statement in the first half of the 'witness' *La ilahe il'allah* and turning our heads rhythmically, in time, from side to side: "There is no Divinity - save God... there is no Divinity - save God..." The sensation was of calm, tranquillity. But gradually, almost imperceptibly, the rhythm and the tempo increased. So gradually did this happen that I was scarcely conscious of it until the physical sensation of it began to affect me. How long this took before I was aware that my pulse was rising uncomfortably fast I can't be sure - probably about a quarter of an hour or more, and by then I wondered whether my chest wasn't feeling too tight. I became anxious about the condition of my heart. Feeling very uncomfortable - in both senses of the word - I got up and left. Was I right, there, to be concerned about my physical state? I didn't know then, nor do I now. What I do know is that, ever since, if I ever feel breathless, or find my pulse is either irregular or too high (or even, occasionally, racing) I repeat the words of that *Zikr*, regularly and rhythmically, while I inhale and exhale deeply in time with the words, conscious both of my physical actions and of the words' meaning. Who can prove an infallible cause or effect? Nevertheless more than a dozen years have passed since that evening and I have very many times found solace and relief in what is for me a spiritual practice.

\*\*\*\*\*\*\*\*\*\*\*

A curious little vignette of what I found when I withdrew from the *Zikr*. There were a few people waiting in the room outside the prayer-hall. Among these was a burly policeman, with what I assumed was a standard, regulation revolver in a belt holster. We chatted amiably, he being curious that a Turk living in England should be present at a *Tekke* (a *Tarikat* meeting place). I, too, was extremely interested in his being there - though I didn't give voice to my curiosity. So far as

300

I knew, the law under which the *Tarikat*s had been closed down in the early years of the Republic more than half a century before had not been repealed. So whether this guardian of the law was there, like any other member of the public, as a visitor or adherent, or in an official capacity of one kind or another - possibly to keep an eye on what went on - it seemed that the State must have reached some kind of unofficial, or tacit, understanding to waive the letter of the law in relation to these places. If so, a pragmatic approach; positively British it seemed to me. All this I naturally kept to myself. Not long afterwards the *Zikr* ended and Lalage emerged with the other women. We returned to the Pera Palas.

\*\*\*\*\*\*\*\*\*\*\*\*

The bus journey to Konya on the morrow took all day. We arrived in the dark, and after dropping our cases at the small hotel in the centre of the town where we registered, we walked to a nearby restaurant. Everywhere on the streets were to be seen, singly and in small knots, men strolling up and down seemingly just filling in time. All were dressed alike in khaki jacket and trousers. It was the week or so leading up to the annual *Hajj* (the Pilgrimage to Mecca) and, as we were to learn, the government's Department for Religious Affairs made provision for organised parties of pilgrims to travel to and from Mecca. The arrangements included cheap 'excursion' fares and also the travelling clothes we had seen (which, on arrival at the Hejaz in Saudi Arabia, were changed for the ritual plain white shroud-like garments of all pilgrims on the *Hajj*). We also learned that it was a long established tradition for pilgrims going from Turkey to travel first to Konya to visit the tomb of *Mevlana* ('Our Master') Jelal ed-Din Rumi there before setting out on the journey to the Holy Places of the *Hajj* itself. This further evidence of pragmatism towards - indeed of accommodation with - the devout Moslems among its citizenry on the part of the strictly secular Turkish Republican government, was to me odd (as being so unexpected) yet, at the same time, wholly admirable.

Rumi's tomb, at the Foundation *Tekke* of the whole *Mevlevi* Order, was naturally one of the main places I had included among those I wanted to see in Konya. The whole complex of buildings is now

301

officially a museum, and a most excellently arranged one for the visitor who might wish to come there in that capacity alone. Though it is sad to see the circular hall of the *Semahane* (where the ritual of the 'dance' used to be performed) now also but part of the area where artifacts are displayed, from different periods - some relating directly to the Order. The tomb chamber itself, however, was still palpably a place of veneration for many - and a place of reverence for all. Although it is no longer celebrated in the *Tekke* as of old, the *Sema* ritual is still publicly performed by the members of the Order with their Sheykh in another building in the town each year on the 17th of December, the anniversary of Rumi's death - the *Şeb-i Arus* (the 'Bridal Night' [of the Union]). This public ceremony is ostensibly permitted by the authorities as a 'cultural' manifestation. Lalage and I have, since that visit, been present at this *Sema* in the Albert Hall in London when the Mevlevi Sheykh of the day and members of the Order came to Britain, as they very occasionally do. It was witnessed and heard by the great audience, which filled the Hall to capacity, quite patently in the reverent atmosphere of a spiritual experience.

In the Istanbul bookshop we had been given the name of a carpet shop in Konya where we might be able to make contact with the *Mevlevi*'s, in the hope that we might be able to meet their Sheykh. We discovered the shop, where we were very soon in conversation with three middle-aged men. Much talk again about ourselves, and after giving our oral introduction we were asked to return the next day at mid-morning with the prospect of a visit to the *Mevlevi* Sheykh. Back we came after breakfast, having first visited some of the other places I had marked down in Konya - including the tomb of Rumi's own dearly beloved 'soul mate' *Şems-i Tebriz*, which, though we had not known this, was customarily visited before going on to Rumi's. In the carpet shop a youth soon arrived to accompany us on foot to our destination. As we left (or was it in the course of conversation just before?) the shopkeeper said to us, in a traditional form of words which I had not until then heard, *Allah bir yastıkta kocatsın* ('God grant you [both] to grow old [together] on one pillow'). A graceful formula; and thirteen years have passed since then, while we now together have passed our allotted span of three score years and ten.

302

The young man and we left the centre of the town and were soon in a quarter of narrower, almost wholly traffic-free, streets. Lalage was, I think, the first to observe that in appearance, and in feel, the place was evocative of the old Nicosia we had known in the early days of our married life in Cyprus, before EOKA was to make such places dangerous. In about ten minutes or so we came to a house much like any of its neighbours. Our guide took us in, and together we entered a room in which an old man - it is strange that I have no memory of his appearance, not even whether or not he was bearded - was lying in bed. My recollection is simply one of frailty and serenity. We did not stay more than a quarter of an hour or so; and I do not remember that anything was said of moment or significance. But I felt that, without being able to communicate why this had been so, the visit had been fulfilling.

**********

The day after our return to Istanbul we paid a final visit to the Sheykh's bookshop. Since we had last been there Lalage had, as I say, written a short verse in commemoration of the episode of the peaches, which I had put into Turkish; and we wanted to give these to him as a parting gift. I quote here the words of Lalage's poem to show how my memory of what had led to it was (as I have recorded above) at variance with what had actually happened. It had not been several peaches, but only one, which had evoked the question to the Sheykh about how to share the fruit among many; and it was only that one which he had cut into several pieces before distributing them in the seemingly inequitable manner which had struck me at the time. Moreover the peach had not been on the table, but had fortuitously fallen to the ground from the tree at the side of the table.

*A peach fell. At a certain time, in a certain place,*
*Unique, that will not come again, a peach fell.*

*What makes this peach, with its familiar sweetness,*
*Its juice, its delectable flesh, unlike any other?*

*It is that it is shared by five people, all different*
*In blood, in tradition, in experience, all linked by longing for God.*

*Did the peach fall up or down?  We only know*
*It came from God, and may perhaps take us back to Him.*

*That moment moves into eternity.  Praise God!*

This time, when we came to pay our farewell visit, the Sheykh was in his shop.  He sat alone at one side with a circle of chairs round the edge of the room.  Some of these were empty but others were occupied, by both men and women, either alone or in twos and threes.  These talked quietly among themselves.  Occasionally someone would address the Sheykh, but I do not recall that he himself ever spoke save by way of response to something said to him.  From time to time a man or woman got up and approached him, speaking to him in an undertone; and he replied in the same way.  The general quiet conversation meanwhile continued.  When I felt that an appropriate moment had come I also rose and gave him the piece of paper with Lalage's poem and my translation of it, saying simply that it was a parting gift from us, as we were travelling to Bursa the day after the morrow, and then going back to England.  He bade us farewell.  I went back to my seat next to Lalage.  He read in silence from the piece of paper.  Then, without looking at us, he kissed the paper and pressed it to his forehead before folding it and putting it away.  We took our leave.  For the last time.

**\*\*\*\*\*\*\*\*\*\***

Our next, and last visiting, day in Istanbul we crossed to the *Üsküdar* side where I had noted, from my reading, two mosques I wanted to see; the *Şemsi Paşa* (a lovely little waterside complex) and the *Atık Valide* (further up the hillside into the town).  The first of these visits was delightful, even happy.  The situation was charming, the atmosphere tranquil.  It suddenly came to me that this was in fact a place we had stumbled upon, in the course of a walk along the edge of the sea, when we had stayed at the Harem Hotel on our visit six years before. Then it had been in need of attention, though the garden was well looked after by a family living in the buildings forming part of the mosque complex. Now these had been restored and were open to the public as a small library and reading rooms. A delightful spot.

From there we made our way on foot to the *Atık Valide* mosque not very far away landward. Just outside the courtyard entrance a group of boys, ten to twelve years old, were kicking a football around. I think it was one of them who first addressed us rather than we them; but however it started, we were soon engaged in the sort of conversation of questions and answers which commonly occurs when curious and inquisitive young people (and often not so young) encounter foreigners in Turkey. As we were talking a couple of men, one of them bearded, came up from behind and walked past us towards the mosque. Whether they were out of normal earshot I couldn't now be certain, but they were a fair distance to one side of our little group as they walked towards the courtyard entrance.

As they approached it the bearded one turned and loudly reproached the boys (in Turkish naturally): "Haven't you ever seen unbelievers before?" (with the implied additional sense of "... that you have to converse with them?"). The word used for 'unbeliever' was the one which more generally signifies *Christian* non-Moslems, rather than, say, a self-professed non-believing 'Moslem'; and is almost as invariably meant, and taken, opprobriously even contumeliously. (Rather, I believe, as *goy* can be used by some members of Judaism). *Gavur* is as offensive as when some Christians once used the word 'infidel' of those who professed Islam, as distinct from other non-Christians - who were more likely to be described as 'pagans', or 'idolaters', or something else similarly merely dismissive or derisive, rather than with the hostility which used to be implicit in 'infidel'. The word *Gavur* is in fact but a corruption of the Arabic *Kafir* - meaning, literally, 'one who denies'. Hearing it from the bearded man, I walked briskly towards him and, catching up, said in Turkish, calmly enough but with no attempt to hide my anger, "From whom was it that you learned I am a *Gavur*? I tell you that I am, like you, a Turk - and a believer." I then returned to Lalage and the boys. I should be surprised if I didn't make some such remark as, "What ill manners!"; though I can't recall whether indeed I commented aloud at all. But what one of the boys said to me is something I have not infrequently since quoted in discussions with other Turks of varying persuasions. The boy's words remained with me as a source of hope for the future, and still do when the young, wherever they may be, are able and prepared to value their own inner convictions against what affronts their sensibilities, however much the affront emanates from supposed 'elders and betters'. The boy said to me wryly, yet matter-of-factly, "What can we do, uncle? He's just an ignorant one."

In fairness to the man, a couple of things should be said. First, that from our general dress and appearance Lalage and I could well have been mistaken for a couple of foreign 'rubber-necks' - which indeed I suppose we were. Second, the man in fact came back to our group and invited me to the mid-day service shortly to begin. (It was actually the weekly Friday Congregational Prayer: I had completely overlooked the day of the week.) I politely declined the invitation; but also reluctantly as well as regretfully. I wasn't at all sure how Lalage would fare among the women members of a completely strange congregation; and I couldn't leave her outside on her own for the quite lengthy period of the *Cuma Namazı*. Moreover I was sneakily apprehensive that my refusal would in fact merely confirm the bearded one in his suspicion that I was, at best, a latitudinarian modernist (which I might be) and, at worst, a devious atheist (which I hope I am not). However, although it ended with the courtesies preserved, the episode was in sad contrast to our encounters with Turkish people at other places of worship.

***********

*It is curious that at almost precisely this time, in the very early 1980s, our daughter (who had of course only relatively recently met again, and known her Turkish, Moslem, grandmother for the first time as an adult), had an experience equally uncharacteristic of most Christian clergymen. She told me that at Holy Trinity, Brompton, in London, to which she occasionally went with some of her young friends, she had heard a youthful priest - I don't recall whether he was a curate, but no matter - inform his congregation that Islam was "the work of the devil". I reflect that none of the faiths is free from the presence of their own - might I say - "satanic" spokesmen. And having so written, I am brought*

306

*up short with a thought. What seems to animate such partisan spokesmen is the conviction of their own rectitude; in which case, do not advocates of outright and wholesale toleration, as a virtual article of faith, actually run the risk of falling into just such a trap of self-righteousness? I do not know how this dilemma is to be resolved, but I feel sure at least that it is healthy - indeed essential - to be constantly aware of the peril. That danger seems to me always to lurk when the much abused word 'fundamentalist' is brought into play. So much so that I am inclined to the view that any of us who find ourselves using it should immediately take it as a warning to stop and think whether we do not in fact intend some other meaning: perhaps 'bigot', or 'zealot'. I can perfectly easily imagine a libertarian bigot or zealot, as much as I can a religious one. I am less sure when it comes to the 'fundamentalist'. As to which there seems to me to be nothing necessarily harmful in anyone delving to the depths of their beliefs, or convictions, to try to discover what lies at their heart; which is how I would understand the sense of that word - so often used pejoratively. I have an image of people in a desert desperate with thirst. Each is digging away to find a water course. The sensible thing is not for each to rush from one place to another making fresh attempts to locate a likely source, but to pursue their individual search patiently, each at their chosen spot. Breaking off from time to time to hurl actual or verbal brickbats at the others is unlikely to be helpful for the others' - and probably still less for one's own - search. (And when each does find a cupful of the water they are seeking, they are likely also to discover that it comes from the same fundamental source.)*

**\*\*\*\*\*\*\*\*\*\*\***

The last place we visited on this Turkish trip was *Yeşil Bursa*, Verdant Bursa. Small wonder that the first Turks to see the place in the 13th century, many of whom were but a few generations removed from their pre-Islamic Shamanistic roots, should have found entrancing this place of greenery, so close also to the Koranic descriptions of paradise as just such a place with flowing waters.

The town itself is strung along the lower skirts of the *Ulu Dağ* mountain rising up above it to the south east, while below is spread out the wide plain stretching down to the southern shores of the Sea of Marmora fifteen miles or so away. Bursa has now grown to be a city, among the five or six most populous in the country, and its expansion below the old town was already well advanced when we were there. Yet the heart of the Bursa of old was still much as it had been - although a good deal of restoration had taken place to repair the ravages of earthquakes over the centuries. But there was one gap of which I was aware from my reading in Goodwin's comprehensive and excellently illustrated great work, *A History of Ottoman Architecture*. "The great loss," he wrote, "was the ancient *Irgandı* Bridge, blown up by the retreating Greek army in 1922. The bridge had a single great arch which carried rows of shops on each side of its highway. Linking, in miniature, Bursa with Florence and London, it was a charming relic of the great days of the town." Since I read that passage twenty years ago I have seen an illustration of another such bridge lined with buildings, which still stood in Kars, nearly a thousand miles away at the other end of Turkey, when Russia occupied those eastern provinces in 1878. Recovered by Turkey once more in the War of Salvation in 1922, the bridge was no more. There comes into my mind that other great single-span bridge which had stood for five hundred years as a symbol of the Ottoman years, whose destruction by Croat artillery was witnessed by millions on their television screens two years ago. What had for centuries joined the Catholic and Moslem quarters of Mostar, in Bosnia-Herzogovina, was wantonly destroyed - for what? There is something peculiarly repellent in the deliberate obliteration of what are symbolic, as much as they are actual, links between human beings.

It is several miles from the mosque and complex of *Emir Sultan* at the eastern end of Bursa to that of *Murad Hüdavendigar* at the western end. Too far to walk, we found; and we began to flag. This was clear to a young lad, who came forward and, when he had learned where we were heading, constituted himself our guide. He walked us to a nearby point, where he put us on a small bus to take us to our destination - and, again entirely matter-of-factly, adamantly refused to accept anything for his trouble.

Once again it would be otiose to do more than just list some of the other places we saw: the Great Mosque; the Green Mosque; the Green Tomb (of Mehmed I, who held the Ottoman state in being during its virtual dissolution as an entity after the rout of the Ottoman army at the battle of Ankara in 1402 by Tamerlaine - *Timurlenk*); the great burial ground of the *Muradiye* (where lies Murad II in his tomb chamber, domed - but open, as he had requested, to the skies). Yet one place does deserve more than a mere mention - for the reason I shall explain: the *Bayezit* Mosque, built by that sultan who had been defeated by 'Tamburlaine' (as dramatised by Marlowe in his play of that name in which the tragic figure of the captured sultan is given the name *Bajazet*).

While Lalage and I were admiring the lofty arched entrance portico of the mosque we came upon an earnest man inspecting the building with a couple of others. They were interested that we, too, were interested, and he told us that he was from whichever office it was (I forget which) that had the responsibility for the maintenance of historic (or was it only of 'ecclesiastical'?) buildings. He was very knowledgeable and, I would judge, capable in his job; and he was pleased that I was, at least to some extent, informed and keen to add to my stock of knowledge about the centuries-old Turkish historical tapestry. The more so when in the course of our conversation he understood that I had spent much more than half of my life in England, only rather less than a third of it in Cyprus, and had never been to a Turkish school. We talked about the state of affairs in Britain. He then took me absolutely by surprise when, learning of the dire economic position which had brought the country to the brink of disaster in the country's 'winter of discontent' under Callaghan, he suddenly burst out with, "So England's in a state of collapse? May she collapse still further! Throughout our history England has been our greatest enemy." There was no point in getting bogged down in an acrimonious argument, for which I had no taste at the time and which I didn't judge would be likely to yield any useful result. We shortly afterwards said good-bye to each other; and Lalage and I resumed our walk, by crossing over to the other side of the road to look at the tomb there of the fallen *Bayezit* who, in death, had been allowed back by his conqueror to be buried in his own country.

\*\*\*\*\*\*\*\*\*\*

309

# Journeying

*I have since reflected on the outburst we heard outside the mosque. What strikes me in retrospect, apart from the vehemence of the man's feelings, is the imbalance of his historical perspective. It is no part of mine to seek to defend Britain's role in relation to the Turkish people over the centuries, but a picture in which she appears as Turkey's "greatest enemy" among the 'Great Powers' of the times, seems to me to be a distorted one. I can only take the man as a sad example of the way some educated Turks have a blinkered view of their own past due, it would seem, to the lack of a deep and panoramic vista when they look back over the years. In the light of events during the lifetime of our interlocutor, and of his parents, they could well have had reason for seeing Britain as a great enemy of their country: the instigator of the Greek invasion of western Anatolia; the encourager of territorial ambitions in eastern Anatolia by Armenians, who were minority populations in those areas; the major beneficiary in the carve-up of the Arab provinces after the First World War, having suborned with gold the Sherif of the Holy Places of Mecca and Medina during it; the moving spirit during that war of the Gallipoli adventure; the chief of the occupying forces in Istanbul from 1919 to 1922. Nor, in recent memory, had there been lacking a pretty persistent stream of animosity and vilification on the part of individual members of institutions of power, authority and influence (in the tradition of such as Gladstone, Lloyd George and T.E. Lawrence) all of whose antipathies to Turkish people, as such, were quite unconcealed. As had been Harold Nicolson's racialist partiality at the time when Curzon was presiding over the Lausanne conference in 1923, and Nicolson was his Foreign Office Private Secretary. Even as I write such a brief summary, I begin to understand what motivated the man at the Bayezit mosque to speak as he did. And yet (though admittedly acting in her own perceived national interests - as have all states in the last couple of centuries during which 'sovereign national states' have been in existence) Britain had in fact quite often tempered her depredations, in relation to Turkey, by perceiving her interests as marching with those of the Ottoman state. So that, for example, she was allied with Turkey in the Crimean War, and for the next sixty years or so she was engaged, at least sporadically, in bolstering the Ottomans against the predatory Czarists. It was, in fact, the Russians against whom, historically, the accusation of being Turkey's greatest enemy could warrantably have been levelled.*

310

*The Russians, too, had acted in what they perceived as their best interests ('religious', dynastic and national); but these had at no time ever been anything but deeply and unremittingly hostile and aggressive to the Turks for the past half millennium. And from the time of Catherine the Great in the late 18th century the loss of Turkish territory to the Russians was inexorable and continuous. And not just Ottoman Turkish lands (from the Balkans to the Caspian) but in other Turkish states from the Crimea, through Azerbaijan, to the furthest lands east beyond Bukhara and Samarkand. If the man in Bursa was not ignorant of all this he gave no sign of having weighed it. Yet were he in fact ignorant, I suppose I really ought not to be too surprised when I consider the quite astonishing lack of knowledge I have encountered in this country among well-educated people about their own relations with other countries - not least Ireland.*

**\*\*\*\*\*\*\*\*\*\***

We were able to clear our minds and refresh our spirits the next day on the summit of *Ulu Dağ* reached by cable car. We lunched at a modest restaurant where we were brought a raised circular charcoal brazier with tongs, together with the meat which you cooked yourself to your own taste - and with no one to blame but yourself - vegetables and salads being produced separately. A novel way of combining the pleasures of a meal out with a home barbecue. The air was alpine; and the place has since, I believe, become even more so, with hotels, *pistes*, and the rest.

Refreshing in a different way was the presence as part of the hotel of a traditional *hamam*, the Turkish Bath. Bursa has for centuries been renowned for its thermal springs where, to quote the Master once more, one can "teach one's liver to take a joke". Our hotel bedrooms were provided, in addition to the famous 'Turkish towelling' in its usual rectangular form adopted in Europe, with hooded dressing-gowns of the same material. We could, at any time, put these on over swimming clothes and saunter down to the *hamam*: a marble-lined thirty foot diameter circular pool of naturally heated water, with assorted tepid, cool and cold douches all around. So passing from enervation through relaxation to invigoration.

311

# ~13~

## Chitterne; Cyprus; Chitterne; Shehri Sebz; Chitterne

I have in this account so far tried largely to avoid segmenting my life by reference to decades; neither those which chronicle a century, as so often happens when historians or commentators on public affairs outline the background against which they survey the vista of their own times, nor yet the successive ten-year periods of my individual past from birth until now, having moved into my own eighth decade. Yet looking back over the years which span our return from Turkey in the autumn of 1982 to the end of the year just passed, although neither of the two decades 1980 to 1990 or 1986 to 1996 seemed at the time to have had any significant objective existence to warrant specific notice, as such, as part of my story, somehow those dozen or so years, more or less, which began with the eighties, do, for me, encompass some particularly meaningful period. Though just what that meaning was, or is, I find very difficult to convey to myself - much less to anyone else.

The time was one during which I see myself becoming bogged down in a metaphorical swamp, the atmosphere heavy and occasionally doom-laden. My mood was one of unfocused apprehension. At first this was no more than a kind of fretful feeling of doubt about the future; but as the years passed this grew into a deeply anxious foreboding. The ominous overhanging clouds were not, it is true, continuously present or unbroken. Had they indeed been so, I would no doubt have been at risk - emotionally, psychically, even physically. From time to time the clouds parted and through the gaps, which were often large and sometimes long-lasting, the warmth and brightness of the sun shone through to uplift the heart. And there were many days when the skies actually cleared and the blue heavens brought the knowledge of joy. But the presence, or the sense, of a threatening darkness, even at noon, was not often completely absent. A couplet of Yunus Emre's would often float into my mind:

*My life together with the Friend is like to the sun in swirling cloud*
*Moments there are His Face is veiled - then, see, His Beauty is revealed.*

On the face of it there were no reasonable grounds for this sense, nevertheless palpably real, of peril or doom. As far as the country was concerned, it seemed indeed to be bathed in a sea of virtual euphoria. Everyone appeared to have as much money as they needed, or even wanted - more markedly so even than when, with an economy roaring ahead, the first housing boom had been in full flood not so many years before. The over-mighty brokers of power in the extreme wings of the great trade unions had been brought within the bounds of legal accountability for their actions, in what most people (to judge from the election results) appeared to think an eminently fair and helpful move towards economic and social stability. Overseas, military aggression by an absolutist ruler had been successfully challenged with a brilliantly conceived and bravely executed campaign thousands of miles away in the south Atlantic, resulting in the defeat of Galtieri and the recovery of the Falklands. To cap all, the seeming impregnability of the menacing Soviet system had been shown to be entirely misjudged, with that empire collapsing as rapidly and unexpectedly as Japanese might had crumbled nearly half a century earlier - and this time without the dreadful use of an overwhelmingly destructive nuclear weapon held by one side only. So why, therefore, that oppressive sense of despondency, seeming to bode a coming disaster, that enveloped me during those outwardly happy years of our time at the Grange in Chitterne?

At the root of my feeling of malaise was fear, which focused on the prospects for overall financial stability and employment security. So far as concerned Lalage and myself, ever since my retirement, we were, and remained, very conscious of our good fortune in having no occasion to worry over money; on the contrary we had every reason to count our personal blessings. So far as a non-expert like myself was able to judge, the general economic state of the country in the early 1980s seemed not to be all that much different from what it had been during that recent earlier period when house prices had first rocketed, and when the credit card had also provided an infallible means of acquiring whatever anyone's heart desired - and whenever. Although on that previous occasion the inevitable swing had arrived, and many people's expectations had been disappointed, nothing really disastrous or cataclysmic had then happened. Yet somehow this time I felt in my bones that something was actually brewing which was different either in its scale or its intensity, and quite probably in both. And this horrible feeling of dread was, as I say, now sensed not in relation to Lalage and myself but on account of the children. How would they fare in this stormy, tempestuous, new world, which seemed to be a throwback to the unbridled 19th century?

A clear recollection I have of the mid-1980s is of saying to Lalage that whether one approved or disapproved of the radicalism of the economic aspects of the Conservative government of that time, it was more than straining reality to regard their ideas as being in the historical tradition of British Conservatism or Toryism: what they were advocating, and seemed to have the will and determination to pursue, appeared to be nothing but simon-pure mercantalist, *laissez-faire*, 'Free Trade', 'Manchester School', Cobden and Bright Liberalism at its most doctrinaire. And what might not flow from that in terms of security of employment for the young in the world of work? As things turned out, both our son and son-in-law were indeed to be struck by the economic blizzard which duly arrived towards the end of the 1980s - in company with millions of others of all conditions and all ages. All that is germane to this story is that they came through; that for this we are most profoundly grateful and thankful; and that we trust that their futures may continue to be blessed.

\*\*\*\*\*\*\*\*\*\*\*

An early break in the encircling clouds came in the latter half of 1983. Within a matter of weeks of each other our son and our daughter announced to us at weekend visits to Chitterne that they were engaged to be married. Which it was of each of the couples who had prevailed upon, or had persuaded, their partner to accept them was never quite clear to me, but that both couples were decidedly in favour of the

314

married state was obvious enough. And our delight at hearing their news goes without saying. It had been three years since the two couples had come out with us to Cyprus on that first return in 1980 which Lalage and I had made, twenty years after we had left the island thinking never to go back; but both our children had known their future spouses for quite a few years before then. And this brings me to reflect on an aspect of my attitude to the relations between the sexes as these have changed over the past generation.

Our son and his future wife had not only known each other for several years before their Cyprus holiday but had lived together during that time. For many, and possibly most, of their contemporaries, this was an entirely normal, almost usual, style of life. My own feelings were not so much neutral as dispassionate. I was certainly very happy that he and his chosen partner had found their own happiness together; but at the same time I nourished an underlying anxious hope that their partnership would lead to a lasting and stable marriage. What I now realise is that I did not at the time consider the position of the girl who was to become our daughter-in-law. Nor did I even entertain the idea that our daughter might ever be in that same position. And I am now conscious that had such a situation in fact arisen I should have agonised and been deeply distressed. Male chauvinism? I do not now try to analyse deeply my inconsistent attitudes in respect of my son and daughter (and more particularly as between my daughter and my daughter-in-law to be), nor to speculate on how far I differed in this regard from other fathers at that time - or now. To the extent that my mind dwells on this at all, it is only to recognise how greatly I respect our daughter-in-law's parents, who never made any reference to their daughter's position before her marriage - other than when her father was to describe our son to me, most feelingly, as "a true gentleman". Which is a designation fittingly applicable to my son-in-law too. In the words spoken to Lalage and me by the man in Konya, may each couple "grow old together on a single pillow", and in their turn find ever-increasing fulfilment in their own children.

\*\*\*\*\*\*\*\*\*\*

Two winters before the children's weddings my mother, in her late

315

seventies, fell gravely ill in Cyprus. The first flight on which I was able to get a seat was more than a week after my brother telephoned to tell me that she was in hospital. I thought I was flying out to her on her death-bed - indeed I did not know whether I should reach her in time. In the event she was to make a remarkable recovery. I flew back to England after ten days, leaving her in my brother's solicitous care. She continued living with him in his flat until she died, eleven years later. For the first four or five years following her recovery she was in reasonably good health, though infirm. But she then had a fall, and thereafter never stepped outside the flat - save once, as I shall tell. During the whole of that time my brother devotedly looked after her, for the last six months of her life nursing her night and day. Those with even a spark of imagination will know that anything else I might say about such care would be pointless to the degree of being insultingly otiose. She never lived in her own house again, which she had had to abandon thirty three years, virtually to the month, before her death. But she was blessed by frequent visits from her grandchildren, accompanied by their own children as these came on the scene in their turn. She saw her fifth great-grandchild, our daughter's second daughter and the youngest of her three children, barely a month before, with all her faculties intact, she died in her eighty-eighth year.

\*\*\*\*\*\*\*\*\*\*

Since our Turkey trip, and after mother's serious illness when I had flown out, Lalage and I had begun to take regular annual fortnightly holidays in North Cyprus, which had been slowly trying to develop tourism there. On our first such visit, the autumn immediately following her recovery, we had been alone, and had stayed in a Nicosia hotel so as to be easily within reach of her and my brother. In subsequent years we had managed to arrange our visits with one or other of the children and their families. We travelled under arrangements for 'package holidays' which were being made by a very restricted number of tourist firms (who were in fact facing very heavy opposition and threats of sanctions by the Greek administration in the South - still recognised by Britain as the lawful government of the whole island). It became our habit to book ourselves into hotels in Kyrenia, which, with Famagusta, was the principal tourist centre; Nicosia didn't feature in such 'package' bookings, and in any case to be in Nicosia for an entire two week period would have been a poor holiday for young people and children for whom such breaks meant the seaside.

**********

For myself, coming out to Cyprus in this way as just another 'package tourist' began increasingly to grate. It weighed on me too when, every time I visited Nicosia and drove or walked from the old city to my brother's flat, I passed in front of the 'Green Line' barricade, just beyond which I could see the Ledra Palace hotel and catch a glimpse of mother's empty and decaying house. I felt more and more affronted by the realisation that I had, in effect, been driven from the land of my birth. And however much it had been my own decision to leave in 1960, my mother's departure four years afterwards had most certainly not been freely willed by her.

There was little rationality in the way my thoughts now developed. After the early 1980s, when there had first seemed to be some faint prospect of the two political leaderships in the island moving towards each other, that hope had faded; and I had ceased even remotely to contemplate the increasingly unlikely possibility of some political 'settlement', or more accurately 'accommodation', which might allow my mother to return to her home. Nor did I ever look to a future in which, were I to survive her, my brother and I would inherit the place jointly. So I was not in the position of feeling an actual deprivation of being able, at some time, to have the use of that house as somewhere to stay when visiting Cyprus - instead of in a tourist hotel. Yet I was irked and resentful that I and my children had been prevented from enjoying a feeling of continuity with our past which could have come from such 'a place of one's own'. However, unlike so many thousands, even millions, of others outside Cyprus driven from their homes, or compelled by circumstances to leave them (and this was before Bosnia), *I* at least could still return to a *part* of my birth-place - however difficult the Greek administration in the South was trying to make such travel to and from the North. So it was that, gradually, I began to conceive and nourish the idea of owning some such place, the key of which I could have in my pocket to let myself in on arrival from the airport.

317

**Journeying**

Wholly unexpectedly, what had been an idle daydream was to become a reality.

**\*\*\*\*\*\*\*\*\*\***

But before I come to that, this picture of homes abandoned in circumstances, and through violent forces, created by megalomaniac politicians brings to me the recollection of one place in Cyprus where Greeks used once to live. This was the village of Zach's family. Some fifteen miles east of Kyrenia, and slightly inland from the coast road, its inhabitants are now all Turkish. After we had known each other for a couple of years Zach asked me if, on my next visit to Cyprus, I would take some photographs of the village for him. He had but dim memories of the place, having come to live in England even before his early teens. Lalage and I accordingly went there some time in the mid-1980s and, wandering about the place, took a dozen and more photographs at random, of houses as well as of the church - a new one built within the previous twenty to thirty years - which was now the village mosque. To my great surprise there were still, more than ten years after the arrival of the Turkish inhabitants, painted slogans on the walls of the kind I remembered from EOKA days calling for *enosis*. I included two or three of these among my snapshots. On return to England I posted all these to Zach observing, light-heartedly, in my letter that I could only account for the continuing presence of these wall daubings - so long after the daubers had gone - by surmising one or more of the following: they were deliberately left so as to serve as a warning to the Turkish villagers to be constantly vigilant; or the Turks were a remarkably tolerant lot of people; or the Turks were too idle a bunch to stir themselves to paint them out or obliterate them! Zach forbore to offer an opinion. But he told me that he had shown the photographs to his father (whom he later was to bring to visit us at Chitterne a few years before the latter died) and had learned from him that none of my haphazard shots had happened to include his own family house. Yet one photograph had been of an uncle's house - and that uncle, he told me, had been a virulent Turkophobe. Such, too, are the inscrutable workings of providence.

318

\*\*\*\*\*\*\*\*\*\*\*

The word "providential" has long since fallen into desuetude, if not actual disuse, in the popular language. So far as it is at all current it carries, more often than not, the unqualified sense of "fortunate" or "lucky", though strictly speaking its meaning ought, so it seems to me, to be taken neutrally, like the word "fortuitous". Providence is, I should have thought, the source of both fortune and of misfortune - whether or not this is to be understood as signifying God at work in the world so that, ultimately, "all things work together for good to them that love God". It is to this belief that I try, at least, to cling . And to the workings of providence as it affected me I now turn.

*There was in Nicosia, within the walls, a house - one of those built by Beligh Pasha at the turn of the century - which had featured in two episodes in my mother's life - separated from each other by some forty years. The first occasion was in 1923 when, nearly eighteen, she and father were preparing to set up house. Until then they had lived with her parents in her mother's great house on the Nicosia ramparts. The house of this little story was only a few hundred yards distant from the latter. It had been chosen by my mother's mother, Hidayet Hanım, for her daughter and son-in-law to live in as their own married home. But it had a tenant of long standing, an Armenian woman with her family who, on hearing of my grandmother's intention, called on her and begged to be allowed to remain in her home. My grandmother was adamant. Mother, who was present when the meeting took place, intervened in a flood of tears and vowed, solemnly and formally, that she would not go through with the public marriage celebration ceremony, the düğün, if the tenant were turned out. My grandmother was forced to relent; and it was in her own house that my mother and father's düğün was in the event celebrated. The years passed. In due course, on the division between mother and her two brothers of their mother's property, ownership of the house passed to my mother. By then the sole tenant of the house was Marie, a daughter of the same Armenian family. (The place was always known to us in our family as 'Marie's house'.) As mother's own tenant, she had always regularly paid her rent - which by the 1950s was the not entirely derisory figure*

319

*of £12 sterling a month! In the uncertain early days of the new-born Cyprus Republic, a trickle began of Turks from some villages, where they felt under threat from their preponderantly Greek neighbours, into Nicosia, which seemed to hold the prospect of greater security within the walls. Forty years after she had opposed her own mother's wishes and so prevented the eviction of the Armenian tenants, mother now came under pressure herself from some self-constituted spokesmen of the Turkish community at street level to get rid of this single Armenian woman. Mother flatly refused to bow to this attempt to intimidate her into putting on the street her old tenant - who had lived all her life in that house. But, not much later, some of Marie's relatives came and took her to live with them on the Greek side of Nicosia. When the flow of Turkish Cypriot refugees into Nicosia became a flood, three such families were billeted there by the separate Turkish Cypriot Administration which had by then been set up; and from then on the house gradually fell into complete disrepair and decay.*

It was, in my understanding of the word, 'providential' that I had inherited from my father's side of the family some fields. Under the Moslem laws of inheritance, which still applied at that time with the Turkish community in Cyprus, my brother and I had no share in other (built-up) property from my paternal grandmother Hurmuz Hanım, which would have been my father's inheritance had he not died before her. When a son predeceased his mother the grandchildren's share on their grandmother's death was limited to unbuilt land only. It had been my share from the sale, at the beginning of the 1950s, of such a field, in what were then the outskirts of Nicosia, which had enabled me and Lalage to buy our Addison Crescent house in 1956. Now, nearly thirty years later, my brother managed to find a buyer for the almost derelict "Marie's house" - and indeed a buyer who was willing and able to preserve the building. (By now the municipal administration in the Turkish part of the capital had introduced town planning and building controls to prevent old buildings from being torn down.)

And so it was that in 1989 with my share from the sale of "Marie's house" (coming to me from my mother's side of the family), I had the resources to realise what had until then been no more than an airy fantasy. In a small field (which had come to me from my father's side)

320

in a village, between Kyrenia and the mountains behind it to the south, I was able to build a two-bedroomed house where we and the children could go for holidays. It was to see this house, when it was nearing completion, that my brother had brought mother from Nicosia in his car on that single occasion when, following her fall, she had during her last few years stepped outside his flat.

And it is that house to which Lalage and I go each spring and autumn, our visits now forming part of the outward pattern of our lives. There, too, we are able to give a measure of peace and tranquillity to our children, and to theirs, when they are able to take holidays from the hustle and stress which seem to be an almost inescapable way of life for young families. We have much indeed for which to be thankful.

Trying to establish trees, both fruit-bearing and ornamental, in soil which had lain largely neglected for so long, has been a daunting but rewarding job - both for me and, I hope, my brother, on whom a great part of the burden falls; especially in the height of the summer when we are in England - a season during which the water supply is only barely adequate for gardening.

**\*\*\*\*\*\*\*\*\*\***

Our autumn visits to our Cyprus house coincide with the annual migration of the cranes. We first hear their approach from the north - with a rising sound like the croaking of a myriad frogs - before we catch sight of the leading wave coming in high over the sea from Turkey to the north. Then, in their hundreds, and sometimes their thousands, flight after flight makes for the castle-crested peak of Hilarion a mile beyond our house where, as they pass right overhead, we see them wheel and re-form between us and the mountains, before they make for the pass a mile further to the east to continue southwards over the Nicosia plains and onwards again across the sea, travelling once more towards Africa. It is an experience which we never fail to feel as both moving and renewing.

**\*\*\*\*\*\*\*\*\*\***

During our time at the Grange I had continued to work on the draft of a verse translation of Yunus Emre's poems. The spirit which suffused

**Journeying**

these - of universal toleration and love, grounded in recognition of the unity of all existence, extending even to the knowledge that the Divine is within every being - was working powerfully on me, though I was scarcely aware of this at the time. When I was, it was but fitfully; and then only at the most superficial of mental levels. But even so I think that my perceptions and understandings were slowly being altered as my mind so often dwelt on Yunus's words. It was comforting (in the old-fashioned, but real, sense of 'strengthening') for me to find in the centuries-old Islamic tradition that which I had not, until then, had the remotest idea was there:

*We need to serve a King who never may be driven from His throne*
*To rest within a place which we may ever feel to be our own*

*A bird we need to be, to fly, to reach the very rim of things*
*To drink that cordial whose drunkenness we never may disown.*

...................

*We drank of that sweet cordial which flows from Truth, praise be to God*
*We have passed over and beyond the seas of power, praise be to God....*

*Parched we were and found refreshment from the lowly we were raised*
*Wings we were granted birds became and rose in flight, praise be to God....*

*Let us now live in reconciliation who had once been foes*
*Our horses saddled stand - we take the Road again, praise be to God....*

*We were a spring, our waters welled, we rose and spilled, became a stream,*
*We flooded, flowed into the standing sea beyond, praise be to God*

...................

*We fell to muse in Meaning's house, from there Existence we surveyed*
*We found that both the worlds are visible in all that Truly is* .....

322

*The Jewish Torah and the Christian Book, the Psalms and the Koran,*
*The Message which they each proclaim we found in all that Truly is*
*....*

*True is the Word which Yunus speaks: devotion we respect in all;*
*For where you want Him there we found is God - in all that Truly is.*

Within the compass of the broad area of my interests, my reading about Islam, Sufism and Turkish history and literature was very largely a matter of chance. In the same haphazard fashion I also began to note down scraps of verse I randomly came across which particularly appealed to me. Very sporadically, and piecemeal, I tried over the years to put these, too, into English verse. The scope of these was even more fortuitously expanded as the result of a journey I made to what were then still the Soviet Central Asian Republics in the year following the children's marriages. I went there unaccompanied by Lalage. She had arranged to attend a short but intensive course at the Jung Institute in Zurich; and I, under the overall command of the Russian Intourist, travelled on a three weeks' package visit to Kazakhstan, Uzbekistan and Turkmenistan.

**\*\*\*\*\*\*\*\*\*\***

I recorded my impressions of that trip as soon as I got back. To recover the general flavour of the atmosphere while we were in Russia itself (which consisted of a few days in Moscow on arrival and departure) I quote from what I wrote about the reception of our party of less than a dozen tourists on arrival by air from London:

*'Clearly one over-riding quality is required of a young man appointed to passport immigration control in the USSR: an absolute determination to give no sign that he shares any humanity with you who, with his every look, every gesture, suggests you have an insufferable nerve trying to enter his country. Despite the fact that his authorities (including the KGB) have granted you an entry visa, you will at the point of entry, having disembarked at Moscow airport, come up against a man whose manner suggests that you presume too much in thinking you can hoodwink him that you are other than the one scoundrel they*

323

*have been scouring the world for. I say 'manner', because speech with any such dregs as yourself is quite beneath him. You enter a narrow aisle, further progress blocked by a turnstile. On your right, in a thick glass-fronted booth, stands your welcoming immigration control officer. Between him and the glass, at waist level, is a shelf or counter. He gives you a piercing, offensive (in every sense of the word) look. This lasts about ten seconds. Then his eyes drop. He is clearly checking you out. Against your passport? The KGB 'wanted' list? Or is he just looking down the better to intimidate with another piercing stare when he eventually raises his eyes again to yours? The only bodily movement he makes meanwhile is when (never letting his eyes leave yours) he picks up a telephone and holds a murmured conversation with someone for a minute or so. Throughout this scrutiny, which seemed to take at least ten minutes, I was only too conscious that my visa application form, made weeks before travelling, had asked all sorts of questions about my background (including that one about whether I had any relatives in the USSR, and whether my name had been different at birth - which, in an access of honesty, I had revealed to be well and truly Turkish, so that, whether or not I might be but another gawping tourist from the hostile and corrupt West, I might well have a more particular, and deleterious, interest). It also occurred to me that my passport photo showed a clean-shaven face. To relieve the tension I smiled weakly and riffled my fingers through my beard - trying to suggest "Yes, it's the same face". Not a flicker. The only look I got in return was a bleak, suspicious, glare with occasional shifting of his eyes to whatever was beneath the counter. Further telephone calls. Eventually passport shoved at you through narrow opening; turnstile opens; and you are free - or out anyway. An English friend tells me that it took 17 minutes with him on a different occasion - but then he was clearly a highly suspicious character, being a clergyman! The friendliest interpretation I can put on this preposterous charade is that, as in everything, Russia has to show that without question she excels the Americans; and that the target she has taken to beat is the notoriously unfriendly US customs officer. She need have no fear: she wins hands down. There is no competition; it is a push-over.'*

**********

It is enough for this present account to refer very summarily to what struck me most about my experience of the other places, which were still palpably part of a Russian empire. There seemed to be little love lost for the Russians by ordinary non-Russian people I met (by which I distinguish those of them who were not *aparatchiks*). In fact there was evidence of a strong resentment at what was considered foreign rule, whatever the nominal 'autonomy' of the separate republics governed by local Communist parties. There were also indications of a virtual Moslem 'sub-culture', which appeared to be in the guardianship of women in the home.

But the thing which most intrigued me was the extent to which both the similarity and the extreme dissimilarity between the local language and the modern one of the republic of Turkey varied enormously from place to place in these Soviet Republics, and even between people in the same republic. It occurred to me, not being an etymologist, that the relationship between these languages would probably be something like that between the Germanic tongues, some being much closer than others to the root language. It seemed to be that the better educated (unless virtually Russianised) were reasonably familiar with western, or Anatolian, Turkish as a sort of literary language. In the Turkic languages I thought I could detect not just the obvious accretions from Russian vocabulary, but also changes in pronunciation due to the imposition of the cyrillic script. That I had been able to acquaint myself with that script sufficiently to be able at least to decipher it led to an entirely unexpected result.

In the town of Shehri Sebz, the birthplace of Tamerlaine, some miles to the south-west of Samarkand, where his beautiful tomb is, I came on a little bookshop. Browsing, I found two books in Uzbek (in cyrillic). One was from a version, by the 16th century Uzbek Ali Shir Nevai, of the 13th century Persian allegorical poem by Farid ed-Din Attar of the soul's journey in search of God (generally translated in the West as *The Conference of the Birds*). The other was a collection of the poems of Babur, the founder of the Moghul dynasty in India, who was born in 1480 at Ferghana in the far south-east of the present Uzbekistan. It was astonishing how, even through the cyrillic veil, a lot of Babur's language was intelligible four and a half centuries later.

325

**Journeying**

So much so that I added not a few of his poems to the list of those others I was translating. One I found of special personal appeal:

*Should exile bring me union with my love*
*Need I a homeland seek by looking back*
*For memory's sake my loved one sent a line*
*My love I need - of memory I've no lack.*

Three others also struck home:

*Let ardent heart obtain that thing on which the soul is set*
*Or all desire forsaking free itself from longing's net*
*Should in our world nor that nor this of these two be our fate*
*Admit no further thought - choose your new road without regret.*

..................

*I came to Being when Your graciousness my spirit made*
*As fellow for it flesh you gave as though its baneful shade*
*So since You have in spirit brought me pure to fleshly home*
*May never dark depression make me feel by You betrayed.*

..................

*Where once was human reverence for all things of worth*
*This marrow joining man to earth such is no more*
*Better by far Babur in times like this to be*
*A simple country squire than twicefold emperor.*

\*\*\*\*\*\*\*\*\*\*\*

On return to Chitterne I resumed my unstructured reading. In the ferment of information, not all of which had been entirely new to me before, simmering and bubbling about in my mind, it seems that my brief glimpse of the central Asian peoples, and my evanescent contact with their culture, had some kind of catalytic effect. A wholly new view of Turkish involvement in world history opened up.

There appeared to me to be a most remarkable parallel between the

326

story of two peoples - the pre-Christian Viking Norsemen (soon to be Christian Normans) and the pre-Islamic Turkic tribes (soon to be Moslem Turks). In 1066 the Normans (Christian converts barely a couple of generations earlier) won the battle of Hastings at the southern edge of England and began the process which led to the British empire and ultimately ended in the emergence of the Britain of today. Only five years after Hastings the Seljuk Turks (as but recently become Moslem) defeated the Byzantines in 1071, at Malazgirt, at the eastern end of Anatolia, and started on the road which led to the Seljuk and Ottoman empires and ultimately to today's Turkish republic.

The Norsemen were sea-wanderers whose journeys and battles took them as far as America, the Mediterranean, and the Ukraine where, at Kiev, was founded the first of the small city states out of which grew Russia. Before their conversion to Christianity they had served in the Byzantine army, and later their Christian Norman descendants were in the forefront of the Crusades. From Britain they spread out by sea to found empires.

The pre-Islamic (Shamanistic, sometimes Buddhist) Turkic people were land-wanderers, horsemen. Their migrations and battles took them as far as India and Persia in the south, and to China in the east. Travelling westward as well, north of the Caspian and Black Seas, down and beyond the Danube, they also came to Byzantium, in whose armies they also served. After conversion to Islam they became the principal troops of the Arab Caliphate in Baghdad and later were the leaders of the counter attack on the Crusaders. Spreading out, overland, they too were empire founders; but under separate dynasties - the Ottomans in Anatolia and Europe, the Safavids in Persia, and the Moghuls in India.

While a lot of this was not wholly unknown to me in piecemeal form, I had only now been able to view it in some kind of perspective.

\*\*\*\*\*\*\*\*\*\*\*

There are nationalist, right-wing Turks for whom the central Asian republics represent a vision - some kind of 'greater Turkey': *Turan*. Insignificantly few such people may be, but their ideas are, to me, comparable in essence with the nationalist Greek concept of a 'greater Greece' - the *Megali Idea*. Such ideas are politically patently futile, pernicious, dangerous and completely counter to the tide of history, which seems to be running in the opposite direction to another shore. In that other world our descendants will, God willing, see that the whole concept of the nation state was but a stage (almost an aberration) in developing different and more fruitful international relationships, structured confederally, and founded on mutual interests - and respect. And, from that perspective, I can see an entirely positive and fruitful possibility for developing links between Turkey and the Turkic republics which would have no political aims but could grow out of recognition of their common historical and cultural past.

**\*\*\*\*\*\*\*\*\*\***

My reading was also bringing me some decidedly new and unexpected snippets of information to dispel well entrenched misconceptions of my own. Such as my assumption that Byron had been an unqualified philhellene and turcophobe, as most people (British and Turkish) seemed also to imagine. It was a revelation to me to read Byron's own *Notes* to his *Childe Harold's Pilgrimage*:

> *If it be difficult to pronounce what [the Turks] are, we can at least say what they are not: they are not treacherous, they are not cowardly, they do not burn heretics, they are not assassins. They are faithful to their sultan till he becomes unfit to govern, and devout to their God without an Inquisition. Were they driven from St. Sophia tomorrow ... it would become a question whether Europe would gain by the exchange. England would certainly be the loser ... Who then shall affirm that the Turks are ignorant bigots when they thus evince the exact proportion of Christian charity which is tolerated in the most prosperous and orthodox of all possible kingdoms [Great Britain] ... And shall we then emancipate our Irish helots? Mahomet forbid! We should then be bad Mussulmans, and worse Christians: at present we unite the best of both - jesuitical faith, and something not much inferior to Turkish tolerance.*

**\*\*\*\*\*\*\*\*\*\*\***

In my retirement I had also been increasingly fermenting in that other, more colloquial, use of that word: seething - at the way a one-sided viewpoint on the Cyprus situation had gained public currency and was now almost universally taken as the truth. Educating myself was one thing; trying to educate others was much different. And trying to get the media to accept contributions, unless one already has some kind of access, was also a very wearing and frustrating business - as many have found. I do not want to unbalance this personal account but, since trying to rebut this prevalent view did in fact much occupy my time and energies, I need to dwell on the matter. The most convenient way of doing so is to let my words at the time speak for themselves - and for me now. Looking through such copies as I kept of what I wrote, I choose now those which seem to serve best in setting issues out as concisely, and in as self-contained a form, as possible.

To the Editor of the Sunday Telegraph, 23 July 1984:

*A reader of last Sunday's advertisement from the "Cyprus Republic" might suppose that ten years ago a harmless and small Greek country had been gratuitously assaulted by an unprovoked large neighbour. The facts, which the Greek community in Cyprus seek to hide, are that it was Greece (no less than Turkey and Britain) which set up the Republic and was a co-guarantor of it; but the Greek Government and the leaders of the Greek Cypriots sought to subvert the Republic and bring about the union (enosis) of Cyprus within Greece, in breach of the Constitution and the Treaty of Guarantee. Finally there was the Greek attempt to murder their own Archbishop/President to allow a usurper, the ex-EOKA killer Sampson, to impose enosis. It was this which compelled Turkey to exercise its right to intervene.*

*The Greek side has managed to shatter what little faith the Turks of the island might have had in their written undertakings of brotherhood and amity enshrined in the 1960 Constitution. Does it imagine that its co-habitants will allow themselves to be exposed again to the contumely and worse of those who wish them nothing but ill?*

*If, in spite of everything, the Greeks truly want to see an island whose two peoples can still be given another chance to live in mutual regard (as, say, in that other small multi-ethnic state, Switzerland) then why do they so resolutely set themselves against such a possible 'Swiss' option? For my part, as a Turkish Cypriot, I can, in truth, see no other possibility save disharmony at best. On the other side of the coin: suppose such a model could, God willing, be found to be possible, what might this not portend for Turkey and Greece themselves - countries which their greatest modern statesmen, Ataturk and Venizelos, tried to transform into friendly neighbours sixty years ago?*

(This was the text as published. It was considerably compressed - and altered in the doing - by the editor. For example, after the words "... *nothing* but *ill* " at the end of the second paragraph, my following words were deleted: *"Not all the Greeks of Cyprus, I do not doubt; but unquestionably the political and religious leadership who determine the course of events. If so they most cruelly mislead - not least themselves."* I was grateful that, even truncated, something had appeared informing the public about the Turkish side; yet, if not exactly mortified, I was also uncomfortable that a wrong message would be conveyed to any Greek Cypriot, not of implacable views, who might read the letter - such as Zach whom, as I have mentioned, I had but recently met at my son's wedding).

In September of 1984 *The Spectator* carried rather more than a full page piece by Christopher Hitchens. I hadn't then known that it was his form not merely to be controversial but, as we have since seen in his television appearances (for example, when he was putting the knife into Mother Theresa), to tend to abrasiveness. My letter to the editor was sent, on the eve of my departure for a visit to Cyprus, under a covering note which ended: *"I have tried to compress my response to this article. If only for this reason it does not attempt to deal with the future - to turn from recrimination to whatever might yet remain of hope for some positive and constructive moves for a settlement, slender though that hope must be. But then nor does the article by Mr Hitchens."* On my return from Cyprus some weeks later I found waiting for me a copy of *The Spectator* which the editor had posted to my address and which carried my letter, but as a separate article - and bearing the heading *Another Cyprus*:

*It is the recourse to bigotry, so cunningly used by Christopher Hitchens to advance a case - rather than the case itself - which affronts a Cypriot Turk brought up wholly in this country and prompts him to reply. As to the case itself, I know nothing of the new airport apparently under construction. Assume, however, that Mr Hitchens's view (or rather Mr Kyprianou's) is correct; then cut through Mr Hitchens's opaque and mannered style and try to strip out the lurking turcophobia. His burden seems to be: America will have the use of an airport in north Cyprus; Mr Reagan is given to parading his Christianity, though hypocritically; the Turks of Cyprus being Moslem have damaged churches; it is, therefore, incongrous(?)/ intolerable(?) that Americans and Turks act in partnership in 'militarising' Cyprus (although there have been two huge UK bases in the south of the island for 24 years). It is not surprising that a mind so attuned should find itself in sympathy with the odious vapourings of Chesterton in 'religious' vein when the fit was on him. But it does shock that, at the tail end of the 20th century, the Spectator should give countenance to such tactics. And it is sad to think that while Chesterton's equally noxious anti-semitic verses should be regarded as out of court these days, the Turks do not warrant similar courtesy and consideration. Mr Hitchens is an atheist. I am not; though possibly we share a conviction that institutional religion has been a damnable cause of much human suffering. Even if we don't it is a cheap trick for Mr Hitchens to seek to exploit either the real religious feelings, or the 'religious' atavism, of his readers in order to blacken the Moslem Turks - after speciously making an avowal of impartiality by way of a disclaimer of religious faith himself.*

*Having lived, off and on, for nearly half a century in this country I know that to the ordinary kindly English man or woman the image evoked by the Greek Orthodox church is more often than not a sort of Anglicanism abroad, made exotically interesting by virtue of a Levantine setting and bearded priests. I have to say, however, that others, more informed and with direct experience, view matters differently. (I have to generalise in what follows as I am dealing with hostility itself couched in generalities. But I am glad first to point to an exception. Some of your readers will have seen the report in* The Times *of 18 August of a Greek family on Castellorizo - a Greek island within hailing distance of Turkey - needing urgent medical help. In the face of obloquy a man crossed to Turkey for it - and was hauled before the Greek courts for behaviour insulting to the Greeks! He was the local priest.)*

*In Cyprus, however, it has not been as men of God that Orthodox archbishops, bishops and priests have presented themselves to the Turks. Not, that is, as men preaching that gospel of love and forgiveness, of penitence and redemption, taught by Jesus whom the Koran, too, venerates in the figure of Isa son of Meryem. What the Turks have seen have been sinister figures urging on courses which look to the obliteration of their community - as was achieved in Crete (where not one Turk remains of the substantial Turkish population of 80 or so years ago), and is under way in Rhodes. Are the Turks of Cyprus being unduly fearful? Am I being unreasonable, or extreme, in trying to voice their fears to the British? When is a church leader in Cyprus on public record as preaching brotherhood with the Turks? Or sorrow, if not contrition, for what has been meted out to them?*

*What that comprised is on record in Mr Hitchens's own book:*

I have visited the mass graves of three little villages ... where hundreds of Turkish Cypriot civilian corpses were dug up like refuse in the ghastly summer of 1974. And I have toured the burned-out ruin of a Turkish Cypriot suburb [*of Nicosia*] that was devastated by Nicos Sampson's gang of terrorists in 1963 ... The Greek irregulars often failed to make any distinction between Turkish mainland soldiers, Turkish Cypriot guerillas and Turkish civilians. It is true that *some* [my italics] detachments did not indulge in pogroms ... Greek arms [did] to Turkish civilians what they could not or dared not do to Turkish soldiers.

*When people use others detestably they are likely to be visited by a similar retribution. And when individuals have been conditioned to disregard others' humanity they will behave inhumanly. To say this is to try to understand, as one looks to the future - not to accuse.*

*It is not as a Christian that Mr Hitchens is distressed by despoliation of churches after 1974. It grieves me too when I see people driven to this as an expression of hate and fear. But I also ask myself why in the present context we do not hear from Mr Hitchens what was done in 1963 (barely three years after a republic was set up in Cyprus and eleven before Turkey intervened) to the Mosque of Bayraktar which had stood on the southernmost point of Nicosia's walls since 1571; or of the desecration and destruction of Turkish cemeteries - of which I was told by a Greek Cypriot speaking, to his honour, in horror only last month in London.*

*What the future holds for Cyprus God knows. But if it is to be another Lebanon or Ireland, then a heavy load of responsibility will rest on outsiders, of whom Mr Hitchens is but the latest in a dismal procession, who (even before the days of EOKA) encouraged the ambitious in unrealistic fantasies and allied themselves with local passions instead of trying to help moderate them.*

(As may be surmised, the Greek Cypriot to whom I had referred was Zach).

Much of what I wrote to the BBC and to Channel 4 television I was of course unsuccessful in getting published. But I also had some correspondence which was not intended for publication. That there are two sides to the Cyprus issue goes without saying, and it is entirely reasonable that, within the bounds of civilised debate, each should try to put forward their case. But what was different about Cyprus was the position of the British government. What I mean is set out in correspondence I had with the FCO. On 6 June 1989 I wrote to Mrs Thatcher:

**Journeying**

*May I please request that the Foreign and Commonwealth Office be asked to give a considered response to my enclosed memorandum.*

The following is the text of the memorandum which I tried to compress into two sides of foolscap:

*Britain and Cyprus*

*1. The purpose of this memorandum is to ask for a statement of the reason for the   position Her Majesty's Government adopts in relation to the matter of Cyprus.*

*2. Having been in North Cyprus as a tourist over several years, I have seen for myself a community working diligently, after years of oppression, to rehabilitate itself in a land where its people can live in safety and self-respect.  They are succeeding admirably despite the attempts of ill-wishers to make things as difficult as possible for them.*

*3. It has been my business to search out for myself the realities of the situation since 1960 by reading what each side has had to say: for example* The Cyprus Dispute *by N.M. Ertekun on the Turkish side, and* Cyprus in Transition *edited by J.T.A. Koumilides on the Greek side; as well as* Burdened with Cyprus *by J. Reddaway writing from the British viewpoint and with the weight of half a century's direct and personal experience.  The picture which emerges is as plain as it is at variance with what is so often represented to us in the media here:*

*(a) From the outset of the British connection in 1878 the Greek leadership in Cyprus proclaimed its goal to be the union of the island with Greece, that is to say 'enosis'.  Enosis was preached in pulpits and taught in schools right up to the 1950s.  The culmination was the EOKA campaign from 1955 to 1959.  Its sole aim was enosis.*

*(b) When Makarios became Archbishop in 1950, he had sworn on oath never to abandon enosis.*

*(c) In 1960 the Republic of Cyprus came into being under international accords subscribed,* inter alia, *by Britain.*

*(d) As part of a comprehensive settlement between all the interested parties, the Republic's Constitution included express provision making unlawful any action promoting enosis.*

*(e) Makarios assumed office as President in 1960 by swearing to uphold and abide by the Constitution. He thus either forswore his 1950 oath as Archbishop, or he perjured himself as President. That the latter was the case is incontrovertible from the scores of times he publicly announced, as President, that enosis was his purpose - as indeed did others of the Greek leadership - right up to 1974.* (Burdened with Cyprus, Appendix II.)

*(f) In 1963 the Greeks in the island embarked on their plan to intimidate the Turks, subvert the Constitution and usurp power.* (Akritas Plan, Op. cit., page 147 and passim.)

*(g) The Turks in the island were systematically excluded from the government and crushed by economic boycott.*

*(h) From 1960 to 1974 Britain was perfectly well aware of these blatant violations of the substance and the spirit of the 1960 Accords.*

*(i) In 1974 the more extreme Greeks in the island, in conjunction with Greece, opted to go for enosis bull-headed, in place of Makarios's tactic of working for it by attrition. To that end they tried to kill Makarios and, by* coup d'etat, *put the notorious EOKA gunman Sampson in his place.*

(j) *The then Turkish Prime Minister flew urgently to London to urge the British government to act, under her legal right and obligation, to put an end to these intolerable illegalities. In face of Britain's refusal so to act jointly, Turkey intervened alone.*

*4. So:*

*The 1960 Accords were upset and the Constitution violated by the Greeks who had, from 1963, even resorted to armed assault on the Turks. Britain appears to have chosen not to intervene, though in a position to do so by virtue of her military presence on the island and her legal right and obligation. (Under Article 2 of the Treaty of Guarantee she had undertaken to "recognise and*

335

guarantee ... *the state of affairs established by the Basic Articles of the Constitution"; and the Foreign Secretary, asked by the Select Committee in 1976 if we had a right to intervene in 1974, said: "I dare say legally we had. In political terms we had none* because the constitution had not been working since the early 1960s". *Which raises the question why Britain as a guarantor failed then to intervene for the eleven years from those "early 1960s".)*

*In face of the continued recognition of the usurping Greek administration as the "government" of the whole island, the Turkish administration in the North declared their own government there in 1983.*

*(If I should be thought to be factually in error in this necessarily brief resumé, I should be grateful to be shown in which particular.)*

*5. In the absence of evidence to the contrary, Britain's determined discrimination to the advantage of Southern Cyprus is as much at variance with the facts as it is contrary to the dictates of justice in allowing the culpable party to appear as the lawfully justified one, and at the same time as the one aggrieved.*

*I can find no record of Her Majesty's Government's having stated the* criteria *by which she adheres to the fiction that the Greek people of Cyprus elect the "government" of the whole island (including the north where its writ does not run and whose people cannot in conscience be expected to owe any allegiance to a wholly Greek administration which has, since the beginning, set them at naught); and why, since there is evidently no government of the whole island, she will not act on the just and pragmatic basis that there are in fact* two separate administrations *which she is prepared to help in searching for a genuine* modus vivendi *in a federation or confederation. May such a statement please now be made.*

This produced an immediate acknowledgement from Number 10, which said that my letter was "receiving attention". Two months later, having heard nothing since my original letter to the Prime Minister, I sent a reminder to Number 10 on 3 August. Still without a reply from the FCO, I wrote to the Foreign Secretary on 1 October.

I now got a first response:

From the desk officer, Southern European Department, FCO, dated 20 October:

*We can find no trace of your first letter. It appears never to have reached us here. But let me apologise for the apparent discourtesy, and for not having been able to get back to you more quickly ...*

*I have read your memorandum with care. The reality of a divided island is, inevitably, a sad one. In common with every other Government in the world, except Turkey, we do not recognise the "Government" of Northern Cyprus as a distinct entity. But we do recognise that the Turkish Cypriot community exists, and that they must be a willing party to any settlement of the Cyprus dispute.*

*Our policy is to bring about a comprehensive just and lasting settlement to the Cyprus dispute. This cannot be imposed. It must be agreed between the Leaders of the two communities. We fully support the initiative of the UN Secretary-General, and the use of his good offices to bring the two sides together to this end. The talks, as you will know, are currently stalled. But the Leaders of both communities had separate meetings with Mr Perez De Cuellar in New York earlier this month, and we hope that this will lead to an early resumption.*

Having waited three and a half months for the "considered" response I had requested (and, I confess, in considerable doubt as to the veracity of the claim that my original letter had been lost - which struck me as being in the same bracket as the legendary assurance from debtor to creditor that the "cheque is in the post"), this farrago of evasion, irrelevance, and bland complacency, staggered me. I had, naturally, no hope or expectation that I was going to get the FCO to admit to the falsity of their position or produce a basic shift in policy; my aim was to try to get out of them some articulation of how they actually justified their position. But I was determined to pursue the matter if only to demonstrate for the record how scandalously British governments (Labour as much as Conservative) had behaved in a matter where Britain had a specifically distinct responsibility quite different from other member states of the UN behind which she tried to skulk. And the patronising tone of the department's letter, with its gracious condescension in telling me that they "recognise that the Turkish Cypriot community exists", took my breath away - and raised my hackles.

Reply to FCO, dated 22 October:

*Your unreferenced letter of 20 October*

*"Is not a Patron, my Lord," asked Dr Johnson of Lord Chesterfield, "one who looks with unconcern on a man struggling for life in the water and when he has reached ground, encumbers him with help?" "Is not a Guarantor," a Turkish Cypriot might ask HMG, "one who undertakes to safeguard the honour and well-being of a people and, when those to whom he has that obligation have, unaided, by him, secured themselves against extirpation, is pleased to recognise that they exist?" The Turkish people of Cyprus would, I surmise, take small comfort from this condescension.*

*That apart, what "every other Government in the world" may choose to do in the matter is scarcely germane to my original memorandum. It was Britain which assumed the obligation of a guarantor in 1960; no "other" governments did so, save that of Greece (which was itself persistently privy to the attempts to subvert the 1960 Accords) and Turkey (which eventually moved to frustrate those attempts). Nor did any "other" government, being a guarantor, encourage (if only by its inaction - see pages 138-9 of Burdened with Cyprus) over a period of eleven years others in their dishonourable courses.*

*If legal (and moral) imperatives count for nothing, does not even expediency, and pragmatism, weigh with our government? Would not a genuine wish to help "bring about a ... settlement" be evinced in treating with each party on the basis of parity? So far from giving the considered response to my original memorandum (which you do not controvert) requested in my letter of 6 June to the Prime Minister, your letter merely restates what is well known: HMG's position. I have asked - and ask again - to know what is so far unknown: the grounds which are deemed to warrant that position. If HMG is unable to make those grounds known, I invite you simply to say so, in terms - and those who care can draw their own conclusions.*

Letter from Head of Southern European Department, FCO, dated 20 November:

*You raise a number of complicated questions about the history of Cyprus since independence and action which the UK might or might not have taken in pursuance of its role as a guarantor of the 1960 constitutional arrangements. These have been, and continue to be, the subject of much debate, and Ministers have stated the Government's position at various times, notably in the evidence which the then Foreign Secretary and Minister of State, the then Mr James Callaghan and Mr Roy Hattersley, gave to the House of Commons Foreign Affairs Committee in 1975-76.*

*In the context of the current intercommunal talks towards a settlement of the Cyprus problem, the Government adopt an even-handed approach to the two communities. But this has to be within limits dictated by our recognition policy. We are satisfied that the Turkish Cypriot community's concerns, particularly over safeguarding their security in an eventual settlement, are fully taken into account when we consider what action we can take in support of the UN Secretary-General's good offices mission. We hope that the separate meetings he is about to hold with the leaders of the two sides will lead to an early resumption of the intercommunal talks, which have been stalled since June, and renewed progress towards a settlement.*

This repetitious, formulaic, language reminded me of a remark which I had heard in my old Commonwealth Relations Office days, attributed to a dour American diplomat commenting on his dealings with, if I correctly recall, the Ceylon government: *"Doing business with these people is like trying to shovel fog!"* However, I simply couldn't let pass this attempt to fob off my specific questions, and especially by being referred back, unspecifically, to the Foreign Secretary's grilling by the Commons Foreign Affairs Committee in

1975-76, to which I had myself invited specific attention when I pointed to Mr Callaghan's admission - on that very occasion - that HMG did indeed have the right to intervene "legally"- even if he believed that honouring her responsibilities was to be ruled out "in political terms" (which he had preferred not to expound).

Reply to Southern European Department, FCO, dated 1 December 1989:

*My memorandum of 5 June last asked for the criteria on which HMG treats the Greek community in the island as electing the "government" of the island as a whole. That request being unanswered by the FCO in its letter of 20 October, my letter in response again sought the "grounds which are deemed to warrant" HMG's position in this matter. Since this unvarnished request remains without reply in your letter I revert to it once more - and now arising directly from your statement that HMG's "even-handed approach to the two communities ... has to be within ... our recognition policy". On what grounds is this general recognition policy based in its application to Cyprus?*

*Is it not a questionable policy (to put it no stronger) which has accorded the status of legitimacy to the direct successors of those who, from 1963, worked to subvert international treaties and agreements, and who oppressed the other community until forcibly restrained? It is surely a very peculiar policy which continues to support as legitimate what is no more than a sectarian* administration *with electoral support from only one of the two communities, and which cannot even claim to control a large part of the territory over which it pretends - apparently with British complaisance, indeed support - to rule? Such a "recognition policy" does not simply put a "limit" on "even-handedness"; rather it utterly vitiates any claim that "even-handedness" is being applied. You will perhaps acknowledge that it is not most people's understanding of even-handedness to treat the one side (and the usurper at that) as the lawfully constituted "government" of the entire island and the other as a marginalised faction to be excluded (with HMG's encouragement) from international organisations of every sort where the usurper has free rein to speak, ostensibly for all the inhabitants of Cyprus, so that* audi alteram partem *no longer has validity? If equity is deemed to be too unrealistically ideal - and even priggish - as the basis for policy decisions, might not the claims of pragmatic expediency weigh?*

*In chronicling a number of* facts *about the past my original memorandum was not intended for sterile debate but in recognition of that apophthegm, attributed to Churchill: "The use of recriminating about the past is to ensure effective action for the future." Since it is common ground that a "comprehensive, just and lasting settlement" can only come by agreement between the "two communities", it is difficult to see how HMG supposes that one side which, during these protracted discussions, is treated not merely as one of the two communities but as being the fully warranted "government of Cyprus"* tout court *has any inducement to yield an inch in pursuance of a "just" outcome of the events of 1963 to 1974 - a state founded on true bi-zonality. Why should they? If, however, HMG were to be bold and decisive in calling the Greek side's bluff, and oppose that administration's being accorded the status of a government of the whole island whenever the Credentials Committee of any international body meets, there might then be some grounds to hope that the Greek side could be induced to realise that the inevitable outcome of their past actions is a cantonal confederation - with the position of Turkey as guarantor enshrined.*

*In the light of this I ask for a FCO statement of HMG's "recognition policy" when a country's legitimate government has been overturned - as in the case of Cyprus - and when there is* de facto *no government in the position of ruling the whole country. I observe, incidentally, that the letters to me on this subject from the FCO bear no reference number. I hope I am wrong in assuming that there are no copies on your departmental files which will in due course be available on the public record. May I ask to be reassured on this point.*

(An interim reply, of 13 December, again unreferenced, acknowledged my letter and added: *May I also assure you that all your letters are kept on our files.* Nothing was said about FCO letters to me, which was what I had asked about).

Letter from Head of Southern European Department, dated 31 January 1990, and now bearing a (manuscript) reference:

*Our recognition of the Republic of Cyprus in 1960 was on the basis of the 1960 Agreements, including the Constitution. We continue to regard these as valid. Of course we acknowledge and regret that certain provisions of the Constitution are not fully in operation. However it does not follow from this that none of its provisions are in operation or that the Constitution itself is invalid ...*

*We do not accept that our recognition of the Republic of Cyprus vitiates our claim to be following a policy of even-handedness to the two communities. On the contrary, we fully acknowledge the rights of the Turkish Cypriots in Cyprus and sympathise with their desire for acceptance of a legitimate status for their community. Our hope is that they will negotiate a settlement with the Greek Cypriots which will bring this about ... Our long-established policy on recognition is not a hindrance to a negotiated settlement which takes full account of the interests and the concerns of both communities. Rather, we believe that any change in our policy would be liable to set back the prospects for an agreement ...*

*Finally, you will I am sure be interested to read the enclosed Hansard record of an Adjournment Debate in the House of Commons on 10 January, in which Mr Francis Maude MP, Minister of State re-iterated the Government's policy on Cyprus.*

The letter was revealing in its admission that the 1960 Constitution was regarded as still being "valid" (despite its conceding that "certain provisions" were "not fully in operation"), and interesting in its evading, by the use of these slippery words, the crucial fact that the "provisions" in question were precisely the ones which entrenched the Turkish population's position and on which their security and prospects rested, as a partner in the establishment of the Republic. Clearly this stone-walling prevarication by mere assertion of policy, instead of explanation or justification, was just going to continue indefinitely; but I decided nevertheless to get on to the record one last missive in strong vein, and at ministerial level in view of the last dismissive paragraph of the letter of 31 January.

Letter of 10 February to Mr Francis Maude, Minister of State, FCO:

*For nearly nine months I have been trying to discover the reason why HMG accords to the Greek side in Cyprus the right to elect the government of the island. The correspondence covers a bare eight pages beginning with my two and a half page memorandum sent to No. 10 last June. If you were to do me the honour, and courtesy, of finding the time to read these brief pages you will see how reasoned argument has throughout been fobbed off by bare assertion. I am left to assume - as I judge would any dispassionate reader - that the points left unanswered are in truth unanswerable. But this correspondence has at last yielded that HMG rests its recognition policy on the intriguing view that the 1960 Agreements, including the Constitution, remain "valid". I judge it pointless to enquire from what weird world of fantasy this perception is derived. Yet, I feel bound to make one last attempt to elicit whether a defensible reason exists to warrant HMG's position in the matter before I am obliged finally to conclude that HMG's intent is merely to adhere to the Greek position - despite all protestations to the contrary of "even-handedness". (It is not without significance that the Department's letter expresses the "hope that [the Turkish Cypriots] will negotiate a settlement": the movement is seemingly to be all from one side).*

*I ask therefore: even if in some metaphysical realm the 1960 treaties can conceivably be taken to be still "in force", by what imperative does it then follow ineluctably that the direct successors of those who from the very beginning openly and persistently worked to destroy those treaties are to be treated as the lawful government of the whole island under the self-same treaties? The process of reasoning,* the 1960 treaties are still in force, *ergo the Greek side comprises the government, eludes this observer for one. How can it be denied that there is* no *government on the island which can claim legitimacy, whether or not the 1960 documents are regarded as still in being? And in so far as the reason for according the Greek side a privileged status vis à vis the Turkish is stated to be the existence of the Turkish Cyprus State in the north, what then was the justification for HMG's maintaining this same unfair distinction during the twenty years before that political entity came into being, while the Greek side exercised their usurped power and a complaisant British government stood by inactive and indifferent to its own status as a guarantor - wholly separate from the position of the other members of the UN behind whom it now shelters?*

The expected brush-off came (from the Department and not from the Minister's office) by a short letter dated 27 February, which contained the standard "I have nothing to add to my replies to your earlier letters". I concluded the correspondence with a letter dated 8 March to the Head of Department:

*May I express my quite genuine sympathy in your unenviable job of seeking to defend the indefensible. Of course "a settlement has to be negotiated by the two sides"; but it is the stance of the pressurising third party which is at issue. You will allow me to detect the very real distinction in nuance - albeit perhaps unconsciously expressed - inherent in hoping "the Turkish side will negotiate a settlement with the Greek side" and hoping that "the Greek side will negotiate a settlement with the Turkish side", or even that "the two sides will ..."; more especially when the hope is expressed by a morally responsible third party which consistently gives aid and comfort to but one side.*

*That HMG's position on Cyprus since 1963 has been discreditable in respect of their obligations to the Turks - as indeed is becoming increasingly apparent to the public at large - will be clear enough to future readers of this correspondence (even if Ministers have no time, nor taste, to do so now). And those whose counsels have yielded a bitter and shameful result will be in as invidious a position as those on whose submissions a knighthood was bestowed - to be shamefacedly withdrawn - on the odious Ceaucescu. For myself, straining to be charitable, I can only deduce that HMG's partial attitude and policies in respect of Cyprus derive as much from a wholly misguided, and as ill-judged, an attempt to stand on pragmatism rather than on principle (leading to a pusillanimous and poltroon preference for the line of least resistance) as it does from mere philhellene sentiment - if that may be considered to diminish the discredit.*

As I re-type this, more than five years after I first did so, I regret that I should have lapsed into the acidulous and sanctimonious; especially as I had quite truly felt the sympathy I expressed at the beginning of the letter. But my letter clearly reflects what I deeply felt at the time. I was obviously angry and frustrated. I remember thinking about this even then, and beginning to question my motives in taking up the cudgels, as I had quite frequently been doing, in a partisan - though fair - way. At one level I was certainly genuinely upset at what were pretty plain injustices - both of substance and because only one side seemed to be getting a hearing, as evinced by Britain's policy as seen in action. But at the same time I began to wonder to what extent I might not also be serving, however unconsciously, some deeper personal and unconscious need.

**\*\*\*\*\*\*\*\*\*\***

This idea had first surfaced in my mind about a year before. The dreadful earthquake in Armenia at the end of 1988 was of course widely and sympathetically reported in the media here. But it was also used to promote political objectives in ways which had again impelled me to remonstrate. (It had not been the first time I had been drawn into this field of bitter controversy: I had responded at some length to a talk at the Royal Asian Society which had in my view transgressed the proprieties of that learned body and my very lengthy letter had been printed in its journal.) In the present case I wrote a very brief letter to *The Independent*:

*The half-page article you published on 14 December,* A Nation which has learned to live with suffering, *was marred by being used not just to evoke sympathy for the victims of a ghastly natural disaster, but as a vehicle for political propaganda made worse by racialist language and undocumented horror stories. To be specific: "Armenians who describe Turkish [tout court] cruelty"; "It is never mentioned in the British press that the Azerbaijanis are, in cultural terms, Turkish and proud of it" (as if being Turkish was in some way defiling); "Armenian women being upended and gang-banged by Azerbaijani youths" (without any evidence). And what has a picture of demonstrators over Karabagh got to do with a report of the earthquake?*

I enclosed with this letter a piece of the same length as the one in *The Independent*. They didn't publish it. It had begun:

*My wife and I made a tour of Turkey last spring. One day we joined a group of tourists on an excursion. Next to us was an American widow. Her husband had often wanted to visit Turkey but had been fearful because he had been brought up to believe the Turks were monsters. He was of Armenian origin. He died without having seen the country, or a Turk. His widow told us how she grieved that he had not been able, as she had, to see the Turkish people as they truly were.*

This was in my mind when I wrote about a year later to Channel 4 about a programme they had screened dealing with Armenians and Turks. My response had included the following:

*It may possibly be that there were a few discerning or sensitive viewers for whom the nastiness may recoil on the heads of those who made the film. The sequence in which a teacher was seen desperately, but unsuccessfully, trying to get a class of cheerful and bright children to regurgitate what she had obviously tried to drum into them - a tale of the attempted extermination of all Armenians, with the class itself being the proof that "the Turks" had been foiled in this plan - was gruesome in its venomous racialism ... It is always deplorable when ethnic fanaticism is manipulated and exploited. It is no less appalling when this is done in pursuit of political ends. It is especially ghastly when this*

346

*is done at a time when, as now, the evidence from Bosnia is before our eyes of where this perniciousness leads...*

*It is more than just a pious hope on my part that Armenians and Turks will one day find release from past bitterness; that, perceiving the demonology which some try to perpetuate - to give their own lives some meaning - for what it is, they will come to recognise their common humanity; that they will even come to accept the truth that for centuries before the 19th century they lived together in such tolerance and harmony that in the Ottoman empire the Armenians bore the honourable distinction of* Millet-i Sadıka: *The Faithful Community. And I would beg those who are neither Turkish nor Armenian to think that they might be able to help each to move in this direction - instead of working against that possibility, even if not deliberately.*

\*\*\*\*\*\*\*\*\*\*

As I now pondered on my own motives for involving myself in public controversy, following my set-to with the FCO, the picture of that Armenian teacher would recur. My own phrase, "- to give their own lives some meaning -", would come back to me. What I had then written began to crystallise thought. Might it not be that there could be in me, too, some compulsion beyond just wanting to defend those whose cases were not being heard? I believed - and still do - that my own interventions, far from being inflammatory, had been attempting to ease paths to reconciliation through improved understanding. But I concluded that, after some ten years, I had by now done all that I could in trying to be a small voice for those whose need for some advocacy seemed so often to go by default. I laid down my pen.

# ~14~
# Samarkand; Yasi; Chitterne; Salisbury . . . Cyprus . . .

My visit to Central Asia, almost a dozen years ago, had yielded other - and even more unexpected - fruits than those I have already described. A feature of many of the old buildings there - mosques, *medrese*'s, old burial grounds and individual tombs - had been the stunning tiling with which these places were faced - sometimes completely covering the structure. The overall effect was highly evocative of the outer tiles which also adorn and distinguish what are often but the remains of buildings from the Seljuk period in Turkey, in such places as Konya, Sivas, and Erzurum - buildings which are lighter and more delicate than the more solid, substantial and majestic monuments of Ottoman times. The predominant hue of both the Anatolian and Turkestan tiling is turquoise; and I now could see why that word had first been used to define the colour. Particularly in its totality, its effect was stupendous - though a lot had seen quite heavy restoration. Three wonderful examples of this Turkestan tiling - all in Samarkand - were, first, at the magnificent and spacious *medrese*'s (each forming one of the three sides of the vast *Registan* square, leaving the fourth side open); second, at Tamerlaine's tomb; and then, most superbly, at the extensive burial ground known as the *Shah-i Zinde* (the Living King).

Apart from the general appeal and overall grace of this style of decoration, the detail of some of the designs especially attracted my attention. The Russian Intourist girl was apparently unaware, seemed indeed to be uninterested, that in very many instances the designs were obviously not merely just some kind of abstract art but, rather, seemed to incorporate calligraphy. For one thing a frequently recurring *motif* in the 'patterns' appeared to be a kind of representation of the word *Allah*. The use of rectangular tiles as components of the lettering

348

meant, of course, that such 'script' was, as it were, necessarily compressed or confined into a highly stylised form, making it very difficult to identify letters even for someone very practised in reading Arabic. For me it was rather more a matter of trying laboriously to decipher. But not all these calligraphic designs were of this nature; many examples were also to be seen of the usual graceful classic cursive script to be found throughout the Moslem world. It was a pleasure to find that I was able to read the encircling words on the drum of the great dome, between its twin minarets, of the *Shir Dar Medrese* on the eastern side of the Registan, the *Ayet el Kursi* ( the 'Throne Verse' ) from the second Sura of the Koran, which was a favourite of my mother's.

The 'stylised' writing did not, however, appear only in linear form. It was very frequently to be seen on walls within a squared space and seemed to run, in spiral fashion, from the outside, moving clockwise inwardly to the centre. The form fascinated me as much as the, unknown, content intrigued. At one of the tombs in the *Shah- i Zinde* I found I was able to unravel one such square. Having got a couple of the opening words I recognised it for what it was; and it then became only a matter of seeing how the remaining words fitted the 'lettering' of a text which I knew. It was, in fact, the Sura *Ihlas*, which is one of the very short and renowned ones most frequently used in the five daily ritual prayers: *Kul huvallahu ahad allahu samad* ... "Say: He, God, is One; God, He is Eternal ...". (This closely parallels the Jewish *Shema*: "Hear, O Israel: the Lord your God is One... - even to the word for 'One' being the same in both the Arabic and the Hebrew.) I determined that on return to England I would try to pursue this art form.

Apart from those in Samarkand, the most impressive examples of this kind of decorative tile-work that I saw were on the colossal broken arch of Tamerlaine's otherwise totally ruined summer palace at Shehri Sebz, and at the massive, partially restored, mosque complex at 'Gorod Turkestan', the modern Russian name for the old city of Yasi, a half day's bus journey to the north of Jambul, the chief town of what is now southern Kazakhstan. Here is the tomb of Ahmed Yesevi, the 12th century Turkish Sufi who is included in the *silsile* - the chain of succession and transmission - of many of the Sufi *Tarikats* (Ways).

**Journeying**

From my notes at the time I record:

> *He died in 1166 at the age of 99, calculated locally in the lunar years of the Moslem calendar as three months short of 100. His mausoleum complex was built in 1394 by the order of Timurlenk ('timur' meaning ' iron' in Eastern Turkish - 'Turki', sometimes called 'Chagatay'). Among Sufi 'Orders' which trace their line to him are the Bektashi and the Nakshbendi, the latter having been widespread, though suppressed, in Russia. He left a work known as the* Divan-i Hikmet *(Compendium of Wisdom) consisting of a long series of verses once known throughout Turkestan.*

In the entrance hall to his actual tomb chamber there was a modern wall-plaque containing one of his verses. I managed to get a local, who attached himself to me as our small group was wandering through the vast building, to vocalise for me the text of the quotation (which was in cyrillic), and I wrote down the words, as best I could, as he spoke them. On paper they were recognisably Turkish enough for me to be able to translate them afterwards:

> *Know beyond doubt without our peopled land abides*
> *This World. In awe stand - all shall slip your hand one day*
> *Father mother womb's companion - where are they*
> *Think then how all your needs a wooden horse provides*
> *The world do not consume - save God no Right presume -*
> *Take not what others claim - through Sirat lies the Way*

['*Sirat el mustaqiym*', is the 'Straight, or Right, Way' to which a Moslem supplicates God's direction each time he recites the *Fatiha*].

***********

Back in Chitterne I decided I would try my hand at actually designing some 'squares' of the sort I had seen so much. I had observed not only that there had been stylisation in the reduction, or compression, into rectangular form of the flowing cursive script itself; it was also clear that a convention was followed (visually apparent but a bit difficult to

350

convey in words) by which the 'writing' and the 'background' each comprise an equal 'area' of the whole. This produced an effect that would sometimes make it difficult, for someone who was unaware that they were looking at writing, to distinguish the 'text' from the 'ground' against which it appeared. I got myself some graph-paper and began, by trial and error, to see whether I might be able to compose such a small square.

The first text I chose was the invocation "In the name of God, the Merciful, the Compassionate" - the opening words of the *Fatiha* (as it is of every Sura of the Koran, save one) which I had memorised so long ago at the Froebel school in Kyrenia. It took not less than a couple of weeks - I don't remember just how long - before a design of sorts, which at least conformed to the 'convention', emerged. I had satisfied myself that I could produce something in this tradition. A nephew - the eldest son of that sister-in-law who had, so many years before, announced that she was the brains of the family, and who was himself extremely brainy, and had won a Winchester Scholarship - saw one of my later such working drafts, uncompleted, on graph-paper. He asked me, to my amusement, as well as some gratification (since the entire world of computers - though they were my son's livelihood - was a sealed book to me then, as it still largely is today), whether I had embarked on computer programming.

There was no way, I thought, that I would be able to produce my texts as tiles; so I chose to work them in wood. This I did by raising the writing through incising, and gouging out, the 'ground' with a narrow chisel, and then painting each separate part in different colours, finished with high gloss varnish. The result, as a kind of mock embossed tile, was not too disappointing. Several years afterwards I was told by a potter I was to meet in Cyprus of the existence of potter's paints which could be applied to plain wall-tiles and then fired in a kiln. I managed to paint the dead straight lines of some of these designs onto such tiles, which she then very kindly fired in her own kiln. She now has one in her house; and half a dozen are fixed to the walls of the surrounding arches to the verandah of our little house in Cyprus. The initial wooden versions of these 'tiles' varied in size. Including the outer frame (the whole being made from a single piece of wood) they varied from between six and ten inches square. A few, including a copy I made (from a photograph), of the Sura *Ihlas* at the *Shah-i Zinde*, were about a foot square. A few years later (working over several months) I managed to work out, and complete, within about a fifteen inch square, the whole of the opening Sura of the Koran, the *Fatiha*. I cannot be exact about these dimensions as I have given them all away, except for one of the smaller ones, which I have here.

In order to pursue what was to develop into an absorbing hobby, after I had managed to produce my very first design, I needed to have texts. Some were ready to hand, like the words of the profession of faith, and the invocation of the *Zikr* and others I have mentioned. I was now to find what I wanted, from the Koran and from the *Hadith* (records of the acts or the sayings of the Prophet). Among those from the former were: "Truly God will not transform a people save that they first transform themselves"; "And I [God] am nearer to him [Man] than his own neck-artery"; "Truly Man shall have insight of his Self"; "God is the Light of the heavens and of the earth"; "No compulsion in religion"; "[There is] no refuge from God - save [only] in Him"; "Truly we are God's, and truly to Him is our return". From the *Hadith* I found: "Die, before you die"; "The most blessed of all works is the middle course" (which is also expressed in the summary, popular, version, "Extremism [or excess] is unlawful"); "Paradise lies at the feet of Motherhood"; "Who knows his Self knows his Lord"; and "A believer is a mirror to a believer". This last has a deeper significance when one knows that the word for "believer" is *mumin*, and that among the Names of God is *El Mumin* - having also the sense of 'The Faithful One'. The process of my seeking out these words, and my thinking about their meanings was, I now see, a stage on the way along which I was travelling.

\*\*\*\*\*\*\*\*\*\*

The second of the Uzbek books which I had bought in Shehri Sebz tells in allegory of the desperate wandering of the birds of the world in search of their king, the Simurgh. Their leader on this quest is the Hoopoe, which makes an appearance, as a messenger between Solomon and the Queen of Sheba, in Sura 27 of the Koran, in which are the words *Mantiq et-Tayyir* ('the speech of birds') which are used by the original writer of the allegorical poem as the title of his work. In the poem the birds travel through the seven valleys of Seeking, Love, Knowledge, Detachment, Unity, Bewilderment and Dissolution. At each stage many give up and turn back. Some become lost. Others perish. Finally thirty alone survive to reach the abode of their king. In the Uzbek version by Ali Shir Nevai the end of their quest is told in words which I translate:

*In that abode of joy and flowers each bloom was as it were a mirror. Wheresoever the birds looked they seemed to be seeing themselves. In this place all was light and simple purity, the outer and the innerness of things being revealed. It was as though all was clear and transparent, in the way of looking into water which at the same time reflected both the seer and the seen. After so much of pain, distress, toil, and hardship, these thirty birds had reached the place of their desire, where the Simurgh would, with his countenance, bestow upon them the transformation of their transitory and illusory state into that in which they would abide for ever. Yet wheresoever they looked, in place of the Simurgh [which means 'thirty birds'] they saw but themselves. And so the great Mystery of "Who knows his Self knows his Lord" was revealed to them.*

The Uzbek book carried an imprint in its endpapers to say: "Delivered to the printing house on 23.12.83. Permission for printing given on 07.09.84." It would seem therefore that the Uzbekistan Communist Party took nearly nine months in deliberating whether or not to allow the book to reach the public. A further imprint states that " 'Bird Tongue' [the Uzbek title of the work] is the sixth and last of the epic works of Ali Shir Nevai renowned for his literary aesthetic genius. The poet illustrates in this work, in a masterfully skilful manner, the way to man's attainment of moral perfection." The word *manevi*, translated as 'moral' (as distinct from 'material'), could also carry the meaning of 'spiritual'. It is interesting to speculate whether the authorities who gave permission for the issue of this book took its *dénouement* to be a powerful demonstration of their own atheist thesis that no God exists but is simply a human projection (an interpretation it is no doubt capable of bearing), or whether they knowingly intended its publication to convey its real, deeply spiritual, message at the core of Sufism - that Divinity is the essence of all things and of every one: that same message conveyed by William Blake when he was asked about the divinity of Jesus. "He is the only God," said Blake; and then he added "And so am I, and so are you."

\*\*\*\*\*\*\*\*\*\*\*

There is a wonderful parable, in the play *Nathan the Wise*, of the man who was given a beautiful ring, and this had the power to make its owner pleasing to God and to all people. At his death the man left it to his favourite son and instructed him and his descendants to do the same, so that the wearer of it should always be the head of the house. It came at last to a father who loved his three sons so much that he could not bear to choose between them. So, without telling the others, he promised the ring to each of them separately. The only way he could escape from his dilemma was by getting a jeweller to make exact copies, so good that no-one besides himself could distinguish them. He then gave one each to his three sons in secret. After he died each son claimed to have been given the ring, but it was impossible for any of them to prove that his was indeed the real one. They put the case to a renowned judge who ruled that since the genuine one had the power to make its wearer pleasing to God and man the real one must clearly have been lost; so the claimants had best trust their father - and seek to show this in their way of life.

As the Koran says: *And had God so pleased He had made you all one community, but He would test you by what He has given to each. Be emulous then in good works. To God shall you all return.*

\*\*\*\*\*\*\*\*\*\*\*

Hardly surprisingly, given the tergiversations over my own religious position, the relationship between religions, and especially that between Islam and Christianity, has been something which has preoccupied me. Over the later years of my retirement I tried from time to time to find a way of making some kind of meaningful connection - unrelated to the formulations of each and without having any direct objective, beyond that of trying to understand. Any idea of syncretism was far from my mind. (Not that I feel entirely at home with the seemingly general idea that syncretism is necessarily to be frowned upon, if not actually condemned. If that term is to be understood as the search for constructive similarities between ostensibly opposing or hostile belief systems - which is how I would see it - it would seem to me to be a worthy and commendable guide to human relationships.) What occupied my thoughts was whether I might possibly be able to discern, at some level or in some dimension, how far the essence of the one religion could be seen as merging with that of the other. For I simply could not find it in me to accept that, at that depth or height, the truths of each did not reflect the ultimate Truth which they each tried to manifest; nor that, in whatever lay beyond the mortal life, the adherents of the one must inevitably be separated from those of the other. I always had in my mind the Koranic verse - one which is reiterated in two different *Suras*: "Truly, those who are Muslims, and the Jews, and the Christians, and the Sabeans - whosoever of these trusts in God and the Last Day and does what is right - shall have their reward with their Lord. Fear shall not come upon them, neither grief." Were I to have reached a contrary, doom-struck, conclusion in the face of that clear Islamic affirmation, I could only have been confirmed in a temptation to cry out "a plague on both your houses"- a temptation to which it was all too easy to succumb when I saw constantly on the television screen, heard on the radio, and read about the things which spokesmen of each were capable of fomenting - and their activists of perpetrating. It was, of course, possible to discount people such as these by simply seeing them as evident traitors to their own cause. But even on such a charitable view the others - the rigidly faithful adherents of that same cause - would (it would seem) be required by that rigidity to deny the validity of other faiths; and so have to believe only themselves to be "saved" and, consequently, all others "lost": in whatever way they might express those two states - in mental imagery or in theological terminology. I could not believe that such a rift was inherent in the Creation of a Divine Being whose existence and presence in the world of time was proclaimed by all faiths - anyway by the two which I had known in part.

\*\*\*\*\*\*\*\*\*\*

355

# Journeying

There came to me the recollection of a verse by the 16th century founder of the Safavid dynasty, Ismail Safevi:

*Heart, it is not restless roaming brings release*
*While yet there are in this world things to you unknown*
*Pass not through life by saying 'Friend' to all you see*
*While yet to **one** a love **complete** you have not shown.*

This brought some glimmering of a perception through an image of two circles, each representing an essential aspect or depth of spirituality. At the core of Christianity, it seemed to me, was the proclamation of itself as the religion of Total Love; and at the core of Islam its proclamation of itself as the religion of Total Unity.

The image developed. Conceive of one circle as "Love, expressed in Suffering Compassion", and the other circle as "Unity of Existence, experienced as Completeness". If the two circles move towards each other, along a line joining their centres, they begin to overlap. The area of overlap expresses and symbolises "Union with the Real". Both circles are 'objectively true' to the extent, and in the measure, of the overlap; but they are 'subjectively true' even outside it. Moreover no overlap (no Union with the Real, the Absolute) is possible from a static position, where the existence of the other circle is denied. Or to put it another way: the one who is moved by a deep sense of the ultimate Unity of Existence and of Being cannot fail to find Love; just as the one whose being is entirely infused with Love will inevitably come to perceive the ultimate Unity of Existence and Being. But in both cases the "inevitability" depends on pursuing the chosen path in total devotion.

In one of his poems Yunus says:

*To none do we deny the faith that guides their steps*
*As faiths fulfilment find so Love again is born.*

And how many of us are capable of this degree and depth of fulfilment?

356

The image of the circles gave me some sense of the "essential" community of the two faiths of which I had some knowledge and experience - of what lies at their essence, outside and beyond their respective formularies, but within the compass of what each professed as its own basic message. And that image also seemed to express what is enshrined in the *Hadith*, "The faith of any one of you is imperfect until you desire for your brother what you desire for yourself." Which truth Yunus expresses:

*What you for self would wish to see wish not for others differently*
*For this the Meaning is, entire, of the Four Books - if such there be.*

***********

As to the nature of the relationship between religions more generally and their truths, another image came to me (which I noted at the time, 9th February, 1986 - ten years ago today, less ten days): the spectrum. It seemed that one might be able to get a glimpse of this relationship through the symbol of refracted light as seen by the human eye. Consider the different religions as various colours in the spectrum - seen most naturally in the rainbow. Some may be in the nature of the three primary colours, others intermediary - but all are contained in the spectrum. If those colours are added to each other, superimposed in the opacity of pigment - applied by brush to the board or canvas - the result is a darkening, and eventually the opposite of light is produced: that in which nothing is seen. But if all the components of the spectrum are, in the form of separate rays of coloured light, projected so as to concentrate and merge on one area? Then the colours, which had been broken up, separated prismatically, *re-unite* in their source - the original white and translucent light, from which they all had come, and in which they all have their being. And so, it seemed to me, was the case with the religions. In the purity of their essences they give us a real, if incomplete, signal of the source; in a way impossible for our partial minds to grasp merely through their 'grosser' formulations - in the 'opacity', as it were, of their doctrines. I think that the source of this idea was in Yunus's:

*The Beloved is made manifest in colours multitudinous*
*But one is His accent which a hundred thousand hearts with joy has*
*filled*

*My life together with the Friend is like to the sun in swirling cloud*
*Moments there are His face is veiled - then, see, His beauty is revealed.*

\*\*\*\*\*\*\*\*\*\*\*

The words *Sharia* (the corpus of Islamic 'Law') and *Tarikat* (used of
Sufi 'Orders') have the same overtones of meaning. The first signifies
a 'road'; the second a 'path' or 'way'. It seems to me that my own life
has indeed been a journey, on which I still travel. But the nature of the
journey has only been dimly apparent. When, some five years ago,
my translation of Yunus was published the book's cover contained my
'square' design of the *Hadith*, "Who knows his Self knows his Lord",
and the title, "The City of the Heart". Those latter words were taken
from the last three couplets of one of Yunus's poems:

*The City of the Heart I entered, in Its depths immersed, thought-free,*
*In wondering love I gazed - and there it was, in Life, I found the trace.*

*I tracked that trace I found and, as I travelled, marked on either side*
*Such things of marvel as may never else be seen upon the earth.*

*Yunus, they who understand will know the Meaning in your words;*
*And may they speak those words according to the times in which they*
*live.*

\*\*\*\*\*\*\*\*\*\*

What Yunus has revealed to me is something I understand in my head.
Only very rarely do I *know* it, truly, in my heart, and sense it in my
being. He also wrote:

*The Ka'aba, know, is but the threshold of yourself;*
*I came not to it in my outward journeying.*

[The Ka'aba, at Mecca, symbolises the annual Pilgrimage].

And, again:

*That which long I sought I found was manifest within my soul;*
*For what my Being searched for outwardly was there, in flesh, within.*

*That which, self-subsistent, never errs, without Which not one lives,*
*Which step by step Its measure takes within the very soul itself.*

*What binds this talisman of power - is told by every tongue on earth -*
*What all the lands and sky cannot contain - has entered in this frame.*

And, again:

*See the hidden sight before you, mystery within the view;*
*To the slave deliverance descends - not he it was who knew.*

*Tell, tell again - you are the Whole, you are not mere material;*
*Of Meaning you the image are, entire - find in yourself the Lord.*

*Come then, take away the veil, flee from self unto the Self;*
*You too will to Mir'aj attain; to you will every path then lead.*

*O sense, where are you to be found? A single mouth speaks every*
*tongue;*
*Each piece of the connected Whole brings tidings of the Total Mind.*

[The *'Mir'aj'* ( 'Ascent' in Arabic) was the mystical Night Journey of
the Prophet mentioned in the Koran.]

And the most shattering of all - resonating with the Koranic *"And I*
*am closer to Man than his own neck-artery"*:

## Journeying

*While on the world I gazed I came upon the wondrous mystery;*
*See then your Self within yourself as I the Friend have seen in me.*

*As one who serves I looked - I looked within myself and saw that One*
*Who on this form had life bestowed, the One Who is at one with me.*

*The Will it was led me to Him; if I were 'He', where might 'I' be?*
*No more distinction was - He I became: no 'I' remained, nor 'He'!*

*For the Beloved is one with me, no hair-breadth's separation now;*
*Why take the distant journey when the Friend within myself I see?*

*The Negative can hear Him not - His soul is sensed by those who grieve;*
*Of them I sing - from Love's rose-garden as a nightingale I came.*

*Not in fire may I be burned nor on the scaffold yield my breath;*
*Let me, my task accomplished here, attain to bliss - for this I came.*

*Possessing nothing, everything I give; all time and space is mine;*
*For east and west and north and south, all earth and heaven I confine.*

*My heart cannot receive the one who cries that form is merely dust;*
*For I have seen the essence of this dust with Majesty combine.*

*My self at last has found my Self, and this because I saw the Truth;*
*My fear was till the finding - free from fear no more do I repine.*

*Yunus, He Who brings you death, it is the Giver takes again;*
*And now the knowledge Who is Governor of every soul is mine.*

['The Truth', *El Haq*, is one of the Koranic names of God.]

**********

At the head of the introductory pages of my translation of Yunus I had quoted a verse from Kipling's 'Kim' (which - by nice synchronicity - in Turkish means 'Who?'):

360

*Something I owe to the soil that grew -*
*More to the life that fed -*
*But most to Allah who gave me two*
*Separate sides to my head.*

But now I know that there are not just two sides. Each of our selves is a multitude. And beyond them all, and at the depth of all, is the Real Self, which is at one with the Unity. As Haji Bayram Veli, who died in 1429, and whose mosque and tomb is at Ankara, wrote:

*If you your self desire to know*
*Search for life in life to grow*
*Beyond a life and find the That -*
*Your Self which self alone can show.*

\*\*\*\*\*\*\*\*\*\*

We knew the right time had come to move from the house at Chitterne and to live in a smaller place more suited to our ages and condition. Our new home turned out to be here in the very spot which, some ten years earlier, I had so dismissively, and as unguardedly, declared to be unthinkable - the Cathedral Close in Salisbury. Before the sale of the Grange had gone through, this quiet and secluded little flat became available, and Lalage and I were wonderfully fortunate in being able to secure it. Here we came two autumns ago; and here it was that I began - and am now finishing - this attempt to set down what I have made of my life. The way still lies ahead. How long, or short, the journey is yet to be remains unknown; the destination shrouded, invisible. Yet: *Inne lillahi ve inne ileyhi rajiyun* - "Truly we are God's and truly to Him is our return."

*Yunus's soul is not beguiled by thoughts of Heaven or of Hell*
*Upon the Path he travels to the Friend - true sunset of the soul.*

\*\*\*\*\*\*\*\*\*\*

361

Meanwhile I recollect, without reflecting on it, that I have twice in my life seen a hoopoe - in each case flying low. The first time, twelve years ago, in Turkmenistan from the window of the small bus taking us back from Khiva to Urgench. And then again, seven years later, with Lalage, in the garden of the house in Cyprus. But were anyone to observe, commiseratingly, that there are no hoopoes here in Britain, I would have to reply: "Well, actually ... they are occasionally to be seen - in human form."

Salisbury
9 Ramazan, 1416 (30 January, 1996)